Jewish Forced Labor Under the Nazis

Forced labor was a key feature of Nazi anti-Jewish policy and shaped the daily life of almost every Jewish family in occupied Europe. For the first time, this book systematically describes the implementation of forced labor for Jews in Germany, Austria, the Protectorate, and the various occupied Polish territories. As early as the end of 1938, compulsory labor for Jews had been introduced in Germany and annexed Austria by the labor administration. Similar programs subsequently were established by civil administrations in the German-occupied Czech and Polish territories. At its maximum extent, more than one million Jewish men and women toiled for private companies and public builders, many of them in hundreds of now often-forgotten special labor camps. This study refutes the widespread thesis that compulsory work was organized only by the SS and that exploitation was only an intermediate tactic on the way to mass murder or, rather, that it was only a facet in the destruction of the Jews.

Wolf Gruner is the Shapell-Guerin-Chair of Jewish Studies and Professor of History at the University of Southern California. He is the author of many works on the history of the Holocaust and Nazi Germany and has held a visiting professorship at Webster University and a fellowship at Harvard University and at the Center for Advanced Holocaust Studies at the United States Holocaust Memorial Museum.

Jewish Forced Labor Under the Nazis

Economic Needs and Racial Aims, 1938–1944

WOLF GRUNER

Department of History, University of Southern California

Translated by
KATHLEEN M. DELL'ORTO

*Published in association with the United States
Holocaust Memorial Museum*

CAMBRIDGE UNIVERSITY PRESS
Cambridge, New York, Melbourne, Madrid, Cape Town, Singapore, São Paulo, Delhi
Published in association with the United States Holocaust Memorial Museum

Cambridge University Press
32 Avenue of the Americas, New York, NY 10013-2473, USA

www.cambridge.org
Information on this title: www.cambridge.org/9780521743570

United States Holocaust Memorial Museum, 100 Raoul Wallenberg Place SW,
Washington, DC 20024-2126, USA

First published 2006
Paperback edition 2008

Printed in the United States of America

A catalog record for this publication is available from the British Library.

Library of Congress Cataloging in Publication Data

Gruner, Wolf, 1960–
[Geschlossene Arbeitseinsatz deutscher Juden. English]
Jewish forced labor under the Nazis : economic needs and racial aims,
1938–1944 / Wolf Gruner; translated by Kathleen M. Dell'Orto.
p. cm.
"Published in association with the United States Holocaust Memorial Museum."
ISBN 0-521-83875-4 (hardcover)
1. Jews – Europe, Central – History – 20th century. 2. Jews – Europe, Eastern – History –
20th century. 3. Forced labor – Europe, Central – History – 20th century. 4. Forced labor –
Europe, Eastern – History – 20th century. 5. Holocaust, Jewish (1939–1945).
I. United States Holocaust Memorial Museum. II. Title.
DS135.E83G72 2006
940.53′18134 – dc22 2005015709

ISBN-13 978-0-521-83875-7 hardback
ISBN-10 0-521-83875-4 hardback

Contents

Abbreviations

AdZ	*Dokumentationszentrum der Staatlichen Archivverwaltung der DDR*
AOK	*Allgemeine Ortskrankenkasse*
AP	*Archiwum Państwowe we Wrocławiu*
BA	*Bundesarchiv*
BA-MA	*Bundesarchiv – Militärarchiv*
BdS	*Befehlshaber der Sicherheitspolizei und des SD*
BLHA	*Brandenburgisches Landeshauptarchiv*
CAHJP	Central Archives for the History of the Jewish People
CCP	Catalogue of Camps and Prisons in Germany and German-Occupied Territories
CJA	*Stiftung "Neues Synagoge Berlin – Centrum Judaicum" Archiv*
DÖW	*Dokumentationsarchiv des österreichischen Widerstandes*
GG	General Government
GIS	*Generalinspektor für das Deutsche Straßenwesen*
HHStA	*Hessisches Hauptstaatsarchiv*
HSSPF	*Höherer SS- und Polizeiführer*
IfZ	*Institut für Zeitgeschichte*
IKG	*Israelitische Kultusgemeinde*
IMT	International Military Tribunal
ITS	International Tracing Service
JNBl.	*Jüdisches Nachrichtenblatt*
LA	*Landesarchiv*
LBIA	Leo Baeck Institute Archive
LHA-SA	*Landeshauptarchiv Sachsen-Anhalt*
NSDAP	*Nationalsozialistische Deutsche Arbeiterpartei*
NW-HStA	*Nordrheinwestfälisches Hauptstaatsarchiv*
OBR	*Oberste Bauleitung der Reichsautobahnen*
OHW	*Oberschlesische Hydrierwerke*
OKH	*Oberkommando Heer*
OKW	*Oberkommando Wehrmacht*
OSOBI	Center for the Preservation of the Historical Documentary Collection (Moscow)

ÖStA/AdR	*Österreichisches Staatsarchiv/Archiv der Republik*
Osti	*Ostindustrie GmbH*
OT	*Organisation Todt*
RAB	*Reichsautobahn*
RABD	*Reichsautobahndirektion*
RSHA	*Reichssicherheitshauptamt*
RWM	*Reichswirtschaftsministerium*
SA	*Sturmabteilung*
SD	*Sicherheitsdienst der SS*
Sopade	*Sozialdemokratische Partei Deutschlands*
SS	*Schutzstaffel*
SSPF	*SS- und Polizeiführer*
StA	*Staatsarchiv*
StadtA	*Stadtarchiv*
SteiLA	*Steirisches Landesarchiv*
USHMM	United States Holocaust Memorial Museum
WiG	*Wehrkreisbefehlshaber im Generalgouvernement*
WL	Wiener Library
WVHA	*Wirtschafts- und Verwaltungshauptamt der SS*
YV	Yad Vashem Archives
ZAL	*Zwangsarbeitslager*
ZwA	*Zwischenarchiv*

Introduction

For millions of people in German-occupied countries in World War II, forced labor was the order of the day.[1] As one of the first persecutory measures after occupation, the National Socialists regularly imposed forced labor on the local Jewish population, whether in Poland, the Soviet Union, Norway, Serbia, the Netherlands, France, or even Tunisia.[2] Utilization of forced labor began in Germany itself after *Kristallnacht* at the end of 1938, with obligatory assignment of German Jews to manual labor in municipalities and private enterprises. Forced labor ended where it began, in Germany, with the exploitation of Hungarian Jews and concentration camp prisoners in underground construction and factories for war production. At the zenith of Jewish forced labor, more than one million Jewish men and women, many of them elderly or young people, toiled for the German economy in occupied Europe.

After the war, Hugo Schriesheimer wrote about his experiences as a forced laborer in the Nazi state: "It was heavy physical labor to which we were not accustomed. . . . I thought of the process in biblical times, when the Jews in Egypt had to perform compulsory labor for the pharaoh and to haul bricks for his temple. . . . Except that our tormentor was not the pharaoh but Hitler."[3] As for Hugo Schriesheimer, forced labor thus shaped the daily lives of countless Jews under Nazi rule. Almost every Jewish family was affected directly or indirectly. Tens of thousands of men and women had to leave their homes and live for months, even years, in labor camps, of which there were far more than one thousand.

The predominant form of forced labor by Jews in Europe, however, was neither exploitation in concentration camps nor in other SS (*Schutzstaffel*) camps, but in "*Der Geschlossene Arbeitseinsatz*," that is, segregated labor

---

[1] For a general discussion, see Mark Spoerer, *Zwangsarbeit unter dem Hakenkreuz: Ausländische Zivilarbeiter, Kriegsgefangene und Häftlinge im Deutschen Reich und im besetzten Europa 1939–1945* (Stuttgart, 2001).

[2] See Martin Gilbert, *Die Endlösung: Die Verfolgung und Vernichtung der europäischen Juden. Ein Atlas* (Reinbek near Hamburg, 1982).

[3] Omissions by the author are indicated with [. . .]; quoted from Hugo Schriesheimer, "Die Hölle von Gurs – Das Ende der badischen Juden," in *Oktoberdeportation 1940*, edited by Erhard Wiehn (Constance, 1990), 182.

deployment, organized by the labor administration. This concept, developed by the labor offices (*Arbeitsämter*), referred to involuntary, segregated, and discriminatory employment of workers who had been selected on the basis of racial criteria. The labor administration's leadership role meant at the same time that compulsory labor was set up with an eye to economic interests. In Germany and the countries it occupied, the "columns of Jews" (*Judenkolonnen*) represented cheap resources for the hard-pressed war-time labor market, resources that were available without need to consider social factors. The laborers' value lay not only in their numbers, but also in the location and type of labor performed. The Jews were purposefully compelled to work in strategic areas where labor shortages were severe, including infrastructure construction, *Wehrmacht* (armed forces) projects, and the armaments industry. Public builders, private enterprises, and government agencies profited from recruitment of the Jews. The Jewish forced laborers, who numbered in the tens and hundreds of thousands, depending on the country, were a significant factor for the labor market and the Nazi economy in Germany, Austria, the Protectorate of Bohemia and Moravia, and Poland.

In stark contrast to these facts presented in this book, research studies have scarcely considered forced labor to be an important factor in Nazi anti-Jewish policy. Instead, historians have regarded forced labor as an intermediate solution or as a separate step on the way to mass murder.[4] The most recent of these scholars, Hermann Kaienburg, maintains, "In all periods and regions, the forced labor of the Jews was considered only temporary and transient."[5] Some authors, such as Daniel Goldhagen, even equated labor from the outset with extermination.[6] Because of these "preconceptions," until now there has been a dearth of independent studies either on planning and organization or on the background and objectives of the forced labor programs.

The fact that compulsory labor for Jews originated in Germany itself has likewise remained unnoticed. A different view still held sway during World War II and in the years that followed. The first books on the Nazi persecution of European Jewry, published in the United States, assumed on the basis of German reports that forced labor for Jews played a key role in everyday persecution from the beginning of 1939 on.[7] This view promptly disappeared

---

[4] See Ulrich Herbert, "Arbeit und Vernichtung," in *Europa und der "Reichseinsatz": Ausländische Zivilarbeiter, Kriegsgefangene und KZ-Häftlinge in Deutschland 1938–1945*, edited by Ulrich Herbert (Essen, 1991), 90–105.

[5] Hermann Kaienburg, "Zwangsarbeit von Juden in Arbeits- und Konzentrationslagern," in *"Arisierung": Volksgemeinschaft, Raub und Gedächtnis*, edited by Irmtrud Wojak and Peter Hayes as commissioned by the Fritz Bauer Institute (Frankfurt am Main and New York, 2000), 219–240, here 236.

[6] Goldhagen supports his hypothesis only with the description of three SS camps at the time of the mass murders; Daniel J. Goldhagen, *Hitlers willige Vollstrecker. Ganz gewöhnliche Deutsche und der Holocaust* (Munich, 1996), 335–382.

[7] Institute of Jewish Affairs, *Hitler's Ten-Year War on the Jews* (New York, 1943), 24; The Jewish Black Book Committee, *The Black Book* (New York, 1946), 170.

when the process of analyzing the historical events began. Indeed, few documents on forced labor turned up at first. During the last phases of the war, the officials in the labor offices – no doubt conscious of their crimes – had, throughout Germany, thoroughly destroyed files on the subject. In his 1961 book *The Destruction of the European Jews*, Raul Hilberg nevertheless outlined the social and historical context of Jewish forced labor in Germany, and in Poland as well.[8] In 1974, H. G. Adler added new details in his unjustifiably neglected study *Der verwaltete Mensch*.[9] At the same time, however, the view spread among historians that forced labor for German Jews had not been introduced until March 1941.[10] This topos influenced not only research, but also became part of the public discussion; it still comes up today in museums and exhibitions. The thesis regarding late introduction of forced labor thus set for a long time the historical stance on the persecution process; as a consequence, the duration, extent, and historical significance of forced labor were inexcusably underestimated. Avraham Barkai, who in 1987 for the first time analyzed material of Jewish institutions and published new information about the implementation of forced labor and the working conditions of the individuals affected in Germany, succumbed to this false assessment.[11] The same is true of Konrad Kwiet, who shortly thereafter advanced the state of research with survivors' statements on forced labor conditions and with source material on the last phase of forced labor, which was affected by deportations.[12] A first monograph on German Jewish forced labor appeared at the end of 1994; the study moves beyond the topos but fails in its detailed representation to analyze the course of events and their background.[13]

---

[8] Raul Hilberg, *The Destruction of the European Jews* (London, 1961); ibid, *Die Vernichtung der europäischen Juden*, new and expanded edition of the translation into German of 1982 edition, Vol. 1 (Frankfurt am Main, 1990).

[9] H. G. Adler, *Der verwaltete Mensch. Studien zur Deportation der Juden aus Deutschland* (Tübingen, 1974), 205–234.

[10] See Joseph Walk (ed.), *Das Sonderrecht für die Juden im NS-Staat. Eine Sammlung der gesetzlichen Maßnahmen – Inhalt und Bedeutung* (Heidelberg and Karlsruhe, 1981), IV/174, 336; Avraham Barkai, "Vom Boykott zur 'Entjudung'. Der wirtschaftliche Existenzkampf der Juden im Dritten Reich 1933-1943," in *Leo Baeck Institute Year Book XXXVI* (1991), 393; Bruno Blau, *Das Ausnahmerecht für Juden in Deutschland 1933-1945*, reworked 3rd edition (Düsseldorf, 1965), 86; Helmut Genschel, *Die Verdrängung der Juden aus der Wirtschaft im Dritten Reich* (Göttingen and Berlin, 1966), 253.

[11] Although he assumed that forced utilization of Jews occurred earlier, his representation focused, using the well-known historiographic topos, on the period beginning in 1941; Barkai, "Vom Boykott zur 'Entjudung,'" 173–181.

[12] Konrad Kwiet, "Nach dem Pogrom. Stufen der Ausgrenzung," in *Die Juden in Deutschland 1933-1945*, edited by Wolfgang Benz (Munich, 1988), 574–596. Kwiet published the part of his study that was devoted to forced labor in 1991 as a reworked article; ibid., "Forced Labor of German Jews in Nazi Germany," in *Leo Baeck Institute Year Book XXXVI* (London, 1991), 389–407.

[13] Dieter Maier, *Arbeitseinsatz und Deportation. Die Mitwirkung der Arbeitsverwaltung bei der nationalsozialistischen Judenverfolgung in den Jahren 1938-1945* (Berlin, 1994).

I published two monographs in German in 1997 and 2000 that for the first time systematically authenticated forced labor as an important element of anti-Jewish persecution in Germany and Austria.[14] As in Germany, the subject of mandatory labor outside the concentration camps has been neglected by historical researchers in Austria as well. In contrast to Germany with its numerous studies, only a very few monographs, document collections, and essays on persecution of Austrian Jews appeared until well into the 1990s.[15] Those works focused on specific aspects of anti-Jewish policies, such as the perpetrators, the theft of property, or the policies regarding segregated housing.[16] In the last decade, a few additional regional studies have been published.[17] Forced labor of Jewish Austrians has been discussed before only in a few pages of Rosenkranz's monumental 1978 work on Jewish persecution.[18] And yet, Austria was where the idea of Jewish forced labor was conceived, as will be shown. For the Protectorate of Bohemia and Moravia, the Czech national territory occupied by Germany, scarcely any systematic studies have been written before now on persecution of Jews and none at all on forced labor. In contrast, a whole series of books on persecution and extermination policies in occupied Poland have appeared in the last few years. These studies, however, seldom devoted any particular attention to Jewish forced labor. Christopher Browning's works, published since the end of the 1980s, are an exception. Browning provided for the first time an overview of the development of forced labor in the General Government.[19] When other historians

---

[14] Wolf Gruner, *Der geschlossene Arbeitseinsatz deutscher Juden. Zur Zwangsarbeit als Element der Verfolgung 1938–1943* (Berlin, 1997); Gruner, *Zwangsarbeit und Verfolgung. Österreichische Juden im NS-Staat 1938–1943* (Innsbruck, Vienna, and Munich, 2000).

[15] Herbert Rosenkranz, *Verfolgung und Selbstbehauptung. Die Juden in Österreich 1938 bis 1945* (Vienna and Munich, 1978); Hans Safrian and Hans Witek, *Und keiner war dabei. Dokumente des alltäglichen Antisemitismus in Wien 1938* (Vienna, 1988). Jonny Moser has published a number of long articles, for example, "Die Katastrophe der Juden in Österreich 1938–1945 – Ihre Voraussetzungen und ihre Überwindungen, in *Der Gelbe Stern in Österreich. Katalog und Einführung zu einer Dokumentation* (Eisenstadt, 1977), 67–133.

[16] Among others, Hans Safrian, *Die Eichmann-Männer* (Vienna and Zurich, 1993); Gerhard Botz, *Wohnungspolitik und Judendeportation in Wien 1938 bis 1945. Zur Funktion des Antisemitismus als Ersatz nationalsozialistischer Sozialpolitik* (Vienna and Salzburg, 1975); Herbert Exenberger, *Kündigungsgrund Nichtarier. Die Vertreibung jüdischer Mieter aus den Wiener Gemeindebauten in den Jahren 1938–1939* (Vienna, 1996).

[17] For example, Friedrich Polleroß (ed.), *"Die Erinnerung tut zu weh." Jüdisches Leben und Antisemitismus im Waldviertel* (Horn-Waidhofen and Thaya, 1996); Robert Streibel, *Plötzlich waren sie alle weg. Die Juden der "Gauhauptstadt Krems" und ihre Mitbürger* (Vienna, 1991); August Walzl, *Die Juden in Kärnten und das Dritte Reich* (Klagenfurt, 1987).

[18] Rosenkranz, *Verfolgung*, 173–174, 208–210, 234–235, 271–273.

[19] Christopher Browning, "Nazi Germany's Initial Attempt to Exploit Jewish Labor in the General Government: The Early Jewish Work Camps 1940–1941," in *Die Normalität des Verbrechens. Festschrift für Wolfgang Scheffler zum 65. Geburtstag* (Berlin, 1994), 171–185; Christopher Browning, "Jewish Workers in Poland: Self-Maintenance, Exploitation, Destruction," in *Nazi Policy, Jewish Workers, German Killers* (Cambridge, New York, and

have taken up Jewish forced labor in Poland in recent years, they have examined either ghettos[20] or the SS labor camps in eastern Poland.[21] While historical researchers have thoroughly explored the development of persecution in the Lublin district during the last decade, no comparable works have been published on the other districts of the General Government. Thus, the Lublin region, in which the SS under Odilo Globocznik developed its own forced-labor program, has until now forged our image of occupied Poland. The most recent studies on the Galicia district have reinforced the impression that the SS controlled forced labor in Poland.[22] Furthermore, interest in utilization of forced labor in the concentration camps of the SS and their economic enterprises has generally continued without interruption until today.[23] Thus, a closed circle connects historical research to public debate, which likewise projects a narrow picture of forced labor directed and organized by the SS.

This perspective must be thoroughly revised. The case studies presented here, which summarize my research over the years as well as recent new investigations,[24] analyze Jewish forced labor as a constituent element of a specific stage of Nazi persecution, which preceded the decisions to commit genocide. In this phase of anti-Jewish policy – whether in Germany, the annexed territories, or the occupied countries – Nazi rule ended the Jews' free access to any given job market by placing prohibitions on employment

Melbourne, 2000), 58–88; Cf. Christopher Browning, *Die Entfesselung der "Endlösung": Die nationalsozialistische Judenpolitik 1939–1942* (Munich, 2003), 209–248 (in English, Nebraska University Press, 2004).

[20] Hanno Loewy and Gerhard Schoenberner (eds.), *"Unser einziger Weg ist Arbeit". Das Getto in Lódz 1940–1944. Eine Ausstellung des Jüdischen Museums in Zusammenarbeit mit Yad Vashem u. a.* (Frankfurt am Main and Vienna, 1990).

[21] Dieter Pohl, "Die großen Zwangsarbeitslager der SS- und Polizeiführer für Juden im Generalgouvernement 1942–1945," in *Die nationalsozialistischen Konzentrationslager. Entwicklung und Struktur*, edited by Ulrich Herbert, Karin Orth, and Christoph Dieckmann, Vol. I (Göttingen, 1998), 415–438; Jan Erik Schulte, "Zwangsarbeit für die SS Juden in der Ostindustrie GmbH," in *Ausbeutung, Vernichtung, Öffentlichkeit. Neue Studien zu nationalsozialistischen Lagerpolitik*, edited by Norbert Frei for the Institute for Contemporary History (Munich, 2000), 43–74.

[22] Eliyahu Yones, *Die Straße nach Lemberg. Zwangsarbeit und Widerstand in Ostgalizien 1941–1944* (Frankfurt am Main, 1999); Hermann Kaienburg, "Jüdische Arbeitslager an der 'Straße der SS,'" in *Zeitschrift für Sozialgeschichte des 20. und 21. Jahrhunderts*, 11, 1 (1996): 13–39; Dieter Pohl, *Nationalsozialistische Judenverfolgung in Ostgalizien. Organisation und Durchführung eines staatlichen Massenverbrechens* (Munich, 1996); Thomas Sandkühler, "Das Zwangsarbeitslager Lemberg-Janowska 1941–1944," in *Die nationalsozialistischen Konzentrationslager*, Vol. 2 (Göttingen, 1998), 606–635.

[23] Most recently, Michael Thad Allen, *The Business of Genocide: The SS, Slave Labor, and the Concentration Camps* (Chapel Hill, 2002).

[24] While the Introduction, Prologue, Chapters 5, 6, and 9, and the Conclusion in this book are entirely new, the author's texts for Chapters 1, 2, 3, 4, 7, and 8, which were published earlier in German, have been reworked and expanded extensively. For the source citations, see the particular chapter.

and trade. As a consequence, the majority of the Jews were without any income and thus dependent on public welfare, so the Nazi state organized forced labor programs. These programs assured a minimum income to Jewish families, provided cheap labor, and at the same time guaranteed strict control over individuals among the Jewish population who were capable of resistance.

Forced labor shaped – decisively and for years – the everyday life of most victims of Nazi anti-Jewish policies. Segregated labor deployment was of course viewed from contradictory vantage points by the people affected, given that they were employed in various jobs in many sectors of the economy. While activities such as garbage sorting, construction, and street cleaning predominated in the beginning, forced laborers soon also were used in agriculture and forestry, then later primarily in industry. Whereas the father of Karla Wolf collapsed physically and mentally while working as a painter's assistant,[25] the writer Gertrud Kolmar regarded her work in an armaments operation as a challenge.[26] Years later, long after the end of the war, survivors' reflections remained just as contradictory. For many German survivors, the memory of the deportations to Poland overshadowed any memory of forced labor in Germany. That was not the case, however, for Marga Spiegel, whose husband lived in an early labor camp. She wrote, "My husband had to perform forced labor. Jews could be deployed only in columns of about 17 men and had non-Jewish supervisors. For many of our acquaintances, the concentration camp existence began at that time. They had supervisors who ordered them around like slaves and harassed them when in the mood."[27]

The fact that hundreds of special forced labor camps existed for German, Austrian, and Polish Jews, entirely independently of the SS-administered concentration camp system, is scarcely known even today. These camps were established and supported by private companies, public builders, the army, even municipal administrative offices. For example, as early as spring 1939, half a year before the beginning of the war, the German city of Kelkheim im Taunus established its own "Jewish camp" in cooperation with the Frankfurt am Main labor office. After being informed about the introduction of the forced labor program, the Bürgermeister requested Jewish laborers for a local road construction project. On his order, the twenty men sent from Frankfurt to Kelkheim were beaten immediately upon arrival. The Jews were allowed to spend their narrowly restricted free time only in a "fifty-meter long and twenty-meter wide patch of woods" on the other side of the camp, in order that their presence "not mar other parts of the woods." They were

---

[25] Karla Wolf, *Ich blieb zurück* (Heppenheim, 1990), 26.

[26] Gertrud Kolmar, *Briefe an die Schwester Hilde (1938–1943)* (Munich, 1970), 158–161, Letter of July 19, 1942.

[27] Marga Spiegel, *Retter in der Nacht. Wie eine jüdische Familie überlebte* (Cologne, 1987), 14.

housed in the large dance hall of the local inn, Taunusblick. The men had to work sixty hours a week; that was not at all usual in the period before the war. Most of the labor recruits had never before performed excavation work and were entirely overtaxed physically. In short order, seven men had to be sent back because of illness. The Kelkheim Bürgermeister did not as a rule release any of the men, most of whom were married, unless they were unable to work. Cases of social need, emigration preparations, or urgent personal requests from relatives went ignored. The difficult living circumstances soon even led to suicides. After half a year, in October 1939, the Kelkheim camp was closed.[28]

As many of these camps existed only for a few months because of the limited duration of the construction projects, they are often forgotten today. They were managed by municipal or forestry administrations and private enterprises, so they do not appear in books on the Nazi camp system, which focus on the SS.[29] Only since the mid-1980s have there been descriptions of the history of local labor programs or individual labor camps in Germany.[30] Hundreds of comparable camps existed in the Warthegau and the General Government as well, supported by the Reich highway authorities or by local hydraulic construction offices; those camps likewise have barely been examined in any detail to date. By describing the extreme conditions in these labor camps, which operated completely independently of the SS, the present study places the issue of compensation for forced laborers in a new light.[31] After the war, for example, the reestablished Republic of Austria refused to compensate Jewish victims for their exploitation as forced labor by the labor administration. According to Rudolf Fischl, who slaved for five years in a camp at a power plant construction site, former forced laborers received no money because such camps were not considered detention facilities.[32] The same applies for Germany, where segregated labor deployment was not compensated until the conclusion of government negotiations in 2000. And even in the case of forced labor for private enterprises in concentration camps or in SS camps, the victims did not receive a penny until

[28] Wolf Gruner, "Terra Inkognita? – Die Lager für den 'jüdischen Arbeitseinsatz' 1938–1943 und die deutsche Bevölkerung," in *Die Deutschen und die Judenverfolgung*, edited by Ursula Büttner (Hamburg, 1992), 131–159 (revised paperback edition, Frankfurt am Main, 2003).

[29] Gudrun Schwarz, *Die nationalsozialistischen Lager* (Frankfurt am Main and New York, 1990), 73–76.

[30] For example, recent publications, such as Hubert Frankemölle (ed.), *Opfer und Täter: Zum nationalsozialistischen und antijüdischen Alltag in Ostwestfalen-Lippe* (Bielefeld, 1990); Joachim Meynert, *Was vor der Endlösung geschah. Antisemitische Ausgrenzung und Verfolgung in Minden-Ravensberg 1933–1945* (Münster, 1988); Margrit Naarmann, *Ein Auge gen Zion . . . Das jüdische Umschulungs- und Einsatzlager am Grünen Weg in Paderborn 1939–1943* (Cologne, 2000).

[31] See Chapters 2–3 and 7–9.

[32] Dokumentationsarchiv des österreichischen Widerstandes (DÖW) Vienna, Doc. No. 20100/2495, no folio numbers, CV of Rudolf Fischl (undated).

recently. Benjamin Ferencz has impressively described the survivors' odyssey and the very embarrassing behavior of German companies in his 1979 book *Less than Slaves*.[33] As the result of international pressure, surviving Jewish forced laborers have recently received monetary compensation from a common fund of the German government and private enterprises.

The following case studies systematically and comparatively analyze the preconditions, planning, and implementation of forced labor programs for Jews in Germany and Austria, as well as in the annexed Czech territories and the occupied Polish territories (see map 1, p. 10). Political, social, and economic motives for the introduction of forced labor systems are discussed, as well as their stage-by-stage development and national and regional characteristics.

Because very few files of the central, regional, and local labor administrative offices with evidential value regarding segregated labor deployment came to light in the archives, I have consulted other collections of national, regional, and local source materials. The documents of some companies, which were freely available in archives of the former German Democratic Republic, were included. In addition, I used Nazi institutional materials held at the Yad Vashem Holocaust Remembrance Authority and at the United States Holocaust Memorial Museum in Washington, DC. The diverse materials were supplemented by documentation of Jewish institutions found in archives in Israel, the United States, and Germany. Diaries, letters, and memoirs of Jewish forced laborers of both genders were also used. Information from contemporary witnesses and the documents scattered in Germany, Israel, the United States, and Austria, pieced together like a puzzle, made possible a systematic description of this hitherto unknown facet of persecution.

I will demonstrate that forced labor was implemented in Germany shortly after the November 1938 pogrom. Initially, in the first years after the assumption of power in 1933, the leading National Socialists had not developed any concept of forced labor, even though the stereotype of the "lazy Jew" had been widespread since the nineteenth century. From 1933 on, the expulsion of Jews was a high priority.[34] Nazi anti-Jewish policy, the development of which I will briefly outline in the prologue, rapidly produced unemployment and poverty in the Jewish population as restrictions on professional activities and trade increasingly obstructed speedy individual emigration. After the March 1938 Anschluss, the inherent contradictions became increasingly pronounced by the radicalized persecutory policy. However, even a Reich-wide, brutal pogrom in November 1938 did not achieve the desired result – the

---

[33] Benjamin Ferencz, *Less than Slaves: Jewish Forced Labor and the Quest for Compensation* (Cambridge, 1979), reprinted in 2002 by Indiana University Press in association with the United States Holocaust Memorial Museum.

[34] For the expulsion priorities, see Philippe Burrin, *Hitler und die Juden. Die Entscheidung für den Völkermord* (Frankfurt am Main, 1993), 12.

immediate and complete emigration of all Jews. The Nazi state thereafter began to redirect its program of persecution: first, to expel as many Jews as possible, and second, to socially isolate the remaining Jews. Under Göring's supervision, persecution was organized centrally and involved division of labor. As the first three chapters will demonstrate, part of the program was forced employment of Jews who had no earnings or income, which was to be arranged by the Reich labor administration. At the end of 1938, the labor offices began to utilize Jews, mostly for excavation work – usually without their consent and without regard to their professions, qualifications, or suitability – in columns segregated from the other workers. Half a year after the November pogrom, yet still before the beginning of the war, 20,000 German Jews were in segregated labor deployment. In 1940, the labor administration extended the forced labor requirement to all individuals capable of working. Many Jews were sent to labor camps, where they had to spend months, sometimes years. Mass recruitment in spring 1941 led to peak exploitation, with more than 50,000 people – men and women, the elderly, and even children – performing forced labor. Those who were deployed in many cases were exempted for a time from the mass deportations. The notorious 1943 *Fabrik-Aktion* (Factory Operation) and the deportation of the last forced laborers ended this chapter of persecution. Soon after, however, the labor administration arranged for the forced deployment of Jews in "mixed marriages," as well as tens of thousands of so-called *Mischlinge* (individuals with a Jewish parent or grandparent).

The system of segregated labor deployment became the model for the forced labor of hundreds of thousands of Jews in all the occupied countries, and beyond that, for the forced labor of millions of so-called foreign workers in Germany. Chapters 4 and 5 show how the labor administration introduced forced labor for Jews in Austria and the Protectorate of Bohemia and Moravia. There, too, thousands of Jews were obligated to work in construction, agriculture, forestry, and industry. Contrary to what was hitherto believed, the SS played no role in the planning and organization of forced labor. Only in the Protectorate, the Central Office for Jewish Emigration (*Zentralstelle für jüdische Auswanderung*) of the SS Security Service (*Sicherheitsdienst* or SD) in Prague controlled parts of the labor program, the result of the relatively late introduction of forced labor in early 1941. The practical planning and organization, however, remained in the hands of the labor administration. Chapters 6 through 9 describe how the regional labor administration and the municipal administration responsible for the Lodz ghetto arranged forced labor of Polish Jews in the territory of the Warthegau. With the establishment of the General Government in the other Polish territories, sole authority for Jewish forced labor passed to the SS for the first time in fall 1939. That lasted only for a few months, however. The SS had to give back responsibility to the civilian administration in summer 1940, because it was incapable of matching the work forces to the requirements of the labor market. After systematic labor programs had been established by the labor offices of the General Government, some of the regional Higher SS and Police Leaders (*Höhere SS- und Polizeiführer* or HSSPF) in Poland, in Lublin, and later in Galicia, attempted to set up their own parallel labor systems. In Upper Silesia, a newly founded SS agency even took over the organization of Jewish forced labor in late 1940. Despite the explicit orders of the Nazi leadership, many of those Jews from Upper Silesia, as well as inhabitants of the Lodz ghetto, were used on German soil as forced laborers for Reich highway and armaments construction. While in the Warthegau the labor administration continued to organize Jewish workers, the SS resumed control in the General Government in summer 1942, in the course of the progressing genocide. However, many laborers were exempted for a long time from mass murder because of the needs of the armaments and defense industries, and many were able to survive because of this.

Persecution of the Jews could not be effected by the NSDAP (*Nationalsozialistische Deutsche Arbeiterpartei*), the SA (*Sturmabteilung*), or the Gestapo alone. The deployment of hundreds of thousands of Jewish forced laborers shows that the persecution process was organized pragmatically, with an eye toward division of labor, contrary to the widespread conception of National Socialist behavior as irrational and motivated by anti-Semitism alone. Agencies of the state (from the Ministry of Labor to the local labor offices), private enterprises (from industrial concerns to small underground engineering firms), as well as public enterprises (from the highway agency to municipal garbage collection services) participated in the organization and exploitation of forced labor. In the occupied territories, the administration and the Wehrmacht were among the entities that profited the most. Far more than has been assumed previously, the requirements of the labor market, interests of the economy, and goals of war production shaped the form and course of the forced labor system. After 1940 the German labor administration managed to push through the mass utilization of Jews in skilled jobs in industry rather than in construction, despite concrete planning for deportation; at the same time the labor administration took over control of forced labor from the SS in the General Government. These circumstances change our previous perception of the conditions and course of anti-Jewish policy. The fact that deportations were modified in favor of forced labor and that the National Socialists even coordinated the genocide program with the requirements of the labor market and the economy in Germany and in Poland fundamentally refutes the thesis that compulsory work was only an intermezzo on the way to mass murder, or rather was only an element of the destruction of the Jews.

I am indebted to my friend Peter Hayes of Northwestern University for encouraging me to write this book. The Center for Advanced Holocaust Studies at the United States Holocaust Memorial Museum and its staff supported my research, especially on the Protectorate, when I was there as the Pearl

Resnick Fellow in 2002–2003. I thank the Director of Academic Publications of that institution, Benton Arnovitz, for arranging cofinancing for the book's translation. I also thank the publisher, Cambridge University Press, and its editor, Frank Smith, for publication. I am deeply grateful to Kathleen Dell'Orto for her translation and to Laura Brahm and Aleisa Fishman for their editing work. And to my family, I owe a much greater debt for this book than I can ever repay.

Prologue

Anti-Jewish Policies in the Nazi State before 1938

Persecution of Jews in Germany did not follow a clear course defined by the NSDAP in or before 1933. It evolved in an open process, with participation of far more German agencies than scholars previously assumed and with active and passive involvement at all levels of society. Anti-Jewish policy was planned, determined, and shaped by a diverse and changing cast of actors. The result was parallel lines of development and, indeed, contradictory elements.[1]

After establishing the dictatorship, the Nazi leadership professed that expulsion of the Jews was its main goal, without, however, formulating clear guidelines for achieving that. As a consequence, central and local administrations, as well as public and private institutions, gained sufficient latitude to develop, or to impede, anti-Jewish measures. Beginning in 1933, not only the government and the NSDAP leadership but also various ministries and other Reich agencies assumed responsibility centrally for conceiving and transforming persecutory policy. At the local level, the municipalities played a subsequently long-overlooked but nevertheless important role in defining anti-Jewish policies, more than local party groups or SA gangs did. A key factor in the rapid radicalization, in addition to widespread anti-Semitism, was the dynamic interchange between local and central administrative offices.

In March 1933, ministries initiated measures to exclude Jews from the legal professions, SA troops directed violent acts against personnel of the universities and courts, and the boycott on "Jewish" businesses began. At the same time a number of municipalities instituted administrative measures. After many Weimar-era mayors were rapidly and forcibly replaced with NSDAP party-liners, especially in big cities, many of the new officeholders presided over the "cleansing" of personnel in the municipal administrative

---

[1] For the prologue, see Wolf Gruner, "Die NS-Verfolgung und die Kommunen. Zur wechselseitigen Dynamisierung von zentraler und lokaler Politik 1933–1941," in *Vierteljahrshefte für Zeitgeschichte*, 48, 1 (2000): 75–126; Wolf Gruner, "Anti-Jewish Policy in Nazi Germany 1933–1945. From Exclusion and Expulsion to Segregation and Deportation. New Perspectives on Developments, Actors and Goals," in *The Comprehensive History of the Holocaust: Germany*, published by Yad Vashem (Nebraska University Press, forthcoming).

offices, prohibited their functionaries' official contact with Jews, and severed commercial ties with Jewish-owned companies and businesses – without any central orders to do so.

Beginning in mid-March, the Nazi leadership prepared a central media campaign that accelerated the spread of municipal anti-Jewish measures. With the April 1, 1933, boycott, which was organized centrally for the entire Reich, the Nazi government succeeded on the one hand in synchronizing local violent acts and municipal actions, and on the other hand in creating an anti-Jewish atmosphere in which the first anti-Jewish laws were launched. For reasons relating to foreign policy and the economy, the Nazi leaders decided against implementing comprehensive plans for discrimination. However, they subsequently issued partial professional and educational restrictions on Jews. As they saw their behavior affirmed by the central authorities, many municipalities introduced new anti-Jewish regulations in the next few months, particularly regulations that restricted access to municipal facilities. Those local initiatives were supported and coordinated by the German Council of Municipalities (*Deutscher Gemeindetag*), which was founded in May 1933 and to which all of the local governments had to belong.

After summer 1933, the Nazi leadership moderated its openly anti-Jewish state policies because of foreign policy considerations. This change brought about a shift of anti-Jewish activities to the regional and local levels,[2] a shift that until now generally has been interpreted by researchers as an abatement of persecution. Despite several central orders against separate local operations, however, in practice the Nazi leadership and ministries tolerated, even encouraged, exclusionary initiatives by city and community authorities. It was specifically in the municipalities that the inequality between Jews and non-Jews first became institutionalized.[3] While Reich laws until the end of 1934 usually affected individual Jewish social or political groups through restrictions on professional activities, education, and trade, all Jewish Germans experienced the concrete stigma of public exclusion at the sight of the sign "*Für Juden verboten,*" posted in front of the entrance to the municipal swimming pool. Putting up anti-Jewish signs was only one of many symbolic acts, such as marking businesses and park benches or prohibiting the Nazi flag from being raised at Jewish homes and businesses, which were intended to create separate worlds for Jews and non-Jews. These initiatives, which in some cases were inspired by local party organizations but in most

---

[2] Uwe Adam's view that there was in this phase no uniform approach to Jewish policy because regional measures predominated is for that reason only half true; Uwe-Dietrich Adam, *Judenpolitik im Dritten Reich* (Düsseldorf, 1972), 74.

[3] Similar observations on the question of individual operations can already be found in Reinhard Rürup, "Das Ende der Emanzipation. Die antijüdische Politik in Deutschland von der 'Machtergreifung' bis zum Zweiten Weltkrieg," in *Die Juden im Nationalsozialistischen Deutschland 1933–1945. The Jews in Nazi Germany 1933–1943*, edited by Arnold Paucker et al. (Tübingen, 1986), 109.

cases originated in the municipalities, served as a warning to the persecuted and as a signal to the rest of the population.

After strengthening Germany's domestic and foreign policies, the Nazi leadership again turned intensively in spring 1935 to anti-Jewish policy, introducing legislation that excluded Jews from the army and from the Reich Labor Service. Measures in the economic sector and measures to prevent contact between non-Jews and Jews were now vehemently discussed in the ministries. The chief of the Secret State Police (*Geheime Staatspolizei* or Gestapo), Reinhard Heydrich, brought forth for the first time his own radical proposals. At the same time the SA, fueled by intensified anti-Jewish internal party propaganda, committed new regional acts of violence, and many municipal administrative offices also initiated new measures. In summer 1935, the Nazi state managed, with an unprecedented anti-Jewish media campaign, to synchronize local violent acts, local separation of Jews in public facilities, and central anti-Jewish law projects. National anti-Jewish policy reached a new level in Nuremberg in September 1935. Introduction of the infamous "racial laws" marked the transition from the stage of state discrimination to that of legal exclusion: On the basis of a racist group definition, Germans of Jewish origin were robbed of their political and civil rights.

While the Nazi leadership announced professional prohibitions with increasing frequency in 1936 and 1937, and imposed further trade and educational restrictions on the Jewish population, persecution on the local level advanced far more rapidly. As a result of laws sanctioning the inequality between Jews and non-Jews, the municipalities now had a "legal basis" for their own initiatives at their disposal. And although at the end of 1935 the Nazi leadership once again officially prohibited individual operations, it tolerated behind-the-scenes radicalization by the local authorities. In reality, the local and central levels were not separated by conflict, but rather interacted dynamically in concert. In 1936 and 1937, the municipalities expanded the range of exclusion of Jewish Germans primarily in the area of public facilities such as baths, libraries, markets, and pawnshops. Jewish welfare dependents were discriminated against; Jews who were sick were isolated in public hospitals. The German Council of Municipalities supported the cities even against individual intervention by ministries. Mayors and municipal officials discussed anti-Jewish ideas in the German Council of Municipalities and its various specialized committees and working groups. This led to the spread and unification of local discrimination standards. Increasingly similar anti-Jewish orders took effect in a growing number of cities. While the centrally devised measures during these two years can be characterized as exclusionary, the Jewish population at the local level had already been systematically separated from the rest of the population. In the Nazi state, there were no "quiet years" for the Jews, despite researchers' previous characterization as such of the years 1934 and 1936–37.

The expectation of war, the doubling of the Jewish population in German territory as a result of the March of 1938 Anschluss, and the rapidly dwindling possibilities for emigration decisively modified the conditions for "Jewish policy." The Nazi leadership resorted to new, tougher administrative measures for the Reich, primarily relating to the economy. Terror produced by violent acts and by mass deportations to concentration camps also played a role. At the same time, a coordinated central approach was designed to bring together the divergent plans of the ministries, the SS leadership, and the Security Police. Beginning in spring 1938, Jewish property was registered. At this point, discussions were underway in the ministries about the state-organized theft of Jewish property. Prohibitions on professional activities and trade were increasingly introduced. Moreover, the first central measures were imposed to ensure isolation within the society, as were the first collective deportation orders for Jews with non-German citizenship. Several anti-Jewish laws and regulations that had long been called for by the municipalities – for example, isolation of Jewish patients in public hospitals – were introduced by summer 1938. As a result, the municipalities and communities lost what had been until now their "innovative" role in the persecutory process, but that did not by any means spell the end of local anti-Jewish initiatives. Increasingly, highly symbolic measures were employed to make apparent the segregation of the persecuted from German society. Municipal administrations used the color yellow for indicating "Jewish benches" or for printing special administrative forms for Jews.[4]

In view of a possible war, by September 1938 the Gestapo and the SS Security Service (or SD), as well as ministries, were discussing ghettoization and forced labor as options. Violence became the means of choice. At the end of October 1938, the police arrested 17,000 Jews of Polish origin and deported these men, women, and children to the Polish border. Only two weeks later, the attempt on the life of a German embassy official in Paris was adequate pretext for Hitler and the Nazi leadership to organize a pogrom against all the Jews in the Reich. On November 9 and 10, synagogues burned all over Germany. The SA and the SS not only destroyed many businesses but also demolished numerous residences and Jewish facilities – a fact barely noticed until now. Considerably more than 100 Jews were murdered. Close to 30,000 men were taken to concentration camps, where many died of beatings, hunger, and cold in the next weeks.

Even so, violence could not solve the basic problem of persecutory policy: An ever-growing number of people without means no longer had any chance of emigrating. Instead of responding to this contradiction by relaxing its own policy, the Nazi leadership agreed in 1938, after the November pogrom, on a radicalization and reorientation of anti-Jewish policy that was to have serious consequences historically. On the one hand, Jews were to be forced out by any means available, and on the other, the remaining individuals were to be dispossessed of all property and isolated from German society. This

---

[4] For the latter in Berlin, see Wolf Gruner, *Öffentliche Wohlfahrt und Judenverfolgung. Wechselwirkungen lokaler und zentraler Politik im NS-Staat (1933–1942)* (Munich, 2002), 135.

marked the beginning of a new phase of central Nazi policy, the transition from a policy of expulsion to one of systematically segregating the Jewish population. In the following months, laws and regulations mandated taxes, expropriation and forced Aryanization of Jewish property, and a total ban on Jewish involvement in business activities. Jews were excluded from the school and welfare systems, and the decision was reached that they were to be ghettoized. The policy redefined in the weeks after the November pogrom not only extended to isolating most of the German Jews who were unable to emigrate, but also to reorganizing their lives, whether in terms of education or social welfare. The vehicle was to be a new compulsory organization, the *Reichsvereinigung der Juden in Deutschland* (Reich Association of Jews in Germany). Germans of the Jewish faith, as well as Germans considered Jews on the basis of racist criteria, were thus systematically separated out by the Nazi state as a compulsory community (*Zwangsgemeinschaft*).

From that point forward, Hermann Göring centrally coordinated the persecutory process, which was organized according to the principle of division of labor. While the Reich Ministry of Economics took charge of the Aryanization of business enterprises and the municipalities took responsibility for concentrating the Jewish population in so-called Jews' houses (*Judenhäuser*), the Gestapo and the Security Service of the SS, charged with forcing emigration, oversaw the means and activities of the Reichsvereinigung. Another important but nevertheless often overlooked element of the new policy was a forced labor system, to be organized by the German labor administration.

GERMANY

1

Segregated Labor Deployment – Central Planning and Local Practice, 1938–1945

PERSECUTORY POLICY IN 1938 AND INITIAL PLANS FOR FORCED LABOR

Historical researchers and the public still usually associate forced labor by German Jews in the Nazi period with work in concentration camps, or sometimes with assignment to industrial enterprises shortly before deportation. The fact that forced labor had already functioned as an integral component of anti-Jewish policy since 1938 was scarcely known until recently. In the concepts and plans for persecution of Jews developed after 1933 by leading Nazis, there was initially no reference to forced labor. The foremost objective was rapid and complete expulsion of Jewish Germans from Germany. However, with the Anschluss, 200,000 additional Jews came under German rule. At the same time, obstacles to mass emigration proliferated. The greater the number of persecutory measures introduced, the deeper the Jews sank into poverty. Without financial means, leaving remained illusory for most Jews. At the same time, willingness abroad to accept refugees diminished. It dawned on the Nazi leadership that their goal of expelling all Jews could no longer be attained with the methods used before.[1]

Thus, ideas about forced labor first evolved primarily as a spontaneous means of exerting pressure to force departure, then later as a planned element of the changed persecutory policy. At the end of May 1938, for example, Hitler demanded that "asocial and criminal Jews" be arrested to "perform important excavation work throughout the Reich."[2] Whether this was intended as a real work project or not is difficult to assess. Heydrich decided in any case to implement this directive, with the raid on "asocials" that he

---

[1] Chapter 1 is an extensively expanded and revised version of the author's essay, "Der geschlossene Arbeitseinsatz und die Juden in Frankfurt am Main 1938–1942," in *"Nach der Kristallnacht". Jüdisches Leben und antijüdische Politik 1938–1945 in Frankfurt am Main*, edited by Monica Kingreen (Frankfurt am Main and New York, 1999), 259–288. Unless stated otherwise, the remarks are based on the study of the author entitled, *Der Geschlossene Arbeitseinsatz deutscher Juden. Zur Zwangsarbeit als Element der Verfolgung 1938 bis 1943* (Berlin, 1997).

[2] Yad Vashem Archive (YV), Jerusalem, 051/OSOBI (Center for the Preservation of the Historical Documentary Collection [Moscow]), No. 88, Fol. 33, June 8, 1938, note from the SD Jewish section on the June 1, 1938, session at the Reich Security Main Office.

had just arranged, to put so-called shirkers, beggars, and so forth, in concentration camps to serve as laborers. Even a one-month prison sentence marked a Jew as an "asocial" or a "criminal"; it could, for example, be the penalty for a traffic offense. In the course of the so-called "Asozialen-Aktion" (Asocial Operation), considerably more than 2,500 "previously convicted" Jews were taken away in June 1938; at that level, the number of Jews affected was disproportionate. In contrast to the other people arrested, no proof of fitness to work was required of Jews.[3]

More repression did little to change the situation of the Jewish population; in this respect, the Nazi policy obstructed itself. The Nazis in charge therefore went in search of new ideas. In response to the growing contradiction between the declared goal of expulsion and the large number of Jews without income and dependent on public welfare – a number that was rapidly growing due to new repressive measures – discussions for the first time raised the possibility of including comprehensive forced-labor measures in future anti-Jewish policy. In light of acute labor shortages and growing welfare expenditures, the Nazi leadership simply had to bring itself to exploit, methodically and compulsorily, the labor potential of about 60,000 unemployed Jews[4] in Germany, if not all able-bodied Jews.[5] Models had been developed since the mid-thirties by the municipal welfare offices. Since that time, Berlin, Duisburg, Leipzig, and Hamburg had as a matter of principle sent all impoverished Jews supported by public welfare to work performing unpaid mandatory labor in separate columns at special work sites or even special camps. In contrast to Aryan welfare recipients, the Jews had to work off the support funds received from the state. Local labor offices also introduced such programs for recipients of unemployment insurance.[6]

The impetus for a Reich initiative came from annexed Austria. There the Viennese labor administration had started in September 1938 "to have Jews supported with public funds perform excavation work, quarry work, etc., until they [were] able to emigrate."[7] In accordance with this idea, which drew upon the compulsory labor model of the welfare administration, the Reich Institute for Labor Placement and Unemployment Insurance

3 The Jews, more than 2,500, made up at least one-quarter of the total of about 10,000 arrestees in the Reich; Gruner, *Der geschlossene Arbeitseinsatz*, 41–45. For the June operation, see Wolfgang Ayaß, *"Asoziale" im Nationalsozialismus* (Stuttgart, 1995), 147–165.

4 Avraham Barkai, "Der wirtschaftliche Existenzkampf der Juden im Dritten Reich 1933–1938," in *Die Juden im Nationalsozialistischen Deutschland. The Jews in Nazi Germany 1933–1943*, edited by Arnold Paucker (Tübingen, 1986), 156.

5 Gruner, *Der geschlossene Arbeitseinsatz*, 40–54.

6 For details, see Gruner, *Öffentliche Wohlfahrt und Judenverfolgung. Wechselwirkungen lokaler und zentraler Politik im NS-Staat (1933–1942)* (Munich, 2002).

7 Österreichisches Staatsarchiv/Archiv der Republik (ÖStA/AdR) Vienna, Bürckel Materials, Carton 24, No. 1762/2, Fols. 40–41, Gärtner (Branch Office of the Reich Institute in Vienna) to the Reich Governor Bürckel, September 20, 1938. See Chapter 4.

(*Reichsanstalt für Arbeitsvermittlung und Arbeitslosenversicherung*, or RAfAA) was already preparing in mid-October for general utilization of all Jewish unemployment relief recipients in Germany.[8] At the same time, the SS had just begun to consider forced labor. In September, during the so-called Sudeten crisis, the SS Security Service made plans to intern all Jews in Germany in forced-labor camps in case of war.[9] If the SS saw in forced labor a means of forestalling the potential security risk of tens of thousands of unemployed men, the labor administration was more interested in the labor potential. Both conceptions of forced labor were in any case based on the assumption that tens of thousands of Jewish men and women would remain for the short and middle terms in Germany.

After the Munich Agreement, the Nazi leadership resorted to force as the instrument for Jewish policy, with the intent of accelerating expulsion. First, 17,000 Jews with Polish citizenship were forcibly expelled at the end of October 1938; then, only two weeks later, an organized pogrom swept the Reich. The actual turning point in persecutory policy, however, was less the resort to violent action than the ensuing fundamental reorientation of Jewish persecution. Forced labor and ghettoization, until then discussed only in the event of war, were integrated into the new conception of "Jewish policy"– *Zwangsgemeinschaft* (the forced community). However, the Nazi leadership assigned the task of organizing a forced labor system not to the SS, but to the labor administration, to guarantee exploitation of unemployed Jewish workers socially dependent on the Nazi state in a manner advantageous to the labor market.[10]

YEAR OF INTRODUCTION, END OF 1938–SUMMER 1939

Segregated labor deployment was first introduced for all unemployed Jews registered at labor offices (*Arbeitsämter*) who received unemployment insurance benefits. While the Nazis understood "labor deployment" to mean quasi-military regulation of the labor market, the term "*Der Geschlossene Arbeitseinsatz*," that is, segregated labor deployment, was used for specific forms of forced labor developed by the labor administration. The December

---

[8] Decree of the Reich Institute for Labor Placement and Unemployment Insurance, October 19, 1938; excerpt in Dieter Maier, "Arbeitsverwaltung und nationalsozialistische Judenverfolgung in den Jahren 1933–1939," in *Beiträge zur Nationalsozialistischen Gesundheits- und Sozialpolitik*, Vol. 8 (Berlin, 1989), 110. For the history of the Reich Institute, see Volker Hermann, *Vom Arbeitsmarkt zum Arbeitseinsatz. Zur Geschichte der Reichsanstalt für Arbeitsvermittlung und Arbeitslosenversicherung 1929 bis 1939* (Frankfurt am Main, 1993).

[9] Gruner, *Der geschlossene Arbeitseinsatz*, 47–48.

[10] At the year change from 1938 to 1939, there were no unskilled laborers for expansion of the infrastructure because foreigners could rarely be employed due to the lack of foreign exchange; Gruner, *Der geschlossene Arbeitseinsatz*, 62–66.

20, 1938, decree of Friedrich Syrup, the President of the Reich Institute for Labor Placement and Unemployment Insurance, states: "The state has no interest in leaving the labor potential of unemployed Jews capable of working untapped and of possibly using public funds to support them without anything in return. The goal is to quickly put to work all unemployed able-bodied Jews. . . . They will be utilized in factories and divisions of factories, in construction and improvement, separated from loyal followers."[11] This decree was not specific about practical organization or legal terms of employment. Nevertheless, the decree was to constitute the basis for German Jews' forced labor over the course of almost three years, until October 1941.

The Reich labor administration[12] had sole responsibility for planning and executing this anti-Jewish measure and, consequently, enormous latitude for creative organization. In practice, Jews in the segregated labor deployment program across Germany were subject to a "separate law" from the outset: in the compulsory labor requirement based on racial criteria; in the principle of deployment in formations (*Kolonneneinsatz*) rather than as individuals; in the nature of the work, which neglected qualifications and professional knowledge; in exploitation as underpaid unskilled workers; and in segregation from non-Jews in the labor office and in the workplace.

To ensure effective organization of compulsory employment, most of Germany's big cities created special offices in the labor administrations. But to implement the forced-labor program at all, labor offices needed extensive help from public institutions and private enterprises. However, they could not force city administrations, regional builders, or private firms to use Jews. From the beginning, regional labor offices attempted to find building sites suitable for planned use of Jewish columns in their area. Regional labor offices arranged transfers preferably to infrastructure construction projects that were important for the national economy (for instance, highway construction and canal, dike, and dam projects). In Hesse, for example, the

---

[11] Complete reproduction of this document (PS-1720 of the Nuremberg Trial materials) in Wolf Gruner, "Der Beginn der Zwangsarbeit für arbeitslose Juden in Deutschland 1938/39. Dokumente aus der Stadtverwaltung Berlin," in *Zeitschrift für Geschichtswissenschaft*, 37, 2 (1989): 139, Doc. No. 1. Syrup was born in 1881 in Lüchow, Lower Saxony. He was the president of the Reich Office for Labor Placement (*Reichsamt für Arbeitsvermittlung*) from 1920 to 1927 and president of the Reich Institute for Labor Placement and Unemployment Insurance from 1927 to 1938. After integration of that Institute in the Reich Labor Ministry, Syrup was appointed to the position of State Secretary (*Staatssekretär*). After the war, he died during his internment in the former Sachsenhausen Concentration Camp near Berlin in 1945.

[12] Until the end of 1938, this was the Reich Institute; after its integration into the Reich Ministry of Labor, the Ministry; and after February 1942, the General Commissioner for Labor Utilization. Labor offices existed at the local level before 1933. These institutions registered unemployed people, kept track of them, and provided state benefits for a limited period of time. Beginning in early 1939, local labor offices became Reich agencies under the Ministry of Labor.

Gauleiter provided assistance. In the Hesse-Nassau Gau, including the city of Frankfurt am Main, 250 Jews could initially be recruited because they had registered as unemployed. On instructions of the NSDAP Gauleiter, 200 Jews were used for an improvement program in Homberg, and part of the remaining fifty for construction projects in Mainz.[13] Many of the unemployed Jews were sent by labor offices to work sites at some distance from their homes. By the summer of 1939, more than thirty camps had been created under the direction of the Reich labor administration for segregated labor deployment of Jews in Old Reich territory (Germany within its 1937 borders) alone, outside and independent of the concentration camp system. The regional focal point of this labor camp system was Lower Saxony.[14] Dike and road construction offices, companies for dam construction, and municipal administrations took responsibility for organizing the Jewish labor camps, and were also the beneficiaries.

City administrations used the cheap forced labor to build streets, collect garbage, and construct parks and sports fields. Whether and how Jews were utilized in municipalities depended to a great extent on the attitude and the involvement of the particular administration. The Kelkheim Bürgermeister who requested Jews from Frankfurt in spring 1939 and set up a labor camp at the local inn was not only interested in racial exploitation of the Frankfurt Jews; he also wanted his city to profit unduly from their labor. Bürgermeister Wilhelm Graf requested authorization from the Frankfurt am Main labor office to be allowed to inflict especially low wages on his "columns of Jews." Furthermore, without even contacting the competent authorities, he simply shrugged off the workers' right to days off and ordered, "The Jews must work on April 20 (the birthday of the Führer)."[15] Comparable special regulations existed in many places, pushed through by public builders and by private companies. Such initiatives represented the informal onset of a separate labor law, as no relevant anti-Jewish decree had been issued centrally.[16] In May 1939, about 10,000 to 15,000 predominantly male Jews were working in

---

[13] Stadtarchiv (StadtA) Kelkheim im Taunus, Record Volume "Labor Utilization of a Column of Jews" (April–October, 1939), no folio numbers, Note of the Kelkheim Bürgermeister, March 6, 1939.

[14] See Chapter 2. For general remarks on what follows, see also Gruner, *Der geschlossene Arbeitseinsatz*, 217–218.

[15] The Bürgermeister turned down the construction businessman Bechtoldt who was seeking Jewish workers from him because Bechtoldt was prepared to pay RM 0.82 per hour to Jews, which was almost 30 Pfennig more than the low rate sought by the Bürgermeister. Only one of the city council members, Josef Herr, later demanded, for example, that the Bürgermeister revalue the work, as most of the married Jews could not get by on the inadequate wages paid; StadtA Kelkheim im Taunus, Record Volume "Labor Utilization of a Column of Jews," no folio numbers, File note on an order of the Kelkheim Bürgermeister, April 17, 1939; ibid., Note, March 31, 1939; ibid., Note of the Bürgermeister, May 20, 1939; ibid., Letter, June 15, 1939.

[16] See Gruner, *Der geschlossene Arbeitseinsatz*.

the segregated labor deployment program. A second Reich Labor Ministry decree on May 19 was designed to remove the remaining ideological barriers, economic problems, and organizational obstacles.[17]

The Nazi census for May recorded 14,461 Jews in Frankfurt am Main, 2.61 percent of the city's residents.[18] As the example of Kelkheim illustrates, the fact that Frankfurt had the second largest number of Jewish inhabitants in Germany clearly influenced planning for local use of forced labor. The local labor office was able to send a number of Jewish laborers to construction projects outside the city. At that point, the forced laborers represented a labor reserve that was doubly interesting, as problems with currency transfer hindered the mass employment of foreigners that was actually intended. Without the utilization of seventy Jews from Frankfurt am Main, arranged in July 1939 by the Hessian state labor office, the Reich Autobahn construction management office in Kassel could no longer have guaranteed procurement of materials to complete Reich grain storage construction projects and high priority stretches of roadway by the beginning of the war.[19]

As a result of interregional labor transfers, the Reich labor administration succeeded through the summer months in increasing the labor force Reichwide to about 20,000 Jewish forced laborers, almost all of them men.[20] In view of this considerable number, the Reich Interior Ministry pressured the Reich Ministry of Labor in summer 1939 to commit to defining the labor status of the Jews. The Reich Interior Ministry favored a definition that held that Jews in segregated labor deployment were not in a formal employment category (*Arbeitsverhältnis*), but instead were in a "de facto employment category."[21] Two years later, in 1941–42, this concept was to be the keystone of the forced labor orders for German Jews, Poles, and Eastern workers employed in the Reich.

DEPORTATION OR FORCED LABOR? FALL 1939–WINTER 1939–40

The beginning of the war was a radical turning point for the development of anti-Jewish policy. The war signaled the ultimate failure of the Nazi leadership's previous persecutory policy, despite all course corrections. After the borders and transit routes had been closed, mass emigration was

---

[17] Gruner, *Der geschlossene Arbeitseinsatz*, 92–107.

[18] YV, Jerusalem, M1DN, No. 76, Fol. 30 and verso, Protocol of an April 11, 1940, meeting with the Frankfurt Oberbürgermeister recorded by the city treasurer.

[19] The workers were to be available on July 17; Bundesarchiv (BA) Berlin, 46.01 General Inspector for German Roadways (GIS), No. 1205, Fol. 62 and verso, Note of the General Inspector for German Roadways, July 8, 1939, and handwritten note, July 13, 1939.

[20] Gruner, *Der geschlossene Arbeitseinsatz*, 92–107.

[21] BA Berlin, 31.01 Reich Minister of Economics (RWM), No. 10310, Fol. 75 and verso, Reich Interior Ministry to the Reich Ministry of Labor, among others, July 23, 1939.

unworkable, even under compulsion. The September 1939 attack on Poland prompted the Nazi leadership to consider what should be done with the mass of impoverished Jews in war time. Plans at the beginning of the year had included "war service of the Jews"; about 200,000 workers from the Old Reich and annexed territories had been anticipated but no concrete preparations were proposed. In the second week after the war began, confusion still reigned. In view of Poland's rapid fall, the Nazi leadership made the radical decision in the third week of September to "resettle" the German Jews there in the near future. As a consequence, the plan to introduce forced labor for all Jews in Germany, which Hitler himself wanted to authorize, did not take effect right away.[22]

Instead, on the Nazi leadership's orders the labor administration was to continue the segregated labor deployment program following the organizational model in use up to that point, until resettlement of the Jews was feasible. As a result of the war-time reform of labor law, the availability of Jewish forced labor increased tremendously. All Jews capable of working but previously supported by public welfare were now entitled to receive unemployment insurance, but at the same time were obligated to register with the labor offices. Many men, and a growing number of women, were thus brought under the control of the labor offices. While the labor offices now had a growing number of Jews at their disposal, the number of work slots in the columns decreased due to many building projects being halted because they were not critical to the war. In addition, the Nazi leadership's persecutory policy was unpredictable for the long term, with the result that the labor offices at this time made only short-term commitments. Hence, they arranged for the allocation of hundreds of Jews to farms to help with the fall harvest, and in the winter primarily to cities for snow removal.[23]

THE YEAR OF EXPANSION, SPRING 1940–SUMMER 1941

When deportations from Germany to the General Government were halted in spring 1940 after the first transports from Pomerania, the Reich labor administration took advantage of the lack of political activity to expand segregated labor deployment. New mobilizations of the *Wehrmacht* (armed forces) and increased armaments production in preparation for the occupation of France had resulted in significant labor shortages in the German market.

[22] Gruner, *Der geschlossene Arbeitseinsatz*, 107–116. Regarding the early decision about the deportation of all German Jews, see Wolf Gruner, "Von der Kollektivausweisung zur Deportation der Juden aus Deutschland. Neue Perspektiven und Dokumente (1938–1945)," in *Beiträge zur Geschichte des Nationalsozialismus, Bd. 20: Deportationen der Juden aus Deutschland. Pläne, Praxis, Reaktionen 1938–1945* (Göttingen, 2004), 21–62.

[23] Gruner, *Der geschlossene Arbeitseinsatz*, 116–117.

Map 1. The Greater German Reich and the General Government (1940)

Approximately 11,500 Jewish citizens still lived in Frankfurt am Main at that time. By the end of April 1940, the pool of able-bodied welfare recipients was depleted. With the changes in labor legislation after the war began, the number of individuals eligible for recruitment had increased to over 2,000 registered with the department established for compulsory labor at the Jewish welfare office in Frankfurt am Main. However, besides more than 100 women (most of whom usually took care of relatives), 840 of 1,961 available male Jews were already over fifty years old. One thousand fifteen were regarded as only capable of working part-time. Nine hundred and forty-six men (more than half in the seventeen-to-fifty age group and a third in the fifty-to-sixty age group) were already employed. Of these, 546 performed forced labor (331 in brick or excavation work; 215 carrying coal or similar jobs); and 400 worked in Jewish organizations. As most of the women attended to relatives in need of care, only 142 Jewish women were registered as suitable for labor. Thirty-nine women worked for the forest management section of the municipal construction office attending to planting in the city forest.[24] As no more people fit to work and supported by public funds or by Jewish offices were available, the local "Gestapo representative in the Jewish welfare office," who was arrogating control of forced labor,[25] pressed for a change in the obligation requirements that were in effect up to that point: He negotiated with the Frankfurt labor office about forced labor "by individuals capable of forced labor but not receiving support."[26] The representative in Frankfurt, however, was the exception. As a rule, the labor offices in German cities and regions arranged for forced labor on their own responsibility, without the intervention of other authorities.

The Frankfurt initiative coincided with the decision of the Reich labor administration above the regional level to include almost all Jews in the forced-labor program, even those not supported with public funds. The decision was made with an eye to the labor required to prepare for the French campaign. The call issued to *all* Jewish men under fifty-five years old and *all* Jewish women under fifty years old to report for segregated labor deployment marked the transition from a labor requirement for selected groups to general forced labor for German Jews. No change in law effected this transition; no special order was issued. The sole basis was the old December 20, 1938, decree.[27]

Beyond this expansion of compulsory service, a further change was evident: Jewish men, and with increasing frequency Jewish women, were for the first time working in large numbers as unskilled laborers in the industrial sector rather than performing support work in construction or the transportation sector, as before. The demands of the armaments industry for another half-million workers was only a secondary factor in this change. At first, the goal of employment of Jews in industry was to release unskilled people of "German blood" for mobilization, vocational training, and reorientation activities. Jewish women were especially sought after on the one hand because of the small percentage of Aryan women in the work force, and on the other because of the specific demands of technology, for example the precision engineering branch of industry. For that reason, women were soon singled out for employment in more skilled jobs than previously.[28]

Mass utilization, which in the meantime affected tens of thousands, and the ever-growing commitment of Jews as unskilled workers in German industry, called for a formal definition of Jews' labor status. The Reich Interior Ministry, the SS, and the Office of the Führer's Deputy required that Jews only

---

[24] *Dokumente zur Geschichte der Frankfurter Juden*, published by the Commission for Research on the History of the Frankfurt Jews (Frankfurt am Main, 1963), XIII 1, 456–457, Report of the Gestapo representative to the Oberbürgermeister of Frankfurt, May 3, 1940.

[25] Ibid., VI 50, 336, Gestapo draft, May 31, 1940.

[26] Ibid., XIII 1, 456–457, Report of the Gestapo representative to the Frankfurt Oberbürgermeister, May 3, 1940.

[27] Gruner, *Der geschlossene Arbeitseinsatz*, 133–151.

[28] Ibid.

be paid the minimum wage without any special benefits. The Wehrmacht, the Economics Ministry, the Commissioner for the Four-Year Plan, and the Ministry of Labor favored a more moderate form of discrimination under labor law so as not to impact negatively the forced laborers' productivity.[29] Even though no agreement was reached despite renewed discussion, the Reich Ministry of Labor could now assume consensus of the ministries on further reducing forced employees' social status. For that reason, the State Secretary of the Reich Ministry of Labor charged the Reich Trustees of Labor (*Reichstreuhänder der Arbeit*) at the beginning of June 1940 with issuing regulations on discrimination against Jews under labor law. A whole catalogue listed which wage and operational benefits, bonuses on special holidays, or maternity and marriage subsidies were to be eliminated for Jews.[30] Labor offices, private companies, and public builders in various places had long since already collaboratively implemented much of what was on the list.

Planning for the attack on the Soviet Union – which had accelerated since the fall of 1940 – and the associated expansion of armaments and new Wehrmacht mobilizations greatly affected the nature of segregated labor deployment in Germany, because a growing number of skilled laborers were missing from production. The labor administration therefore finally began including the Jewish labor force in its long-term planning. The transformation in labor policy that had begun in spring accelerated after October 1940. In a new wave, compulsory commitments of Jews to workplaces in industry rose precipitously, and from this point on were of unlimited duration. Jews were now often trained for skilled workers' positions. This was a fundamental departure from the dictum of 1939, that Jews were only to be utilized for unskilled labor. At New Year's in 1941, the labor administration even withdrew Jewish forced laborers from the construction sector to be allocated to industry instead.[31] In Frankfurt as well, recruitment became intense at this time, and the labor office there, as in other cities, made use of the local Jewish community. The latter sent out forms and required that even the few people still allowed to work as professionals report for forced labor. In January 1941, for example, Mathilde Cahn received an order to report. She worked as the office assistant to her husband, the attorney Dr. Robert Cahn, one of the few legal consultants for Jews still permitted to work independently. Without the help of his wife, however, he was unable personally and financially to maintain his office operation.[32]

---

[29] For a detailed discussion and description of development, see Gruner, *Der geschlossene Arbeitseinsatz*, 152–160.

[30] BA Berlin, R 43 II Reich Chancellery, No. 548 a, Fol. 73–74 verso, June 3, 1940, circular letter of the Reich Ministry of Labor, with the June 3, 1940, circular decree to the Reich Trustees of Labor attached.

[31] Gruner, *Der geschlossene Arbeitseinsatz*, 161–178.

[32] Hessisches Hauptstaatsarchiv (HHStA) Wiesbaden, Dep. 474/2, No. 271, no folio numbers, Cahn to the Jewish Religious Association, Labor Utilization Department, January 15, 1941.

Short-term recruitment in Frankfurt am Main was for assignment both to industry and to the municipal administration; the same was true in other cities as well (see photo 1, p. 20). The Jewish Religious Association (*Jüdische Kulturvereinigung*) sent out the following circular on January 19, 1941: "According to information provided by the authorities, the number of Jews who have reported so far for emergency operations (removing snow and collecting garbage) is entirely inadequate. To avoid drastic action by the competent offices, an *urgent* request is going out to all men under sixty years of age who are not yet being utilized as labor but are somehow in a position to be, to make themselves available voluntarily for emergency measures, in return for the usual remuneration. . . . *Labor utilization of women*. Female workers under fifty years old who have not yet reported to our labor allocation department are asked to report immediately to the Labor Allocation Department, Röderbergweg 29, II, Room 17."[33] Many private enterprises not only replaced workers lost as soldiers but also through the new recruitment efforts even increased production and turnover by establishing new "Jewish departments" or introducing third "Jewish shifts." For companies, Jewish forced laborers were attractive because in practice they had already long since been in a "special employment category."

Since 1939, both the administrative acts mentioned[34] and labor courts' discriminatory legal decisions had established a special status for German Jews under labor law. For example, in September 1940 the Frankfurt am Main labor court denied the suit of a compulsory employee for vacation wages because Jews only had a right to wages for work performed. The judge justified the decision with the argument that in the Nazi state the entrepreneur and the loyal follower (*Gefolgsmann*) were bound by a relationship of mutual loyalty and assistance under personal law that was unthinkable between an Aryan and a non-Aryan. Wage rate determinations based on this obligation to be loyal and to provide assistance, also including paid vacation, therefore did not apply in the case of Jews.[35] The SS journal *Das Schwarze Korps* picked up and publicized this decision at the beginning of October 1940,[36] reigniting the central discussion – smoldering since 1939 – regarding a special legal status for Jewish employees. In January 1941, the competent Reich ministries finally agreed officially to classify the Jews in the Old Reich as forced labor. A draft order stated, "§ 1 Jews are obligated to accept the employment assigned to them by the labor office. § 2 (1) The employment

---

[33] (Emphasis in the original.) Announcement No. 7 of the Jewish Religious Association in Frankfurt, January 19, 1941. (The document was very kindly made available by Mrs. Monika Kingreen.)

[34] Gruner, *Der geschlossene Arbeitseinsatz*, 92–107 and 151–161.

[35] Ernst Noam and Wolf-Arno Kropat, *Juden vor Gericht 1933–1945. Dokumente aus hessischen Justizakten*, preface by Johannes Strehlitz (Wiesbaden, 1975) 99–100, Court decision of September 4, 1940 (short version).

[36] *Das Schwarze Korps*, October 3, 1940: 4.

relationship with Jews is not a work relationship in the meaning of labor law as it applies to German workers."[37] This order, which of course only legalized what had long since been practice at labor offices, was not issued initially for a variety of reasons. Its contents were nevertheless circulated to the public at the beginning of March in articles of daily newspapers.[38]

Those publications are the basis for the topos, still widely held today, regarding the March 1941 introduction of forced labor. In reality, no new order appeared at that point,[39] and utilization of forced labor had not just begun. A month earlier, at the beginning of February, segregated labor deployment in Germany already included 41,000 German and stateless Jews, 24,500 men and 16,500 women. With that, the pool of available Jewish workers was considered exhausted. The Reich labor administration had expanded the Jewish work program initiated at the end of 1938 into the perfect forced-labor organization within two years.[40]

In reality, what occurred in March 1941 was just another round of forced recruitment. The difference from the mustering of 1940 was that the Reich Security Main Office (RSHA) and the labor administration worked together for the first time in this operation. In contrast to the situation in the General Government, the influence of the SS on the Jewish forced-labor program in Germany had remained limited because of the way in which persecutory activities were distributed organizationally.[41] The RSHA only controlled the work of several hundred Jewish inmates from a few dozen camps for forestry and agriculture that were nominally subordinate to the Reichsvereinigung.[42] Because of the anticipated attack on the Soviet Union, however, Hitler had abandoned previous post-war planning efforts and instructed at the beginning of December 1940 first that Austrian Jews were to be "evacuated" to

37 *Akten der Parteikanzlei der NSDAP*, published by the Institut der Zeitgeschichte, Part II, Vol. 4 (Munich, and Vienna, 1983), Microfiche No. 044769, Note from the Reich Ministry of Justice, January 9, 1941; excerpt in Kurt Pätzold (ed.), *Verfolgung, Vertreibung, Vernichtung. Dokumente des faschistischen Antisemitismus 1933–1942* (Leipzig, 1983), 280–281, Doc. No. 256.

38 Gruner, *Der geschlossene Arbeitseinsatz*, 199–204.

39 On March 4, 1941, State Secretary Syrup authorized the labor administration to ignore "objections of the sort relating to population, national characteristics, or racial policies in implementing labor utilization measures necessary for the war economy." This was cited in research literature as the decree that initiated forced labor for Jews, without Jews even being mentioned in it; see Joseph Walk (ed.), *Das Sonderrecht für die Juden im NS-Staat. Eine Sammlung der gesetzlichen Maßnahmen – Inhalt und Bedeutung* (Heidelberg and Karlsruhe, 1981), IV/174, 336. The citation does not go back to the original, but instead provides an inaccurate interpretation of the Reich Minister of Labor's March 14, 1941 decree. The latter sought to bring about the special utilization of Polish Jews in Germany. See Paul Sauer (ed.), *Dokumente über die Verfolgung der jüdischen Bürger in Baden-Württemberg durch das nationalsozialistische Regime 1933–1943*, Part II (Stuttgart, 1966), 203–204, Doc. No. 421.

40 Gruner, *Der geschlossene Arbeitseinsatz*, 176.

41 For a detailed discussion, see Chapters 6–9 of the present study.

42 See Chapters 2–3 and 7–9.

Poland during the war. The RSHA then attempted to tighten the budgets of the German Jewish institutions in preparation for coming deportations. To that end, the Gestapo ordered in February and March 1941 that the personnel of all Jewish organizations in the Reich be reduced by several thousand employees, and that training courses and camps be shut down. All persons dismissed were sent to labor offices for use as forced labor.[43]

The situation was similar in Frankfurt am Main, where the number of personnel in the Jewish Community dropped considerably. The Gestapo representative's report states, "If the people in question were fit for employment in the general market, they were sent to German businesses." The Gestapo's objective was at the same time to reduce expenditures for Jewish welfare by increasing use of forced labor, and the effort apparently met with success.[44] In Frankfurt, some individuals attempted to resist recruitment by petitioning to be allowed to practice the professions that they had been forced to give up. The Gestapo, however, pressured the municipal police to reject such petitions, because "the Jews [were] urgently needed for forced labor."[45] In this case, too, the RSHA and the labor administration acted together – even if with different motives.

In April 1941, a total of 1,628 Jewish forced laborers (1,104 men and 524 women) were working in Frankfurt am Main. By May, the number had grown to 1,802. This increase, only marginally attributable to personnel dismissals in Jewish organizations, was due instead to increased use of young people.[46] The underlying reason was that even minors fourteen years old and above were being recruited Reich-wide as the last reserve. From April to June 1941, the number of Jewish young people under eighteen years old being utilized for labor in Frankfurt rose from 98 to 134; two-thirds of the total were girls.[47] While a few workers still seemed to be available in Frankfurt am Main, the labor pool suitable for industry in the Reich capital Berlin was to all appearances exhausted, despite the new initiatives. The labor administration therefore negotiated with the RSHA in March 1941 in hopes of employing Jewish girls from other regions in the Berlin armaments factories. Employment of almost 200 women from Frankfurt am Main in the Siemens-Schuckert Werke AG in Berlin was a pilot operation. The RSHA made establishment of a company-owned camp a condition for transfer of outside Jews to Berlin – that is, ruled out the housing of individuals privately. Consequently, the only verifiable Jewish labor camp within the city

---

[43] Gruner, *Der geschlossene Arbeitseinsatz*, 178–184.

[44] The number of households dropped by 230, the number of people by 445; *Dokumente Frankfurter Juden*, XIII 2, 461–462, Report of the Gestapo representative at the Jewish welfare office, July 12, 1941.

[45] Ibid., IV 27 C, 209, Gestapo to the Municipal Police, April 18, 1941.

[46] Stadtarchiv (StadtA) Frankfurt am Main, F Main Records 7020/11, no folio numbers, Attachment to the report of the Gestapo representative, July 12, 1941.

[47] Ibid., Attachment to the report of the Gestapo representative, July 12, 1941.

of Berlin was established for this operation.[48] The girls worked for Siemens at minimum wage rates and took their midday meal in the factory canteen, while a "simple evening meal" was served in the camp. The Gestapo, with the help of the company, subjected the girls to special harassments such as a prohibition on returning home to Hesse during Easter vacation;[49] the fear of being reported by the foreman or other factory workers dominated their everyday lives, as reports of survivors demonstrate.[50]

The drift in the power relationship between the labor administration and the Security Police was especially evident in Frankfurt am Main because of the Gestapo representatives' unique position there. While the labor office had previously recruited by themselves as in other cities or by working through the labor allocation department of the Frankfurt Jewish community, the control and demands in the meantime obviously came directly from the Gestapo representative's labor allocation department at the Jewish welfare office. After another recruiting operation in mid-May 1941, affecting both self-employed persons and persons employed in businesses (among them the aforementioned wife of attorney Cahn[51]), the Frankfurt am Main Gestapo representative once again, at the beginning of June, used the labor administration to tighten his control over forced labor. In a circular of Administrative Inspector Ernst Holland, he ordered that commencement of work by any Jewish forced laborer after assignment by the labor office, or departure from a company, was to be reported to his department, as was any laborer's incapacity to work. Any illness that lasted longer than three days had to be registered with him, verified by a medical certificate and a prognosis for the outcome.[52]

At this time, the plant management of the Voltohm Seil- und Kabelwerke AG (wire and cable manufacturers) in Frankfurt am Main replaced workers who were consistently absent with Jewish forced laborers. By May 1941, the Jewish forced laborers constituted 40 percent of the work force. But at that point the firm reported to the competent local armaments command (*Rüstungskommando*) of the Wehrmacht that its "initially good experiences with Jewish workers" had "steadily deteriorated."[53] In March the company

---

[48] BA Berlin, R 8150 (earlier 75 C Re 1), No. 45, Fol. 50, Note 18/41 of Eppstein about the telephone call of the RSHA, March 7, 1941; see Gruner, *Der geschlossene Arbeitseinsatz*, 226.

[49] BA Berlin, R 8150, Film No. 52407/23, Fol. 215, Note about the telephone call of the Stapo headquarters in Berlin, May 30, 1941.

[50] See Christine Zahn, "Jüdische Zwangsarbeiterinnen im Siemenslager. Kommandantenstr. 58/59," in *Juden in Kreuzberg. Fundstücke, Fragmente, Erinnerungen*, edited by the History Workshop (Berlin, 1991), 167–170.

[51] HHStA Wiesbaden, Dep. 474/2, No. 271, no folio numbers, Dr. Cahn to the labor utilization department, May 19, 1941.

[52] Ibid., Circular letter, June 4, 1941.

[53] Bundesarchiv – Militärarchiv (BA-MA) Freiburg im Breisgau, RW 21–19, No. 7, no folio numbers, War diary of the armaments command in Frankfurt am Main, Entry of May 29, 1941.

had already complained for the first time that the "initially satisfactory will of Jewish columns to work" had "waned considerably." The level of illness had also risen sharply.[54] The employer attributed the change to a "lack of will to work resulting from wages that were too low compared to the wages of Aryan employees." In contrast to the practice of reducing the minimal wages of Jews still further, which prevailed everywhere else, the company's head initiated negotiations with the Reich Trustee of Labor "for the purpose of improving the wage rates" for his Jewish forced laborers.[55] The minimum wage for unskilled laborers was RM 0.50 per hour. In a six-day week, that added up to about RM 24. However, wages at the lowest levels were also widespread in Berlin industry. Thus, for example, the Jewish women working at AEG in Schöneweide in summer 1941 only received RM 20 to 22 per week, despite the piecework rate; the situation was similar at Siemens. At Ehrich & Graetz AG, the women earned even less, RM 14 per week;[56] the men received a bit more. Interestingly enough, a forced laborer working in construction or as a painter for a small business could earn more than in large-scale industrial operations – between RM 25 and 30 per week.[57]

Low wages – since January 1941 further reduced by a special anti-Jewish tax, the "Social Equalization Tax" (*Sozialausgleichsabgabe*) of 15 percent – had a negative effect on the productivity of Jewish forced laborers in private businesses but, because of the disappearing labor pool, so did the increasing tendency to assign workers "with limited work capacity."[58] In the months before, men and women fully capable of working but usually without any experience in forced labor had been allocated by labor offices; in the meantime, sick, old, or physically incapacitated Jews were procured with increasing frequency for requesting private enterprises because no others were available. By the end of June 1941, the labor administration in Frankfurt am Main again had increased the number of workers slightly in this manner; at that point, 1,851 of 10,803 Jewish inhabitants were being used for forced labor. A total of 2,696 were employed; 69 percent of them worked

---

[54] Ibid., No. 6, Fol. 58, War diary of the armaments command in Frankfurt am Main, Entry of March 22, 1941.

[55] Ibid., No. 7, no folio numbers, War diary of the armaments command in Frankfurt am Main, Entry of May 29, 1941.

[56] Stiftung "Neue Synagoge Berlin – Centrum Judaicum" Archiv (CJA) Berlin, 75 A Be 2, No. 375, Fol. 14, Care report, May 11, 1942; ibid., No. 395, Fol. 131, Care report for the Mendelsohn siblings, July 11, 1941; ibid., No. 446, Fol. 24, Jewish welfare office, Berlin-Mitte, to the Central Office, April 30, 1941.

[57] CJA Berlin, 75 A Be 2, No. 417, Fol. 2, Jewish welfare office, Berlin-Mitte, to the Central Office, July 1, 1941; ibid., No. 364, Fol. 3, Questionnaire, June 19, 1942.

[58] *Dokumente Frankfurter Juden*, XIII 2, 470, Report of the Gestapo representative at the Jewish welfare office, October 22, 1941 (July 1–September 30, 1941). See also "Second Decree for Implementation of the Decree on the Imposition of a Social Compensation Charge," December 24, 1940, *Reichsgesetzblatt*, 1940 I: 1666. See Gruner, *Der geschlossene Arbeitseinsatz*, 194–200.

for German businesses (that is, private companies or offices of the municipal administration) and only 31 percent for Jewish offices.[59] In July, the number of compulsory employees in Frankfurt could once again be increased to 1,941; 722 of them were women. Even women who actually had to take care of relatives were assigned to half-day work.[60]

The labor offices in Germany recruited about another 10,000 male and female forced laborers in this manner. With intensified recruiting methods and the support of the RSHA, labor offices succeeded in virtually exhausting the potential of able-bodied Jews. In the summer of 1941, segregated labor deployment in Germany encompassed 51,000 to 53,000 people. Even the majority of male and female Jews as young as eighteen and as old as seventy were in the meantime utilized as forced laborers.[61] In order to win the Aryan population over ideologically to the growing mass utilization of Jews in many German cities and communities, the German weekly news in review in the last week of May 1941 showed footage of Serbian Jews who were forced to perform clearing work in Belgrade. The film obviously achieved the desired effect on the Aryan population, as a report of the SS Security Service evinces. The public, for example in Dresden, "had made the statement a number of times that the Jews, who were finally feeling on their own hides what work means in Germany, should also be taught 'German tempo.'"[62]

As throughout the Reich, almost every third Jew was in the meantime utilized in Frankfurt for forced labor. By September 1941, the authorities had used increasingly extreme methods to employ on a compulsory basis a total of 2,020 Jews, 1,265 men and 755 women.[63] A number of them were put to work in the immediate vicinity of the city, for example, in the Hofheim-Taunus *Kreis* (county-size unit of government). In that Kreis, eight Jews worked at each of two building sites of the Firma Hammel & Westenberger, in Breckenheim and Hofheim-Marxheim. People employed there had to travel every day from Frankfurt to the building sites and back again in the

---

[59] *Dokumente Frankfurter Juden*, VIII 2, 461, Report of the Gestapo representative at the Jewish welfare office, July 12, 1941; StadtA Frankfurt am Main, F Main Records 7020/11, no folio numbers, Attachment to the report of the Gestapo representative, July 12, 1941.

[60] *Dokumente Frankfurter Juden*, VIII 3, 470, Report of the Gestapo representative in the Jewish welfare office, October 22, 1941 (July 1–September 30, 1941); StadtA Frankfurt am Main, F Main Records 7020/11, no folio numbers, Attachment to the report of the Gestapo representative, July 12, 1941.

[61] Gruner, *Der geschlossene Arbeitseinsatz*, 178–194, 204–217.

[62] *Meldungen aus dem Reich 1938–1945. Die geheimen Lageberichte des Sicherheitsdienstes der SS*, edited and with an introduction by Heinz Boberach, Vol. 7 (Herrsching, 1984), 2397, Report no. 192, June 9, 1941.

[63] *Dokumente Frankfurter Juden*, XIII 3, 470, Report of the Gestapo representative in the Jewish welfare office, October 22, 1941 (July 1–September 30, 1941); StadtA Frankfurt am Main, F Main Records 7020/11, no folio numbers, Attachment to the report of the Gestapo representative, October 22, 1941; see H. G. Adler, *Der verwaltete Mensch. Studien zur Deportation der Juden aus Deutschland* (Tübingen, 1974), 222.

evening.[64] Seventy-one percent of all 2,865 Jewish employees of Frankfurt were considered forced laborers; only 29 percent were employed in Jewish organizations. However, in the meantime even Jewish vocational training was in the service of the war economy. As in all parts of the Reich, Jewish training sites were only allowed to continue to exist if they financed themselves with paid work in industrial enterprises,[65] with the consequence that even the Frankfurt Jewish Community's vocational school was directly affiliated with the segregated labor deployment program.[66]

Statistics on German Jews in Segregated Labor Deployment, 1939–41

		Germany		Berlin	
		Jewish population	In forced labor	Jewish residents	In forced labor
1939					
	May	213,457	10,000–15,000	82,788	
	July		20,000		
1940					
	September			72,327	20,000
	October		40,000		
1941					
	February	170,000	41,000		
	March				
	End of July	167,245	51,000–53,000	73,465	26,000–28,000

FORCED LABOR AND DEPORTATIONS, FALL 1941–JANUARY 1942

While the *Einsatzgruppen* were already shooting Jews by the tens of thousands in the occupied territories of the Soviet Union, the Jews within Germany lived in a compulsory community. The introduction of the stigmatizing yellow Star of David in September 1941 that all Jews, including forced laborers, had to wear in public demonstrated that fact openly. Only at the point shortly before mass deportations began did the Nazi leadership officially define the German Jews' forced labor status. The October 3, 1941, order (already outlined months before) legalized "the special employment

---

[64] HHStA, Wiesbaden, Dep. 425, No. 432, Fol. 52, Bürgermeister Hofheim to the Frankfurt-Höchst State Counselor with a report of a master sergeant of the Municipal Police, November 8, 1941.

[65] Gruner, *Der geschlossene Arbeitseinsatz*, 186–187.

[66] *Dokumente Frankfurter Juden*, XIII 3, 471–472, Report of the Gestapo representative, October 22, 1941 (July 1–September 30, 1941).

Photo 1. German Jewish forced laborer in Hanau, spring or summer 1941 (note the armband with a Star of David, at this time still not compulsory in Germany)

classification" of "Jews utilized for work."[67] After three years of forced labor in practice, the new order replaced the December 20, 1938, decree.

In the meantime two million foreign laborers were working in Germany, so in the Nazi leadership's view, 50,000 Jewish forced laborers was no reason from the labor policy perspective to halt deportation. Consequently, new mass deportations began in mid-October 1941. In contrast to what occurred at the national level, however, problems arose immediately regionally and in industrial management. In the first transport out of Frankfurt, the Gestapo carried off Jewish forced laborers without regard to companies such as Voltohm Seil- und Kabelwerke AG, where the laborers represented 40 percent of the personnel. The war diary of the local armaments command (*Rüstungskommando*) of the Wehrmacht responsible for the city states, "Several armaments factories, among them Voltohm Seil- und Kabelwerke AG in Frankfurt am Main, Radio Braun in Frankfurt am Main, and others, report that, when Jews were suddenly transported out of Frankfurt to the General Government on October 19, 1941, without prior notice to the armaments command, a number of their Jewish workers were deported, too, which has negatively affected production for the Wehrmacht

[67] *Reichsgesetzblatt*, 1941 I: 675, reproduced in Adler, *Der verwaltete Mensch*, 213–215.

in that particular sector, because replacement workers cannot be provided at the moment."[68]

Because of protests by private firms and also by labor offices and Wehrmacht offices at various industrial locations, representatives of the economic armaments office (*Wirtschaftsrüstungsamt*) of the Wehrmacht met with Adolf Eichmann (RSHA) and the expert for Jewish matters of the Reich Interior Ministry, Bernhard Lösener, on October 23, 1941, to confer on participation of the Wehrmacht armaments inspection offices (*Rüstungsinspektionen*) in decisions regarding forced laborers. Eichmann and Lösener now assured the Wehrmacht economic armaments office that "not one single Jew employed in the segregated labor deployment program would be deported without consent of the responsible armaments inspection office and the competent labor office."[69] Two days later the armaments inspection offices and commands received guidelines that had been developed by Heydrich on "Carrying Out the Evacuation of Jews." The guidelines set down that Jews in the segregated labor deployment program were not to be deported, but with a critical qualification: "only when timely completion of urgent armaments orders is in jeopardy." Thus, the RSHA had decisively weakened the compromise of October 23 to favor deportations, which would affect the next transports.[70] Contrary to the myth circulating among the Jewish population at the time and to the assertion made by authorities, the proportion of compulsory employees deported from the armaments industry for the time being continued to be little less than from other sectors, both in Berlin and in elsewhere.[71] Of course, that situation was primarily the result of local power relationships. What remained decisive at the particular location was the discussion and coordination of forced-laborer transports among the Gestapo, the labor office, enterprises, and the Wehrmacht armaments commands. With the rigorous approach taken during the first transport still a clear memory, the Frankfurt am Main armaments commands, to forestall unanticipated removals "in light of the substantial shortage of workers," took the precautionary measure of sending the local Gestapo lists of the names of Jewish workers employed as forced laborers "in segregated units at twelve companies producing important articles for the Wehrmacht." The transport of these 360 persons was supposedly postponed for "at least as long as no replacement workers [could] be made available."[72] This statement did

[68] BA-MA Freiburg im Breisgau, RW 21–19, No. 9, no folio numbers, War diary of the armaments command in Frankfurt am Main, Entry of October 20, 1941.

[69] According to a circular of the economic armaments office (Wirtschaftsrüstungsamt), October 23, 1941; Raul Hilberg, *Die Vernichtung der europäischen Juden*, new and expanded edition of the translation into German of 1982 edition, Vol. 2 (Frankfurt am Main, 1990), 460.

[70] BA-MA Freiburg im Breisgau, RW 21–19, No. 9, Fol. 15, War diary of the armaments command in Frankfurt am Main, Entry of November 2, 1941.

[71] Gruner, *Der geschlossene Arbeitseinsatz*, 276–282.

[72] BA-MA Freiburg im Breisgau, RW 21–19, No. 9, Fol. 15, War diary of the armaments command in Frankfurt am Main, Entry of November 2, 1941.

not, however, reflect the facts. As in Düsseldorf, but in contrast to Würzburg, the Gestapo deportations in Frankfurt am Main were especially brutal. By the end of January 1942, the Security Police had deported another 526 male and 162 female forced laborers "without regard to their work." For the men, that was 41.6 percent, and overall, 34 percent of all Jewish men and women performing forced labor in Frankfurt during fall 1941. After the first wave of deportations, only about 7,000 Jews still lived in Frankfurt am Main. Of the remaining 1,332 compulsory employees, 739 were men and 593 were women.[73]

EXCURSUS: STANDARD WAGES FOR JEWS IN HESSE

The forced labor order was followed on October 31, 1941, by an implementation order in which the Reich Ministry of Labor summarized all the special provisions in labor law developed so far, in order to supplement the paragraphs on compulsory labor new to the existing laws of the Old Reich. Jews only received wages "for labor actually performed," that is, without paid vacations or disability, and with all supplements, subsidies, and overtime payments eliminated. All public and private social benefits were eliminated. And social protections for Jewish women and young people were reduced. The companies could terminate Jewish forced workers any day without notice. Nor were the companies obligated to hire the Jewish forced laborers.[74]

Contrary to the myth still in circulation today, a commentary – reprinted in daily newspapers – stated openly and unequivocally several weeks later, "The Jew's obligation to accept the position assigned does not mean that the employer has one. . . . Businesses cannot be compelled by labor offices to employ Jews."[75] A one-day term of notice, the absence of social benefits, and low pay had long been among the advantages to companies using Jews as their work force. However, the Reich Trustee of Labor in Hesse took the introduction of forced-labor law as the occasion for once again generally reducing the private sector wages of Jewish compulsory employees, who were mostly employed as unskilled workers and as such were on the lowest end of the pay scale anyway. Instead of industrial branch, type of work, and

---

73 StadtA Frankfurt am Main, F Main Records 7020/11, no folio numbers, Attachment to the report of the Gestapo representative, October 22, 1941; *Dokumente Frankfurter Juden*, XIII 4, 478, Report of the Gestapo representative, April 15, 1942; StadtA Frankfurt am Main, F Main Records 7020/11, no folio numbers, Attachment to that report.

74 The implementation order was promulgated together with the order on November 4, 1941; *Reichsgesetzblatt*, 1941 I: 681–682. For a discussion of the orders, see Gruner, *Der geschlossene Arbeitseinsatz*, 276, 284–285.

75 *Reichsgesetzblatt*, 1941 V: 570–574, No. 32, November 15, 1941; *Kölnische Zeitung*, December 2, 1941; *Jüdisches Nachrichtenblatt* (JNBl), January 9, 1942.

wage scale, only age counted for Hessian Jews in the times ahead.[76] Even forced laborers in mixed marriages were subject to "standard wages for Jews," although special labor law actually applied to them only in part. In provincial Hesse, pay was even 15 percent lower than in Frankfurt proper.[77] Only when the wages for unskilled workers were lower than the new Jewish wages were the forced laborers to be paid according to a wage scale.[78]

Wages for Jewish Forced Laborers in Hesse from
November 1941 on[79]

	Standard wages	Wages for reduced performance
Men		
Over 23 years old	RM 0.60	RM 0.50
Over 20 years old	RM 0.54	RM 0.45
Over 18 years old	RM 0.45	RM 0.38
Over 16 years old	RM 0.36	RM 0.30
Under 16 years old	RM 0.27	RM 0.23
Women		
Over 21 years old	RM 0.45	RM 0.38
Over 19 years old	RM 0.38	RM 0.32
Over 18 years old	RM 0.34	RM 0.29
Over 16 years old	RM 0.27	RM 0.23
Under 16 years old	RM 0.20	RM 0.19

Frankfurt am Main city administration also found this all-inclusive wage reduction highly attractive, but could not use this provision because it was only valid in the Hessian private sector. At that time, the municipality employed a total of 100 Jews in the municipal cemetery, nursery, and forests, and for streetcar and street-cleaning operations. Frankfurt therefore complained in Berlin at the Council of Municipalities in March 1942 that the regional maximum wage limit for Jews of RM 0.60 per hour did not apply to their compulsory employees because municipal institutions were subordinate to the Reich Trustee for Public Service (*Reichstreuhänder für den Öffentlichen Dienst*). The German Council of Municipalities should,

[76] BA Berlin, R 36, No. 516, no folio numbers, Order of November 21, 1942.
[77] BA Berlin, R 22, No. 2057, Fol. 247, Note, July 11, 1942; ibid., Fol. 249 verso – 254, Decision, August 24, 1942.
[78] Circular letter 2/41 of the German Labor Front – Gau Administration of Hesse-Nassau, quoted in Sven Beckert, *Bis zu diesem Punkt und nicht weiter. Arbeitsalltag während des zweiten Weltkriegs in einer Industrieregion Offenbach-Frankfurt* (Frankfurt am Main, 1990), 147.
[79] Guidelines of the Reich Trustee of Labor for the remuneration of Jewish forced laborers in the Hessian economic region after November 1941; follows the table in Beckert, *Arbeitsalltag*, 147.

the municipality continued, establish uniform principles through the Reich Interior Minister.[80]

Although the German Council of Municipalities pressed for a decision by the Reich Interior Ministry on Frankfurt's behalf, the response was delayed.[81] The Reich Trustee for Public Service had simultaneously appealed to the Reich Minister for a general wage reduction in public operations. Until the Ministry made a final decision, however, the Reich Trustee ordered at the beginning of June 1942 that the across-the-board wage reduction for Jewish forced laborers in effect at the Reich Railway be adopted as a temporary measure. The reduction was to apply to all municipal operations in the Reich.[82] In January of that year, the Reich Minister of Transportation had issued an employment order for "Jews at the German Reich Railway" that included general wage reductions. Regardless of their activities, Jews only received wage group C pay, and female employees only 75 percent of C; regardless of location, Jews were always in the lowest-paying locality classification.[83] In August, the Reich Interior Ministry officially gave the green light to the actually illegal procedure of adopting the order, for everyone wanted to spare himself the trouble of issuing his own order because of the quickly progressing deportations, and in consequence, the problem's rapid loss of significance.[84]

The city of Frankfurt thus not only had succeeded in lowering the wages of the Jewish forced laborers in its employ, but with its initiative had set a precedent for all the municipalities and communities in the Reich to do the same. The irony of the story, however, was that the Hessian municipality itself derived scarcely any benefit from the new ruling because of the rapid deportation practices of the local Gestapo.

THE YEAR OF DESTRUCTION, SPRING 1942–SPRING 1943

At the January 20, 1942, Wannsee Conference, Heydrich repeated his assurance that armaments workers would be exempted – which, contrary to

---

[80] BA Berlin, R 36, No. 516, no folio numbers, Oberbürgermeister of Frankfurt am Main to the German Council of Municipalities, March 3, 1942.

[81] Ibid., German Council of Municipalities, department I, to the Reich Interior Ministry, March 31, 1942; ibid., German Council of Municipalities, department I, to the Oberbürgermeister of Frankfurt am Main, May 21, 1942.

[82] StadtA Kelkheim im Taunus, Record Volume "Labor Utilization of a Column of Jews," no folio numbers, Reich Trustee for Public Service in Hesse to the president of the Wiesbaden administrative district, June 16, 1942, regarding the Reich Trustee's June 8, 1942, order.

[83] BA Berlin, R 36, No. 516, no folio numbers, Circular letter of the Reich Ministry of Transportation, January 15, 1942. See Gruner, *Der geschlossene Arbeitseinsatz*, 287–288.

[84] BA Berlin, R 36, No. 516, no folio numbers, Reich Trustee for Public Service, August 19, 1942; ibid., Reich Interior Ministry to the German Council of Municipalities, September 17, 1942; ibid., German Council of Municipalities to the Oberbürgermeister of Frankfurt am Main, October 13, 1942.

previous assumptions, was obviously a deliberate lie to avert the predictable intervention of the labor offices and Wehrmacht armaments inspection offices. The deportations, briefly suspended in February because of transportation problems, resumed at the end of March, and the Gestapo continued the forcible removal of industrial and armaments workers everywhere. The RSHA proceeded with the intent of keeping deferment of transports to a minimum. At the end of May 1942, Hitler further demanded, for the first time personally, that Jewish forced laborers be withdrawn from the armaments industry, and he emphasized that repeatedly on later occasions.[85]

Because of the especially strict deportation practices since fall 1941, several Hessian private enterprises feared even before the resumption of deportations that "Jews in a short time [would] again be removed from Frankfurt am Main by transport without regard to their use as labor." To ensure continuation of operations without losses, the Firma Osterrieth, which had about 150 Jewish employees, and the Firma Wäscherei Seibel (lavndry), Dönigheim, Hanau rural Kreis, with about thirty, made application for assignment of "a corresponding number" of foreign employees.[86]

At the beginning of April 1942, the forced laborers in Frankfurt am Main numbered 1,345: 755 men and 590 women. A month later, 220 firms, 80 of them companies that were important for the war, still employed 1,281 Jews. The Gestapo coordinated the deportations with the city and the labor administration. To remove obstacles to deportation, the Gestapo reached an agreement with the city administration that all its forced laborers would be transferred to companies that were not important for the armaments industry. Inspector Holland, who worked as the Gestapo's representative at the Jewish welfare office, prepared the necessary lists.[87] On May 16, the regional labor office, the armaments inspection office of the Defense Economic Office, and Inspector Holland participated in a meeting at the Gestapo office. For the next transport, the Gestapo requested an additional 200 Jews, "who would have to be pulled out of companies." The meeting participants decided first to remove the forced laborers from the Frankfurt city administration, from several chemical dye works, and from smaller companies – that is, to spare large companies and companies critical to the war effort.[88] After this transport, only 688 Jews (438 men and 250 women) were still in segregated labor

---

[85] Gruner, *Der geschlossene Arbeitseinsatz*, 299–300, 303, and 307.

[86] *Dokumente Frankfurter Juden*, XIII 4, 478, Report of the Gestapo representative at the Jewish welfare office in Frankfurt am Main, April 15, 1942.

[87] Ibid.; and StadtA Frankfurt am Main, F Main records 7020/11, no folio numbers, Attachment to the report. Wolfgang Wippermann, *Das Leben in Frankfurt zur NS-Zeit, Bd. I: Die nationalsozialistische Judenverfolgung* (Frankfurt am Main, 1986), 230, Doc. 4a, Note for party comrade K(och), May 12, 1942; see Beckert, *Arbeitsalltag*, 148.

[88] Wippermann, *Das Leben in Frankfurt*, Vol. I, 230, Doc. 4b, May 18 note for Gau Office Head party comrade A. regarding a meeting on May 16, 1942; see Beckert, *Arbeitsalltag*, 148.

deployment at the end of May – half the number from the beginning of April. At the end of June, only 469 forced laborers (287 men and 182 women) were left, in 54 companies. Thus, the Gestapo had diminished the number of forced laborers by a third in three months. Over 150 businesses, probably most of them small, had lost their forced laborers. The Jews still present constituted just 23 percent of the fall 1941 compulsory employees. At the same time, 38 percent of the Jewish residents of Frankfurt were forced laborers. Something less than 4,100 of the Jewish residents still lived in the city;[89] they were not spared, either. More than 3,000 people were taken away in several transports over the summer, most of them to Theresienstadt (Terezin). By fall 1942, hardly any Jewish forced laborers were present in Frankfurt am Main.[90]

When at the end of December 1942 just 706 of the previously 14,000 Jewish residents remained,[91] the Gestapo established "community housing" (*Gemeinschaftsunterkunft*) for Jews who until now had been exempted from deportation – mostly Jews with relatives of German blood, as well as for the district Reichsvereinigung office and the infirmary in Frankfurt am Main. This signaled the relatively early conclusion of deportations in Frankfurt.[92] Similar institutions were established in other cities, although often not until months later, for example in Cologne,[93] in Breslau,[94] and even later in Berlin at the Jewish Hospital.[95]

Instead of the 50,000 German Jews employed in the segregated labor deployment program during summer 1941, only 20,000 were still left at the end of 1942. The number of Jewish forced laborers had been reduced everywhere by transports, but for economic reasons not nearly so blatantly in all cities as in Frankfurt or Hamburg. Most of the rest, over 15,000, thus lived in Berlin, an area of industrial concentration where deportations were orga-

---

[89] *Dokumente Frankfurter Juden*, XIII 5, 484, Report of the Gestapo representative, July 14, 1942; and StadtA Frankfurt am Main, F Main Records 7020/11, no folio numbers, Attachment to the report.

[90] *Dokumente Frankfurter Juden*, IX 2, 420, Statistics from October 1, 1939, to September 30, 1944, according to the biannual reports of the police president to the Oberbürgermeister of Frankfurt am Main.

[91] Ibid.

[92] *Dokumente Frankfurter Juden*, XIII 6, 495, Report of the Gestapo representative at the Jewish welfare office in Frankfurt am Main, April 16, 1943; see BA Berlin, R 8150, No. 762, Fol. 25 and verso, Gestapo representative at the Jewish welfare office in Frankfurt am Main to the Reichsvereinigung, December 28, 1942.

[93] The Reichsvereinigung district office for the Rhineland was moved to the Cologne-Müngersdorf labor and residential camp; BA Berlin, R 8150, No. 762, Fol. 10, District office for the Rhineland to the Reichsvereinigung, February 24, 1943.

[94] Andreas Reinke, "Stufen der Zerstörung. Das Breslauer Jüdische Krankenhaus während des Nationalsozialismus," in *Menora. Jahrbuch für deutsch-jüdische Geschichte 1994* (Munich and Zurich, 1994), 379–414, here 403.

[95] Here, however, not until the second quarter of 1943; Wolf Gruner, "Die Reichshauptstadt und die Verfolgung der Berliner Juden 1933–1945," in *Jüdische Geschichte in Berlin. Essays und Studien*, edited by Reinhard Rürup (Berlin, 1995) 229–266, here 254.

nized from the beginning by the Gestapo in regular contact with the Berlin labor administration. According to SS statistics, other major German cities with more than 200,000 residents, such as Dresden, Munich, Düsseldorf, and Duisbug, but also cities such as Kassel and Wiesbaden, still had a few hundred Jewish compulsory employees, as the following table shows.

Number of German and Austrian Jewish Forced Laborers on January 1, 1943[96]

Security Police and SD Inspector's area		Security Police and SD Inspector's area	
Berlin	15,100	Königsberg[97]	96
	110	Munich	313
Braunschweig			
Breslau[98]	2,451	Nuremberg	89
Dresden	483	Stettin	18
Düsseldorf	673	Stuttgart	178
Duisbug	497	Wiesbaden	139
Kassel	259		
		Salzburg	7
		Vienna	1,126
Total			21,539

At the end of 1942, the RSHA was preparing for the conclusion of German mass deportations. After transports in January and February 1943, a large-scale raid was directed primarily against forced laborers spared until then for economic reasons. In the Third Reich's capital, the Gestapo, with the help of the SS, brutally snatched thousands of people on one day from more than a hundred businesses and crammed them into collection camps. The raid, called the *"Fabrik-Aktion"* by the survivors, was not limited to Berlin. Across the entire Old Reich beginning on February 27, 1943, Jewish men and women were taken from their places of work, arrested at agencies, on the street, at their homes, and in camps, and then interned for transport at collection points that included synagogues, caserns, private inns, municipal slaughterhouses, and forced-labor camps. In the massive raid at the beginning of March, the Gestapo took away primarily male and female forced laborers, but also all so-called "full Jews" not protected by a mixed marriage. Thus, forced laborers' relatives were taken away at the same time, as well as hundreds of employees of Jewish institutions and their relatives, until

[96] The total number included 18,546 Jews with German citizenship, 107 persons from the Protectorate, 487 foreigners, and 2,519 stateless persons; LBIA New York, Microfilms, Wiener Library, 500 Series, No. 526, Inspector for statistics with the RFSS, January 1, 1943 (Korherr Report), 14 (also in BA Berlin, NS 19, No. 1570).

[97] This number does not include the Soviet Jewish forced laborers in this region.

[98] This number does not include the Polish Jews exploited by the SS Organisation Schmelt.

mid-March. The number of men, women, and children deported from the Reich in March 1943 – 12,496 – was one of the highest for a month since the onset of deportations in Germany. By summer 1943, the large extermination transports out of Germany had finally been completed.[99]

FORCED LABOR FOR JEWS IN MIXED MARRIAGES, 1943–45

Even though in the spring of 1943 the Nazi leadership had no real intention of deporting Jews from mixed marriages, it at least wanted – after removal of most of the other Jews – radically to step up persecution of Jews remaining in the Reich. After deportation of most Jewish Germans, the persecutory concept of the forced community was to be applied to the Jews partly spared thus far because they lived in mixed marriages. These people had long since been performing forced labor, usually in the armaments industry. The Gestapo had used the Fabrik-Aktion to remove this group from the companies involved in the war economy so that the compulsory employment program could be reorganized. Instead of working in industry as before, Jews living in mixed marriages now had to perform forced labor in physically demanding jobs. From March 1943 on, the labor administration employed them primarily in unskilled excavation, transport, or cleaning work – in keeping with the original intention of segregated labor deployment. In Berlin, the labor office committed Jewish men and women from mixed marriages to the Reich Railway, to garbage collecting, and to demolition companies; the pattern was the same in other cities.[100] Soon many labor offices expanded the use of Jewish forced-labor columns and pulled in additional Jews not affected so far, for example Victor Klemperer, who from mid-April forward had to slave in a tea factory. Klemperer left behind the most impressive description to date of everyday life under forced labor in that period.[101]

In Frankfurt am Main, an operation for identification "of racially and non-practicing Jewish individuals who had not previously been registered" was also used to check their fitness for labor. Due to stricter regulations, the labor office had in the meantime brought almost 50 percent of the remaining Jewish residents into the forced-labor program; in the previous years it was 20–30 percent. Two hundred fifty-four of the 542 remaining Jewish citizens of Frankfurt, 105 men and 149 women, toiled in forced-labor jobs. Two-thirds of the men worked for the municipality of Frankfurt (37 for the city interment

---

99 For a detailed description, see Wolf Gruner, *Widerstand in der Rosenstraße. Die Fabrik-Aktion und die Verfolgung der "Mischehen" 1943* (Frankfurt am Main, 2005); and Gruner, "The Factory-raid and the Events at the Berlin Rosenstrasse, Facts and Fiction about 27 February 1943–60 years later," in *Central European History*, 36, 1 (2003): 179–208.

100 Gruner, *Der geschlossene Arbeitseinsatz*, 322–326.

101 Victor Klemperer, *Ich will Zeugnis ablegen bis zum letzten. Tagebücher 1933–1945, Bd. 2: Tagebücher 1942–1945*, edited by Walter Nowojski, with the assistance of Hadwig Klemperer, 2nd Edition (Berlin, 1995), 353, Entry of April 18, 1943.

system and 29 for the city street-cleaning authority), the rest in small groups for companies such as Frankfurt Asbestwerke, Voltohm Seil- und Kabel-werke AG, Firma Max Braun Radio, or Firma Kulzer & Co. The latter produced false teeth with the help of eighteen female forced laborers. The Osterrieth company alone employed 95 Jewish women, who put together parcels for the *Winterhilfswerk*, the Nazi charity and relief organization. Fif-teen women were employed in the sewing shop and hospital laundry, a public welfare workshop of the city administration. As the Gestapo in the meantime had disbanded all Jewish organizations, 87.6 percent of all Jewish employees in Frankfurt worked in the segregated labor deployment program.[102]

While the labor office continued to run its forced-labor program on its own authority, the RSHA increased so-called "agency use" after March 1943. In Berlin, but also in other locales, the RSHA began employing Jews in activities ranging from Gestapo library positions to bunker construction. For that work, Jews were moved to Berlin from other regions. In summer 1943, a group from Frankfurt am Main reached the capital, where they were employed at construction companies, other enterprises, and the Gestapo.[103] An employee of the Reichsvereinigung noted on the occasion of a roll-call at the forced laborers' housing in fall 1943 that their performance was poor, they lacked the tools for this work, and their number included scarcely any skilled workers.[104]

Until the war's end, forced labor was a basic component of persecution for Jews living in mixed marriages; at the same time, they were crammed together in buildings for Jews, for example, in Hamburg, Halle an der Saale, Bremen, and Frankfurt am Main.[105] A year after the Fabrik-Aktion, on Himmler's orders the Gestapo first deported to Theresienstadt those Jewish men and women whose mixed marriages no longer existed because of divorce or death of the partner.[106] After further deportations, only 242 Jews still lived in Frankfurt in the fall of 1944.[107] A few months before the end of the war, the RSHA joined in the last act of persecution. On January 15, 1945, the RSHA ordered that all Jews "living in mixed marriages and fit to work, and all stateless Jewish men and women . . . are to be transferred, regardless of their work situations at this time, . . . to the ghetto for the aged in Theresienstadt for segregated labor deployment."[108] In this case, forced labor apparently

---

[102] *Dokumente Frankfurter Juden*, XIII 6, 490–495, Report of the Gestapo representative, April 16, 1943.
[103] Bruno Blau, "Vierzehn Jahre Not und Schrecken," Memoir Collection, LBIA New York.
[104] BA Berlin, R 8150, No. 61, Fol. 48, Neumann report, October 8, 1943.
[105] Gruner, *Der geschlossene Arbeitseinsatz*, 321–331.
[106] Gruner, "The Factory-action," 179–208.
[107] *Dokumente Frankfurter Juden*, IX 2, 420, Statistics from October 1, 1939, to September 30, 1944, according to the biannual reports of the police president to the Oberbürgermeister of Frankfurt am Main.
[108] Sauer, *Dokumente*, Part II, 383, Doc. No. 550, RSHA decree of January 15, 1945, in the order of the Security Police of Baden-Alsace, January 26, 1945.

served as a Gestapo front for new transports. In Frankfurt am Main, where the persons affected were to appear at the great market hall on February 14, 1945, the written order contained the camouflage statement, "This order is not to be viewed as one of the evacuations that were usual earlier."[109] In those days and weeks, even though not all cities were able to arrange for transports, a dozen trains carried far more than 1,600 people from German cities to Theresienstadt ghetto.[110]

SUMMARY

Until 1938, ideas about forced labor did not play a role in the conception of anti-Jewish policy. Only when the objective of expelling the Jewish population became increasingly remote because of growing poverty did the Nazi leadership, after the November 1938 pogrom, undertake a fundamental reformulation of anti-Jewish policy, with emphasis on forcing emigration by any means and on keeping completely separate from German society any Jews who were incapable of emigrating. As laws had forbidden Jews from engaging in trade or any profession since the end of 1938, in the new conceptual framework the labor administration was to arrange for Jews who had no future income to perform forced labor. Forced labor was thus a fundamental element of the newly directed persecutory process.

Two phases of segregated labor deployment can be demonstrated. In the first phase, the December 20, 1938, decree issued by the Reich Institute for Labor Placement and Unemployment Insurance first obligated all Jews supported by unemployment insurance to work in regional and local infrastructure construction but also at municipal garbage disposal sites and in snow removal operations. (See photo 2, p. 37.) In segregated work groups or columns, Jews were assigned to mandatory heavy physical labor as unskilled workers for private construction or transport companies, or for municipal agencies. By summer 1939, there were already 20,000 forced laborers in Germany. In the second phase, from spring 1940 on, the labor offices recruited *all* German Jews fit for work, but now preferably for industry or for skilled activities. Enterprises established Jewish departments or Jewish shifts for this purpose. In 1941, Nazi Germany employed over 50,000 male and female Jewish workers.

The transformation of forced-labor policy clearly demonstrates how the labor administration's specific interests reshaped a persecutory measure in practice. The change was only possible, however, because the overall policy after the 1938 pogrom was implemented with responsibility distributed

---

[109] *Dokumente Frankfurter Juden*, XIV 13, 531, Circular of the Reichsvereinigung agent, February 8, 1945.

[110] Gruner, *Der geschlossene Arbeitseinsatz*, 328–329; *Theresienstädter Gedenkbuch. Die Opfer der Judentransporte aus Deutschland nach Theresienstadt 1942–1945*, published by the Institute of Theresienstadt Initiatives (Prague, 2000), 89.

among multiple agencies. Hence, the Reich labor administration was able to organize a forced-labor program independent of the SS and the concentration camp system. For three years, the labor administration administered segregated labor deployment solely on the basis of the December 30, 1938, decree. German Jews were employed with individual work contracts, a feature specific to this approach to forced labor, but the Jews generally entered the contracts involuntarily. Furthermore, Jews' working situations were subject in practice to a special law that evolved from a succession of administrative decrees and court decisions and was first codified by an October 1941 order.

Frankfurt am Main was no exception with regard to the objective and the course of segregated labor deployment. Barely 600 men and women worked as forced labor in spring 1940, but after the labor administration's recruitment efforts in fall 1940 and pressure from the Security Police, coupled with preparation for the spring 1941 deportations, the number rose to over 1,600. In fall 1941, before the first transports departed, over 2,000 Jewish men and women worked for approximately 220 companies. The city administration also employed forced laborers. As in other big cities, Jewish men and women from Frankfurt were sent to outside construction sites of other municipalities or private enterprises where they had to live in specially constructed segregated labor camps.

One unusual local feature is the position of the Gestapo representative at the Jewish welfare office, an office that only existed in Frankfurt am Main. The Frankfurt Gestapo's position of power, apparent from this function, clearly influenced forced labor in that city significantly after 1941, in contrast to other cities. The labor allocation department in the representative's office monitored the forced placement of Jewish workers arranged by the local labor office. After the initiation of transports in fall 1941, the Gestapo conducted deportations much more vigorously than in other big cities, not only from the private and municipal economic sectors but especially from the armaments industry. By mid-1942, hardly any forced laborers remained in Frankfurt, in sharp contrast to Berlin, for example. As 15,000 Jewish forced laborers still working in the capital of the Third Reich at the end of 1942 demonstrate, the course of the deportation transports was clearly influenced by the demands of the regional and local labor market and war industry. On the other hand, during fall 1941 in the eyes of Hitler the overall number of 50,000 Jewish forced laborers in comparison to over a million foreign workers already in Germany seemed no argument against the decision to deport the German Jews.

The example of forced labor establishes that the persecution of Jews could not be effected by the NSDAP, the SA, or the Gestapo alone. Participants in the organization of forced labor in Germany were state agencies and private or public enterprises. For countless German Jews, their exploitation as forced labor dictated the course of their days for as many as four years and was at the same time a structural element serving the purpose of social isolation and state control.

2

German Jews in Forced Labor Camps, 1939–1943[1]

THE LABOR CAMPS UNTIL THE DEPORTATIONS IN 1941[2]

Under the direction of the Reich labor administration, a network of at least forty now-confirmed camps arose on German territory – independent of the concentration camp system – between 1939 and 1941; that camp system, mostly for German but also for Austrian Jews, has not been described in the literature before now (see map 2, p. 35). In 1939, the Security Main Office wrote in its first situation report, which was intended for a broader audience, "Many Jews became unemployed when Jewish commercial establishments were shut down. In many places, establishment of collective labor camps for Jews became necessary."[3] While this sounded rather laconic, and the measures haphazard, the Jewish section of the SS Security Service openly expressed the underlying intent in an internal report some months later: "In the businesses in which Jews must work directly with Germans," it stated, contacts occurred "even though separate eating and changing facilities for Jews had been established," which indicated "how little effect the National Socialist views on race have had," especially in Catholic regions. For that reason, the report continued, the SD was pleased that on large construction projects, "use of Jewish labor" could "be effected smoothly," because "the Jews were housed in camps where they could be kept completely separate from the population living in the vicinity."[4]

---

[1] Chapter 2 is the modified and updated version of the fifth chapter of the author's study; Wolf Gruner, *Der geschlossene Arbeitseinsatz deutscher Juden. Zur Zwangsarbeit als Element der Verfolgung 1938–1943* (Berlin, 1997).

[2] For all the camps mentioned in the following pages of this chapter or in the footnotes, the source citations and additional details can be found in the camp lists in Wolf Gruner, "Die Arbeitslager für den Zwangseinsatz deutscher und nichtdeutscher Juden im Dritten Reich. Einleitung und 1. Kapitel: Zu den Arbeitslagern für deutsche und österreichische Juden im Altreich (1938–1943)," in *Gedenkstättenrundbrief*, published by the Foundation for the Topography of Terror, 78 (1997): 1–17.

[3] First quarterly situation report of the Security Main Office in 1939, in *Meldungen aus dem Reich 1938–1945. Die geheimen Lageberichte des Sicherheitsdienstes der SS*, edited and with an introduction by Heinz Boberach, Vol. 2 (Herrsching, 1984), 222.

[4] Vad Yashem (YV) Jerusalem, 051/OSOBI (Center for the Preservation of the Historical Documentary Collection [Moscow]), No. 47, no folio numbers, SD situation report (II 112) for the period June 16–30, 1939.

Initiatives of municipal welfare offices had established separate camps for anti-Jewish labor programs even before segregated labor deployment was established. In 1937, Hamburg's social welfare agency planned segregated housing for forty non-Aryan support recipients in one camp for river control work.[5] After the project in Sulinger Swamp failed because of opposition from the Lower Saxony regional labor office, which was in charge, the city pushed for the opening of a camp in the Nordmark regional labor office's region.[6] The Hamburg welfare agency was at the same time interested in "finding outside labor projects" for Gypsies.[7] In early summer 1938, Hamburg opened the first two separate labor camps near the city.[8] Around seventy-five Jews receiving social welfare were mandated to perform physically difficult drainage work in Wohlerst near Harsefeld and to built a bucket conveyor in Buxtehude. In August, Hamburg senators gathered information on-site regarding the new labor measures for non-Aryans.[9] In Buxtehude, the Jews were housed in the *Herberge zur Heimat,* a facility providing travelers' assistance and run by the evangelical Inner Mission (*Innere Mission*). The people in charge behaved inconsistently. The deacon at the hostel checked on the one hand to see that the Jews he supervised remained in the camp after work, and on the other he criticized the overcrowding in the camp to city officials. City officials reminded several mining crew supervisors who found fault with the performance of the columns of Jews that a period of adjustment was necessary. But then the same officials paid strict attention to segregation of the compulsory workers. The Jewish holidays were still respected, and the workers were allowed to go home every weekend to their families, although their wages as unskilled workers were often not sufficient to cover the trip after the costs of room and board had been subtracted.[10]

---

[5] Staatsarchiv (StA) Hamburg, 351–10 Social Agencies I, AW 40.30, no folio numbers, Bassum labor office to Hamburg labor welfare office on September 8, 1937.

[6] StA Hamburg, 351–10 Social Agencies I, AW 40.30, no folio numbers, Letter of the Hamburg labor welfare office to the Bassum labor office, October 27, 1937; ibid., Hamburg labor welfare office to the Hamburg labor office, November 1, 1937.

[7] Ibid., Protocol of a meeting with the Hamburg labor office by the Hamburg labor welfare office, November 22, 1937.

[8] Ibid, Note of the Hamburg labor welfare office, July 13, 1938.

[9] They complained about the lack of securable lockers for the personal effects of Jewish workers; ibid., Note of the Hamburg labor welfare office, August 15, 1938.

[10] The twenty-five Jews living in a wooden barracks in Wohlerst received the unskilled worker rate of RM 0.50 per hour. The approximately fifty Jews from Hamburg in Buxtehude received RM 0.62–0.68 per hour from the hydraulics cooperative, of which RM 1 was subtracted every day for food. For that reason, they applied for subsidies from the Jewish religious community; ibid., 351–10 Social Agencies I, AW 40.30, no folio numbers, Note of the Hamburg labor welfare office, July 16, 1938; ibid., Note on measures in the Stade labor office district, August 6, 1938; StA Hamburg, 522–1 Jewish Community, No. 985 a PK, 70 and 80, Protocols of the Jewish Religious Association in Hamburg, Sessions of August 9 and 31, 1938.

Regardless of local activities, the SS Security Service prepared in summer
1938 for interning the Jewish population of Germany in forced-labor camps
if war broke out, as Chapter 1 described. When the Nazi conception of
persecution was reformulated in the fall, however, the SD plan was not pursued further; for the time being, the decision was made instead to have the
labor administration organize a program putting unemployed Jews to work.
Although never explicitly stated in the Reich Institute's decrees, measures
since the end of 1938 implied establishment of special labor camps for Jews,
as the majority of the work sites suitable for planned use of columns – street
and hydraulic construction projects, for example – were located outside the
city, and segregated utilization was assumed. Individual labor office officials thus immediately made deployment of Jews dependent on the construction of separate camps. The head of the Mannheim labor office had refused
in October 1938 to utilize columns without camps. After the November
pogrom, he proposed collecting all of Baden's unemployed Jews in one special
labor camp.[11] The president of the Berlin-Brandenburg regional labor office
instructed his labor offices at the beginning of 1939 to establish without delay
the "conditions for housing in a camp-like arrangement," so that "as many of
the mass of Berlin Jews as possible" could "be put to use in the province."[12]

A total of at least twenty-three labor camps for German Jews, sixteen
camps for Austrian Jews, and two for both German and Austrian Jews were
constructed from 1939 to 1941 in Germany. Actually, about forty more
camps established in Silesia between 1939 and 1940 must probably be added
to the following list of camp locations; before now the camps were attributed
to the SS Organisation Schmelt. However, that organization, which will be
discussed in more detail in subsequent chapters, was not founded until late
1940.[13]

Planning, construction, and maintenance of labor camps in Germany were
at first, in 1939, associated with mostly short-term building projects. The
camps often existed only for a few months, which makes confirming their
existence very difficult today. The labor offices specifically assigned Jews
from big cities to Reich or state construction projects, but also to some
municipal projects. The scope ranged from utilization in a city (for example,
Jews from Frankfurt am Main in nearby Kelkheim[14]) to employment in the

---

[11] See Paul Sauer (ed.), *Dokumente über die Verfolgung der jüdischen Bürger in Baden-
Württemberg durch das nationalsozialistische Regime 1933–1943*, Part II (Stuttgart, 1966),
207, No. 173, Report of the Director of the Mannheim Labor Office, October 26, 1938; and
Sauer, *Dokumente*, Part II, 72, No. 328, Report of the Mannheim labor office to the regional
labor office for Southwestern Germany, January 13, 1939.

[12] Gruner, "Der Beginn der Zwangsarbeit," 140–141, Doc. No. 2, Cover letter from the president of the Brandenburg regional labor office, December 24, 1938, regarding the December
20, 1938, decree.

[13] For more detail, see Chapters 6–9.

[14] StadtA Kelkheim im Taunus, Record Volume "Labor Utilization of a Column of Jews"
(April–October, 1939), no folio numbers.

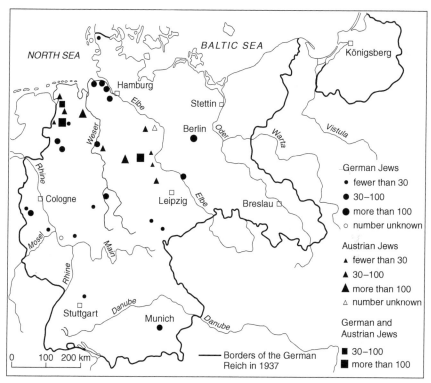

Map 2. Labor Camps for German and Austrian Jews in Germany, 1938–43

region (for example, for Hamburg Jews), to sending hundreds of Viennese Jews to Lower Saxony and East Friesland.[15]

LABOR CAMPS FOR GERMAN JEWS[16]

Berlin–Siemens camp
Buxtehude an der Röbke
Dumpte near Borghorst, Steinfurt Kreis (Westphalia)
Haina Monastery, Frankenberg Kreis (Hesse)
Hohenwarte, Saalfeld Kreis (Thuringia)
Höringshausen, Sauerland (Hesse)

---

[15] Österreichisches Staatsarchiv/Archiv der Republik (ÖStA/AdR) Vienna, Bürckel Materials, Carton 74, 2160/7, Fol. 11 verso, Report of the Austrian branch office of the Reich Ministry of Labor to the Minister, July 18, 1939; Rosenkranz, *Verfolgung*, 209.

[16] List of camps with source citations and additional details in Gruner, "Arbeitslager für den Zwangseinsatz, 1.Kapitel," in *Gedenkstättenrundbrief*, 78, 1–17. For Höringshausen, see Hans Frankenthal, *Verweigerte Rückkehr. Erfahrungen nach dem Judenmord*, with assistance from Andreas Plake, et al., 2nd edition (Frankfurt am Main, 1999), 39–41.

Jößnitz, Vogtland
Kelkheim, Taunus (Hesse)
Laer, Münster Kreis (Westphalia)
Lahde, Petershagen
Lohhof near Munich
Oersdorf, Stade Kreis
Otterndorf near Cuxhaven
Prettin, Torgau Kreis
Rongard near Kelberg (Koblenz)
Söhre near Bergshausen (Kassel)
Sprakebüll, Südtondern (Schleswig-Holstein)
Stolberg-Atsch near Aachen
Walheim near Stolberg
Walsheim, Waiblingen Kreis
Welterod, Rheingau
Wendefurt near Blankenburg (Harz Mountains)–Jewish camp II
Werlte I, Aschendorf-Hümmling Kreis (Lower Saxony)
Werlte–Rastdorf Construction camp II (Lower Saxony)
Wohlerst near Harsefeld, Stade Kreis

The sizes of camps for Jews in the Old Reich varied. Camps existed for
about twenty to thirty men, as in the vicinity of Saalfeld (Thuringia) for construction of the Hohenwarte Dam[17] or in Wohlerst near Harsefeld, Stade
Kreis, where Hamburg Jews performed excavation work for Firma Emil
Schmidt Tief- & Straßenbau (underground and road construction).[18] The
Reich highway agency employed around seventy Jewish men in Söhre camp
near Bergshausen (Kassel).[19] Even larger camps were built specifically for
Austrian Jews:[20] In May to June 1939, the water resources office (*Wasser-
wirtschaftsamt*) opened a camp for over 100 Jews in Leer;[21] the Prussian
Department for Land Development (*Preußische Kulturbauabteilung*), a
camp for over 150 Jews in Hölingen;[22] and the Straßenbaugesellschaft
Kemna-Lenz GmbH, (roadway construction), a camp for 150 Jews at the

---

[17] Harald Mittelsdorf, "Die Geschichte der Saale-Talsperren (1890–1945)," Dissertation
(Berlin, 1991), 100–204.
[18] BA Berlin, Zwischenarchiv (ZwA) Dahlwitz-Hoppegarten, former Archiv des Dokumentationszentrums der Staatlichen Archivverwaltung der DDR (AdZ), Doc./K 839, 1, Attachment
5 to the census of May 1939, Table on labor camps and the like.
[19] BA Berlin, 46.01, No. 1170, Fol. 242, Kassel central construction management office for
Reich highways, Information regarding the existing residential camps and housing, status as
of July 31, 1939.
[20] See Chapter 4.
[21] Niedersächsisches StA Aurich, Rep. 32, Rural District Leer, No. 2249, no folio numbers, Letter from Leda-Jümme construction department to the president of the Aurich administrative
district, June 1, 1939.
[22] Werner Meiners, *Geschichte der Juden in Wildeshausen* (Oldenburg, 1988), 304.

Photo 2. German Jews performing forced labor for Hanau Municipality, Winter 1941–42

Hildesheim-Hanover Reich Road Construction Office (*Reichstraßenbau*),[23] all with the help of the Lower Saxony regional labor office.

Immediately after the war began in 1939, construction projects classified as unimportant to the war effort were halted, and for that reason a whole series of camps for Jews closed down. Builders were able for a time to continue using some of the camps for large projects, such as Hohenwarte Dam.[24] A few existed until the end of the war, such as the camp for marshland cultivation at Werlte in the Emsland and the camp for the Rappbode Dam at Wendefurt in the Harz Mountains.[25] The Nazi leadership had in the meantime cancelled the forced-labor camp plans prepared for wartime and favored instead the idea of deporting German Jews to Poland. Soon the labor administration increasingly assigned German Jews to industrial centers, so that by the end of 1940 there was little need to supplement existing labor camps for segregated labor deployment in the Old Reich by building new ones.

[23] BA Berlin, 46.01, No. 136, no folio numbers, Attachment 1 of the report of the Oberpräsident of Hanover Province, September 14, 1939, Compilation of the Reich highway building projects to be carried out in case of mobilization.
[24] Mittelsdorf, "Saale-Talsperren," 202 and 204.
[25] Rastdorf until 1944 and Wendefurt until the beginning of 1945; see Hans-Donald Cramer, *Das Schicksal der Goslarer Juden 1933–1945. Eine Dokumentation* (Goslar, 1986), 110 and 143.

Although from the outset the tactical rule had been to establish camps for Jews on the fringes of cities or in rural areas – outside the German population's visual field[26] – the construction capacities were already limited before the war's onset. Hence, builders, or the private companies engaged to handle construction for the building owners, seldom built camps. They rented empty barracks to house Jews and increasingly used large rooms in inns or hostels meant for travelers or young people.[27] The Jews of Höringshausen Camp, for example, lived from 1941 to 1943 in the Lahrmann company's construction trailer in Meschede. Young Jewish Germans from Dortmund also performed road construction work for the same company after the training workshops were closed.[28]

In the first half of 1939, some municipal welfare offices still operated camps. As Jews receiving public support were then to work exclusively in the segregated labor deployment program, the Reich Institute for Labor Placement and Unemployment Insurance no longer made public funds available for Jews working on emergency projects. Thus the Hamburg camp programs, which had been operating since 1938, suddenly experienced financial difficulties.[29] When the Reich Institute adjusted its negative attitude after outside intervention, Hamburg's special projects then continued seamlessly within the framework of segregated labor deployment and even expanded.[30] Hamburg resident Heinz Rosenberg recalls, "After the end of my apprenticeship in March 1939, I was immediately sent to a labor camp for Jews, Wohlerst near Buxtehude. . . . I lived in a barracks with 50 other Jewish employees. The food and the living conditions were terrible. Once a month we were allowed to visit our families, provided that we had met our work quota."[31] The Hamburg social services administration employed about seventy Jews in Oersdorf and Wohlerst (Stade labor office district) in the first quarter of 1939 and also planned to use a third camp in Rendsburg, Schleswig, which had been built earlier for convicts.[32]

Dike and road construction agencies and companies for dam construction and also many municipal administrations were, as organizers and beneficiaries, responsible for the camps built in Germany. As already shown with

---

[26] See StA Hamburg, 351–10, Social Agencies I, AW 40.30, Bassum labor office to the Hamburg labor welfare office, September 8, 1937.

[27] See Ruth J. Wolff, "Verheiratet mit einem Juden – Erinnerungen an meinen Mann," in *Juden in Aachen*, edited by Manfred Bierganz and Annelie Kreutz (Aachen, 1988), 141.

[28] Frankenthal, *Verweigerte Rückkehr*, 39–41.

[29] StA Hamburg, 351–10, Social Agencies I, AW 40.30, no folio numbers, Note of the labor welfare office, December 17, 1938.

[30] Ibid., Excerpt from a report on an official meeting at the labor office, January 25, 1939.

[31] Heinz Rosenberg, *Jahre des Schreckens* (Göttingen, 1985), 12.

[32] StA Hamburg, Social Agencies I, AW 40.30, no folio numbers, Note of the labor welfare office, February 22, 1939; ibid., Note on the meeting with the labor office, February 24, 1939.

the example of Kelkheim, strict restrictions on freedom of movement were already in effect at some camps in summer 1939. The situation was similar at Jewish camp II in Wendefurt in the Harz Mountains, as a survivor describes, "We were robbed of our freedom, we were only allowed to go visit our relatives after a certain amount of time, and . . . all because we were Jews."[33] As control by local agencies working hand in hand with the Gestapo was considered adequate, additional guard personnel generally were not used until 1941. In Kelkheim, the foreman watched the Jews at work; in the camp, they were constantly guarded by a policeman residing by chance in the inn. Every week one of the city councilmen inspected the camp. One councilman complained in his report that "the Jews had to use the guest toilets of the Taunusblick inn."[34] Only once in a half year did the SS Security Service inspect the inmates of the camp.[35]

The labor camp network in Germany clearly gave concrete expression to the new anti-Jewish concept of a physical, social, and political forced community (*Zwangsgemeinschaft*). Further radicalization since the beginning of the war in September 1939 also affected camp inhabitants. In the Old Reich, for example, the imposition of a prohibition on going out in the evening caused almost complete isolation of the camp inhabitants, who could no longer leave the camp except on Sundays and to go to work. Discrimination through labor law also increased. The example of the Leer camp, established in spring 1939, illustrates the virtually friction-free, committed racist collaboration between administration offices and private industry. The Firma Wurpts-Loga construction enterprise, charged with dike construction work, was permitted by the labor office to go to Vienna to select Austrian Jews fit for work itself.[36] The Leer labor office had announced that a special-rate order was being prepared by the Reich Trustee of Labor to make the use of Jewish labor more profitable.[37] Later the labor office discussed with the water resources office and the construction company how they could strip away more benefits to which even compulsory employees were still entitled. The labor office let the building contractors designate which workers would be allowed in the future to take family trips home only every twenty weeks and

---

[33] Letter from Charly J. to Martin W., November 23, 1949, in a copy from the papers of the Mahlert family, Berlin, in the hands of the author.

[34] StadtA Kelkheim, Record Volume "Labor Utilization of a Column of Jews," no folio numbers, Note of a council member for the Kelkheim Bürgermeister, June 18, 1939.

[35] Ibid., Notes of the Bürgermeister, March 31 and May 5, 1939.

[36] Niedersächsisches StA Aurich, Rep. 16/3, No. 196, no folio numbers, Note of the Leer water resources office, April 24, 1939.

[37] Paid trips home were supposed to be curtailed by the wage scale. The Leer labor office also assured the enterprises which utilized Jews that their Aryan workers would not be taken away; Niedersächsisches StA Aurich, Rep. 32, Leer, No. 2237, no folio numbers, Note on the meeting with the Leer labor office on March 27, 1939; Niedersächsisches StA Aurich, Rep. 16/3, No. 196, no folio numbers, Leda-Jümme construction department in Leer to the president of the Aurich administrative district, April 3, 1939.

which were to have their family separation pay eliminated.[38] Despite all the concessions, the labor office ultimately demanded a surcharge for expenses from the water resources office; the latter refused to pay.[39] Such behavior often occurred at the local level. In spring 1939, the Bürgermeister of Kelkheim sent a notice regarding special rates for Jews to the labor administration,[40] and one year later the "work group of Upper Saale" refused to pay for the vacation days of their construction workers in Hohenwarte camp.[41]

To ensure that Jewish workers were not paid below the poverty level as a result of such arbitrary measures, labor offices intervened correctively in some cases: No public funds were to support "making cheap labor available to companies."[42] In early summer 1940, the labor office responsible for Jewish camps of the Stade district sought to make "all employers pay a hardship allowance" because the Jews, who worked fifty-four hours a week at an hourly wage of RM 0.50, had scarcely any money left for their families after the builders or companies took out up to RM 1.80 per day for food. Hamburg's Jewish welfare offices already had been compelled to provide additional support.[43] The workers' social situation continued to worsen in 1940–41 because of new, discriminatory deductions for Jews, such as the social equalization tax. Increasingly, Jews living in labor camps, or their families, had to apply for public welfare services.[44]

Public institutions, private enterprises, and many individuals – regardless of their personal views – profited from use of camp labor. In the Kelkheim labor camp, for example, the beneficiaries included the master butcher, who supplied the groceries; the owner of the inn, who rented out his dance hall; the town brick works owner, who rented out beds; and Miss Margarete Walter, who arranged for the camp's supplies. She lived in Taunusblick, and her salary came not from the city's coffers but from the Jews' wage deductions for housing.[45] The discriminatory utilization of German Jews in camps took place under the eyes of the public. Furthermore, even without having a role in the party or the administration, many local inhabitants actively participated

---

[38] Niedersächsisches StA Aurich, Rep. 32, Leer, No. 2237, no folio numbers, Note of the president of the Aurich administrative district, June 26, 1939.

[39] Niedersächsisches StA Aurich, Rep. 16/3, No. 196, no folio numbers, Leer water resources office to the Wurpts construction company, March 12, 1940.

[40] StadtA Kelkheim, Record Volume "Labor Utilization of a Column of Jews," no folio numbers, Note of March 31, 1939.

[41] BA Berlin, R 8150, No. 761, Fol. 79, Reichsvereinigung, welfare department to the Reichsvereinigung, Erfurt district office, November 6, 1940.

[42] StA Hamburg, 351–10 Social Agencies, AW 40.30, no folio numbers, Note of June 17, 1940.

[43] Ibid., and ibid., Office for Jewish economic assistance to the Hamburg social service administration, June 19, 1940.

[44] See BA Berlin, R 8150, No. 2, Fols. 69 and 72, Protocols of the Reichsvereinigung board meetings, December 20, 1940, and January 6, 1941.

[45] StadtA Kelkheim, Record Volume "Labor Utilization of a Column of Jews," no folio numbers.

and profited in a variety of ways in the persecutory process. That was probably one reason why so few examples of support for Jews by non-Jewish Germans are known.[46]

Scarcely any new labor camps were established in 1940 and 1941, as the majority of the Jewish workers had been put to work in industrial enterprises in the cities. In a very few cases, the labor administration got by with special transfers to armaments centers, as in the aforementioned case of the Jewish women from Frankfurt who ended up in a labor camp on Siemens's company property in Berlin.[47] Fear ruled those women's lives: The foreman or other employees could report them at any time for suspicion of sabotage, weak performance, or having sausage on their bread during breaks; completely unknown individuals might denounce them to the Gestapo for illegally purchasing a roll.[48] The Berlin camp personnel supplied by Siemens AG decisively influenced the women's living situation; critical was how consistently the personnel implemented the countless prohibitions that regimented the daily life of German Jews. The survivors still remember the head of the camp, Mrs. Krurup, in a positive light because she lightened their heavy load by, for example, not stringently enforcing the restrictions on leaving the camp and on food.[49]

Favored as workers at this time, Jewish women now suffered acutely under the everyday conditions within the camp system, which in 1941 were growing increasingly repressive. In May 1941, over 150 Viennese women were sent to harvest asparagus in the Magdeburg administrative district. Camps for this operation have been confirmed so far in Aschersleben, Nordhausen, Stendal, Siems near Mieste, and Haldensleben and Osterburg.[50] To avoid

---

[46] The Kelkheim city council members, among them a master mason and a furniture manufacturer, who because of their control had all the information at their disposal, widened the circle of individuals who approved of persecution; ibid., Letter, June 15, 1939, and Note of the Bürgermeister, May 20, 1939.

[47] BA Berlin, R 8150, No. 45, Fol. 50, Note 18/41 of Eppstein regarding the telephone call from the RHSA on March 7, 1941; BA Berlin, R 8150, Film No. 52407/23, Fol. 215, Reichsvereinigung Note A 11 regarding a telephone call from the Berlin State Police headquarters on May 30, 1941.

[48] C. Neumann makes similar reports about their work for the Blaupunkt-Werke GmbH Berlin, where a supervisor turned many Jewish forced laborers over to the Gestapo; Camilla Neumann, "Report on Experiences from the Hitler Period, First Part," 3–5, Memoir Collection, LBIA New York, 3–5. Similar information is reported about Zeiss-Ikon Görtz, Berlin; ibid., "Memoirs of Valerie Wolffenstein up to 1945, Andrea Wolffenstein 1938 to 1945" (manuscript edition), 73.

[49] Zahn, "Jüdische Zwangsarbeiterinnen im Siemenslager," 167–170.

[50] Two groups left Vienna on May 16 and 17 on order of the Gestapo. They actually belonged to Alijah Youth (preparation for emigration to Palestine); Gabriele Anderl, "Emigration und Vertreibung," in *Vertreibung und Neubeginn. Israelische Bürger österreichischer Herkunft* (Vienna, Cologne, and Weimar, 1992), 249. For more details on this deployment, see Wolf Gruner, *Zwangsarbeit und Verfolgung. Österreichische Juden im NS-Staat 1938–1943* (Innsbruck, Vienna, and Munich, 2000), Excursus VIII, 226–234.

undermining the Jewish women's willingness to work, the Magdeburg State Police headquarters wrote into the regulations set times for leaving the camp: "two hours on Saturday and . . . two hours on Sunday morning and three hours on Sunday afternoon." Later, at the end of June, the agency gave the green light to eliminating time off completely, to prevent "all too close contact" with the rest of the population.[51] The Vienna labor office gave its assurance that the female forced laborers, whose number was increasing rapidly, actually would be released at the end of June or beginning of July 1941. After the harvest, however, the labor administration responsible for Nordhausen and the other locations assigned over 300 of the women to local private enterprises; tragically, many of them had volunteered.[52] Fifty-seven Viennese women then worked for the Vereinigte Nordhäuser Kautabakfabriken-Hanewacker company (chewing tobacco factories). They were only allowed to leave their camp (an old house) in groups of ten regardless of whether they were going to the factory or to the mailbox across the street. They were forbidden from entering local stores, as well as certain streets and squares; taking a walk required authorization. Visits to the camp and contact with the Nordhausen Jews were prohibited. In August 1941, daily rations consisted of a few slices of bread. That weakened the female forced laborers so much, despite food sent from Vienna, that diphtheria and skin diseases were rampant in the camp. After intervention of the Viennese Jewish community, the agencies relaxed conditions somewhat, but an attempt to offer the women to the Vienna labor office for mandatory employment failed.[53] The majority had to perform forced labor at the camp until their deportation in 1942.[54]

Another camp was built for women in June 1941 at the instigation of the representative of the Munich Gauleiter at Flachsröste GmbH. in Lohhof. Twenty-five young people prepared flax there; they were supplemented by older, completely overtaxed women: "The piles of flax [had] to be completely separated, the individual stems checked for their strength. . ., many piles

---

[51] Verwaltungsarchiv Landkreis Oschersleben, Registration Hornhausen No. 184, Fols 4–8, Circular letter of the Magdeburg Gestapo, May 23, 1941, and Addendum to the circular letter, June 20, 1941.

[52] Central Archives for the History of the Jewish People (CAHJP), Jerusalem, A/W, No. 180/2, no folio numbers, Letter to Löwenherz (Office Director of the Jewish Religious Community [*Israelitische Kultusgemeinde*, IKG] in Vienna), August 23, 1941; and Landeshauptarchiv Sachsen-Anhalt (LHA-SA) Magdeburg, Rep. C 20 I b, No. 3293, Fol. 107 and verso, president of the regional labor office for Middle Germany to the Saxony Oberpräsident, April 18, 1942.

[53] The Nordhausen Jewish community was now allowed to take care of the Viennese women; CAHJP Jerusalem, A/W, No. 180/2, no folio numbers, Anonymous report, August 17, 1941; ibid., Letter to Löwenherz, August 23, 1941.

[54] LHA-SA Magdeburg, Rep. C 20 I b, No. 3293, Fol. 107 and verso, president of the regional labor office for Middle Germany to the Saxony Oberpräsident, April 18, 1942.

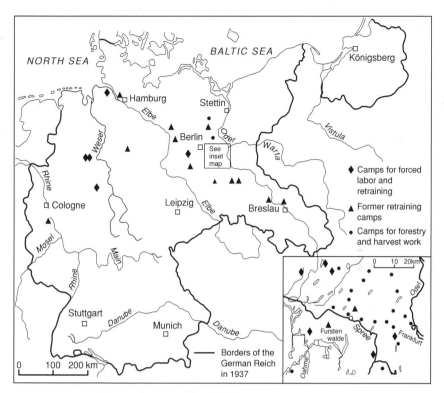

Map 3. Camps of the Reichsvereinigung, 1939–43

[were] completely moldy and [exuded] a terrible stench. . . . But most difficult to bear [was] the eternal standing in the burning heat of the sun."[55] Contrary to all wage scale provisions and even to all special regulations, the camp inhabitants were only granted barracks housing, food, and a daily allowance of RM 0.20 for work that was detrimental to their health; they had no health insurance.[56]

Until the beginning of 1941, German, stateless, and Austrian Jews in the Old Reich were employed and housed in two categories of camp, which represented two different types of organization for labor utilization – camps for segregated labor deployment controlled by the labor administration, and the "independent" camps of the Reichsvereinigung for forced labor and retraining. The latter will be described in the following pages.

[55] Mrs. Rosenfeld had a lame arm; Else Behrend-Rosenfeldt, *Ich stand nicht allein. Erlebnisse einer Jüdin in Deutschland 1933–1944*, 3rd printing (Cologne and Frankfurt am Main, 1979), 101.

[56] BA Berlin, R 8150, No. 760, Fol. 10, Letter draft for Dr. Eppstein (Reichsvereinigung), February 23 (?), 1942; Behrend-Rosenfeld, *Ich stand nicht allein*, 102.

FROM RETRAINING ESTATE TO LABORER BARRACKS: THE REICHSVEREINIGUNG CAMPS[57]

Retraining Camps before and after 1939

Between 1939 and 1943, the Reichsvereinigung operated about fifty work and retraining camps (see map 3, p. 43). At least half of those camps, which were involved in the forced-labor program in an unusual way, already existed before 1938. Jewish organizations had been developing vocational training programs since the 1920s, especially for agricultural training at so-called "teaching estates"; those programs were greatly expanded after 1933 in reaction to the Nazis' policy of expulsion.[58] Many Jewish youths and unemployed adults considered so-called "retraining"– learning cattle breeding and gardening for an extended period in completely different living circumstances – to be solid preparation for emigration, as emigrants with agricultural qualifications were accepted more readily in many places.[59] The reactions of the Nazi state to such counter-strategies on the part of the Jews were contradictory.

Because of the dominant goal of expulsion, early Nazi plans to transform the camps into long-term forced labor sites had come to naught. In summer 1938, however, the possibility was again raised, this time against the background of the Nazi leadership's increasingly concrete war plans. The SD Jewish section addressed the situation with a plan that was to take effect in case of war: The twenty-nine retraining camps in the Old Reich, each with an average capacity of forty to fifty, would be transformed into forced-labor

---

[57] For all of the camps mentioned in the following pages of this chapter or in the footnotes, the source citations and additional details can be found in the camp lists in Wolf Gruner, "Die Arbeitslager für den Zwangseinsatz deutscher und nichtdeutscher Juden im Dritten Reich. 2. Kapitel: Zu den Lagern der Reichsvereinigung (ab 1941 Arbeitslager) im Altreich," in *Gedenkstättenrundbrief*, published by the Foundation for the Topography of Terror, 79 (1997), 3–17.

[58] Among the best-known training spots were the Neuendorf agricultural operation, which was founded in 1932, a rural estate about 40 kilometers from Berlin with cultivated land, cattle raising, and vegetable gardening; the Groß-Gaglow training estate near Cottbus, founded in 1928 and cultivating fruit and vegetables; and the Winkel estate (formerly owned by the Schocken family) that educated about 100 trainees; Alexander Szanto, "Im Dienste der Gemeinde 1923–1939," Memoir Collection, LBIA New York; excerpt in Monika Richarz (ed.), *Jüdisches Leben in Deutschland. Bd. 3: Selbstzeugnisse zur Sozialgeschichte 1918–1945* (Stuttgart, 1982), 225–226. For the history up to 1939, see also Adler-Rudel, who as a Jewish social worker helped shape the development of the vocational reorientation; S. Adler-Rudel, *Selbsthilfe unter dem Naziregime 1933–1939. Im Spiegel der Berichte der Reichsvertretung der Juden in Deutschland* (Tübingen, 1974).

[59] LBI/A New York, Memoir Collection, Szanto, "Im Dienste der Gemeinde 1923–1939," 168. See also *Dokumente zur Geschichte der Frankfurter Juden*, published by the Commission for Research on the History of the Frankfurt Jews (Frankfurt am Main, 1963), VI 1, 241; Willy Mainz, *Gemeinde in Not 1933–1938*, in ibid, VI 1, 241; for what follows, see Werner T. Angress, *Generation zwischen Furcht und Hoffnung* (Hamburg, 1985), 29–33.

camps guarded by the SS. The particular focus would be Jews in need of assistance, who "would have practical work to perform there and would have to arrange their own supplies."[60] The project, proposed to Heydrich in September 1938, did not materialize, as the critical pre-war situation became for a short while more relaxed with the Munich Agreement, but it was not forgotten.

During the November 1938 pogrom, the male trainers, and the trainees as well, were arrested in many retraining camps. The Steckelsdorf agricultural operation was demolished, seventy youths were "chased into the fields," and the male personnel were placed in Buchenwald Concentration Camp.[61] Many camps remained closed for a time, and others were put up for sale. The Reich representation (*Reichsvertretung*) first appealed to the Gestapo office without success.[62] Then, under pressure from the SD, the Gestapo finally ordered at the end of November that all the arrested "leaders of the retraining camps, . . . and the trainees as well," were to be released "because of their activities to promote emigration."[63] After the pogrom, only sixty-one of the previous year's ninety-four training camps and sites were still in existence; the remaining twenty camps had 1,190 slots.[64]

Because of the general changes in the prosecution program by the beginning of December 1938, the SD Jewish section wanted a final ruling on administration of the training estates for Jewish emigrants. The main problem was the burgeoning number of unemployed Jews without any particular chance of emigrating. In Göring's opinion, which the SD also vigorously supported, the camps should remain in existence and be expanded still further for that group. As the first step, the SD had to ward off efforts to close the training estates in the interest of forced Aryanization. An agreement with the Reich Farm Leader (*Reichsbauernführer*) established as a minimum that regulations would place restrictions on leaving the camp, thereby preventing

---

[60] YV Jerusalem, 051/OSOBI, No. 92 (Moscow 500/1/387), Fol. 37, Note of the SD Jewish section II 112, September 16, 1938.

[61] There were arrests, for example, in Ellguth, Silesia; Freienstein, Pomerania; Gehringshof near Fulda; Groß-Breesen, Silesia; Grüsen near Frankenberg; Neuendorf near Fürstenwalde; Silingthal, Silesia; Halberstadt and Jägerslust near Flensburg. Bomsdorf, Bitterfeld District, and Sennfeld, Baden, among others, were closed; YV Jerusalem, 051/OSOBI, No. 92 (Moscow 500/1/387), Fols. 64–67, Reich representation list, December 9, 1938, with handwritten notes on destruction and arrests. For Steckelsdorf, Kreisarchiv Rathenow, Friedrich Löwenthal Report, 1–2. For arrests in Groß-Breesen, see Angress, *Generation*, 69–71.

[62] YV Jerusalem, 051/OSOBI, No. 92 (Moscow 500/1/387), Fol. 43, Note of the Security Service (SD) of the SS, Ref. II 112, November 19, 1938.

[63] Ibid., Fol. 58, Teletype of the Reich Security Main Office to the SD *Oberabschnitt*, December 1, 1938.

[64] At the beginning of 1939, the capacity had dropped to 1,100 persons, and there were only 804 trainees; "*Arbeitsbericht der Reichsvertretung der Juden in Deutschland für das Jahr 1938*," Manuscript (Berlin, 1939), 37–38; Wiener Library (WL) London, Microfilms, Doc. Section 606, 500 Series, Reel 2, No. 38, Reichsvereinigung financial report, August 8, 1939, 6.

any contact between Jews and non-Jews.[65] At the beginning of February 1939, a meeting with the Gestapo and "the future leader of central Jewish emigration," Reinhard Heydrich, was finally to settle the matter in a manner amenable to the SD. However, Kurt Lischka of the Berlin headquarters of the Gestapo[66] wanted to wait on "consultations with the ministers."[67] In March, Heydrich finally complained personally to the Minister of Agriculture about his Aryanization efforts. Although Heydrich explicitly referred to Göring's directive favoring preparation for emigration, that did not prevent the ministerial officials from planning for the "Jews' school" to be leased back after the property had been transferred and thus to remain in Jewish hands.[68] At this point, a decision had obviously been made about the use of the retraining camps in the Old Reich. Subordinate in the meantime to the Reichsvereinigung, the camps were to become a factor in the new strategy of persecution and were examined by the Gestapo in that context.[69] Both the Gestapo and the SD were interested in both control and isolation of the occupants, and in certificates confirming months of agricultural work and therefore usefulness for emigration. The agricultural and gardening businesses not shut down underwent significant transformation, however, they increasingly lost "their training site character."[70]

That was the case, even though the need of many Jews for short-term vocational training had risen sharply due to persecution. The retraining camps, together with a few artisan training workshops, afforded the last chance to obtain vocational qualifications after trade was prohibited and training restricted. Consequently, the Reichsvereinigung, with the consent of its supervisory agency, expanded existing facilities by adding barracks and built new

[65] In a meeting with the envoy of the Farm Leader, the SD representatives emphasized that the camps for training emigrants had to continue to exist because Göring had demanded that "first and foremost emigration and welfare of the Jews [should] be promoted in solving the Jewish problem"; YV Jerusalem, 051/OSOBI, No. 92 (Moscow 500/1/387), Fols. 61–63 verso, Note of the SD section II 112, December 8, 1938.

[66] Born on August 16, 1909, in Breslau; studied law and political science, employed in local courts and as an attorney; from 1933 on, a member of the SS; from 1935 on, in the Geheimes Staatspolizeiamt (Gestapa); in 1938 leader of the Gestapa Jewish section II B 4; in January 1940, leader of the Gestapa in Cologne; in November 1940, deputy commander of the Sipo and SD in France; in 1943 in the RSHA; from 1945 to 1950, under arrest; convicted of war crimes in France and the Federal Republic of Germany.

[67] YV Jerusalem, 051/OSOBI, No. 92 (Moscow 500/1/387), Fol. 87 and verso, Note of the SD Jewish section, February 7, 1939.

[68] BA Berlin, R 14, No. 301, Fols. 217–218, Heydrich (Chief of the Security Police and SD) to the Reich Ministry for Nutrition and Agriculture (*Reichsministerium für Ernährung und Landwirtschaft*), March 6, 1939 (including the handwritten note of an official); excerpt in Kurt Pätzold (ed.), *Verfolgung, Vertreibung, Vernichtung. Dokumente des faschistischen Antisemitismus 1933–1942* (Leipzig, 1983), 223–224, Doc. No. 187.

[69] StadtA Göttingen, Police directorate in Göttingen, 156, No. 5, Fol. 340, Circular letter of the Hildesheim Stapo Central Office, March 23, 1939.

[70] Angress, *Generation*, 33.

camps. As Aryanization advanced, private Aryan estates increasingly had to be leased in order to house "segregated Jewish groups" that worked under the direction of a leader appointed by the Reichsvereinigung.[71] In the Ostmark, the approach was somewhat different: Retraining occurred at self-supporting estates that were "neither leased nor rented by Jewish organizations." The Viennese authorities even planned to set up two "retraining camps in the Lower Danube region"– each for over a thousand Jews – that were intended to exploit the inmates' labor until the time they were expelled.[72]

In Germany, the capacity of the twenty-one camps had increased to almost 1,600 slots by summer 1939, and all were filled.[73] However, this approach only seemed promising to the responsible authorities as long as "enough work [was] available for the expanded work force or could be created, for example, by leasing land or accepting work for pay."[74] The need for work coincided with growing interest in separate, compulsory employment for Jews. Existence of the Reichsvereinigung camps at this stage was contingent on the central condition that the trainees could at any time be called up for the segregated labor deployment program operated by the labor offices since the beginning of the year, or could be put to work just outside the camp.

The size of the Havelberg work force increased after April 1939 because the trainees could be used in the public forest;[75] Skaby, an estate employing about forty Jews for agricultural labor, was first set up in May.[76] The Paderborn barracks camp was established in June; the Jews there worked for the city administration, as the Reichsvereinigung's contract with the municipality demonstrates: "The purpose of this labor and reorientation camp is to utilize Jews for labor and to train and reorient Jews for physical, primarily agricultural and horticultural work as preparation for their emigration. Work and reorientation will be associated with soil improvement, water pipe installation, garden lay-out, sports field complexes, streetcar construction, sewer systems, and auxiliary tasks in residential construction, as well as with the municipal nursery. . . . In addition, in cooperation with the competent

---

[71] Adler-Rudel, *Selbsthilfe*, 67.

[72] YV Jerusalem, 051/OSOBI, No. 92 (Moscow 500/1/387), Fol. 88, Order of the SD section II 112, February 10, 1939. For the lack of influence of the Jewish side in Austria, see the statement of Bar Gedallah in a letter to the author, March 29, 1992.

[73] While there were several new openings, three camps were also closed at the end of 1938; WL London, Microfilms, Doc. Section, 500 Series, Reel 2, No. 38, Reichsvereinigung financial report from January 1, 1939, to July 31, 1939, Attachment of report to JOINT, August 8, 1938, 6–8. See *"Arbeitsbericht der Reichsvereinigung der Juden in Deutschland für das Jahr 1939,"* Manuscript (Berlin 1940), 24–25.

[74] *Arbeitsbericht der Reichsvertretung 1938*, 41.

[75] BA Berlin, R 8150, No. 47, no folio numbers, Reichsvereinigung report to the Gestapo for April, April 28, 1939, 4.

[76] WL London, Microfilms, Doc. Section, 500 Series, Reel 2, No. 38, Reichsvereinigung financial report from January 1, 1939, to July 31, 1939, Attachment of report to JOINT, August 8, 1938, 7.

office of *Reichsnährstand* [the Reich nutrition office, here the Kreis farm leader], work will also be performed for local farms that do not belong to the city."[77]

Activities in Paderborn thus had very little to do with training or reorientation. In a rosy description of the "emigration preparation site" in Paderborn, the only allowed official Jewish news bulletin, the *Jüdisches Nachrichtenblatt*, later wrote that "retraining and productive work" were combined there in the context of labor utilization. The Paderborn inmates "began in July 1939 by laying out a large park. The construction of an open-air theater by the group followed; at the same time, another group of workers was deployed to various locations in late fall to help with the harvest. In early fall, the work on installing a game preserve began. . . . Other *chaverim*[78] worked in winter on tasks associated with snow, hacking up ice blocks to obtain usable ice, and clearing rails. Since the beginning of the warmer season, about fifty people from the Hachsharah Kibbutz[79] have been performing underground excavation. Others are assisting with construction of an auction hall. The work sometimes has been very difficult for unskilled workers, but the *chaverim* proved their worth. . . . Such *hachsharah* sites, where reorientation and work go hand in hand, are no longer rare today."[80]

After the war began in 1939, a series of additional camps was set up – under the control of the RSHA – for forced employment in agriculture and forestry. New labor agreements with the forestry offices and the Kreis farmers' associations required that the Reichsvereinigung provide short-term laborers and housing. About 1,200 Jews sixteen to forty-five years old resided in camps working for the Lebus Kreis farmers' association between September and December, to help with the harvest in the Berlin area. Several smaller camps in the Mark Brandenburg had been added by the end of the year, when "a large number of young and especially strong Jews" performed forestry work in segregated groups of twelve to forty men at various sites in the territory of the Fürstenwalde district forestry office.[81] A survivor recalls his involuntary experience as a tree cutter: "No Labour office was involved. . . . We were originally indoctrinated by some Jewish fellow, who arranged that. . . . We

---

77 Margrit Naarmann, *Die Paderborner Juden 1802 bis 1945* (Paderborn, 1988), 464–465, Attachment 34, Agreement of June 23, 1939; see *Arbeitsbericht der Reichsvertretung 1939*, 25. A more detailed publication on this camp is Margrit Naarmann, *Ein Auge gen Zion. . . . Das jüdische Umschulungs- und Einsatzlager am Grünen Weg in Paderborn 1939–1943* (Cologne, 2000).

78 *Chaverim* means "friends" in Hebrew.   79 *Hachsharah* means "preparation" in Hebrew.

80 *JNBl*, Berlin, 58 (July 19, 1940); p. 2. For the work conditions, see Erwin Angreß, "Im Arbeitslager am Grünen Weg in Paderborn," in *Opfer und Täter. Zum nationalsozialistischen und antijüdischen Alltag in Ostwestfalen-Lippe*, edited by Hubert Frankemölle (Bielefeld, 1990), 75–78.

81 *Arbeitsbericht der Reichsvereinigung 1939*, 25.

only had a kerosene lamp, we had nothing to read. No books, no newspapers, no magazines . . . and no radio. And we worked long hours, came home, went to bed, and went out next morning."[82] As a result of the change in course, twenty-eight Reichsvereinigung camps existed in Germany by the end of 1939; the camps had a total of 1,800 slots and had already been officially designated "reorientation camps for agriculture, gardening, forestry, and other forms of cultivation."[83]

REICHSVEREINIGUNG CAMPS[84]

Ahlem near Hanover (*Israelitische Gartenbauschule* [Jewish Horticultural School])
Ahrensdorf near Luckenwalde
Altlandsberg (Altlandsberg Domain) in Niederbarnim Kreis (Brandenburg)
Altmahlisch, Lebus Kreis (Brandenburg)
Assel near Stade
Beerfelde, Lebus Kreis near Fürstenwalde an der Spree
Behlenfelde, Mark Brandenburg
Berkenbrück, Lebus Kreis (Brandenburg)
Berlin-Wannsee
Bielefeld Camp, 4 Koblenzer Street, later 73a Schloßhof Street
Boosen, Lebus Kreis (Brandenburg)
Eichow, Krieschow post office, Cottbus Kreis
Ellguth near Steinau, Falkenberg Kreis (Silesia)
Garzau, Straußberg near Berlin
Garzin, Lebus Kreis (Brandenburg)
Gehringshof near Hattendorf, Fulda Rural Area
Groß-Breesen,Obernigk (Silesia)
Hangelsberg an der Spree, Wulkow Estate (Brandenburg)
Hasenfelde, Lebus Kreis (Brandenburg)
Havelberg, Mark
Hohenwalde near Frankfurt an der Oder
Jakobsdorf, Mark, near Frankfurt an der Oder
Jessen-Mühle near Sommerfeld, Niederlausitz
Kaisermühl, Lebus Kreis (Brandenburg)
Kersdorf near Briesen (Brandenburg)

---

[82] He worked in a group of ten to twelve youths between Jüterborg and Finsterwalde; interview of the author with Mr. Eisenstädter on December 7, 1991, 2.

[83] *Arbeitsbericht der Reichsvereinigung 1939*, 26; see Adler-Rudel, *Selbsthilfe*, 66.

[84] List of camps with detailed references and source citations and additional details in Gruner, "Arbeitslager für den Zwangseinsatz, 2. Kapitel: Zu den Lagern der Reichsvereinigung (ab 1941 Arbeitslager) im Altreich," in *Gedenkstättenrundbrief*, 79, 3–17.

Markendorff, Jüterbog Kreis
Müncheberg, Mark
Neuendorf near Fürstenwalde an der Spree
Neumühle, Lebus Kreis (Brandenburg)
Neumühle Estate near Straußberg (Brandenburg)
Neutrebbin, Oberbarnim Kreis (Brandenburg)
Obersdorf, Lebus Kreis (Brandenburg)
Oderbruch, Seelow National Research Estate (Brandenburg)
Paderborn, 86 Grüner Weg
Pillgram, Lebus Kreis (Brandenburg)
Polenzwerder
Radinkendorf, Jewish Labor Home
Reppen (Brandenburg)
Rissen near Hamburg
Rüdnitz near Bernau, Barnim Kreis (Niederlausitz)
Schneeberg near Beeskow (Brandenburg)
Schniebinchen near Sommerfeld (Niederlausitz)
Schönfelde, Lebus (Brandenburg)
Skaby near Friedersdorf, Beeskow Kreis
Steckelsdorf expansion, Steckelsdorf, Jerichow Kreis II
Steinhöfel, Uckermark
Teuplitz, Jewish labor group
Treplin, Lebus Kreis (Brandenburg)
Urfeld, Bonn Kreis
Wallnow, Lebus Kreis (Brandenburg)
Winkel, Spreenhagen (Brandenburg)

While only young people between fourteen and thirty years old had lived in the Neuendorf retraining camp in 1933–34,[85] the situation now changed. From September 1939 on, a Bielefeld labor and retraining camp was located in a private residence, then after 1940, in an old inn. Of the seventy-five people on average who lived in the camp until 1942, about 38 percent were women; furthermore, the proportion of older persons increased.[86]

The presence of the elderly, families, and children is a serious indicator for a lack of training, also the fact that Jews usually were in a training camp for a few months, but often in Reichsvereinigung camps for longer, and later always for an indefinite period. Forty percent of the inmates lived in Bielefeld for longer than a year, a total of fifty-eight Jewish men and women

---

[85] Adler-Rudel, *Selbsthilfe*, 60.

[86] The male inmates were housed in the ballroom of the inn, where two to three old, primitive beds stood one above the other. On the first floor were bedrooms for women. The sanitary facilities were outside the building; Joachim Meynert, *Was vor der Endlösung geschah. Antisemitische Ausgrenzung und Verfolgung in Minden-Ravensberg 1933–1945* (Münster, 1988), 236–240. For Paderborn, see Angreß, "Arbeitslager," 74–75.

Age Distribution in the Camp in Bielefeld,
1939–43

Age	Number	Percent
00–15 years old	12	5.9
16 –30 years old	124	61.1
31–45 years old	36	17.7
45–60 years old	13	6.4
Over 60 years	16	7.9
Unknown	2	1.0
Total	203	100.0

for more than two years, and some Jews for a total of three years before their deportation.[87]

Inmate transfers among the Reichsvereinigung camps were frequent. Of the ninety-eight men and women who had been transferred to Paderborn until the end of 1942, over half came from another camp, some already in fall 1939.[88] At thirty-seven years of age, Herbert N. was sent in August 1939 from Breslau to Neuendorf camp and then transferred to Jänichendorf, to Winkel in November 1939, and from there to the camp in Rüdnitz in March 1940.[89] The way out of a Reichsvereinigung camp thus generally led into yet another camp, not to emigration.[90] Some Jews came from labor camps;[91] the Gestapo sent others directly from a concentration camp.[92]

[87] At twenty years old, Herbert L. arrived from the Winkel estate camp in Bielefeld in August 1940 and was deported from Bielefeld on March 2, 1943; StadtA Bielefeld, House Records, Inmate List, Fols. 11–19; also Meynert, "Endlösung," 237.

[88] Naarmann, *Die Paderborner Juden*, 468–472, Attachment, List of inmates in Paderborn (Status as of December 31, 1942).

[89] Brandenburgisches Landeshauptarchiv (BLHA) Potsdam, Rep. 36 A Senior President for Finance (*Oberfinanzpräsident*), No. 2730, no folio numbers, Various letters to the senior president for finance, 1939–1940.

[90] Only five young people were able to emigrate in August 1940 with one of the special transports of the Palestine Office, and in addition a few to Yugoslavia, Holland, or the United States; Meynert, "Endlösung," 236–240. In Paderborn, five Jews apparently succeeded in emigrating in 1939, and twenty-four in 1940; Naarmann, *Die Paderborner Juden*, 351.

[91] Two inmates, for example, came to the Bielefeld camp from the camp in Rastdorf, Werlte, to which one of the two had to return again after seven months; StadtA Bielefeld, House Records, Inmate List, Fols. 17 and 19.

[92] See the file of the Jewish woman Itla Magier, who was interned in a concentration camp after May 1940 and was transferred in March 1941 from there to Bielefeld: "She was told to register immediately with the Jewish Community here; from there she was to be sent to a Jewish agricultural retraining camp in preparation for her emigration"; BA Berlin, RSHA St. 3, No. 800, Fol. 131, Note of the Düsseldorf Gestapo, March 14, 1941. See StadtA Bielefeld, House Records, Inmate List, Fol. 19. Examples are also to be found in Meynert, "Endlösung," 238.

The Reichsvereinigung camps were not guarded in the narrow sense, but they were strictly monitored, as the RSHA centrally supervised the Reichsvereinigung, the institutional umbrella of the camps, and the Gestapo had reports sent every day from on-site.[93] A roll call was held before and after work.[94] Fences enclosed Bielefeld and Paderborn, because they were located on the peripheries of cities.[95] The camp inmates were prohibited from shopping in town.[96] Only if a pass was issued by the Gestapo-controlled camp leadership was it possible to go out. Of course, it is doubtful whether forced laborers would have had the time and strength to leave camp when the work day lasted until 7:00 p.m. After the beginning of the war, the curfew started at 8:00 p.m., and additional work sessions frequently were held on Sunday.[97]

How exactly was the forced labor of the camp inmates set up? In Paderborn, according to the June 1939 contract between the Reichsvereinigung and the city, "The workers employed by the city are paid by the city according to a standard wage scale. In addition to the number of workers requested by the city, the Reichsvereinigung is to supply an equal number for the purpose of reorientation without compensation. The city is to pay the wage total to the camp leader appointed by the Reichsvereinigung. The wages, with some spending money subtracted, will be applied exclusively as a contribution to the camp costs."[98] In real terms, that meant that the city administration got two workers for the price of one unskilled worker.[99] Despite the heavy labor of approximately 100 trainees working at the municipal garbage collection facility or for private companies in Paderborn, the parties to the contract had stipulated that "there [was] no obligation to provide social insurance, no labor records are to be kept, and the labor office is not to be involved in employment." The labor office and the health insurance provider had agreed to this extra-legal determination. While accident insurance was a given, the Reichsvereinigung insisted on health insurance with the General Local Health Insurance Provider (*Allgemeine Ortskrankenkasse*

---

93   For Bielefeld, ibid., 236–240. For Paderborn, see Angreß, "Arbeitslager," 74–75.

94   Naarmann, *Die Paderborner Juden,* 350.

95   Rita Klussmann, "Die 'Jüdische Arbeitseinsatzstelle' Schloßhofstr. 73a," in *Einwohner-Bürger-Entrechtete. 7 Jahrhunderte jüdisches Leben im Raum Bielefeld-eine Ausstellung des Stadtarchivs, 9. Oktober bis 9. Dezember 1988, zum 50. Jahrestag des Novemberpogroms von 1938, Katalog von Monika Minninger* (Bielefeld, 1988), 197; see also Angreß, "Arbeitslager," 74.

96   That was already the case in Steckelsdorf in December 1939. Groceries were obtained there for the camp in the company of a responsible person; Joel König, *David. Aufzeichnungen eines Überlebenden* (Göttingen, 1967), 134.

97   Julius Bendorf, "Lager Grüner Weg von Paderborn," manuscript in possession of the author; see also Klussmann, "Die 'Jüdische Arbeitseinsatzstelle,'" 202.

98   Naarmann, *Die Paderborner Juden,* 465.

99   Apparently the camp leadership received between RM 0.17 and 0.19 compensation per hour net per person; Angreß, "Arbeitslager," 72–86; see also Bendorf, "Lager Grüner Weg," 1.

or AOK) and assumed the costs for it.[100] The conditions in Bielefeld were similar. The camp retained three-quarters of the wages of Jews employed at the Firma Nebelung & Söhne performing rail construction for room and board.[101] In harvest and forest camps, exploitation was even more blatant. In 1940, the Radinkendorf local farmers' association paid the Jews only RM 0.25 per hour for harvest work,[102] exactly the same as the Prussian state forest administration for forest work.[103]

The Hangelsberg forestry office in the Mark Brandenburg had requested workers from the Neuendorf camp in March 1940. When the Reichsvereinigung promised twelve Jews,[104] both parties decided to establish a camp at Hangelsberg an der Spree, where ten to twenty Jews later lived. The Jews' housing was rented for RM 75 per month from the Wulkow farm administration.[105] The contract was obviously similar to that of other forestry and harvest camps: "Housing is for a closed group. Supplies and leadership for the group are the business of the Reichsvereinigung." The latter provided the camp leader and was responsible for order and discipline. The forestry office supplied the "leadership for the work project and the work tools." In this situation, too, Jews were not in a formal employment classification and therefore were not subject to any social insurance obligation; nor could they be placed by the labor office. The forestry office, which was interested in extremely cheap labor, committed itself to obtaining the consent of the insurance institution and the labor office on the unusual collective labor contract; authorization of the Potsdam Gestapo central office was of course necessary.[106]

The compensation agreed to was primarily used to cover the cost of food and housing; for that reason, it was transferred by the Prussian forestry administration directly to an account of the Reichsvereinigung.[107] This appears to have been the normal procedure. As the payments were minimal, they often were not sufficient to maintain the camp. Families thus also had to pay maintenance fees for family members regularly performing forced

---

[100] Naarmann, *Die Paderborner Juden*, 465–466; Angreß, "Arbeitslager," 72–86.

[101] Meynert, "Endlösung," 243; Klussmann, "Die 'Jüdische Arbeitseinsatzstelle,'" 203.

[102] For help with the harvest by women from the "Radinkendorf Jewish Labor Home," the Reichsvereinigung was to receive RM 0.20, with the authorization of the Potsdam Gestapo; BA Berlin, R 8150, No. 483, Fol. 134, Reichsvereinigung letter to the Potsdam Gestapo on July 16, 1940.

[103] BLHA Potsdam, Pr. Br. Rep. 15 C Hangelsberg, No. 5, no folio numbers, Prussian forestry office in Hangelsberg and the Neuendorf agricultural operation, March 15, 1940.

[104] Ibid., Neuendorf to the Reichsvereinigung, March 17, 1940; ibid., Handwritten note on a Reichsvereinigung letter, March 21, 1940.

[105] The rent was RM 50 plus a RM 25 inventory-use fee; ibid., Contract, February 6, 1941.

[106] Ibid., Reichsvereinigung to the Prussian forestry office, April 8, 1940, with an attachment, Agreement regarding the utilization of Jewish trainees.

[107] Ibid., Hangelberg Jewish retraining camp to the Prussian forestry administration, October 31, 1940.

labor, which in 1939–40 was RM 30 to 75 per month for self-payers and RM 30 to 60 for Jews in need of support.[108] Although Jewish social offices bore the costs for those in need of assistance,[109] the Jewish communities were compelled to initiate investigations at the office of the Senior President of Finance (*Oberfinanzpräsident*) and other agencies in order to establish their clients' ability to pay based on family income.[110]

This situation did generate protests. The example of Jews in the segregated labor deployment program, who were usually paid according to a standard wage scale, even if on the lowest level, prompted demands: The forced labor in Reichsvereinigung camps utilized everywhere since 1939–40 for "productive work on Aryan estates [and] in forest operations" should be compensated. In July 1940, the Reichsvereinigung was compelled to announce publicly regarding the classification of the two work situations that the organizer of the one type was the labor administration, and the institutional sponsor of the other was the Reichsvereinigung. The inmates of the latter's camps thus did not fall in any formal employment classification, were not entitled to wages for their work, and had to defray the costs for their "training." The Reichsvereinigung acknowledged that even when camps produced "earnings as the result of their trainees' productive work in outside businesses" – which most of the camps did at that point – the inmates were to receive no wages, but instead, after cost settlement, only "bonuses."[111]

Experience with this cheap approach probably also won over the control authority. In April 1940, the RSHA laid plans to expand the use of forced labor in agriculture and forestry – ostensibly to promote illegal emigration to Palestine. As the estimate of existing camps was too small, the RSHA wanted the Reich Minister of Agriculture, Richard Walther Darré, to place a number of large estates at its disposal. Able-bodied Jews were to be collected on a large scale for six months of "work training" following the model used thus far for forestry work.[112] The Jewish partner would handle organization and housing in the "community camps" (*Gemeinschaftslager*) and would

---

[108] WL London, Microfilms, Doc. Section, 500 Series, Reel 2, No. 38, Reichsvereinigung financial report to JOINT, August 8, 1939, 9. For the stay in the labor and retraining camp in Assel near Stade that was opened on April 1, 1940, the Reichsvereinigung demanded RM 30 per month per person, as well as a *kupah* amount (in Hebrew, a donation box for the poor, also a cashbox) of RM 3; CAHJP Jerusalem, JCR/S 7, no folio numbers, Reichsvereinigung circular, March 28, 1940.

[109] That was the case for trainees in Havelberg in 1939 and 1940; BLHA Potsdam, Pr. Br. Rep. 36 A Senior President for Finance, No. 2714, Fols. 1–26. 58 and verso, 107, Various letters to the senior president for finance, also from Beerfelde; ibid., No. 2713.

[110] StA Leipzig, Leipzig Exchange Office (*Devisenstelle*), No 331, no folio numbers, IKG, emigration office, to the senior president for finance on September 30, 1940.

[111] CAHJP Jerusalem, JCR/S 7, no folio numbers, Circular of the Reichsvereinigung, vocational training and vocational reorientation, July 8, 1940.

[112] In the forestry camps, there were not even attempts at preparation for emigration. The inmates performed unskilled forest work exclusively.

receive in exchange "the trainees' work compensation . . . as a contribution to costs." The RSHA's other ideas, however, were illusionary, if the conditions in the existing camps are any indication. "To the extent possible, instruction in trade skills could be given on these estates. Furthermore, language courses and all other events sponsored by emigrant transit facilities could be provided there. . . . In this manner, emigration demands, labor utilization, and pedagogical and cultural activities could be tied to one another through the Reichsvereinigung."[113] Of course this viewpoint may only have been presented to motivate Jewish support for smooth implementation of the labor camp project. Ultimately, the undertaking bogged down in the planning stage. While in June 1940 the Reichsvereinigung still maintained twenty-seven labor and retraining camps as well as fourteen forestry camps in the Old Reich,[114] by October these numbers had fallen to twenty-three and twelve.[115]

Although the Reichsvereinigung maintained in its work report for 1939 that the emphasis in the camps had "primarily [been] on practical training," that was more wishful thinking than reality.[116] In the 1939 Paderborn camp contract, the Reichsvereinigung had still promised "to provide, at its expense, instruction suitable as preparation for emigration, for example, technical or language training,"[117] yet this passage reveals that in fact labor for the municipal administration was not viewed as preparation for emigration. The 1940 contract with Hangelsberg forestry camp contains no significant training clause at all.[118]

The implementation of forced labor for all German Jews at that time did influence such changes. The Reichsvereinigung recommended to camp inmates capable of working that they take advantage of the new developments and make themselves indispensable, as in Steckelsdorf: "The manager of the agricultural operation [Steckelsdorf] also took this advice. . . . In the farm building there was considerable activity. Nurserymen and farmers came and went. Even factory owners from Rathenow came to call. . . . The number

---

[113] The RSHA wanted to have "intensified forestry utilization" implemented on a decentralized basis from the camps; BA Berlin, R 8150, No. 45, Fol. 215, Summons to the Gestapa, April 24, 1940.

[114] Ibid., No. 31, Fol. 207, Reichsvereinigung statistics (January 1940 to October 1941). According to other statistics, the Reichsvereinigung was in charge of thirty camps, eleven of them forestry camps, BA Berlin, 80 Re 1, No. 5019, Fol. 30, Reichsvereinigung organizational diagram (Status as of June 30, 1940), Attachment to the report of *Deutsche Revisions- und Treuhand AG* (German Auditing and Trustee, Inc).

[115] BA Berlin, R 8150, No. 31, Fol. 207, Reichsvereinigung statistics (January, 1940, to October, 1941).

[116] *Arbeitsbericht der Reichsvereinigung 1939*, 26.

[117] Naarmann, *Die Paderborner Juden*, 464–465, Attachment 34.

[118] BLHA Potsdam, Pr. Br. Rep. 15 C Hangelsberg, No. 5, no folio numbers, Reichsvereinigung to the Prussian forestry office, April 8, 1940, with an attachment, Agreement regarding the utilization of Jewish trainees.

of 'outside workers' soon surpassed the number of 'inside workers.' . . . A large group drove daily to Rathenow, where they were employed in the optical industry. . . . The estate preparing [Jews] for Palestine had become a worker barracks."[119]

Camps with their own agricultural production on leased estates, such as Steckelsdorf and Gehringshof, thus sent a good part of their labor resources to do outside work.[120] With ten-hour workdays and long distances to travel to work, little time was left for instruction. Exhaustion and hunger did the rest. On Sunday, additional work had to be performed for the workers' own estates, or coal transports elsewhere, or emergency work for companies.[121] Despite these circumstances, people in some camps (for example, Schniebinchen or Steckelsdorf) were able to pursue so-called "cultural work," usually consisting of Hebrew instruction, after their forced labor was done. However, the courses were usually taught by inmates rather than teachers and thus constituted informal education, provided and organized by the inmates themselves, and therefore unusable as a formal credential.[122] A former inmate of the camp in Eichow recalls the fall 1940, "Awakened at 5:00 a.m. Breakfast at 5:30 a.m. Then departure for the fields to gather potatoes . . . until 6:00 p.m. Then we were so tired that we could hardly move. . . . After that, we wanted to offer Hatti a bit of culture, but we were no longer capable of registering. . . . We were only fifteen-, sixteen-, and seventeen-year-old slave laborers, who were exploited to the edge and beyond."[123] Despite the lack of any regular education, the forced laborers organized their own activities (including religious celebrations and song and dance evenings, for example) in Bielefeld, Neuendorf, Steckelsdorf, and Schniebinchen.[124]

Despite everything, the name "retraining camp" was retained to serve as a deceptive mask. Even the first camp built in Poland for deportees from Vienna and Mährisch-Ostrau was euphemistically designated the "Central Office for Jewish Retraining, Nisko am San."[125] Under the control of the RSHA, the inmates of the Reichsvereinigung camps were deployed as labor in agriculture and forestry without any involvement of the labor administration. For the employers, who did not have to pay camp support or to observe wage scale and social insurance regulations, exploitation of the camp

---

[119] König, *David*, 156–157.   [120] Ibid., 134 and 184.

[121] For Steckelsdorf, see ibid., 169. For Groß-Breesen, see Angress, *Generation*, 46. For Paderborn, see Angreß, "Arbeitslager," 76. For Eichow, see Klaus Scheurenberg, *Ich will leben* (Berlin, 1982), 63.

[122] Scheurenberg, *Ich will leben*, 59, and König, *David*, 148–149.

[123] Scheurenberg, *Ich will leben*, 62–63; likewise, see König, *David*, 163.

[124] For Bielefeld, see Meynert, "Endlösung," 243. For Neuendorf, see Mine Winter, "Zehn Jahre später," 7, Memoir Collection, LBIA New York. For Steckelsdorf, see König, *David*, 163. For Schniebinchen, see Scheurenberg, *Ich will leben*, 59.

[125] For this camp, see Seev Goshen, "Nisko – Ein Ausnahmefall unter den Judenlagern der SS," in *Vierteljahrshefte für Zeitgeschichte*, 40, 1 (1992): 95–106.

inmates remained extremely profitable. Forced labor deployment increasingly dominated everyday life in the camps. By 1941, Reichsvereinigung camps included only two independent operations and twelve leased operations, but a total of twenty operations purely for "labor deployment."[126] Actually, the Reichsvereinigung camps should be subsumed in the category of "labor camps for Jews," but to preserve the distinctions they remained separate here for the period extending from 1939 until their formal integration into the labor offices' forced-labor program in 1941.

INTEGRATION IN THE FORCED-LABOR PROGRAM, EARLY SUMMER 1941

After preparing for deportations and subsequently reevaluating the forced-labor program of the labor administration, the RSHA in spring 1941 began reorganizing the camp system controlled until then by the Gestapo. The Reichsvereinigung's agricultural operations and lease-based camps that could not be transformed completely into profitable forced-labor operations or were geographically too far from Berlin, such as Ellguth and Groß-Breesen, were to be closed or sold to save costs.[127] In the future, the inmates of camps sold were to be employed only in accordance with the conditions of segregated labor deployment at the formerly leased estate, at neighboring estates, or at outside companies. Camps would only be permitted to exist if they were financially self-supporting.[128] The RSHA was interested at that point only in cost reductions, not in special agreements anymore, as the following document of the Reichsvereinigung-Vocational Training and Vocational Reorientation Department reveals: "We have been instructed by our supervisory agency to transform all vocational training into a forced labor program. Consequently, workers previously engaged as trainees now can work only for standard wages, they must receive their labor assignment from the competent labor office, and all the costs for room and board are to be borne by the operation in which the workers are employed (and are to be passed on to the workers). . . . According to the instructions that we have received, the Reichsvereinigung is no longer to be the renter of housing space, thereby precluding any financial obligation on the part of the Reichsvereinigung."[129]

---

126 BA Berlin, R 8150, No. 125, Fols. 259–261, Reichsvereinigung statistics, July 1, 1941.

127 BA Berlin, R 8150, No. 45, Fol. 36, Reichsvereinigung file note about inspection of the Reichsvereinigung Central Office by representatives of the RSHA and the State Police Central Office in Berlin on February 26, 1941.

128 Ibid., Fol. 35; File note of Eppstein (Reichsvereinigung) on his summons to the RSHA on March 11, 1941; ibid., Fol. 18, File note of Eppstein (Reichsvereinigung) on his summons to the RSHA on March 19, 1941.

129 BLHA Potsdam, Pr. Br. Rep. 15 C Hangelsberg, No. 5, no folio numbers, Reichsvereinigung letter to the Hangelsberg head forester's office, July 29, 1941.

In May 1941, the funds for "vocational training" were reduced in the course of events to 10 percent of the original RM 180,000. While a few camps were able to adapt to the conditions of segregated labor deployment, others had to shut down.[130] At the end of May, the RSHA decided to close Reichsvereinigung camps based on lease contracts, for example, those in Ahrensdorf, Ellguth, Jessen, Rissen, Rüdnitz, and Havelberg.[131] In the case of Havelberg, the critical measure coincided with the plans pushed by the town and the *Landrat* since the end of 1940 to Aryanize the camp.[132] On June 25, the RSHA ordered "termination of all lease operations except for Wannsee" by July 15;[133] later the number of exceptions was expanded to include Ahlem, Gehringshof, and Steckelsdorf.[134] In cases requiring lease payments for a transition period, for example Schniebinchen, or subsidies such as the RM 350 per month for Eichow, the RSHA refused to release the money, threatening shut-down.[135]

On June 25, 1941, the motto was only, "No more expenditures by the Reichsvereinigung for labor camps that exist." Then on July 17 the RSHA ordered that the Reichsvereinigung sever all connections to "labor camps and forestry camps."[136] Only a few days later the death knell tolled for the Reichsvereinigung's labor operations:[137] "Workers from retraining operations to be closed down" are to report to the "competent labor office for assignment." In the future, there would be only one organizational form of labor allocation. The Reichsvereinigung "could register persons from the vocational training program" but would no longer be involved in any way with the practice of allocating labor; for that reason, camp inmates would no longer be designated as "trainees." No objections would be raised, however, to the Jewish organization providing "social services and disciplinary control" in the camps.[138] On August 16, 1941, the RSHA emphasized once again that "continuation of labor operations" was contingent on integration into the segregated labor deployment program. Strangely

[130] BA Berlin, R 8150, No. 2, Fol. 47, Reichsvereinigung board meeting, May 26, 1941.

[131] Ibid., No. 125, 253–254 verso, Chronicle on the closing of the facilities of the Reichsvereinigung, vocational training department, April 22 to August 8 (1941).

[132] StadtA Havelberg, Records of the Julianenhof Hunters' Lodge, Records No. 924, Vol. 12, No. 6, no folio numbers, District administrator in Perleberg to the Havelberg Bürgermeister, December 20, 1940; also Letter of the Havelberg Bürgermeister to the Oberpräsident of the Mark Brandenburg Province, August 18, 1941.

[133] BA Berlin, R 8150, No. 125, Fol. 253 verso, Reichsvereinigung chronicle (from the end of August 1941).

[134] Ibid., Report, July 28, 1941.

[135] BA Berlin, R 8150, No. 46, Fol. 216, Record note on consultation in the RSHA, September 3, 1941.

[136] BA Berlin, R 8150, No. 125, Fol. 253 verso, Reichsvereinigung chronicle (from the end of August 1941).

[137] Ibid., Order, July 27, 1941.

[138] Ibid., Fols. 253 verso – 254, Declaration, July 28, 1941.

enough, the designation "Jewish labor camp" for such operations was prohibited.[139]

The RSHA had already decided about the future of the Brandenburg forestry labor camps: They could continue to exist if they were fully self-supporting.[140] At the end of July, the Reichsvereinigung made new agreements with the Fürstenwalde district forestry office. In the future, the latter would report its needs to the labor office, which would procure Jews for interregional transfers either through other labor offices or through the Reichsvereinigung. The district forestry office would be the employer both of the Jews used in the forest and of the camp leader and staff – their status as employees of the Reichsvereinigung would then be rescinded – and the forestry office from that time forward would be the managing institution for the forestry camps. As the district forestry office could not act as a party to the rental contract, formalities would be dispensed with and rents covered, as previously, from the work earnings of the forestry laborers. A branch location of the district forestry office would be set up in the Neuendorf camp to administer the forestry camps and to allocate Jewish workers.

Jews with family members provided for by the Jewish welfare office were afforded the opportunity to be transferred from forest work to much-better-paid industrial work, in order to relieve pressure on the Reichsvereinigung's budget.[141] The camp inmates were now registered with the labor office for subsequent allocation. Thus, the Jews not only obtained work documents but also were automatically obligated to contribute to social insurance (disability and health insurance).[142] The wage conditions changed. For assistance with leveling work from July 28 to August 6, 1941, the Bürgermeister of Hangelsberg paid the forestry camp an average of RM 30–35; of that, insurance premiums of about RM 4 went to the insurance provider. Obviously standard unskilled laborers wages, only about RM 0.50, were now paid for the inmates.[143] In the Schönfelde Jewish forestry camp, Walter Kahn received about RM 20 gross per week in July 1941, but RM 15 of that was withheld for room and board.[144] One year later, at the Kersdorf Jewish forestry camp, Heinz Jacoby earned RM 60–80 per month.[145] A new contract had also been set up for the Paderborn camp, in this case with the city; in the contract, the labor office retained authority over the workers and their allocation, with

---

[139] Ibid., Fol. 254, Declaration, August 16, 1941.   [140] Ibid., Fol. 253.

[141] Ibid., Fols. 265–266, Reichsvereinigung to the Reich Agriculture Office and Fürstenwalde district forestry office, July 31, 1941.

[142] BLHA Potsdam, Pr. Br. Rep. 15 C Hangelsberg, No. 5, no folio numbers, Hangelsberg forestry office to all officials, May 30, 1941.

[143] According to the varying wages cited, the maximum number of work hours was seventy and a minimum number, thirty-five; BLHA Potsdam, Pr. Br. Rep. 15 C Hangelsberg, No. 5, no folio numbers, Worksheets for calculating wages, September 30, 1941.

[144] CJA Berlin, 75 A Be 2, No. 364, Fol. 6, Schönefeld camp to Michaelis, July 31, 1941.

[145] Ibid., No. 440, Fol. 5, Acknowledgement of paternity, June 25, 1943.

all the associated consequences, including wage scales and insurance obligations.[146]

By the end of August 1941, the Reichsvereinigung no longer maintained
any "retraining" facilities; the vocational education department was closed,
and its staff dismissed.[147] The camps, "if they were not closed or just on
the verge of being closed," had been "converted to independent operations,
barring any further collaboration with the Reichsvereinigung or financial
obligation to that organization for labor."[148] The camp contracts had been
modified accordingly. For the harvest of the Lebus Kreis farmers' association, normally handled in Brandenburg by inmates since 1939, the labor
office now had to assign workers,[149] which immediately created problems
because in 1941 the Berlin labor office was not releasing any Jews to outside
offices.[150]

As a result of the reorganization, the Reichsvereinigung had lost any
chance to exercise future influence on the camps' labor and living conditions. The circumstances of the inmates worsened dramatically: "Our farming operation [Steckelsdorf] suddenly had to take in ten *chaverim* from a
Hessian Palestine preparation camp that had been closed. . . . The oldest of
the group was twenty-one years old. . . . How great was our horror when
shortly after that a second group of seventeen *chaverim* arrived from a camp
in Hamburg! Where were they all going to sleep . . .? How were a hundred
people to find space in the dining room? . . . They were considerably younger
than we were. We felt tempted to ask, 'But children, what are you doing in
a labor camp? You still belong on the school bench!'"[151]

In 1939 at Bielefeld the food was already inadequate for the physically
demanding work of the men;[152] by 1941, under the conditions resulting
from intensified persecution, the inmates suffered increasingly from extreme
hunger. Camps that produced their own agricultural products generally had
to give them up. The camp kitchens, which because of the inspections performed had to get along on the reduced "Jewish rations," complained of
omnipresent shortages. In Steckelsdorf, the alternative was to distribute the
food differently, so instead of bread for breakfast, there was only watery
soup. As a result, outside workers could be given three double slices of
bread to take along, and in the evening, a meal of rutabaga, carrots, and
bad potatoes stewed together awaited them.[153] Despite forced labor and the

[146] Naarmann, *Die Paderborner Juden*, 466–467, Attachment 35, Contract, July 5, 1941.

[147] BA Berlin, R 8150, No. 125, Fol. 254, Report, August 21, 1941.

[148] Ibid., 229–230, Attachment to the Reichsvereinigung letter to the Berlin labor office, central
office for Jews, August 23, 1941. In some cases, for example, for Neuendorf, the Reichsvereinigung remained responsible for certain aspects during the wind-down phase; ibid., No.
46, Fol. 209 verso, File Reichsvereinigung note F 4 on consultation at the RSHA, September
9, 1941.

[149] Ibid., No. 125, Fol. 254, Order, August 18, 1941.

[150] Ibid., Fol. 224, Letter of the Berlin labor office, central office for Jews, August 25, 1941.

[151] König, *David*, 172.   [152] Meynert, "Endlösung," 236–240.

[153] König, *David*, 134 and 184–185.

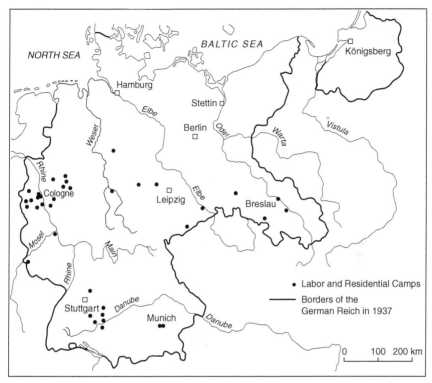

Map 4. Labor and Residential Camps in Germany, 1941–44

prohibition on going out,[154] many Jews still considered the camps "respite(s) from anti-Jewish neighbors in the city and from the merciless conveyor belts of the armaments industry."[155]

LABOR AND RESIDENTIAL CAMPS FOR GERMAN JEWS, 1941–43[156]

In addition to labor camps and the Reichsvereinigung camps, a third camp network had been created by the summer of 1941 during preparations for

---

[154] After the closing of Ahrensdorf, Esther Bejarano was sent to Neuendorf forced labor camp. Most of the inmates worked outside the camp during the day; they were not allowed to leave the camp on private business; Esther Bejarano, *Man nannte mich Krümel* (Hamburg, 1989), 15.

[155] König, *David*, 173.

[156] For all of the camps mentioned in this chapter or in the footnotes, the source citations and additional details can be found in the camp lists in Gruner, "Die Arbeitslager für den Zwangseinsatz deutscher und nichtdeutscher Juden im Dritten Reich, 3. Kapitel, Zu den Arbeits- und Wohnlagern für deutsche Juden im Altreich (1941–1943/1944)," in *Gedenkstättenrundbrief*, published by the Foundation for the Topography of Terror, 80 (1997), 27–37.

total deportation of Jews from the Old Reich. For this system, consisting later of forty camps, the old idea of connecting internment of Jewish families to forced labor in camps was revived, because in the meantime the Nazi leadership also wanted to complete the so far slow process of expelling Jews from their residences in one radical step (see map 4, p. 61). While the Nazi party openly called upon regional authorities to clear residences in March 1941, the RSHA at the same time rejected local proposals to turn out Munich, Aachen, and Brandenburg families and to house them in camp-like barracks or small summer garden houses.[157] The RSHA continued to favor the Berlin model of "more dense occupation of existing Jewish living space."[158] As "formation of ghettos [was] not permitted in Germany," the Cologne Gestapo, as late as mid-May, prohibited establishment of a camp.[159]

A short time later, previous reservations were dropped. From the end of May or beginning of June on, the Gestapo offices, in collaboration with the city administrations or district administrators, converted to housing segments of the Jewish population in so-called "residential communities" (*Wohngemeinschaften*). In cities, newly established camps on the fringes held families interned for an open-ended period in isolated circumstances. In rural areas, Jews, especially those not engaged in forced labor, had to move into camps.[160] Of course, the actors on the scene gave the impression that the prospect of making room for "national comrades of German blood" motivated their expropriation of property.[161] The actual objectives, however, were concentration of Jewish families in preparation for the coming deportations, monitoring of those families, and using them for forced labor. The establishment of new camps was handled by the Gestapo, usually in collaboration

---

[157] BA Berlin, R 8150, No. 45, Fol. 13, Reichsvereinigung file note 30/41 and summons to the RSHA, March 21, 1941; ibid., Fol. 47, Reichsvereinigung file note 19/41 and summons to the RSHA, March 8, 1941. In Munich, building was continued anyway; Behrend-Rosenfeld, *Ich stand nicht allein*, 96.

[158] BA Berlin, R 8150, No. 45, Fol. 13, Reichsvereinigung file note 30/41 and summons to the RSHA, May 21, 1941. In Berlin, the Jewish housing office had to perform checks starting in March 1941 to create the basis for the concentration of thousands of Jews. The Jews became victims of the clearing operations in which Speer had four city sectors cleared and rendered "cleansed of Jews" from March to November 1941; see Gruner, "Reichshauptstadt," 245–248. For details, see the recent publication of Susanne Willems, *"Der entsiedelte Jude". Albert Speers Wohnungsmarktpolitik für den Berliner Hauptstadtbau* (Berlin, 2002).

[159] Nordrheinwestfälisches Hauptstaatsarchiv (NW-HStA) Düsseldorf, RW 18, No. 18, Fol. 142, Circular letter of the Cologne Stapo Office, May 12, 1941; see BA Berlin, R 8150, No. 45, Fol. 9, File Note 33/41 of the Reichsvereinigung on consultation at the RSHA on March 24, 1941.

[160] NW-HStA Düsseldorf, RW 18, No. 18, Fol. 141, Circular letter of the Cologne Gestapo Office, May 12, 1941; and ibid., Fol. 192, Letter of the Cologne Gestapo, June 3, 1941. For Bonn, see BA Berlin, R 8150, No. 129, Fol. 21, Reichsvereinigung report to the RSHA, August 20, 1942 on the development of the Bonn camp. See also Maria Zelzer, *Weg und Schicksal der Stuttgarter Juden* (Stuttgart, 1964), 221.

[161] See NW-HStA Düsseldorf, RW 18, No. 18, Fol. 142, Circular letter of the Cologne Gestapo Office, May 12, 1941.

with the NSDAP Gau leadership. The camps should be called "labor and residential camps," to differentiate them from the labor and Reichsvereinigung camps.

In the first two months alone, labor and residential camps were built in Tormersdorf near Görlitz, initially for Breslau families[162] and later also for Görlitz families;[163] in Friedrichssegen near Koblenz for Jews from the Lower Lahn–Limburg Kreis, Rheingau–St. Goarshausen, and Westerwald;[164] and in Essen-Steele,[165] Munich-Milbertshofen,[166] and Bonn–Kapellen Street[167] for the Jews living in those cities. Soon more than 400 people lived in some of the camps, for example, in Munich-Milbertshofen and Tormersdorf.[168]

LABOR AND RESIDENTIAL CAMPS[169]

Aachen – Grüner Weg
Ahlem – Horticultural School

---

[162] Facsimile of the decree of the Breslau police president, July 26, 1941, in Karel Jonca, "Die Deportation und Vernichtung der schlesischen Juden," in *Die Normalität des Verbrechens. Festschrift für Wolfgang Scheffler zum 65. Geburtstag* (Berlin, 1994), 153–155. See Franciszek Polomski, *Ustawodawstwo rasistowskie II Rzeszy I jego stosowanie na Górnym Slasku* (Katowice, 1970), 327, note 93. For the events, see Willy Cohn, *Als Jude in Breslau 1941. Aus den Tagebüchern von Studienrat a. D. Dr. Willy Israel Cohn*, edited by Joseph Walk 2nd edition (Gerlingen, 1984), 80 and 86, Entries of July 26, 1941, and August 8, 1941.

[163] Roland Otto, *Die Verfolgung der Juden in Görlitz unter der faschistischen Diktatur 1933–1945* (Görlitz, 1990), 61.

[164] For more details, see Walter Rummel, Ein Ghetto für die Juden im Tal der Verbannten. Die Umwandlung der ehemaligen Bergarbeitersiedlung in Friedrichssegen (Lahn) zum Wohnlager für jüdische Zwangsarbeiter und -arbeiterinnen 1938–1942, in *Jahrbuch für westdeutsche Landesgeschichte* 30 (2004): 419–507.

[165] Herman Schröter, *Geschichte und Schicksal der Essener Juden* (Essen, 1980), 54.

[166] The camp, which had been under construction since March, was finished at the end of June 1941; Behrend-Rosenfeld, *Ich stand nicht allein*, 93–96. See *Die Jüdischen Gemeinden in Bayern 1918–1945*, edited and revised by Baruch Z. Ophir and Falk Wiesemann (Oldenburg, 1979), 55.

[167] The camp in the seized monastery "Zur ewigen Anbetung" (For eternal worship) in Bonn-Endenich (6 Kapellen Street) was occupied by Bonn Jews until the end of June 1941; Otto Neugebauer, "Ein Dokument zur Deportation der jüdischen Bevölkerung Bonns und seiner Umgebung," in *Bonner Geschichtsblätter*, published by the Bonn Homeland and Historical Society and the Bonn City Archives, 18 (1964): 159. See BA Berlin, R 8150, No. 129, Fol. 21, Reichsvereinigung report, August 20, 1942.

[168] *Die Jüdischen Gemeinden in Bayern*, 55; StadtA Görlitz, Rep. III, S. 990, No. 4, R 20, F 33 Magistrate of the city of Görlitz, 0150 Economic Office, Report on labor utilization in the Görlitz administrative district for December 1941, 4–5.

[169] Camp lists with source citations and additional details can be found in Gruner, "Die Arbeitslager für den Zwangseinsatz, 3. Kapitel: Zu den Arbeits- und Wohnlagern für deutsche Juden im Altreich (1941–1943/44)," in *Gedenkstättenrundbrief*, 80, 27–37. Based on recent research, a barracks camp in Jena can be added to the thirty-nine listed; BA ZwA Dahlwitz-Hoppegarten, ZA I, No. 7928, A. 4, no folio numbers, Siegfried Singer to the legal office of the city of Jena, August 4, 1941.

Photo 3. Jews forced to construct their own labor camp in Munich-Milbertshofen, spring 1941

Blaschkowitz near Aussig (Sudeten)
Bonn – 6 Kapellen Street
Breslau – New Graupen Street
Burg Veynau, Euskirchen near Bonn
Cologne – 18–22 Cäcilien Street
Cologne-Ehrenfeld (85 Otto Street)
Cologne-Müngersdorf (Fort V)
Dellmensingen, Ulm Kreis
Dresden-Hellerberg
Eschenau near Heilbronn
Eschwege near Kassel
Eschweiler-Stich near Aachen
Essen-Steele – Holbeckshof Camp
Friedrichssegen near Koblenz
Grüssau near Waldenburg, Silesia
Haigerloch, Württemberg
Halle an der Saale – 24 Boelcke Street
Hamm, Westphalia
Hüpstedt in Eichsfeld
Irsch, Saarburg Kreis, Rhineland
Jena, Thuringia
Kassel-Niederzwehren – Wartekuppe camp
Laupheim near Ulm, Württemberg

Much, Siegkreis, Rhineland
Munich – Berg am Laim
Munich-Milbertshofen
Neheim Hüsten, City of Arnsberg – Im Ohl 76, Westphalia
Niederbardenberg near Aachen
Oberstotzingen near Ulm
Plettenberg, Altena Kreis, Wesphalia
Quirrenbach near Siegburg, Rhineland
Riebnig, Brieg Kreis, Lower Silesia
Schönwald, Erz Mountains
Schwerte near Dortmund
Sophienhöhe, Bergheim near Cologne
Tigerfeld near Ulm
Tormersdorf, Rothenburg, Oberlausitz
Weissenstein, Württemberg

In Berlin, the very scope of the plan articulated in mid-August 1941 to concentrate 10,000 Jewish families in barracks camps[170] must have overwhelmed planners. Although a large number of forced evacuations occurred, no labor and residential camps were established. Nevertheless, the new camp system had been expeditiously expanded outside the Reich capital by fall. After the establishment of a first camp in Munich, a second project was already underway at the beginning of July, the Berg am Laim camp, which was occupied by the end of the month.[171] The president of the Breslau administrative district held negotiations in August with the Brieg district administrator about the second Silesian camp for about 400 to 500 Jews. Construction of this camp, however, was delayed; not until the end of October could about 200 Jews from Breslau and Brieg be housed in Riebnig, Brieg Kreis.[172] The Gestapo was also resettling large portions of the Jewish citizenry of Aussig (Sudetengau) to Schönwald in the Erz Mountains to

[170] Note of the session in the Ministry of Propaganda, August 15, 1941, quoted in Bernhard Lösener, "Das Reichsministerium des Innern und die Judengesetzgebung," in *Vierteljahrshefte für Zeitgeschichte*, 9, 3 (1961): 264–313, here 302–303.

[171] Behrend-Rosenfeld, *Ich stand nicht allein*, 102 and 104, Entries of July 6 and 27, 1941; Konrad Kwiet, "Nach dem Pogrom. Stufen der Ausgrenzung," in *Die Juden in Deutschland 1933–1945*, edited by Wolfgang Benz (Munich, 1988), 635.

[172] Archiwum Panstwowe we Wrocław (AP), Rejencja Wroclawska, No. 9985, Fols. 1–3, District Administrator in Brieg to the President of the Breslau Administrative District, September 19, 1941; ibid., Fol. 11, *Oberbürgermeister* of Breslau, Nutrition Office, to the District Administrator of Brieg District, September 19, 1941; ibid., No. 8391, Fol. 3, Copy of the camp regulations, November 7, 1941 (thanks to Andreas Reinke, Berlin, for these documents). For the Riebnig camp overall, see Tomasz Kruszewski, "Obóz dla Ludosci Zydowskiej w rybnej kolo Brzegu (1941–1943)," in *Acta Universitatis Wratislaviensis*, No. 1207 (Wroclaw, 1992), 315–341.

live in a dilapidated castle that had previously served as a prisoner-of-war camp.[173]

In addition, the camp "Im Ohl 76" was built in Neheim Hüsten, Arnsberg, in September; the camps in Grüssau near Waldenburg, at Wendelinsgrube near Laupheim, and in Stolberg-Atsch near Aachen in October; and the camps in Hüpstedt in Eichsfeld and Hamm, Westphalia, in December.[174] During late October 1941 in Hamm, the deputy NSDAP Gauleiter for Westphalia demanded isolation of the Gypsies living there, whereupon the city administration and the NSDAP Kreis leadership decided to put all the Jews in barracks as well. Seventy-eight Jews had to hand over their property to the city administration for sale; their residences were offered to "Aryans deserving advancement." The authorities carried out resettlement quickly, without regard to family circumstances, because they wanted to have "notification to that effect" sent to the NSDAP functionaries.[175] The situation was different in Hanover; there the attempt to establish a barracks camp for 280 Jewish families (about 1,000 people), planned by the city administration and the NSDAP Gau leadership since March, failed in October. The majority of the families, who were crammed together temporarily in "Jewish houses" and in the Ahlem Horticultural School during September based on an eviction plan, were taken away to Poland in the first deportations.[176]

Housing in labor and residential camps was put into effect virtually everywhere. The authorities sent the inhabitants of Jewish old-age or nursing-care homes to such camps,[177] and sent even Jews still protected because

---

[173] After a barracks camp project was rejected, the local Gestapo obtained authorization for resettlement after the fact at Stapo Headquarters in Reichenberg; BA Berlin, R 8150, Film 52439, No, 362, Fol. 38, Letter of the Reichsvereinigung district office in Sudetenland, September 2, 1941.

[174] Werner Saure, *Geschichte und Schicksale jüdischer Mitbürger aus Neheim und Hüsten* (Balve, 1988), 63–65 and 81; Ambrosius Rose, *Kloster Grüssau* (Stuttgart, 1974), 192; Sauer, *Dokumente*, Part II, 194–196, Doc. No. 414 b), Laupheim city council session of October 17, 1941; see Kwiet, "Nach dem Pogrom," 635; Manfred Bierganz, "Jüdische Zwangsarbeiter in Stolberg und der Leidensweg der Stolberger Juden während der Nazi Herrschaft," in *Die Menorah, Zeitschrift der Jüdischen Gemeinde Aachen*, 3 (December 27, 1986): 17–18; see Wolff, "Verheiratet," 142; Carsten Liesenberg, "Juden in Mühlhausen – ihre Geschichte, Gemeinde und bedeutende Persönlichkeiten," manuscript (Mühlhausen, 1990), 95; Max Gonsirowski, "Bericht über die Geschichte der jüdischen Gemeinde der Stadt Hamm/Westf. seit 1932 für die Stadtchronik," in *Spuren zur "Reichskristallnacht" in Hamm* (Hamm, 1988), 10; and Rita Kreienfeld, "Bilder und Zeugnisse einer Familie," in *Spuren zur "Reichskristallnacht" in Hamm*, 29.

[175] CAHJP Jerusalem, Inv. 1648, no folio numbers, NSDAP district leader in Unna to the Hamm Oberbürgermeister, November 11, 1941.

[176] Marlis Buchholz, *Die hannoverschen Judenhäuser* (Hanover, 1987), 27–39. Jews evicted once again at the beginning of 1942 were sent to Ahlem; ibid., 155–160.

[177] For example, from the Beathe Guttmann Home in Breslau to Tormersdorf; Otto, *Verfolgung*, 61.

they lived in mixed marriages.[178] The organization of the resettlement process varied at the local level. In Siegkreis, movers handled the moves to Much.[179] While the Görlitz Jews were conspicuous for their "overloaded furniture trucks" (eighteen families are said to have shared a truck for their household goods) the Breslau Jews traveled to Tormersdorf on the Reich Railway.[180]

People ordered to go to the camps had to build, or at least repair, the camps themselves. The Munich NSDAP leadership had forced the Jews "voluntarily" to build barracks for the Milbertshofen community settlement "at their own expense."[181] (See photo 3, p. 64.) In other places, the authorities used shut down mines (Essen, Friedrichssegen, Hüpstedt, Laupheim), confiscated and vacated monasteries (Bonn, Grüssau, Munich–Berg am Laim), abandoned institutional buildings (Tormersdorf), empty Reich Labor Service camps (Much, Riebnig), and run-down castles (Schönwald, Dellmensingen, Oberstotzingen) for the labor and residential camps. Fort Cologne-Müngersdorf was provided for Jews from Cologne and the vicinity.[182] From the standpoint of hygiene and construction, the old housing was usually dilapidated. During the preliminary inspection of the shut-down Reich Labor Service Camp in Riebnig, Silesia – actually the expanded barn of a former government estate – the following statements were made: "After the closing, the most important furnishings were removed. The building has many deficiencies. No cooking facilities, water, lighting, heating equipment, or bathroom facilities are present."[183]

In order to correct the almost identically miserable condition of the Schönwald facility, the Sudetenland district office of the Reichsvereinigung had to apply not only for the moving costs, but for RM 25,000 to 30,000 just to perform structural alterations. In addition to kitchens, toilets, and a laundry, rooms for fuel storage had to be built because Schönwald was "located

---

[178] For example, in the Munich camps at Berg am Laim and Milbertshofen; Behrend-Rosenfeld, *Ich stand nicht allein*, 162 and 171.

[179] NW-HStA Düsseldorf, RW 18, No. 18, Fol. 257–277 verso, Siegkreis district administrator to the Cologne Gestapo, April 17, 1941.

[180] Otto, *Verfolgung*, 62; Bernhard Brilling, "Die Evakuierung der Breslauer Juden nach Tormersdorf bei Görlitz, Kreis Rothenburg, Oberlausitz, 1941/42," in *Mitteilungen des Verbandes ehemaliger Breslauer und Schlesier Juden in Israel*, 46/47 (1980): 16.

[181] Behrend-Rosenfeld, *Ich stand nicht allein*, 93; see Avraham Barkai, "Vom Boykott zur "Entjudung". Der wirtschaftliche Existenzkampf der Juden im Dritten Reich 1933–1943," in *Leo Baeck Institute Year Book XXXVI* (1991), 175; Kwiet, "Nach dem Pogrom," 577.

[182] BA Berlin, R 8150, No. 46, Fol. 125, Note F 38 of Eppstein (Reichsvereinigung), January 6, 1942; ibid., No. 2, Fol. 38, Protocol of the Reichsvereinigung board meeting, August 11, 1941.

[183] AP Wrocław, Rejencja Wroclawska, No. 9985, Fol. 2, Letter August 19, 1941. A large-scale kitchen also first had to be installed in the monastery building at Munich-Berg am Laim; Behrend-Rosenfeld, *Ich stand nicht allein*, 104.

so disadvantageously that in the winter months it [was] cut off from contact for days at a time."[184] The castle at Oberstotzigen, which had been provided as a camp for the Jews from Ulm, had to be renovated at a cost of about RM 10,000, which in this case the city of Ulm, under pressure from the NSDAP Gauleiter, first had to pay out in advance.[185] Haigerloch camp was also in need of repair.[186] Jews were housed in the Zoar Monastery and Nursing Home (*Brüder- und Pflegeanstalt Zoar*) in Tormersdorf despite similarly deplorable conditions. As survivors recalled, "None of the windows could be opened, none of the doors closed, the toilets did not work, and water had to be carried from the street."[187] In the Much camp, the inmates had to put up with a barracks roof that was not water-tight and a cellar that was flooded; in the Grüssau monastery, there was still no heating in the winter of 1941–42.[188]

Despite such miserable living conditions, the people quartered involuntarily not only had to pay exorbitant rents but even had to accept unusual rental clauses. After the inmates in Much had already borne the moving costs, they were collectively liable, under the contract signed with the Siegkreis municipal association, for a monthly rent of RM 500. At first glance that does not seem especially high for about 100 camp inmates. That perception changes, however, with the knowledge that in Much, as in Tormersdorf, three families were squeezed together in one room. Furthermore, the Jews, in violation of established law, were obligated to maintain the entire camp, which was in need of repair, and were not allowed to collect any rent from the company that set up its machines for the inmates to use for work at their living site.[189] The inmates of the Bonn camp had to deposit RM 11,000 in a savings account at the city savings bank as security; RM 500 was deducted each month from that amount until the balance was exhausted as "compensation for the use of the kitchen and laundry facilities." Those facilities were then to become the property of the "residential facility," which of course never happened

---

[184] BA Berlin, R 8150, Film 52439, No. 362, Fol. 34, Attachment to the letter of the Reichsvereinigung district office for Sudetenland, September 5, 1941.

[185] Heinz Keil, *Dokumentation über die Verfolgungen der jüdischen Bürger von Ulm/Donau* (Ulm, 1961), 237 and 244.

[186] "Significant structural changes (and) restoration" had to be accomplished by the Jewish Religious Association of Württemberg; Benigna Schönhagen, *Tübingen unter dem Hakenkreuz* (Stuttgart, 1991), 339.

[187] Quoted in Brilling, "Evakuierung der Breslauer Juden," 16.

[188] Bruno H. Reifenrath, "Die 'Evakuierung' der Juden des Siegkreises unter besonderer Berücksichtigung ihrer Internierung im RAD-Lager Much," in *Juden am Rhein und Sieg*, edited by Heinrich Linn (Siegburg, 1983), 245. For Grüssau, Tormersdorf, and Riebnig, see Andreas Reinke, "Stufen der Zerstörung. Das Breslauer Jüdische Krankenhaus während des Nationalsozialismus," in *Menora. Jahrbuch für deutsch-jüdische Geschichte 1994* (Munich and Zurich, 1994), 398–400.

[189] Reifenrath, "Die 'Evakuierung' der Juden des Siegkreises," 243–246. For Tormersdorf, see Brilling, "Evakuierung der Breslauer Juden," 16.

after the deportations.[190] In Munich, the deputy of the Gauleiter had at first demanded a rent payment of one Reich Mark per day from the 320 inmates of the "home facility" in the Berg am Laim- monastery; RM 0.80 was to go to the NSDAP, and RM 0.20 to the monastery that supplied the building. After the Reichsvereinigung intervened in Berlin with the help of the RSHA, the amount demanded was reduced to RM 0.50. The rent was then about RM 15 per month per person; the Party still collected a share amounting to just under RM 2,900.[191] In the case of Riebnig, the city of Breslau had leased buildings from the state forestry administration and assumed the task of equipping the camp and making structural modifications.[192] The organization "Gemeinnützige Grundstücksverwaltung Breslau GmbH (Property Management for the Public Benefit in Breslau, Ltd.)"[193] then ran the businesses of the Jewish camps in Riebnig and Grüssau on commission. Under the arrangement, "monthly compensation of RM 10.00 per head" was collected from the Reichsvereinigung district office in Silesia for housing use.[194] Authorities as well as modalities were thus regionally different, but rent requirements were generally excessive. In addition, several clever German Bürgermeisters charged the involuntarily resettled Jews fees for ostensible administrative expenses – in Haigerloch,[195] Grüssau,[196] and elsewhere, for example, "head taxes" were levied to cover ostensible community losses for "increased Jewish settlement."[197]

One of the main considerations for the Gestapo and the other authorities involved in opening these camps was recruitment for forced labor. Jewish organizations had still tried to prevent construction of the Schönwald labor and residential camp with the argument that "people allocated to labor will be wrenched from their work and will have to be supported by the Reichsvereinigung because of their lost earnings."[198] Nevertheless, on order

---

[190] BA Berlin, R 8150, No. 129, Fol. 21, Reichsvereinigung report to the RSHA, August 20, 1942.

[191] Behrend-Rosenfeld, *Ich stand nicht allein*, 117, Entry of October 26, 1942.

[192] AP Wrocław, Rejencja Wrocławska, No. 9985, Fol. 2, Letter August 19, 1941.

[193] This name is very reminiscent of the SS enterprise names.

[194] AP Wrocław, Urzad Skarbowy Provincji Dolnoslaskiej we Wroclawiu (Senior President for Finance in Lower Silesia, Breslau), No. 1395, Fols. 252 and 250, Property management for the public benefit in Breslau to the senior president for finance in Silesia, June 22 and 24, 1943.

[195] Every person who was involuntarily resettled paid RM 6 to the Bürgermeister; Schönhagen, *Tübingen*, 338.

[196] BA Berlin, R 8150, No. 46, Fol. 93, Reichsvereinigung note F 47 and consultation in the RSHA on February 3, 1942.

[197] Sauer, *Dokumente*, Part II, 199–200, Doc. No. 418 a) and b), Letter of the Stuttgart Jewish center to the district administrator in D., October 28, 1941, and Bürgermeister B. to the district administrator in D., November 10, 1941.

[198] BA Berlin, R 8150, Film 52439, No. 362, Fols. 38–39, Letter of the Reichsvereinigung district office in Sudetenland, September 2, 1941.

of the local Gestapo, twelve men were dismissed from their jobs so that they could build the camp in Schönwald under supervision of the municipal construction office.[199] This local order does not contradict the overall importance attributed to the forced-labor program by the authorities. Instead, forced labor had now been linked to preparations for deportation, and the latter in the meantime had gained political priority.

Over 100 Jews from communities in the Siegkreis were housed in the Much camp on the pretext of pressing previously unemployed Jews into service as forced labor.[200] In one of the first meetings in the Siegburg district administrator's office, it was already noted that "labor allocation [would] be regulated by the competent labor office as soon as the people are up there."[201] After resettlement early in July 1941, the district administrator and the Bürgermeister negotiated with the labor office and private enterprises about swiftly organizing the forced-labor program. They won over, among others, Metallwerke Elektra GmbH (metal works) in Gummersbach, which employed Jews in the camp with home work from July 21 on.[202] Problems were also eliminated to ensure an effective labor program. Thus, after Jews were prohibited from using public transportation, the forced laborer inmates from Milbertshofen, located far from the workplace, were rehoused at a closer site, the Berg am Laim-camp in Munich.[203]

Forced labor utilization in the labor and residential camps extended to all Jews capable of working. In the Bonn camp, a third of the inmates were engaged in compulsory heavy labor by early September 1941; the remaining people were over seventy years old or "children and partial or complete invalids who were sick and incapable of working."[204] The situation seems to have been similar in other camps. In Riebnig, half the inmates were over sixty-five years old.[205] About 320 Jews lived in the Tormersdorf camp in November: "Of those, 140 are employed. The rest are Jews

---

[199] Ibid., Fols. 33–35, Attachment to the letter of the Reichsvereinigung district office in Sudetenland, September 5, 1941.

[200] NW-HStA Düsseldorf, RW 18, No. 18, Fol. 238, Much Bürgermeister to the Siegkreis district administrator, June 17, 1941; see Reifenrath, "Die 'Evakuierung' der Juden des Siegkreises," 238–250.

[201] File note April 10, 1941, reproduced in Reifenrath, "Die 'Evakuierung' der Juden des Siegkreises," 242–243.

[202] NW-HStA Düsseldorf, RW 18, No. 18, Fol. 239, Much Bürgermeister to the Siegkreis district administrator, July 4, 1941; ibid., Fol. 240, Much Bürgermeister to the Siegkreis District Administrator, July 17, 1941; see Reifenrath, "Die 'Evakuierung' der Juden des Siegkreises," 246.

[203] Behrend-Rosenfeld, *Ich stand nicht allein*, 117, Entry of October 26, 1942.

[204] StadtA Bonn, File Pr. 14/3, not folio numbers, Community at 6 Kapellen Street to the Bonn economic and nutrition office, September 6, 1941.

[205] Of a total of 350 Jews who were interned in Riebnig from 1941 to 1943, 160 were between sixty-five and ninety-one years old, and 18 were children under seven years old; Appendix with table in Kruszewski, "Obóz," 340.

who can no longer be utilized because of their advanced age. After the agricultural work is complete, the Jewish women will be used for housework. The camp is to be filled up again in the course of this week. Even the expected 150 Jewish men and women are mainly older workers who can no longer work."[206] In December 1941, the Görlitz Gestapo forced all Jews not employed in the armaments industry to move to the Tormersdorf camp, along with the non-working family members of Jewish armaments workers.[207] In March 1942, 195 Jews of 441 Tormersdorf camp inmates worked on road construction, on development of the Neisse River, at Christoph & Unmack AG in Niesky, and at the Sägewerk Müller & Sons (sawmill) in Rothenburg; children sewed buttons on laundry for the Firma Eduard Riedel Mechanische Knopffabriken (button factories) in Görlitz.[208] In Görlitz, plans were even made to have fifty-nine camp inmates "not entirely fit to work" dig out and sort potatoes on manors, so that "all workers who can work do so."[209] In the Bonn camp, too, the proportion of forced laborers had increased by the end of April 1942. Of 374 inmates, 150 Jews, 57 of them women, were in the meantime performing mostly heavy labor.[210]

In the labor and residential camps, families lived in an especially repressive microcosm of the Jewish forced community of Germany. The Much camp was immediately enclosed by a fence in early summer 1941, when the Jews moved in. The camp regulations, written by the local Bürgermeister in consultation with the Gestapo, demonstrated the inmates' extreme isolation and the restrictions on their freedom of movement:

1. "It is prohibited for Jewish inmates of the camp to enter the town of Much.
2. Jews are not allowed to enter any kind of business in Much and the vicinity. The camp administration is to appoint. . . one person to do the shopping.
3. Jews are prohibited from visiting restaurants and taverns.

---

[206] StadtA Görlitz, Rep. III, S. 990, No. 4, R 20, F 33 Magistrate of the city of Görlitz, 0150 Economic Office, Report on labor service in the Görlitz administrative district for November 1941, 3–4.

[207] After that, 217 of the 445 camp inmates were deemed fit for labor service and about one quarter of those were employed; ibid., Report on labor service in the Görlitz administrative district for December 1941, 4.

[208] Ibid., Report on labor service in the Görlitz administrative district for March 1942, 4; ibid., Report on labor service in the Görlitz administrative district for February 1942, 4; Otto, *Verfolgung*, 64.

[209] StadtA Görlitz, Rep. III, S. 990, No. 4, R 20, F 33 Magistrate of the City of Görlitz, 0150 Economic Office, Report on labor service in the Görlitz administrative district for March 1942, 4.

[210] StadtA Bonn, File Pr. 14/3, no folio numbers, Community at 6 Kappellen Street to the economic office, April 24, 1942.

4. Park benches in the community of Much are only for the use of natives and spa guests.
5. The prescribed times for Jews to go out are to be observed (from April 1 to September 30, between 6:00 a.m. and 9:00 p.m., and from October 1 to March 31, between 7:00 a.m. and 8:00 p.m.).
6. Men and women can only be assigned to labor with authorization of the local Bürgermeister, acting as the local police authority.
7. Furthermore, any contact of Jews with the population is prohibited.
8. It is prohibited to accept groceries as remuneration for performing work of any kind. Work performed can only be compensated in cash.
9. Failure to observe the preceding instructions will result in police measures."[211]

Such restrictive regulations were the rule, as the surviving records on Riebnig, Tormersdorf, Munich, Bonn, and others, confirm. The Gestapo installed Jewish camp managers in each labor and residential camp, carried out inspections, and only handed out authorization certificates for purchasing supplies in the surrounding towns to a few people. In Tormersdorf, Jews were only allowed to go walking on a "Jewish path." The inmates were always prohibited from entering the towns except for forced labor; contacts were to be strictly prevented.[212] Nevertheless, there were contacts and even gifts of food.[213] As a countermeasure, restrictions on going out were tightened by various authorities. That was the case from May to July 1942 in the Boelcke Street camp in Halle an der Saale.[214] Likewise, after May 1942, weekly rollcalls were held in Munich-Berg am Laim, and a gate guard was introduced, together with absolute prohibitions on having visitors or going out.[215]

Obtaining supplies was a serious problem in the labor and residential camps. "Trustworthy" merchants from the particular town were designated

---

[211] NW-HStA Düsseldorf, RW 18, No. 14, Fol. 289, Camp regulations, August 15, 1941.

[212] For the Riebnig camp, see AP Wrocław, Rejencja Wroclawska, No. 8391, Fols. 3–5, Camp regulations, November 7, 1941. For the Tormersdorf camp, see Otto, *Verfolgung*, 63–64. For the camp at Munich-Berg am Laim, see Behrend-Rosenfeld, *Ich stand nicht allein*, 108. The Bonn camp had Jewish camp management and limitations on leaving the camp; Neugebauer, "Ein Dokument zur Deportation," 160. See LBIA New York, Alfred Phillipson Collection, no folio numbers, Release certificate of the camp leader, September 18, 1941; see BA Berlin, R 8150, No. 129, Fols. 21 and verso, Reichsvereinigung report, August 20, 1942.

[213] For Much camp, see Reifenrath, "Die 'Evakuierung' der Juden des Siegkreises," 247. For the Paderborn camp, see Angreß, "Arbeitslager," 76.

[214] According to a Gestapo order; "Dreihundert Jahre Juden in Halle. Leben-Leistung-Leiden-Lohn," *Festschrift zum Jubiläum des 300 jährigen Bestehens der Jüdischen Gemeinde zu Halle,* published by the Jewish Community in Halle (Halle, 1992), 157. In Much, the district administrator requested that the Gestapo impose a prohibition on going out. There is no evidence of such a prohibition being implemented; NW-HStA Düsseldorf, RW 18, No. 14, no folio numbers, Letter of the Siegburg district administrator, March 13, 1942.

[215] Order of the Gauleiter's commissioner; Behrend-Rosenfeld, *Ich stand nicht allein*, 159.

to provide the inmates with food. For the Riebnig camp, the Breslau Gestapo, together with the district administrator and the NSDAP Kreis leader, made that determination.[216] In addition to a laundry, three businesses for groceries, dairy products, and meat were assigned to the camp at Munich–Berg am Laim; the store owners recorded marked increases in earnings.[217] But as decisions of the authorities further shrank the limited supplies, the Jewish leader of the Kapellen Street camp in Bonn, for example, had to fight from the very beginning for food products to be supplied on a regular basis. Despite the fact that both forced laborers and old and sick camp inmates were dependent on adequate food, they were already forced in September 1941 to live exclusively – in violation of the official regulations of this period – on vegetables and potatoes that were only "C-class" products, with 40–60 percent waste.[218] In January 1942, the camp leader wrote to the Bonn Economic and Nutrition Office (*Wirtschafts- und Ernährungsamt*): "We request allotment of 150–200 centners of potatoes. With the arrival of the Jews from the rural Kreis, our population is increasing to about 380 people. A large percentage of them are being utilized for labor. Almost 100 of them are heavy laborers but do not receive any additional food for heavy labor. In the last allotment for the current rationing period, we only received rutabaga instead of vegetables. We thus do not have any vegetables, either, and therefore must have potatoes to maintain the people's strength for work."[219] Nevertheless, the camp remained without potatoes. After consultation with the NSDAP Kreis leader in March, the city administration only approved beets for the heavy laborers.[220] But the Kreis farmers' association did not even provide beets, with the result that not even one meal per day could be guaranteed in the camp. At the end of April, the camp leader appealed to the food office, referring to the Cologne camp, where every inmate received five pounds of potatoes per week.[221] Finally, the city of Bonn granted "150 centners of potatoes that could not be considered for normal distribution" because they were partly

---

[216] AP Wrocław, Rejencja Wroclawska, No. 8391, Fols. 3–5, Camp regulations, November 7, 1941.

[217] Behrend-Rosenfeld, *Ich stand nicht allein*, 108–109 and 111, Entries of August 10 and 17, 1941.

[218] No legumes, rice, baked goods, or farina products were supplied; StadtA Bonn, File Pr. 14/3, no folio numbers, Community at 6 Kapellen Street to the Bonn economic and nutrition office, September 6, 1941; ibid., Community at 6 Kapellen Street to the Bonn district farmers' association, October 5, 1941.

[219] Ibid., Community at Kapellen Street to the Bonn economic and nutrition office, January 29, 1942.

[220] Ibid., Note of the Bonn economic and nutrition office about a telephone call of the community at Kapellen Street, March 13, 1942; ibid., Note of the Bonn economic and nutrition office, March 18, 1941.

[221] Ibid., Community at Kapellen Street to the Bonn economic and nutrition office, April 24, 1942.

spoiled.[222] The Bonn case was not an exception. The Halle an der Saale Kreis farmers' association retrieved almost half of 30 centners of potatoes stored at the camp, with the justification that the Jews were not entitled to them.[223]

An inadequate food supply, poor living conditions, and psyches damaged by persecution resulted in a high mortality rate among older Jews in the labor and residential camps.[224] The German authorities had made provisions bureaucratically for deaths, as has been recorded for Much and Riebnig.[225] Based on all these circumstances, the cancellation of allotments of meat, wheat-flour products, eggs, or milk that had been ordered in September 1942 was for the inmates of the labor and residential camps nothing more than confirmation of the inadequacy of their current provisioning.[226] The disproportion between growing exploitation and the glaring lack of food for the "Jewish men and women who [were] housed in camps for forced labor and [were] fed together" must have been so evident, and must have had such an inhibiting effect on productivity, that the Minister of Agriculture rescinded his decree on December 1, 1942, in order to maintain "the work strength" of the persons utilized "for work critical to the war." He also ordered that inmates were to receive 300 grams of meat and, further, 30 grams of rye or bread flour, 60 grams of cereal products, and 80 grams of soup products every week.[227] The order, hastily prepared by the Minister of Labor, would have brought about little improvement, as the camp was shut down within a few months and the inmates were deported.[228]

---

[222] Ibid., Note of the Bonn economic and nutrition office, May 18, 1941.

[223] "Drei Hundert Jahre," 211.

[224] The majority of the twenty-five interned persons who died in the Tormersdorf camp in one year were over seventy years old. A list of the twenty-four Jews who died between September 1941 and September 1942 is included in Brilling, "Evakuierung der Breslauer Juden," 16. See Otto, who only reports four names, three of which overlap with the list; Otto, *Verfolgung*, 64.

[225] Even during the planning of Much camp, the responsibilities for burials were set; File Note, April 10, 1941, reproduced in Reifenrath, "Die 'Evakuierung' der Juden des Siegkreises," 242–243. The rules for official medical certification of deaths, for cremations, and for "burials without ceremony in the Jewish cemetery" were included in the Riebnig camp regulations; AP Wrocław, Rejencja Wroclawska, No. 8391, Fols. 1–5, Letter of the Brieg health office, December 5, 1941.

[226] Sauer, *Dokumente*, Part II, No. 435, 225–229, Decree of the Reich Ministry for Nutrition and Agriculture, September 18, 1942.

[227] Decree of the Reich Ministry for Nutrition and Agriculture, December 1, 1942, in *Der ausländische Arbeiter in Deutschland*, edited by Carl Birkenholz u. Wolfgang Siebert, (Berlin, 1943), Vol. II, D I 13, 854–857, Twenty-eighth supplement; BA Berlin, NSD 3 1–1943, Party Chancellery, II B 4, Confidential information, March 22, 1943, Series 12, Article 159, Provisions for the Jews in the labor utilization program.

[228] NW-HStA Düsseldorf, Reg. Aachen, No. 14421, no folio numbers, Decree of the Reich Ministry of Labor, December 7, 1942.

THE CAMP INMATES AND THEIR DEPORTATION, 1941–1943

The German Jews' lives had been completely reorganized in the forced-labor community by summer 1941. Instituting the new policy had brought the conditions in labor camps, former Reichsvereinigung camps, and labor and residential camps into conformity at the most degrading level. The number of German Jewish camp inmates had reached its peak in the Old Reich with the establishment of the labor and residential camps: In the Mark Brandenburg alone, the Reichsvereinigung registered eighteen Jewish labor camps with 845 persons in early November 1941.[229] In the rest of Germany, former Reichsvereinigung camps held about 320 inmates and labor camps held several hundred. At least 3,200 Jews lived in labor and residential camps between December 1941 and spring 1942.[230] A total of about 5,000 German Jews were thus subjected at that time to a labor camp regime entirely separate from the concentration camp system.

Since the beginning of the deportations, the Gestapo had also pulled Jews from Old Reich camps and sent them to the Occupied Eastern Territories, despite any labor obligations. No distinction was made among the inmates of the various camp types; Jews were transported from the labor and residential camps at Laupheim, Haigerloch, and Munich–Berg am Laim in November 1941, just as they were from the Bielefeld labor camp (a former Reichsvereinigung camp) in December.[231] By the end of 1941, Jewish forced laborers had been taken from the labor camp at Hohenwarte–Saale Dam, which had existed since 1939,[232] but also thirty-five women, including the female camp leader, from Lohhof camp, built only months before. Sixty-eight Polish Jewish women from the Bavarian labor camp at Unterdiessen were sent there as replacements.[233]

At the end of January 1942, the Reich Security Main Office had the Reichsvereinigung report on the camps at Neuendorf, Steckelsdorf, and Berlin-Wannsee, on Berlin "labor residential homes," on Paderborn and Bielefeld, on the other forestry and labor camps, and on the Radinkendorf labor home, clearly with the intention of including the Jews from those

---

[229] Most of them were former Reichsvereinigung camps; BA Berlin, R 8150, No. 7, Fols. 166 and verso, Report of the district office to the Reichsvereinigung, November 19, 1941.

[230] (Estimation of the author) Ibid., No. 55, Fol. 178, Reichsvereinigung list of the personnel of the settlement institutions and residential communities (around March 1942). In addition, information from the literature about local history presented here is included. For a number of camps, however, no figures have been unearthed to date.

[231] Waltraut Kohl, "Die Geschichte der Judengemeinde in Laupheim," manuscript (Laupheim, 1965), 22; Schönhagen, *Tübingen*, 342; Behrend-Rosenfeld, *Ich stand nicht allein*, 120; Meynert, "Endlösung," 241.

[232] Mittelsdorf, "Die Geschichte der Saale-Talsperren," 202 and 204.

[233] BA Berlin, R 8150, No. 760, Fol. 10, Draft letter for Eppstein (Reichsvereinigung), February 23 (?), 1942.

camps when deportations (which had been halted in the meantime) were resumed.[234] The Gestapo was sending Jews to camps in the same context and at the same time. Families from the vicinity – from towns including Beuel, Bornheim, Godesberg, and others – were forced to move into the Kapellen Street labor and residential camp in Bonn,[235] and all the Jews from the Saale Kreis moved into the Boelcke Street camp in Halle.[236]

In the meantime, the Gestapo in Berlin tried to resolve the area-specific contradiction between the political priority of deportations and significant labor shortages in the armaments center there with a project that involved interning Jewish forced laborers in camps maintained by private companies.[237] In two meetings in February and March 1942, the Gestapo informed all the Berlin industrial enterprises employing more than 100 Jews (there were apparently more than fifty such enterprises) that forced laborers living apart from their families would be locked up separately by gender in factory camps and would be treated like prisoners of war. They would have to "provide their labor . . . in exchange for free room and board"; their wages were to be paid to the Gestapo after deduction of the costs for food and use of the barracks. These conditions were clearly to apply to already existing forced-labor systems for non-German Jews, for example the SS Organisation Schmelt.[238] "Very severe penal regulations" were to prevent the total deprivation of wages from potentially resulting in deteriorating performance, a possibility criticized by the companies. The companies would have to arrange and be responsible for the Jews' provisions and for their "being guarded by factory security service officers." The majority of the company heads questioned the feasibility of constructing barracks camps for about 16,000 Berlin Jewish armaments workers on short notice, so the Gestapo suggested that the German Labor Front be tasked to construct common barracks camps, thereby distributing the costs over several companies. The Gestapo was also willing to consider ghetto housing, a solution welcomed by the "business managers present" because of its advantages. The companies were to look for property and partners to establish the camps while Hitler was reaching a

---

[234] Berlin labor utilization homes were located at 16 Lützow Street and 26 Rosenthaler Street; ibid., No. 46, Fol. 101, Note F 45 of Eppstein (Reichsvereinigung) on consultation in the RSHA on January 28, 1942.

[235] There were transports to the East on June 14 and 15, 1942, and on July 19 and 27, 1942; Neugebauer, "Ein Dokument zur Deportation," 164–221. See BA Berlin, R 8150, No. 129, Fol. 21.

[236] According to a letter from Hirsch to the Reichsvereinigung in Leipzig, February 5, 1942; "Drei Hundert Jahre," 209.

[237] BA ZwA Dahlwitz-Hoppegarten, AdZ Dok/K568/1, Fol. 55, Note of Aceta, Ltd., Berlin, February 9, 1942; Excerpt in Dietrich Eichholtz and Wolfgang Schumann (eds.), *Anatomie des Krieges. Neue Dokumente über die Rolle des deutschen Monopolkapitals bei der Vorbereitung und Durchführung des zweiten Weltkrieges* (Berlin [GDR], 1969), 380, Doc. No. 195. For what follows, see Gruner, "Reichshauptstadt," 249.

[238] See Chapter 8.

decision on the suggestion that families be separated by interning the forced laborers and deporting the family members.[239] As an intermediate solution, the Gestapo offered the Berlin companies housing for forced laborers in the August Street collection camp. This fact possibly explains the recorded information that 300 Jews, after having been picked up, had to live for months on August Street under the most primitive circumstances until their deportation in December 1942, but continued to go every day to perform forced labor.[240] That was only a stop-gap solution; by May 1942 the Berlin industrial camp project had been relegated to the files. Hitler finally ordered that the principle of transporting family groups together be retained in Germany.[241]

Despite everything, a large number of Jewish labor and residential camp inmates were deported in the spring and summer of 1942 – at the end of April from the Hamm camp, in June from the camp at Stolberg-Atsch near Aachen, and at the end of July from the Much and Bonn camps, to mention just a few.[242] The camps were then shut down. To render further areas *"judenrein"* (cleansed of Jews), families from various rural Kreise were once again sent to nearby camps, for example, at the end of June from Sundern to the camp at Neheim-Hüsten in the city of Arnsberg, or in mid-July from Euskirchen to the Bonn camp.[243] Sometimes it was now only a short time until they themselves were carried away in transports. In some places, Jews were transported in stages: from the two Munich camps in April and July 1942; from Hüpstedt in Eichsfeld in June and September 1942; and from Neheim-Hüsten in July 1942 and March 1943.[244] The Gestapo also used large labor and residential

[239] Only two companies with factories outside Berlin could, according to their own statements, house their forced laborers in the planned manner. In the second meeting, the Gestapo argument was that barracks would be made available for sale "in an adequate quantity" and later, after "final evacuation of the Jews," could "be put to some use"; BA ZwA Dahlwitz-Hoppegarten, AdZ Dok/K568/1, Fol. 55, Note of Aceta, Ltd., Berlin, February 9, 1942; ibid., Fol. 46, Note (Aceta, Ltd., Berlin [?]) about a meeting of March 11, 1942.

[240] See Camilla Neumann, "Erlebnisbericht aus der Hitlerzeit," Part I, 14, Memoir Collection, LBIA New York, 14; Scheurenberg, *Ich will leben*, 86 and 90.

[241] See *Die Tagebücher von Joseph Goebbels. Teil II: Diktate 1941–1945*, edited by Elke Fröhlich as commissioned by the Institut für Zeitgeschichte and with support of the State Archive Service of Russia, Vol. 4 (Munich and others, 1995), 273, Entry of May 11, 1942.

[242] Gonsirowski, "Bericht über die Geschichte," 10; Kreienfeld, "Bilder und Zeugnisse," 29; Bierganz, "Jüdische Zwangsarbeiter," 17–18; see Wolff, "Verheiratet mit einem Juden," 142; NW-HStA Düsseldorf, RW 18, No. 18, Fol. 21, Letter of the Bürgermeister of Much to the Siegkreis district administrator, July 28, 1942; see Reifenrath, "Die 'Evakuierung' der Juden des Siegkreises," 247–249; Neugebauer, "Ein Dokument zur Deportation," 164–221. See BA Berlin, R 8150, No. 129, Fol. 21.

[243] Irmgard Harmann-Schütz and Franz Blome-Drees, *Die Geschichte der Juden in Sundern. Eine geschuldete Erinnerung an die Familie Klein* (Sundern, 1988), 78; Neugebauer, "Ein Dokument zur Deportation," 164–221.

[244] Behrend-Rosenfeld, *Ich stand nicht allein*, 130–168, Entries of April 12 and July 26, 1942; Liesenberg, "Juden in Mühlhausen," 95; Harmann-Schütz and Blome-Drees, *Die Geschichte der Juden in Sundern*, 78; Saure, *Geschichte und Schicksale*, 63–65 and 81.

camps, such as Munich-Milbertshofen and Cologne-Müngersdorf, as transit
and collection camps.

A comparable plan of approach is evident in the former Reichsvereinigung camps that had been transformed into labor camps. One special case
is noteworthy: At the request of the Ministry of Agriculture, Eichmann personally ordered in April 1942 that the labor forces of the Oderbruch camp
at Seelow National Research Estate be excluded from the next transport,
but demanded that the Minister find replacement workers because exemption of the Jews from general evacuation was only *temporary*.[245] In this
period alone, more than half the inmates were taken from the Brandenburg
forestry labor camps.[246] Deportations from Hangelsberg and Kaisermühl
have been confirmed for the beginning of April.[247] Some of the inmates
were taken away from the Neuendorf camp at the same time, and likewise from Steckelsdorf in May. By August, only fifteen of sixty-five Jews
remained in Steckelsdorf; those fifteen were performing forced labor in the
Rathenow optical industry.[248] The Gestapo conducted deportations from
Groß-Breesen, Silesia, in October 1942 – with Grüssau camp as the intermediate destination – and again at the end of February and the beginning of
March.[249]

To intern the last unprotected Jews living in Dresden before their transport,
the local Gestapo carried out a special operation to build a camp in mid-
November 1942, literally at the last moment.[250] As forced labor was not
to be abandoned until the very last minute, the Dresden-Hellerberg labor
and residential camp was built in direct cooperation with Zeiss-Ikon AG in
Dresden. The company and the Gestapo decided jointly that a "*Selbstver-
waltung*," that is, an inmate self-administration subordinate to the Gestapo,
would run the barracks camp; the Gestapo would draft the camp regulations and oversee their enforcement. Construction, housing, and food for the
camp were the responsibility of Zeiss-Ikon AG, which collected the excessive
monthly rent of about RM 18 per head. Both parties agreed, extraordinar-
ily, that the "Jews sent will remain in the camp and have their economic
needs met, even if they are no longer employed by Zeiss-Ikon AG until the

[245] Underlining is in the original; BA Berlin, R 14, No. 49, Fol. 174–175, Eichmann (Chief of
the Security Police and SD) on April 14, 1942.

[246] Ibid., Fols. 213–214, Reich Ministry for Nutrition and Agriculture to RSHA, April 1, 1942.

[247] BLHA Potsdam, Pr. Br. Rep. 15 C Hangelsberg, No. 5, no folio numbers, Prussian forestry
office in Hangelsberg to the regional forestry official in Frankfurt an der Oder, April 2,
1942; Adler, *Der verwaltete Mensch*, 422.

[248] Letter from Neuendorf, April 3, 1942, in Clara Grunwald, "*Und doch gefällt mir das
Leben*". *Die Briefe der Clara Grunwald 1941–1943* (Mannheim, 1985), 51; König, *David*,
220–226 and 264.

[249] Angress, *Generation*, 83–85.

[250] Victor Klemperer, *Ich will Zeugnis ablegen bis zum letzten. Tagebücher 1933–1945, Bd. 2:
Tagebücher 1942–1945*, edited by Walter Nowojski, with the assistance of Hadwig Klemperer, 2nd Edition (Berlin, 1995), 273, Entry on November 13, 1942.

transports take them away. The Gestapo is free to fill unoccupied slots at the camp with Jews who are not employed at Zeiss-Ikon."[251] There were about 300 Jewish men and women housed in the Hellerberg camp. In the words of Victor Klemperer, "They are held. . . like prisoners: communal camps, communal meals, taken in groups to work – otherwise kept in the camp, . . . no communication with the world."[252] There was a curfew, only one common room for every nine married couples, and only toilets open to public view. The inmates' furniture that had been left behind was auctioned off, but the money was put in their savings accounts, they could receive mail, and the Jewish Community set up a camp library.[253] Dresden-Hellerberg is the first evidence of a labor and residential camp that was supported jointly by the Gestapo and private industry and at the same time regarded as a collection camp for deportation.

In Brandenburg Province early in 1943, the Frankfurt an der Oder Gestapo blocked any transfer of labor forces between the labor and forestry labor camps that existed there. In mid-February, the Prussian forestry administration learned that measures were being taken to shut down camps, for example, Neuendorf camp with its 160 inmates.[254] However, a few days later, the RSHA – in preparing for the large-scale raid to finish deportations in the Old Reich – made a decision: "Jews employed in businesses, as long as they are housed in segregated camps such as Neuendorf an der Spree, forestry labor camps, etc., are not to be seized in this operation."[255] The inmates of several former Reichsvereinigung camps thus received a temporary reprieve, but despite provisions of the RSHA decree to the contrary, the February 27 Fabrik-Aktion cleared out and closed the Winkel Estate and Skaby.[256] In Paderborn as well, the Gestapo locked up the labor camp and brought the inmates as a group to Bielefeld, from where they were deported in the first days of March together with most of the Jews from the Bielefeld camp.[257] On February 28, the inmates of the labor and residential camp at Neheim-Hüsten were deported. The Gestapo also closed the camps in Dresden and in the Silesian towns of Riebnig, Tormersdorf, and

---

[251] BA, ZwA Dahlwitz-Hoppegarten, AdZ Dok./K, No.785/I, Fols. 2–3, Protocol of meeting, November 10, 1942.

[252] Klemperer, *Tagebücher 1942–1945*, 273, Entry of November 13, 1942.

[253] Ibid., 277–282, Entries on November 19 and 26, 1942.

[254] BLHA Potsdam, Pr. Br. Rep. 15 C Hangelsberg, No. 5, no folio numbers, Reich Agriculture, Fürstenwalde district forestry – Küstrin forestry office to the Hangelsberg forestry office on February 17, 1943.

[255] BLHA Potsdam, Pr. Br. Rep. 41 Großräschen, No. 272, Fol. 84, Decree of the Gestapo in Frankfurt an der Oder, February 24, 1943. See Wolf Gruner, *Widerstand in der Rosenstraße. Die Fabrik-Aktion und die Verfolgung der "Mischehen" 1943* (Frankfurt am Main 2005).

[256] Anneliese-Ora Borinski, *Erinnerungen 1940–1943* (Kwuzat Maayan and Zwi, 1970), 38.

[257] Angreß, "Im Arbeitslager," 78; Naarmann, *Die Paderborner Juden*, 353. Bielefeld was closed at the earliest in June 1943; StadtA Bielefeld, House Records, Inmate List, Fols. 11–19. In contrast, see Meynert, "Endlösung," 246.

Grüssau at this time.[258] The Reichsvereinigung camps at first spared by the Brandenburg Gestapo during the February raid were included in the general "evacuation" a few weeks later: "In the meantime, many young people from other estates had been sent to Neuendorf, as these estates were all being shut down. We were again approximately 250 people. . . . We were all collected in the big home on Hamburger Street in Berlin. . . . Accompanied by SS [men] with loaded revolvers, we were then taken to a Berlin railway station and loaded into freight cars there. The next morning we arrived in Auschwitz."[259] On April 19, the Jewish men and women from Neuendorf, as well as those from the labor camps and forestry camps in Hangelsberg, Kersdorf in Briesen, Kaisermühl, Jakobsdorf, Schönfelde, Behlenfelde, Teuplitz in Niederlausitz, Boosen, and the Neumühle Estate in Straußberg were deported with the thirty-seventh eastern transport according to the RSHA's organization of their operations.[260] To conclude this four-year-long chapter, Himmler ordered that by June 30, 1943, the last "Jews housed in camps be transported" out of Reich territory "to the East and to Theresienstadt."[261]

SUMMARY

Between 1939 and 1943, several labor camp systems differing in structure, function, and practices were established for the use of Jewish forced labor in Germany; their emergence was entirely independent of the concentration camp system. The labor administration organized a program of segregated labor deployment in the Old Reich that depended on labor camps; the existence of at least forty such camps for German, Austrian, and stateless Jewish men and women can be confirmed today for the period between 1939 and summer 1941.[262] Municipalities, representatives of public construction projects, and private enterprises maintained the labor camps, the majority of which came into being in 1939 and only existed for a few months. A regional center was located in Lower Saxony. Camps used for road, improvement,

[258] Harmann-Schütz and Blome-Drees, *Die Geschichte der Juden in Sundern*, 85; Klemperer, *Tagebücher 1942–1945*, 339–340, Entry of March 4, 1943; AP Wrocław, Senior president for finance in Lower Silesia, No. 1395, Fols. 250–252; Otto, *Verfolgung*, 65.

[259] Mine Winter, "Zehn Jahre spater," 9, Memoir Collection, LBIA New York. See also Anneliese Borinski, "Wir sind die letzten hier," in *Erinnerungen deutsch-jüdischer Frauen, 1900–1990*, edited by Andreas Lixl-Purcell (Leipzig, 1992), 336–353; Bejarano, *Man nannte mich Krümel*, 18.

[260] Landesarchiv Berlin, Rep. 92 Senior President for Finance, Acc. 3924, No. 631, no folio numbers, Lists of the thirty-seventh transport to the East.

[261] Teletype of the RSHA, May 21, 1943, Excerpt in *Verzeichnis der Haftstätten unter dem Reichsführer SS 1933–1945. Konzentrationslager und deren Außenkommandos sowie andere Haftstätten unter dem Reichsführer SS in Deutschland und deutschbesetzten Gebieten*, published by the International Tracing Service of the Red Cross (Arolsen, 1979), LXII.

[262] About forty camps in Silesia should possibly be added to that number, see Chapter 8.

and dam projects housed between 20 and far more than 100 inmates. Many camps shut down after only a few months because construction projects were cancelled in wartime. Until 1941, no central regulations existed on forced labor and camp conditions. Local officials combined pragmatic requirements of the work organization with segregation and guarding of the Jews; in that process, arbitrary discrimination was an element of the daily routine. Only a few new camps were later established in 1941, in most cases for female Jewish forced laborers.

In the first half of 1941, several camps that had previously belonged to the Reichsvereinigung camp system were reorganized on the model of the labor administration's labor camps. A network of over fifty Reichsvereinigung-supported camps had existed since 1939 under the control of the Gestapo; their purpose was exploitation of Jewish labor in agriculture and forestry. After the Pogrom, a number of Jewish organizations' retraining camps had been placed under the Reichsvereinigung to serve as agricultural training sites. The Reichsvereinigung expanded the existing camps and established new ones as labor sources for harvest and forestry work. The geographic center of the Reichsvereinigung camps was the Mark Brandenburg; in that area there were fifteen camps whose inmates worked for the Prussian forestry administration in Frankfurt an der Oder alone. Employment in forestry and agriculture was organized on the basis of collective contracts arranged by the Reichsvereinigung with forestry offices, city administrations, the Reichsnährstand, and private companies, without any involvement of the labor administration. The partners profited from the fact that camp inmates were in fact outside labor law. The partners paid "reimbursement" rather than wages according to a standard wage scale and did not deduct any insurance contributions, all with the approval of the competent authorities.

In the first half of 1941, the RHSA reorganized the camp system. Expensive camps based on lease agreements were closed and the remaining camps were officially converted to labor camps. The inmates were now subject to deployment by the labor administration, while their minimum-rate wages continued to flow into the coffers of the Reichsvereinigung.[263] By integrating the camps into the segregated labor deployment program, the RSHA killed two birds with one stone: While preparing for deportations, the RSHA simultaneously reduced to a minimum both the Reichsvereinigung's administrative costs and expenditures for camp inmates' social support.

The reorganization also involved degrading conditions to the level of a new type of camp, the labor and residential camp: While preparations were made for deportations, a new camp system emerged in Germany during early summer 1941. The Gestapo, usually collaborating with the Gau leadership, combined recruitment and internment of forced labor with housing for Jewish families. The existence of forty such labor and residential camps has

---

[263] König, *David*, 186.

been confirmed so far. Regional clusters were located in the Rhineland, in Württemberg, and in Silesia. District administrators, the Gestapo, and representatives of NSDAP Gau leadership groups placed families evicted from their homes in various rural Kreise and large cities in quarters frequently consisting of dilapidated facilities. The inmates had to repair spaces in former mines, monasteries, or Reich Labor Service camps and pay generally excessive rents. In these Gestapo-controlled camps, leaving the camp was strictly regulated and contact with the population prohibited. In contrast to earlier labor camps, each of these camps had a Jewish camp administration subordinate to the authorities. Forced labor for everyone capable of working shaped everyday life; at the same time, the proportion of forced workers grew steadily. Between 1941 and 1942, the problem of qualitatively and quantitatively substandard food for the inmates became acute, as it did in other types of camps. Cities and communities profited from the system of labor and residential camps because the residences of evicted Jews became available, merchants either directly supplied the camps or were approved as shopping destinations for the inmates, and of course companies were able to exploit forced laborers until they were deported. Beginning in fall 1941 and increasingly in 1942, the Gestapo deported the inmates of labor and residential camps, but also those of labor camps. Some camps in the vicinity of construction projects crucial to the war effort and the Cologne-Müngersdorf labor and residential camp, however, continued to exist until 1944, when a further camp system was created for forced labor of Jewish Mischlinge.

3

"Special Service" – Forced Labor of Jewish *Mischlinge*, 1942–1945

PERSECUTION AFTER THE NOVEMBER POGROM[1]

Although forced labor by people discriminated against by the Nazis for being so-called *Mischlinge*, that is, offspring of mixed Jewish and non-Jewish parentage, frequently has been documented in local studies on the persecution of Jews, neither older nor more recent academic research has focused in any depth on this subject.[2] Only Dieter Maier devoted cursory attention to some forced-labor measures and a few organizational details, but no attention is given to forced labor's origins, development, and background. That author frequently does not even distinguish between the different measures against Jews in mixed marriages and against Mischlinge.[3] Thus until now, research has not examined how the decision to introduce forced labor for Mischlinge came about, who made the decision, and when it occurred. Likewise, studies are lacking on what motivated this kind of forced labor, who organized it, and how it was carried out. Forced labor must, however, be viewed as a basic element of Nazi anti-Jewish policy, and for that reason the following discussion will attempt to close the existing gaps in knowledge about the persecution of Jewish Mischlinge and the so-called *jüdisch Versippte*, that is, Aryan partners married to Jews.

[1] This is a reworked and expanded version of the author's article, "Die NS-Führung und die Zwangsarbeit für sogenannte jüdische Mischlinge. Ein Einblick in Planung und Praxis antijüdischer Politik in den Jahren 1942 bis 1944," in *Rassismus, Faschismus, Antifaschismus: Forschungen und Betrachtungen gewidmet Kurt Pätzold zum 70. Geburtstag*, edited by Manfred Weißbecker and Reinhard Kühnl with assistance from Erika Schwarz (Cologne, 2000), 63–79.

[2] The first to discuss the general persecution of this group (without forced labor) was S. Fauck, "Verfolgung von Mischlingen in Deutschland und im Reichsgau Wartheland," in *Gutachten des Instituts für Zeitgeschichte*, Vol. 2 (Stuttgart, 1966), 29–31. The subject was later examined in detail by Jeremy Noakes, "The Development of Nazi Policy towards the German-Jewish *Mischlinge* 1933–1945," in Leo Baeck Yearbook XXXIV (1989), 291–354. Finally, Beate Meyer, *"Jüdische Mischlinge." Rassenpolitik und Verfolgungserfahrung 1933–1945* (Hamburg, 1999). She at least describes the practice of forced labor utilization in Hamburg; ibid., 240–246.

[3] Dieter Maier, *Arbeitseinsatz und Deportation. Die Mitwirkung der Arbeitsverwaltung bei der nationalsozialistischen Judenverfolgung in den Jahren 1938–1945* (Berlin, 1994), 203–234.

Since the first persecutory measures, racial classification of the victims had been an ongoing problem for the Nazi leadership. The Nuremberg Laws furnished an accepted hierarchy of full Jews, half-Jews, and so on, but in subsequent years the Nazi leadership had to decide each time anew which groups would be subjected to new anti-Jewish orders. The discussion of the policies affecting the Mischlinge (in 1939, about 52,000 of the first degree, and 33,000 of the second degree)[4] constantly ranged back and forth between the alternatives of placing them on equal footing with the Aryans and integrating them in the Nazi national community, or persecuting them as Jews. Implementation of persecutory policies had cost 10,000 Mischlinge their jobs and left them dependent on public social support. As a consequence, plans were being laid at the ministerial level for their mandatory employment. Ultimately, however, Mischlinge were not included in the forced-labor program instituted for all unemployed Jews after the pogrom in late 1938.[5] To the contrary, labor offices were ordered not to interfere with this group's free access to the labor market.[6]

In practice, the order did not prevent discrimination either by the administration or by private industry. Jewish Mischlinge were no longer appointed to public service in 1939–40. The German Council of Municipalities made clear in its response to an inquiry of the Potsdam Oberbürgermeister that the status of Mischlinge as "provisional citizens of the Reich" did not change the fact that as non-Aryans they could not be employed in the municipal economy either as employees or as laborers.[7] The armaments industry was not yet so strict. Of course, Mischlinge had already been proscribed from employment in "special jobs" or "elevated positions" since summer 1939.[8]

Although service of the Mischlinge in the army was controversial, their general military obligation at the beginning of the war in 1939 was initially still indisputable.[9] At the same time, that fact caused a conflict of interest. On

---

[4] Figure according to the census of 1939 in Maier, *Arbeitseinsatz und Deportation*, 205. Mischlinge were categorized by the Nazis according to the number of their grandparents who were Jewish: In the case of two, they were so-called half-Jews (Mischlinge of the first degree) and in the case of one, quarter-Jews (Mischlinge of the second degree).

[5] BA Berlin, R 26 IV Commissioner for the Four-Year Plan, No. 5, Fols. 53–54, Thirty-third session of the General Council on the Four-Year Plan (Working Committee) on November 10, 1938.

[6] Noakes, "The Development of Nazi Policy," 328. On that subject, with more examples, see Maier, *Arbeitseinsatz und Deportation*, 206–207.

[7] BA Berlin, R 36 German Council of Municipalities, No. 405, Fol. 127 verso, Handwritten note of the German Council of Municipalities, June 11, 1940, on an inquiry of the Potsdam Oberbürgermeister (signing as deputy, Beyrichen), May 30, 1940.

[8] Quoted according to the General Army Reports, August 21, 1939; BA Berlin, 50.01 Reich Propaganda Ministry, No. 859, Fols. 53–54, Circular of the defense office (*Abwehrstelle*) in Military District (*Wehrkreis*) III, Berlin, September 25, 1939.

[9] In 1936, the decision was made that Mischlinge were not allowed to hold leadership positions. For a detailed discussion, see Noakes, "The Development of Nazi Policy," 329–330.

the one hand, the Nazi leadership was interested in having Mischlinge serve in the war,[10] and on the other, it wanted to avoid elevating their position by doing so. Discussions on the subject between the Reich Interior Ministry and the Chancellery of the Führer dragged on until 1940. The Ministry – where State Secretary Leonardo Conti (rather than State Secretary Wilhelm Stuckart) took a sharply negative position with regard to Mischlinge – waited for a fundamental decision by Hitler.[11] At the end of March 1940, the Chancellery of the Führer proposed directly to Hitler that half-Jews be excluded from the army.[12] On April 8, Wilhelm Keitel, chief of the Wehrmacht High Command (*Oberkommando Wehrmacht*, or OKW), announced to the Wehrmacht Hitler's quick decision: Both so-called half-Jews and "men who were married to Mischlinge who were half Jewish or to Jewish women" were to be transferred out of active service into the reserves, with the special file note, "Not to be used." So-called quarter-Jews or men married to women who were one-quarter Jewish were to remain in the Wehrmacht.[13] Hitler's decision, which considerably intensified the persecution of Mischlinge and at the same time pulled in the so-called "people related by marriage to Jews," could not take effect immediately because a new phase of the war, the Western campaign, was just beginning. Most of the persons in the Wehrmacht who were affected were not discharged until after the conquest of France.[14]

In summer 1941, when large numbers of Jews were already being murdered in the occupied territories and the Nazi leadership decided to deport all the Jews from Germany to the East in short order, the Party and the SS pushed to subject Mischlinge to the same planned measures.[15] Thus, on August 21, the ministries and the Security Police discussed the modalities of the "final solution to the Jewish question," and in this context, the inclusion of half-Jews and Jews living in mixed marriages in the deportations. It was announced that the *Reichsleiter*, Martin Bormann, had informed Heydrich of Hitler's view that half-Jews were now to be treated like full Jews, and

---

[10] With the beginning of the war in 1939, the Reich Interior Ministry drafted a Hitler order according to which Mischlinge who were to serve at the front as soldiers were to be placed on equal footing with persons of German blood, except in the matter of authorizations to marry; Noakes, "The Development of Nazi Policy," 331.

[11] BA Berlin, 62 Ka 1, Chancellery of the Führer, No. 83, Fols. 204 and verso, File note of the Chancellery of the Führer for the Reich Office Leader Brack, March 19, 1940. See Noakes, "The Development of Nazi Policy," 331.

[12] According to a letter March 28, 1940; Noakes, "The Development of Nazi Policy," 331.

[13] Officers and exceptions subject to authorization by Hitler remained excluded; BA-MA Freiburg im Breisgau, RH 15, No. 219, Fol. 33, OKW circular, April 8, 1940.

[14] Noakes, "The Development of Nazi Policy," 331. In the summer of 1941, the Army High Command (OKH) had a check run to ascertain whether all the half-Jews and all the men married to half-Jewish women had been excluded from active service. If not, these persons were to be released with furloughed status; BA-MA Freiburg im Breisgau, RH 15, No. 219, Fol. 33 verso – 34, OKH circular, July 16, 1941.

[15] See Noakes, "The Development of Nazi Policy," 340.

that in the cases excepted from deportation, Mischlinge of the first degree were generally to be sterilized. Mischlinge of the second degree, on the other hand, would later be placed on the same footing as Aryans.[16] The Wehrmacht and others voiced objections, however, and the Nazi leadership backed down for a short time from this planned radical approach: They feared the measures would have negative effects on the morale of the Mischlinge of the second degree who continued to serve in the Wehrmacht, as their fathers would be deported as Jews.[17] After the beginning of the deportations, the Reich Interior Ministry provided information internally about the current policies: "Jewish Mischlinge and (for the time being) Jews living in mixed marriages will not be affected by the expulsion of Jews from the Reich territories. . . . Intensification of the pressure to label the Jewish Mischlinge is not intended. Only in the Protectorate have the exceptions specified for Mischlinge not been put into effect."[18]

The decision not to deport half-Jews did not slow the persecutory planning for this group at all. In early October 1941, Reich Minister Hans Lammers and Walter Groß, the chief of the NSDAP's Racial Policy Office, had met to discuss the matter. Groß now wanted to see all Mischlinge of the first degree remaining in Germany sterilized. That would still have to be coordinated with the Wehrmacht, but Lammers thought it entirely possible that the chief of the OKW, Keitel, would agree to the policy. After that, a final decision by Hitler would have to be arranged.[19]

FORCED STERILIZATION, FORCED COMMUNITY, AND FORCED LABOR

It was still by no means certain that Mischlinge would not be deported. At the Berlin Wannsee Conference on January 20, 1942, Heydrich (RSHA) appealed again to have Mischlinge of the first degree given the same status as Jews. State Secretary Stuckart, however, favored forced sterilization rather than "evacuation." After a follow-up meeting on March 6 where the sterilization issue was debated,[20] Stuckart wrote once again to all the participants in the Wannsee Conference, arguing against eviction and for

[16] Bernhard Lösener, "Das Reichsministerium des Innern und die Judengesetzgebung," in *Vierteljahrshefte für Zeitgeschichte*, 9, 3 (1961): 306; Noakes, "The Development of Nazi Policy," 339.

[17] Noakes, "The Development of Nazi Policy," 340.

[18] Landesarchiv (LA) Berlin, Rep. 142/7, 1-2-6/ No. 1, Vol. 1, no folio numbers, Teletype of Zeitler to Fiehler in Munich, October 28, 1941.

[19] BA Berlin, Nuremberg Trials, Case XI, No. 371, Fols. 197–199, October 13, 1941, note of Dr. Groß on October 2, 1941, consultation with Lammers (Doc. NG-978).

[20] See Kurt Pätzold and Erika Schwarz, *Tagesordnung: Judenmord. Die Wannseekonferenz am 20. Januar 1942. Eine Dokumentation zur Organisation der "Endlösung"* (Berlin, 1992); Raul Hilberg, *The Destruction of the European Jews* (London, 1961); – , *Die Vernichtung der europäischen Juden*, new and expanded edition, Vol. 2 (Frankfurt am Main, 1990), 437–449; Uwe-Dietrich Adam, *Judenpolitik im Dritten Reich* (Düsseldorf, 1972), 319–326;

"natural extinction of half-Jews within Reich territory." His main point was that causing distress to Aryan family members must be avoided.[21] However, in the March 1942 meeting it was clearly stated that discrimination would not stop even after sterilization. The discussion was about isolating sterilized Mischlinge in a city, like the old Jews in the Theresienstadt's fortress walls.[22] After Hitler announced stricter measures against Jewish Mischlinge in mid-May,[23] the assassination attempt on Heydrich in Prague and the attack of Jewish resistances fighters on the exhibition "The Soviet Paradise" in Berlin provided justification for radicalization of the anti-Jewish policy as a whole from the end of May on. Over the summer, at Hitler's personal insistence,[24] the exclusionary provisions affecting Mischlinge in the Wehrmacht were again made more restrictive.[25] The Nazis proceeded vigorously against this group in other areas as well.[26] When the RSHA campaigned intensively for a radical "solution to the Mischlinge question" at the end of August,[27] a concerned Stuckart wrote in September directly to Himmler: The news "that Mischlinge of the first degree are also to wear the Star of David in the future and in other ways to be placed on exactly the same footing as Jews, that is, they are also to be evacuated," had caused considerable unrest, "not only among the Mischlinge themselves but also in other segments of the population." According to Stuckart, those fears had to be allayed and Hitler had finally to make up his mind about the future of the Mischlinge.[28]

The fear of unrest in Germany's own hinterland during wartime saved the Mischlinge from being included in the mass deportations that had just

---

H. G. Adler, *Der verwaltete Mensch. Studien zur Deportation der Juden aus Deutschland* (Tübingen, 1974), 285–288.

[21] Pätzold and Schwarz, *Tagesordnung: Judenmord*, 121–122, Doc. No. 35, Letter of Stuckart, March 16, 1942; see Noakes, "The Development of Nazi Policy," 341–342.

[22] Noakes, "The Development of Nazi Policy," 344.

[23] Henry Picker, *Hitlers Tischgespräche im Führerhauptquartier 1941–1942*, 2nd printing (Stuttgart, 1965), 324, No. 109, Record of May 10, 1942, afternoon (Wolfsschanze).

[24] Ibid., 425, no. 162, Record of July 1, 1942, midday; BA Berlin, 62 Ka 1, No. 83, Fols. 131–132, Bormann to Bouhler, July 2, 1942. See Noakes, "The Development of Nazi Policy," 333.

[25] Now even quarter-Jews could only remain if they had served before May 8, 1940, and only with special permission from Hitler; BA-MA Freiburg im Breisgau, RH 15, No. 219, Fol. 34, Change from 1942 on circular of the Armed Forced High Command (OKW), July 16, 1941. See Noakes, "The Development of Nazi Policy," 334. In October, Hitler decided that petitions for exception of half Jews to be taken into the armed forces would no longer be processed; ibid., 335.

[26] For examples, see Noakes, "The Development of Nazi Policy," 349. In the municipal administrations such as Berlin's, all the offices and internal operations were checked once again to sift out Mischlinge and persons related to Jews by marriage; LA Berlin, Rep. 208, Acc. 2651, No. 9301, Fol. 84, Order of the Oberbürgermeister (signed as deputy, Plath), November 5, 1942.

[27] Noakes, "The Development of Nazi Policy," 344.

[28] Reproduced in Lösener, "Das Reichsministerium des Innern," 298–299. See Noakes, "The Development of Nazi Policy," 345.

reached a new high point. Nevertheless, the question remained for the Nazi leadership of what to do in the meantime with the Mischlinge still in the country; the policies against them were growing increasingly rigid. At the end of 1938, in a comparable situation, they had agreed on a persecutory program that intended to reorganize Jews' lives, isolating them in a forced community separate from Nazi society. The intention of the Nazi leadership was obviously to use a similar approach for the Mischlinge. Forced labor was thus discussed for the first time as a possible measure in summer 1942.[29] After the OKW had supplied the requisite statistics, high-ranking representatives of the Party Chancellery, the Reich Interior Ministry, and the Wehrmacht met in the Ministry of Propaganda on September 28 to discuss in concrete terms the "call-up . . . of Jewish Mischlinge and individuals related by marriage to Jews for service in the war." The plan for both groups was to organize "labor battalions" for separate utilization of the Mischlinge, possibly analogous to the so-called "individuals unworthy to bear arms" and possibly primarily to clear away the damage from the air war. State Secretary Stuckart and the representatives of the Party Chancellery criticized the plan because it would spark "an immediate, undesirable discussion of whether the Mischlinge would in the future also have to go the way of the full Jews."[30] As forced labor had been a basic element of persecuting Jews since the end of 1938 both in Germany and in Austria, this fear seemed to the participants in the meeting to be founded. The Party Chancellery was therefore supposed to approach Bormann with "the question of how this group was to be dealt with further." Without abandoning the forced-labor project on that account, the plan was to procure in the meantime, by the beginning of 1943, more precise documentation on the current use of the individuals in question by the labor administration and the Wehrmacht.[31]

At the end of 1942 it was still not yet clear in which direction the scales of policy on Mischlinge would tip. The idea of reclaiming these groups, numbering in the thousands, for military service still did not seem at all inappropriate even to many ministerial representatives.[32] All in all, the deportation plans were, for the time being, off the table; however, the fact of considering

---

[29] Noakes places the date of the idea of forced labor utilization only in June 1943; Noakes, "The Development of Nazi Policy," 351.

[30] *Akten der Parteikanzlei der NSDAP*, Part II, Vol. 4, Nos. 066018–19, Note of the Reich Propaganda (Dr. Gussmann), February 10, 1943; BA Berlin, R 43 II Reich Chancellery, No. 695, Fols. 53 and verso, Goebbels to Lammers on September 4, 1943. The session is also mentioned in Meyer, *Jüdische Mischlinge*, 237–238.

[31] The material was to have been gathered by January 7, 1943; *Akten der Parteikanzlei der NSDAP*, Part II, Vol. 4, Nos. 066018–19, Note of the Reich Propaganda Ministry, February 10, 1943; BA Berlin, R 43 II Reich Chancellery, No. 695, Fols. 53 and verso, Goebbels to Lammers on September 4, 1943.

[32] *Akten der Parteikanzlei der NSDAP*, Part II, Vol. 4, Nos. 066018–19, Note of the Reich Propaganda Ministry, February 10, 1943.

for the first time the organization of forced labor potentially signaled a new stage of persecution.

THE DECISION ABOUT FORCED LABOR

By the beginning of 1943, the majority of the German and Austrian Jews had been deported. Both Mischlinge and persons living in mixed marriages were among those excepted from the transports. In the infamous Fabrik-Aktion at the end of February, persons living in mixed marriages were removed from their forced-labor slots in industry and armaments. On the orders of the RSHA, they would only be utilized further for unskilled, manual jobs.[33] The question of how to handle the Jewish Mischlinge still awaited clarification.[34] Probably encouraged by reorganization of the forced labor of Jews in mixed marriages, the head of the RSHA revived the idea of labor battalions for Mischlinge that had been discussed in the previous summer. Only a few days after the Fabrik-Aktion, on March 3, Ernst Kaltenbrunner informed the OKW and the propaganda, labor, and armaments ministries about his ideas regarding compulsory employment of Mischlinge. In contrast to individuals unworthy to bear arms who were serving in special formations in the Wehrmacht, Jewish Mischlinge (but also persons related to Jews by marriage, as well as Gypsies, traitors, and previously convicted homosexuals) should, in Kaltenbrunner's view, be given no opportunity to prove themselves in war. The recruiting offices were therefore to advise the labor offices that these people were unfit for special military formations: "The labor offices will then immediately conscript these people for service in the Organisation Todt. This organization will then put the conscripted individuals together in special formations and arrange for their assignment to especially difficult work."[35]

Despite the fact that Keitel, Goebbels, and Speer had been approached directly, no quick decision was made. The Party Chancellery, besieged by the Ministry of Propaganda, wanted a decision about the plan by the end of March 1943, but the matter dragged on into April.[36] After the Reich propaganda managers of the NSDAP had intervened and pressed Goebbels's ministry about whether the most recently proposed option was good enough to keep, that ministry took the question directly to Kaltenbrunner.[37] However,

---

[33] See Chapter 1.

[34] At the beginning of February 1943, the OKW informed the Nazi leadership that with the reintegration of 20,000 persons unworthy to bear arms the problem for the army was resolved, without addressing the open question of utilization of Mischlinge for forced labor; mentioned in BA Berlin, R 43 II, No. 695, Fol. 53 verso, Goebbels to Lammers on September 4, 1943.

[35] *Akten der Parteikanzlei der NSDAP*, Part II, Vol. 4, Nos. 066023–25, Express letter of the Chief of the Security Police and SD (II A 2), March 3, 1943.

[36] Ibid., Nos. 066020–22, Notes of the Reich Propaganda Ministry, March 12 and 22, 1943, and April 13 and 17, 1943.

[37] Ibid., No. 066026, Note of Tießler for Passe on May 25, 1943.

it was learned from the RSHA at the end of May that Kaltenbrunner's proposals had been put on the back burner by Himmler because he was undecided,[38] on account of the Warsaw Ghetto uprising, as to whether separate
Jewish special formations might not be too risky. In addition, the RSHA
still had to establish how many Mischlinge of the first degree and persons
related to Jews by marriage could be considered for forced labor at all.[39]
The Organisation Todt (OT) was in any case occupied with the appropriate
preparations.[40] On May 22, 1943, Himmler sent a proposal of Professor
B. K. Schulz, office chief of the SS Race and Settlement Main Office, on
sterilization of Mischlinge – in cases of "racial inferiority" – within the next
three to four generations to Martin Bormann, with whom he had recently
discussed the Mischling issue.[41]

To some degree opposed to the forced-labor plans of the RSHA – clearly
under the influence of the recent defeat at Stalingrad – the OKW meanwhile developed a project "for military use of Jewish Mischlinge until then
excluded from military service and of citizens related by marriage to Jews."
According to figures of the Reich Interior Ministry, there were an estimated
26,000 men of an age suitable for military service. At the beginning of June,
Hitler's Chancellery welcomed any means of "removing Jewish Mischlinge
from the economy," but in no case should a military call-up have the final
effect that Mischlinge would later be placed on equal footing with persons
of German blood. Hitler's Chancellery made it absolutely clear that if there
were to be any utilization of Mischlinge in the Wehrmacht, it would be
in construction labor battalions. The Mischlinge would have to be specially
marked by wearing captured uniforms and deployed "to especially unhealthy
swamps."[42]

In mid-June 1943, Hitler finally instructed Goebbels to submit to him concrete proposals for forced labor of Mischlinge not inducted into the army,
with the argument that they should not be spared "the rigors of war."[43]
Only days later, a meeting took place for that purpose in the Ministry of
Propaganda with the representatives of the OKW. Unlike what Kaltenbrunner had proposed in March, but also unlike what the OKW had evidently

---

[38] The heroic uprising of the Jewish resistance fighters in the Warsaw ghetto began on April
19, 1943, and was not until mid-May put down by German SS units by means of systematic
destruction of the ghetto, with much bloodshed.

[39] *Akten der Parteikanzlei der NSDAP*, Part II, Vol. 4, Nos. 066027, Note of the Reich Propaganda Ministry for Tießler, May 28, 1943.

[40] BA Berlin, 62 Ka 1, No. 83, Fol. 84, Undated handwritten note on the note of the Chancellery
of the Führer, June 3, 1943.

[41] *Reichsführer! . . . Briefe von und an Himmler*, edited by Helmut Heiber (Munich, 1970),
268, No. 235.

[42] BA Berlin, 62 Ka 1, No. 83, Fol. 84, Undated handwritten note on the note of the Chancellery
of the Führer, June 3, 1943. For the figures, see ibid., Fol. 83.

[43] BA Berlin, R 43 II Reich Chancellery, No. 695, Fol. 53 verso, Goebbels to Lammers on
September 4, 1943.

planned initially, the two sides agreed that Jewish Mischlinge should be utilized by the Wehrmacht in labor battalions, but should wear "neither uniforms nor national emblems, but only work clothes." These columns could be given a "status similar to the prisoner-of-war battalions." Hitler agreed to this option, which had been developed by Goebbel's subordinates,[44] and in July officially ordered that "Mischlinge of the first degree and Jews' relatives by marriage be taken out of businesses," that they be inducted into the Wehrmacht, and that they be utilized "in the form of labor battalions for clean-up work under supervision of the Wehrmacht in areas damaged by bombing."[45] On July 27, 1943, the Reich propaganda managers of the NSDAP let it be known publicly that both groups would have to clear away bomb damage because they had ostensibly evaded military service.[46]

Hitler's order regarding the forced-labor utilization of Mischlinge under the supervision of the Wehrmacht was given just at the moment when the two-year-long mass deportations of Jews out of the German Reich were considered complete. Reichsführer SS Himmler described his and Hitler's perspectives on persecution on October 6, 1943, in Posen (Poznán): "The Jewish question in the countries that we occupy will be settled by the end of this year. . . . The question of Jews married to non-Jewish partners and the question of half-Jews will be examined appropriately and sensibly, decided, and then resolved."[47] In 1943–44, the living circumstances both of Jews in mixed marriages and of Mischlinge were to be drastically restricted.[48] In addition to the crowding together of these families in "Jewish houses" (as, for example, in Hamburg[49]), forced employment played an important role in that change.

THE ORGANIZATION OF FORCED LABOR

The chief of the OKW, Keitel, suddenly and unexpectedly refused to agree to use of Mischlinge for forced labor under the control of the army. This occurred not because he rejected the idea, but from wounded vanity. Keitel felt that Hitler had passed him over (as he complained later to the head of the Reich Chancellery) because Goebbels alone, as chairman of the Committee on Damages from the Air War (*Luftkriegsschädenausschuß*),

---

[44] The Propaganda Minister once again informed Generaloberst Fromm of the OKW about these results through official channels on July 3; ibid.

[45] No decision had been made about forced utilization of Gypsies, homosexuals, etc.; that was viewed as purely a matter for the Security Police; *Akten der Parteikanzlei der NSDAP*, Part II, Vol. 4, Nos. 066028, Note of the Reich Propaganda Ministry, July 17, 1943.

[46] According to Noakes, "The Development of Nazi Policy," 351.

[47] Heinrich Himmler, *Geheimreden 1933 bis 1945 und andere Ansprachen*, edited by Bradley F. Smith and Agnes F. Peterson (Frankfurt am Main, 1974), 170.

[48] See Adam, *Judenpolitik*, 330–332.   [49] See Meyer, *Jüdische Mischlinge*, 240.

had brought about Hitler's decision.[50] On August 10, 1943, the Ministry of Propaganda officially learned that the Wehrmacht refused to be involved, except for making available the records of the military replacement offices.[51]

Without further ado, the Nazi leadership then went back to the Kaltenbrunner proposal of March, and in the next weeks transferred the responsibility of creating the forced-labor columns not to the Wehrmacht but instead to the labor administration and to the Organization Todt, which was directly subordinate to Hitler.[52] In mid-October 1943, Göring informed the Gau labor offices about a new Hitler order regarding OT utilization of "half-Jews with no military obligation (Mischlinge of the first degree)" and "Aryans married to fully Jewish women."[53] Evidently at the beginning of November 1943, the General Commissioner for Labor Utilization (*Generalbevollmächtigter für den Arbeitseinsatz*), Sauckel, who was actually in charge, formally commanded the "segregated allocation of Jewish Mischlinge . . . on orders from the highest levels."[54]

At a meeting in Austria on November 8, 1943, between the labor administration and the authorities responsible for armaments, the following statement was made: "Regarding the treatment of persons unworthy to bear arms, Jewish Mischlinge, and persons related to Jews by marriage, the labor office has already conducted investigations of these persons using its own card file resources and those of the military replacement offices. Whether it is possible to release these men for utilization in the OT will be determined in consultation with armaments command."[55] At the end of November in Vienna, the responsible armaments office and the labor office reviewed possibilities "for release of the forced laborers employed in part in the armaments industry."[56] In Germany as well, the labor offices, in association with the responsible armaments command, registered these groups categorized by expendability for assignment to the OT. Only Berlin Armaments Command V reported 120 persons from armaments operations, including engineers.[57] Nevertheless, the Gau labor offices still recruited both groups sporadically rather than consistently toward the end of 1943 for deployment

[50] Keitel later had to admit to Lammers that the Armed Forces had been decisively involved in the planning from the outset; BA Berlin, R 43 II Reich Chancellery, No. 695, Fol. 43, Keitel to Lammers on August 16, 1943; ibid., Fol. 68, Keitel to Lammers on October 4, 1943.

[51] Ibid., Fols. 53 verso – 54; Goebbels to Lammers on September 4, 1943.   [52] Ibid., Fol. 54.

[53] Letter, October 13, 1943, quoted by Fauck, "Verfolgung von Mischlingen," 29.

[54] No decree has been found to date. However, the order is mentioned in BLHA Potsdam, Rep. 41, Großräschen, No. 272, Fols. 114 and verso, Decree of the Gestapo in Frankfurt an der Oder, October 9, 1944.

[55] BA-MA Freiburg im Breisgau, RW 21–63, No. 5, no folio numbers, War diary of Vienna armaments command, November 8, 1943.

[56] Ibid., War diary Vienna armaments command, November 27, 1943.

[57] According to Maier, *Arbeitseinsatz und Deportation*, 218.

to occupied France, where the OT already employed around 10,000 French Jews as forced laborers.[58]

In order to accelerate the planned forced-labor deployment, General Commissioner Sauckel issued two new decrees on March 21, 1944, and April 17, 1944.[59] The first of the two instructed the labor administration specifically regarding the combined deployment of persons unworthy to bear arms, Mischlinge of the first degree, persons related to Jews by marriage, and Gypsies for expansion of military positions in northern France.[60] In Baden, 2,000–3,000 still had to be recruited in March for that purpose.[61] In Vienna, 2,500 Mischlinge and Aryans living in mixed marriages were registered in April for use as forced labor.[62]

The labor offices everywhere thus reported the men suitable to be considered.[63] The men were placed in OT stand-by units of 100 forced laborers each and sent to Paris.[64] Erich Balzer, born in 1901, arrived by train to the OT's Eichkamp collection camp; from that location, he was taken with 196 men to France at the beginning of April 1944. There they lived in a camp in Boulogne that was enclosed by a barbed-wire fence and guarded by Dutch SS men.[65] Transports also left Duisburg and Koblenz.[66] Two transports in a row departed from the Cologne Gau labor office's area, the first on May 12 to France and the second on August 1 to Bedburg in Germany, where an underground hydrogenation plant was being built.[67] The second transport did not go west because of a transport stoppage imposed for the time being due to the war situation.[68] From Hamm, Mischlinge were taken in May 1944

---

[58] Franz Seidler, *Die Organisation Todt. Bauen für Staat und Wehrmacht 1938–1945* (Koblenz, 1987), 130 and 142.

[59] The decrees are mentioned as a reference in BA Berlin, R 3901 (former R 41) Reich Labor Ministry, No. 463, Fol. 22, Teletype of the Reich Ministry of Labor, General Commissioner of Labor, August 25, 1944. See Maier, *Arbeitseinsatz und Deportation*, 219; Seidler, *Die Organisation Todt*, 130.

[60] This decree became known in Hamburg on March 31, 1944; Meyer, *Jüdische Mischlinge*, 238.

[61] Maier, *Arbeitseinsatz und Deportation*, 219.

[62] BA-MA Freiburg im Breisgau, RW 21–63, No. 6, no folio numbers, War diary of Vienna armaments command, April 15, 1944.

[63] For Hamburg in April 1944, see Ingeborg Hecht, *Als unsichtbare Mauern wuchsen. Eine deutsche Familie unter den Nürnberger Rassengesetzen* (Munich, 1987), 142–145.

[64] Seidler, *Die Organisation Todt*, 131–132.

[65] CJA Berlin, Collection 4.1 Application Files of Victims of Fascism, No. 75, no folio numbers.

[66] Maier, *Arbeitseinsatz und Deportation*, 219.

[67] Mentioned in BA Berlin, R 3901 (former R 41) Reich Labor Ministry, No. 463, Fol. 22 verso, Circular of the Gau labor office, Reich Trustee of Labor, in Cologne-Aachen, August 26, 1944. The fate of a half-Jew in the camp at Bedburg, Erft, is briefly documented in Ernst Schmidt, *Lichter in der Finsternis. Widerstand und Verfolgung in Essen 1933–1945*, Vol. 2 (Essen, 1988), 25.

[68] Mentioned in BA Berlin, R 3901 (former R 41) Reich Labor Ministry, No. 463, Fol. 22, Teletype of the Reich Ministry of Labor, General Commissioner of Labor, August 25, 1944.

to Bergkamen to lay streetcar rails. A camp was established for them in the inn *Zur Grünen Eiche* (The Green Oak).[69]

On June 20, 1944, the Army High Command (OKH) finally declared employment of Jewish Mischlinge of the second degree in the army also to be unacceptable. The persons subject to discharge were "to be assigned to labor without delay."[70] When assignment to forced labor was still not effected Reich-wide to the desired extent, the General Commissioner for Labor Utilization once again sent a teletype to the Gau labor offices. The OT, he said, had provided information that large numbers of Jewish Mischlinge and persons related to Jews by marriage were still "available to be called up" at the labor offices. The transports to France then resumed, but, as a modification to the procedure, the Gau labor offices no longer dispatched persons obligated to perform forced labor directly to Paris, but instead routed them first to the Falkenberg-Westmark camp.[71]

Possibly encouraged by these events, transports accelerated within Germany as well. In August and September 1944, Mischlinge from Breslau were taken to labor camps in the Silesian *Kreis* (county-size unit of government) of Trachenberg.[72] In September, 180 Mischlinge were taken to the OT camps in Zeitz and Elben, and Mischlinge from Dortmund to Weissenfels and Halle an der Saale.[73] Clearly the failed assassination attempt on July 20, 1944, had contributed once again to the policies being made more severe: Citing that event as justification, Hitler instructed that the ministries' administrative offices finally be cleansed of the last Mischlinge, even of those who in an act of clemency had been given the status of Aryans.[74] In Hamburg, the Gau chamber of commerce now called upon the enterprises important to the war effort to report individually employed Mischlinge. Exemptions from forced labor granted previously to the few individuals still working in management positions or in specialized jobs in private industry were to

---

[69] Rita Kreienfeld, "'Sie haben uns zu Juden gemacht.' Ein Familienschicksal aus Hamm," in *Spuren der "Reichkristallnacht" in Hamm* (Hamm, 1988), 32.

[70] Quoted according to Maier, *Arbeitseinsatz und Deportation*, 222.

[71] BA Berlin, R 3901 (former R41), No. 463, Fol. 22, Teletype of the Reich Labor Ministry, General Commissioner of Labor, August 25, 1944. Facsimile in Maier, *Arbeitseinsatz und Deportation*, 224.

[72] Kreisarchiv Rudolstadt, Records of Persons Persecuted during the Nazi Regime, Various Personal Histories and Forms; Report of Ruth Pilz, in Roland Otto, *Die Verfolgung der Juden in Görlitz unter der faschistischen Diktatur 1933–1945* (Görlitz, 1990), 103, Attachment 8; YV Jerusalem, 01/ No. 61, no folio numbers, Letter of Ludwig Laubhardt, January 6, 1947.

[73] Meynert, "Endlösung," 262–272. For Dortmund, see Ulrich Knipping, *Die Geschichte der Juden in Dortmund während der Zeit des Dritten Reiches* (Dortmund, 1977), 134.

[74] Noakes, "The Development of Nazi Policy," 352. The Armed Forces had in the meantime ordered that Mischlinge of the first and second degree were no longer permitted to work as employees and laborers in the Army. The persons released were transferred to labor service; Sauer, *Dokumente*, Part II, 380, Doc. No. 548, Order of the OKH, June 20, 1944, quoted in Order of the Württemberg *Gau* Labor Office, September 21, 1944.

be reviewed yet again.[75] The action was taken because only 310 of the 775 Mischlinge registered until then in the Hanse city were performing forced labor.[76]

Segregated labor deployment had still only been implemented to a limited extent despite a number of decrees addressed to the labor administration. As "many Jewish Mischlinge" continued to work "in protected businesses," Heinrich Himmler ordered a second Fabrik-Aktion in early October 1944. Just as in the first large-scale operation against Jews and Jews in mixed marriages at the end of February 1943, now all Mischlinge working in industry and armaments were to be removed and used in the future only for manual labor, in segregated columns.[77] On October 6, 1944, Kaltenbrunner instructed the Gestapo offices that the police, in collaboration with the labor administration, were to pull all "able-bodied male Jewish Mischlinge of the first degree and persons related to Jews by marriage . . . out of businesses within three days" and transfer them "to the OT for segregated labor deployment in construction battalions." The labor offices were to utilize physically unsuitable men and female Mischlinge "in segregated groups for manual labor" in the areas where they lived. The course and results were to be reported to the RSHA.[78] On October 14, 1944, General Commissioner Saucel informed the labor administration of the new Fabrik-Aktion and the necessary cooperation with the Security Police.[79]

The operation to reorganize forced employment was evidently carried out quickly in some cities. In Hamburg, many of the persons targeted were removed from enterprises, and others had to give up their independence.[80] In the Aschaffenburg labor office district, the operation affected twenty-three

---

[75] For such complaints in Berlin, see Maier, *Arbeitseinsatz und Deportation*, 219–222.

[76] At that time, fifty men who had until then been exempt from the obligation to perform forced labor still worked in large businesses in Hamburg; most of them were exempt because of their service in the war, and some because of requests from the authorities, etc.; see the description of individual cases in Hamburg in Meyer, *Jüdische Mischlinge*, 239.

[77] In contrast, Beate Meyer interprets the operation only as a means of meeting private enterprises' requests for release in a way favorable to the Mischlinge; Meyer, *Jüdische Mischlinge*, 238.

[78] Further employment in previous places of work was only possible for physical labor in sectors not important for the war effort; BLHA Potsdam, Rep. 41, Großräschen, No. 272, Fol. 114, Decree of the Gestapo in Frankfurt an der Oder, October 9, 1944, in the decree of the Calau district administrator, November 11, 1944; reproduced in *Kennzeichen J. Bilder, Dokumente, Berichte zur Geschichte der Verbrechen des Hitlerfaschismus an den deutschen Juden 1933–1945*, edited by Helmut Eschwege (Berlin, 1981), 316. Partial reproduction of the RSHA decree in Meyer, *Jüdische Mischlinge*, 238–239.

[79] Excerpt reproduced in Maier, *Arbeitseinsatz und Deportation*, 225–226. See also BA ZwA Dahlwitz-Hoppegarten, AdZ Dok/K, No. 4, no folio numbers, Circular letter of the Organisation Todt at Kyffhäuser – Group Commissioner of the Construction Industry, Labor utilization (Schmidt), November 5, 1944.

[80] For details about several cities, see Maier, *Arbeitseinsatz und Deportation*, 226–231. For Hamburg, see Meyer, *Jüdische Mischlinge*, 241.

Jewish Mischlinge who actually were not working any longer in protected businesses. They all were to be taken to an OT construction site in Altenburg, Thuringia, on November 4.[81] Bavaria, however, had not entirely completed the seizure operation by the beginning of November.[82] And in Frankfurt am Main, the NSDAP local groups were still being asked at the end of November to report all their Mischlinge of the first degree "whom the Gestapo intends to collect and transport to labor camps."[83] In Vienna, "the induction of the Mischlinge and persons related by marriage to Jews" into the OT did not occur until December 1944. "The operation encompassed . . . 5,000 workers, among them many skilled employees whose departure the businesses had not anticipated."[84]

FORCED LABOR IN THE CAMPS

The majority of the persons seized in the course of the new Fabrik-Aktion were transported to forced-labor camps of the OT, for the most part within the German Reich. An exception was Klaus Bloch, who was taken in fall 1944 to the Amersfoort OT camp in Holland. Arthur Briesemeister was sent in October 1944 to the Sarstedt camp near Hanover in Lower Saxony, where he had to work in a salt mine. Dietrich Byk was recruited in October by *Aktion Hase* (Operation Rabbit) for forced labor at the Jülich camp; Werner Bach was recruited for forced labor in the Birkesdorf camp near Aachen. Various men were taken in October and November to the Wuppertal-Wichlinghausen camp. Gerhard Baur, who had already performed forced labor living in the casern Mortier in Paris, was sent from France to Wichlinghausen. As can be seen from applications, preserved in Berlin, for the certification of survivors as victims of fascism, some fled after the demand that they report to the transports; others fled after their arrival in the camp.[85]

Many new camps were established during the operation in the Saxony-Anhalt region. Individuals from Duisburg and Braunschweig performed

---

[81] Maier, *Arbeitseinsatz und Deportation*, 226.

[82] Monthly report of the president of the Upper and Middle Franconia administrative district, November 8, 1944, in *Bayern in der NS-Zeit, Bd. I: Soziale Lage und politisches Verhalten der Bevölkerung im Spiegel vertraulicher Berichte*, edited by Martin Broszat, Elke Fröhlich, et al. (Munich and Vienna, 1977), 486.

[83] *Dokumente zur Geschichte der Frankfurter Juden*, published by the Commission for Research on the History of the Frankfurt Jews, XIV, 12 (Frankfurt am Main, 1963), 531, Note of cell leader 08 of the Dornbusch local group about the cell leader meeting, November 29, 1944.

[84] BA-MA Freiburg im Breisgau, RW 46, No. 470, no folio numbers, Situation report of the defense economic officer for Military District (Wehrkreis) XVII for December 1944, January 5, 1945.

[85] See various statements, especially of Richard Bielefeld, Günter Bielefeld, Hermann Beermann, in CJA Berlin, Collection 4.1 Application Files of Victims of Fascism.

forced labor in the Blankenburg OT camp in the Harz Mountains.[86] Günther Breitkreuz had to go to the Braunlage camp. According to statements of survivors, 500 Mischlinge were sent to the Zerbst camp alone. Herbert Bamberg was taken in November in *Aktion Mitte* to Borstel near Stendal, and later to Burg near Magdeburg. Persons related to Jews by marriage were also sent to the Borstel camp. They were likewise taken to the Gardelegen camp, where Georg Blumenstein, whose wife was Jewish, ended up on November 1, 1944, along with 175 other men. A massacre of 1,016 concentration camp prisoners and forced laborers took place in the town of Gardelegen in spring of 1945.[87]

Various forced-labor camps for Mischlinge were also established in Saxony, for example, at Leuna and Halle an der Saale, and at Untertannwald in the Erz Mountains.[88] Kurt Budy began his forced-labor assignment in the medical depot of the OT hospital at Rathen an der Elbe.[89] In Thuringia, there was a camp in the city of Jena, according to the statement of Günter Becker, on the factory grounds of the famous glass company Schott & Genossen. He worked for Karl Walter und Co. GmbH.[90] Further camps for the forced utilization of Mischlinge were maintained at Sitzendorf in Thuringia and at Groß-Kamsdorf, the latter for the OT *Aktion Mitte B*. Ostensibly the letter "B" stood for "*Bewährung*," that is, "probation."[91]

Many forced laborers remained in their home regions. Both Mischlinge and Jewish women from mixed marriages who came from Arnstadt and Hamm were taken to Kassel-Bettenhausen, where they lived until 1945 in a barracks camp and worked in a spun-fiber factory.[92] Men were transported from Rudolstadt in Thuringia on October 16 to the nearby labor camp at Weissenfels; young women were sent to Saalfeld.[93] Nighttime telephone calls of the Gestapo had ordered the women to go to the labor office. In Saalfeld, they had to do the heaviest jobs, even though they were still minors: digging trenches for air raid protection, sweeping streets, cleaning air raid shelters and the municipal slaughterhouse, felling trees, clearing debris after air raids

---

[86] Günther von Roden, *Geschichte der Duisburger Juden* (Duisburg, 1986), 887; *Brunsvicensia Judaica. Gedenkbuch für dir jüdischen Mitbürger der Stadt Braunschweig 1933–1945* (Braunschweig, 1966), 151.

[87] See the statements of Karl Basch, Artur Balzer, Hans Joachim Bocj, and others in CJA Berlin, Collection 4.1 Application Files of Victims of Fascism.

[88] See the statements in CJA Berlin, Collection 4.1 Application Files of Victims of Fascism; StadtA Dresden, Hellerau Municipal Administration, No. 145/05 d, no folio numbers, Hellerau local committee on victims of fascism to the main committee, November 18, 1946.

[89] See the statements in CJA Berlin, Collection 4.1 Application Files of Victims of Fascism.

[90] CJA Berlin, Collection 4.1, No. 115, no folio numbers.

[91] Statements in the CJA Berlin, Collection 4.1 Application Files of Victims of Fascism.

[92] Werner Saure, *Geschichte und Schicksale jüdischer Mitbürger aus Neheim und Hüsten* (Balve, 1988), 97; Kreienfeld, "Sie haben uns zu Juden gemacht," 33.

[93] Kreisarchiv Rudolstadt, Records of Persons Persecuted during the Nazi Regime, Various Personal Histories and Forms.

and putting on roofs, construction work for emergency housing projects, and other heavy excavation work. A survivor describes this work, which lasted six months, until liberation in April 1945: "We often worked under police supervision with Russians, Frenchmen, and Italian civilian workers who were prisoners of war and in their treatment ranked higher than we did. The police and the city administration held attempts to converse with these people, our fellow workers, against us. My wages were 32 Pfennig per hour."[94] The Krüger brothers, Answald and Helmut, arrived with a Berlin transport at Miltitz-Roitzschen in Saxony at the beginning of January 1945. The OT was having underground halls for production of synthetic fuels built there by the forced laborers. They were guarded in a barracks camp by Ukrainian auxiliaries.[95]

Thus, thousands of Mischlinge and persons related to Jews by marriage lived in the meantime in labor camps, under conditions that varied considerably.[96] In the view of survivors, the situation in some of these camps resembled that in concentration camps.[97] However, there were fundamental organizational differences from the concentration camp system. Just like Jews in the segregated labor deployment program between 1939 and 1943, the Mischlinge were considered "free" (that is, voluntary) workers, even though they were employed against their will in separate columns. The OT Kyffhäuser operational group used the term *"Sonderdienstverpflichtete"* (persons obligated to special service) to camouflage them. The rules of their forced labor were decided in consultation with the RSHA: "The men must be housed separately in camps and may not be employed as individual workers. They are to be utilized as a separate group, whenever possible, of not less than 100. It is clearly established that the workers are not to be treated as prisoners, but as free workers. However, strict discipline shall prevail in the camps; the men are to be taken firmly in hand, but are to be treated fairly. When individual laborers get out of line and don't go along, they are to be reported immediately to the competent local Gestapo office." The threat of internment in a concentration camp hung over their heads. Letters could be written once a week, but the camp leadership censored the mail, both letters and packages. Visits of relatives and leave (for example, in cases of illness, bomb damage at home, or deaths) could be authorized in individual cases. The inmates were to be guarded by OT men.[98] A short time later,

---

94 Kreisarchiv Rudolstadt, Records of Persons Persecuted during the Nazi Regime, Personal Histories of Rosemarie (born 1929) and Wilhelmine (born 1906).

95 Helmut Krüger, *Der halbe Stern. Leben als deutsch-jüdischer "Mischling" im Dritten Reich* (Berlin, 1993), 101–102.

96 On the conditions, see Fauck, "Verfolgung von Mischlingen," 29. In contrast, see the very apologetic representation by Seidler, *Die Organisation Todt*, 131.

97 Noakes, "The Development of Nazi Policy," 353; Meyer, *Jüdische Mischlinge*, 247.

98 BA ZwA Dahlwitz-Hoppegarten, AdZ Dok/K, No. 4, no folio numbers, Circular letter of the Kyffhäusser OT – group commissioner of the construction industry, labor utilization

the RSHA made the already drastic guidelines more stringent in significant points: Without regard to prior education, the Mischlinge were only allowed to perform "manual labor at construction sites." In the camp, on the way to work, and at work, they were guarded. They were prohibited from leaving the camp in their time off, or from taking leave or receiving visits from relatives, especially from their wives.[99]

The schizophrenia in the classification of Mischlinge and persons related to Jews by marriage is clear from some of the other conditions of their forced labor. First, they could receive from the labor offices a compensatory payment up to the level of their previous earnings as a supplement to their wages for forced labor, which actually occurred in some cases.[100] Furthermore, they were allowed by the OT to use the Hitler greeting.[101] And finally, in November 1944, Himmler (correcting his own decree) ordered that officials, employees, and workers in public service – which of course by then included only persons related to Jews by marriage – were exempted from forced labor. He did so even though that employment sector had as a priority been cleansed of Mischlinge.[102] The clergy, too, could be excused from mandatory allocation.[103] On the other hand, relatives of both groups still working as physicians were to be interned in camps.[104]

As already stated, not all of the persons seized in the second Fabrik-Aktion were sent to distant labor camps. In Kassel, forty Mischlinge were transferred to an OT camp in the vicinity of the city. There they slaved at constructing bunkers and at clearing debris.[105] The city of Hamburg even managed – because of the destruction to the city – to arrange for the 1,000 persons seized there to be assigned to its own construction administration rather

---

(Schmidt), November 5, 1944; ibid., Guidelines on the labor utilization of Mischlinge of the first degree and persons related to Jews by marriage.

[99] Ibid., Circular letter of the OT at Kyffhäuser and group commissioner of the construction industry (Wagner) with instructions of the RSHA, November 20, 1944. Sick forced laborers and forced laborers who were not up to the heavy construction activities were not allowed to be released to go home; they were handed over to the Gestapo; ibid., Circular letter of the OT at Kyffhäuser – Börde senior construction management in Halberstadt, December 19, 1944.

[100] For Hamburg, see Meyer, *Jüdische Mischlinge*, 241.

[101] BA ZwA Dahlwitz-Hoppegarten, AdZ Dok/K, No. 4, no folio numbers, Guidelines on the labor utilization of Mischlinge of the first degree and persons related to Jews by marriage.

[102] Decree of the Reich Interior Ministry, excerpt printed in Maier, *Arbeitseinsatz und Deportation*, 230. The decree applied to state agencies, municipalities, and insurance carriers; see Sauer, *Dokumente*, Part II, 381, Doc. No. 549, Decree of the Reich Interior Ministry, December 8, 1944; LA Berlin, Rep. 208, Acc. 1651, No. 9301, Fol. 150. Order of the Berlin Oberbürgermeister, January 6, 1945.

[103] Bormann circular, December 31, 1944; Maier, *Arbeitseinsatz und Deportation*, 230.

[104] Reich Health Leader Conti had agreed to their forced utilization on the condition that withdrawal would proceed gradually and breakdowns in care for the population would be avoided; BLHA Potsdam, Rep. 41, Großräschen, No. 272, Fols. 113 and verso, Decree of the Gestapo in Frankfurt an der Oder, November 13, 1944.

than to the OT operational detail in Weimar.[106] Forced laborers were to be housed in several of the city's own camps, for example, those at the Ohls-dorf cemetery and the Horner Racetrack. In the end, however, evidently only the Ohlsdorf cemetery camp was occupied by about 100 inmates who all worked on the grounds there. The Firma Roggenbuck & Söhne man-aged the camp under a contract with the Hamburg's cemetery office. Here, too, the recruits were considered "free workers," although they were not allowed to leave the camp after 8:00 p.m. or to receive visitors.[107] In the Hamburg forced-labor group called "*Sonderkommando J*" to disguise its purpose, Mischlinge worked under guard at private construction firms or for the municipal gardens and parks office or cemetery office. A total of thirty-seven operational groups were present in Hamburg, many of them removing debris and performing heavy transport work. Many Mischlinge worked for the city works; others were employed by private companies or by property owners whose houses had been destroyed. The heaviest work was beyond the strength of most of the persons obligated to perform forced labor. Room and board were inadequate, and the treatment by fore-men and guards was often discriminatory.[108] In addition, the Mischlinge were required to fill out forms that contained questions about the living space that had become available as a result of their internment, or about their property – which reminded them alarmingly of impending deporta-tions.[109]

Mischlinge of the first degree, who were considered Jews (*Geltungsjuden*) by the Nazis because they were members of a Jewish religious community or married to a Jew, were finally included at the end of the war in the last deportation operation of the RSHA. In big cities, they had to arrive for trans-port between February 12 (Stuttgart) and 19 (Vienna), 1945; among them were even some Mischlinge who were not Geltungsjuden. In some places the victims could flee; in other places, the transport capacity was insufficient.[110]

---

[105] Maier, *Arbeitseinsatz und Deportation*, 230.   [106] Meyer, *Jüdische Mischlinge*, 240.

[107] StA Hamburg, 325-1 Cemetery Administration, No. 175, no folio numbers, Note, October 19, 1944; ibid., Municipal above-ground building construction department to the clearing office, October 30, 1944; ibid., Senior garden inspector to Roggenbuck & Sons Com-pany on November 16, 1944. For this and the following, see also Beate Meyer, "Das Sonderkommando 'J' – Zwangsarbeit der 'Jüdisch versippten' und der 'Mischlinge ersten Grades' in Hamburg, "in: *Beiträge zur Geschichte der nationalsozialistischen Verfolgung in Norddeutschland, Heft 8: Zwangsarbeit und Gesellschaft* (2004), 102–110; see also Meyer, *Jüdische Mischlinge*, 245–246.

[108] StA Hamburg, 325-1 Cemetery Administration, No. 175, no folio numbers, Note, Octo-ber 19, 1944; ibid., Circular note of the municipal above-ground building construction department, October 25, 1944. See Meyer, *Jüdische Mischlinge*, 241–246.

[109] Meyer, *Jüdische Mischlinge*, 242.

[110] For a detailed description, see Wolf Gruner, *Der Geschlossene Arbeitseinsatz*, 329. For Vienna, see Herbert Rosenkranz, *Verfolgung und Selbstbehauptung. Die Juden in Österreich 1938 bis 1945* (Vienna and Munich, 1978), 310.

Two months later, when defeat loomed, the RSHA stopped both the Theresienstadt transports and the effort to reorganize forced labor of Mischlinge underway since October. Measures that had been implemented, however, remained in effect; the individuals affected performed forced labor until the end of the war.[III]

SUMMARY

The decision regarding the deportation of German Jews stimulated discussion in the Nazi leadership about inclusion of Mischlinge in deportation measures; Mischlinge were exempted from transports in fall 1941, but in exchange were supposed to be sterilized forcibly later. Mischlinge of the first degree who were not deported were segregated with increasing frequency from Nazi society. Forced labor, which was discussed for the first time on the ministerial level in the summer of 1942, was to become a basic element of that process. Whether the planned labor battalions were to be formed under supervision of the Wehrmacht or the labor administration was a subject of debate. Following proposals of Goebbels, Hitler decided in July 1943 that Mischlinge of the first degree and persons related to Jews by marriage were to be mustered by the army and subsequently used to clear bomb damage. However, when the chief of the OKW rejected the plan, Hitler, in fall 1943, transferred recruitment and allocation to the more experienced Reich labor administration, as the Chief of the RSHA, Kaltenbrunner, had previously intended.

Utilization was to be for construction projects of the OT. The labor administration organized segregated labor deployment of Mischlinge and persons related to Jews by marriage on the model of forced labor for Jews – the decrees for the two groups in fact had the same record number, 5431. Forced labor of Mischlinge was planned primarily for defensive construction projects in occupied France but initially could be put into effect only partially because of events of the war. The General Commissioner for Labor Utilization, Sauckel, attempted to force implementation with several decrees. However, in the beginning of October 1944, an operation initiated by Himmler to transfer all Mischlinge to OT construction work and to manual labor in general finally led to radically increased allocation for forced labor. Labor camps used forced laborers for underground armaments construction projects inside Germany, but sometimes cities also put them to work clearing away bomb damage. Although the Mischlinge were considered "free" workers, they were subject to discriminatory regulations: They were guarded at all times and were prohibited from leaving the camps. With the segregated labor deployment of Mischlinge and persons related to Jews by marriage

---

[III] Sauer, *Dokumente*, Part II, 383, Doc. No. 550 c), Gestapo in Stuttgart to district administrators, March 25, 1945.

for OT construction projects, the Nazi leadership achieved the persecutory policy objective of isolating two groups that could not be deported for fear of unrest in the population and, simultaneously, the economic objective of making available tens of thousands of unskilled workers as cheap forced labor. In sum total, between 10,000 and 20,000 persons, mostly men, were affected, several thousand of them in Hamburg and Vienna alone – the latter the location where, six years before, the idea of segregated labor deployment was first conceived.

AUSTRIA

4

Initiatives in Vienna – Austrian Jews in the Segregated Labor Deployment Program, 1938–1945[1]

ANNEXATION, ANTI-JEWISH POLICIES, AND THE LABOR MARKET

Photographs in which Jewish men and women can be seen cleaning Vienna's streets, forced to do so by the SA and SS and surrounded by curious onlookers, illustrate the reports on Austria and persecution in the Nazi era. These images of public humiliation rituals from the days after Austria's annexation to the German Reich dominate our historical memory today. At the same time, scarcely any pictures or reports from the special labor camps for Jews established after 1939 have entered public consciousness, despite the fact that thousands of Austrian Jews had to perform the most strenuous possible forced labor there for months or years. Studies on the persecution of Jews in Austria, or Vienna, ignored this subject.[2] So far, Austrian research on the National Socialists has in fact associated forced labor with the concentration camps alone.[3]

As already stated, the expulsion of Jewish Germans was regarded within the Nazi leadership as the uncontested objective of persecution, even after Austria's annexation in March 1938. Not until summer 1938 did the concept of forced labor surface, initially more as a spontaneous means of applying pressure, the way it was in Austria, with the objective of forcing departure. The reasons for reorienting persecutory policies emerged earlier and more noticeably in Austria than in the Old Reich, because Austrian Jews' social situation was traditionally far worse than that of German Jews and deteriorated enormously after March 1938 as an effect of brutal persecution.

---

[1] Chapter 4 is the reworked and expanded version of the author's article, "Der geschlossene Arbeitseinsatz österreichischer Juden im NS-Staat 1938–1942," in *Dachauer Hefte, Bd. 16: Zwangsarbeit* (Dachau, 2000), 36–53. On this subject, see the author's extensive study, *Zwangsarbeit und Verfolgung. Österreichische Juden im NS-Staat 1938–1943* (Innsbruck, Vienna, and Munich, 2000).

[2] See the Introduction.

[3] For a summary of the state of research, see Florian Freund and Bertrand Perz, "Fremdarbeiter und KZ-Haftlinge in der 'Ostmark,'" in *Europa und der "Reichseinsatz". Ausländische Zivilarbeiter, Kriegsgefangene und KZ-Häftlinge in Deutschland 1938–1945*, edited by Ulrich Herbert (Essen, 1991), 317–350. Karl Stuhlpfarrer, Bertrand Perz, and Florian Freund (eds.), *Bibliographie zur Geschichte des Konzentrationslagers Mauthausen* (Vienna, 1998).

Photo 4. Austrian Jews forced to clean up streets in Eisenstadt, spring 1938

Consequently, practical plans for a forced-labor program evolved there first. Economic factors also played a role. The Nazi state wanted to increase iron ore production for Austrian armament, expand hydroelectric power production, and adapt the road and railway networks to meet war requirements.[4] On April 7, 1938, Hitler had already broken ground for construction of the Reich Autobahn near Salzburg.[5] It quickly became apparent, however, that the Ostmark's human labor pool could only satisfy the new requirements for a short time.[6] Thus, in September 1938, the Austrian labor administration hit upon the idea of forcing unemployed Jews to work on construction projects. Inspired by the idea, Reich Commissar for the Reunification of Austria with the German Reich (*Reichskommissar für die Wiedervereinigung Österreichs mit dem Deutschen Reich*), Josef Bürckel, proposed to utilize forced labor for modernization of the infrastructure. Use of Jews for road construction in Vienna provided the model for forced employment Reich-wide. By 1945, a total of 20,000 Austrian Jews are thought to have performed forced labor.[7]

---

[4] According to plans of the Reich Office for Expansion of the Economy in the Reich Ministry for the Economy, March 13, 1938; reference in Norbert Schausberger, *Rüstung in Österreich 1938–1945* (Vienna, 1970), 34.

[5] Hans Kernbauer and Fritz Weber, "Österreichs Wirtschaft 1938–1945," in *Die NS-Herrschaft in Österreich 1938–1945*, edited by Emmerich Tálos, Ernst Hanisch, and Wolfgang Neugebauer (Vienna, 1988), 65, Note 31.

[6] Schausberger, *Rüstung in Österreich*, 25–39.

[7] Yad Vashem Archive (YV) Jerusalem, 030/No. 22, Fol. 19, Anonymous report from Vienna (around 1947).

SCOURING GROUPS AND CLEANING COLUMNS, SPRING 1938

After the *Anschluss*, Austria – and Vienna in particular – held a special place in the development of the Nazis' anti-Jewish policies. With annexation, the Nazis' statistically measured success in expelling Jews vanished, because twice as many Jews as had emigrated since 1933 now came under the regime's control. In the 1930s, about 190,000 Jewish persons lived in Austria, 90 percent of them in Vienna.[8] The process of catching up hastily to the persecutory policies that Germany had been developing since 1933, and the first year's institutional confusion because the lines demarcating state, party, and municipal jurisdictions were not yet clearly drawn, spawned pogrom-like acts of brutality in Austria, particularly by SA and the Party formations. Persecution was thus loosed on the Jewish population in March 1938 with hitherto unknown force. Terror in the streets, searches of houses, seizure of property, and arbitrary Aryanization or shut-down of businesses and factories characterized the first days and weeks of the new regime.

The so-called "scouring groups" (*Reibepartien*) etched themselves indelibly in the survivors' memory; Jewish women and men, the elderly, and children were pressed into service.[9] The humiliating rituals took place in many Austrian towns[10] (see photo 4, p. 106) and were especially prevalent in the various sectors of Vienna.[11] The SA, the SS, and Hitler Youth forced Jews to scour the Schuschnigg election slogans or Teutonic crosses from the street pavement, to wipe them from walls, or to remove the same type of posters from fences and pillars. The work frequently had to be performed with unsuitable tools, sometimes even with bare hands, but usually accompanied by the onlookers' derision. Aryan Austrians were often an enthusiastic audience; in the words of an eyewitness, "'Work for the Jews, finally work for the Jews,' the crowd howled. 'We thank our Führer; he made work for the Jews.'"[12] Ehud Nadir, who was spit upon and kicked by the onlookers,

---

[8] Figures for 1934 according to Jonny Moser, "Die Katastrophe der Juden in Österreich 1938–1945 – Ihre Voraussetzungen und ihre Überwindungen, in *Der Gelbe Stern in Österreich. Katalog und Einführung zu einer Dokumentation* (Eisenstadt, 1977), 67.

[9] On this subject, see *Jüdische Schicksale. Berichte von Verfolgten*, published by the Dokumentationsarchiv des österreichischen Widerstandes, and selected, edited, and reworked by Brigitte Bailer, Florian Freund, et al. (Vienna, 1992), 99, 104, 112, 114–115, 131, 144, 153–154, and 160.

[10] Robert Streibel, *Plötzlich waren sie alle weg. Die Juden der "Gauhauptstadt Krems" und ihre Mitbürger* (Vienna, 1991), 45. Walzl does not note incidents of this sort in Carinthia; August Walzl, *Die Juden in Kärnten und das Dritte Reich* (Klagenfurt, 1987), 149.

[11] See Hans Safrian and Hans Witek, *Und keiner war dabei, Dokumente des alltäglichen Antisemitismus in Wien 1938* (Vienna, 1988), 20–26; Wolfang Platt (ed.), *Voll Leben und voll Tod ist diese Erde. Bilder aus der Geschichte der jüdischen Österreicher (1190–1945)* (Vienna, 1988), 234–235.

[12] G.E.R. Gedye, *Die Bastionen fielen* (Vienna, 1947), 295–296. See also *Deutschland-Berichte der Sozialdemokratischen Partei Deutschlands (Sopade) 1934–1940)*, edited by

also had to listen to choruses saying such things as, "Who is giving the Jews work? Adolf Hitler!"[13]

The "punishment work" sometimes dragged on for weeks, depending on the inclination of the local SA. In April 1938 as well, men and women were pulled from their dwellings or stopped on the street. Increasingly, the workers, whose labor cost nothing, were used to clean caserns, schools, Hitler Youth homes, and SA or Party meeting rooms.[14] For example, Hedy Hollitscher was stopped with two friends by an SA man in Vienna: "He asked, 'Are you Austrians?' 'Yes.' 'Jewish?' 'Yes.' 'Then come along with me.' And then all three of us were taken to an office building where the SA and SS worked. There we were given a bucket of water and rags and brushes, and had to scrub the floors in the offices."[15] While the harassment of scouring groups gave way to more rational utilization of Jews in cleaning columns, the new measures could hardly be called well-organized, and the random seizure of victims on the street continued.

ARRESTS FOR FORCED LABOR IN CONCENTRATION CAMPS

Jews were not only detained on the street for cleaning columns at that time. In the second half of May 1938, large-scale raids swept through Vienna. The *Times*, the British newspaper, wrote that hundreds of Jews were loaded into special trains and transported from Vienna to Dachau Concentration Camp.[16] This was clearly not a local Gestapo operation, as previously assumed, but rather the result of a Hitler order.[17] At the beginning of the last week in May, he personally ordered that "asocial and criminal Jews would be arrested to perform important excavation work."[18] The State Police head-

---

Klaus Behnken, 7th edition, Vol. 5 (Salzhausen-Frankfurt am Main, 1989), 738, No. 7, July 1938.

[13] Report of Ehud Nadir, in *Jüdische Schicksale*, 131.

[14] Safrian and Witek, *Und keiner war dabei*, 23 and 45. Also mentioned in the Central Zionist Archive (CZA) Jerusalem, S 25, No. 9703, no folio numbers, Summary of a verbal Report made by Sir Wyndam Deedes, April 25, 1938, 2. See the reports on the cleansing of an SA restaurant and an SA casern in Robert Breuer, *Nacht über Wien* (Vienna, 1988), 51–55.

[15] Report of Hedy Hollitscher, in *Jüdische Schicksale*, 114.

[16] *Sopade*, Vol. 5, 736, No. 7, July 1938.

[17] The explanation given up to date for the internments was that the Gestapo wanted to arrest 5,000 young, "unpleasant" Jews capable of working in *"geschlossener Arbeitseinsatz* in the western border areas." The first 650 prisoners were not to have arrived at Dachau Concentration Camp until after the operation was halted by Göring's intervention; Herbert Rosenkranz, *Verfolgung und Selbstbehauptung. Die Juden in Österreich 1938 bis 1945* (Vienna and Munich, 1978), 86–87.

[18] YV Jerusalem, 051/OSOBI, No. 88 (Moscow 500/1/261), Fol. 30, Note of Hagen (SD Jewish section), June 8, 1938. For more details, see Wolf Gruner, *Der Geschlossene Arbeitseinsatz deutscher Juden. Zur Zwangsarbeit als Element der Verfolgung 1938–1943* (Berlin 1997), 43.

quarters in Vienna had already issued an almost identically worded decree on May 24.: "It has been ordered that unpleasant Jews, especially those with prior criminal convictions, are to be arrested and transported to Dachau Concentration Camp."[19] In the last days of May, the Viennese Police arrested 650 Jews. As is evident from a note of Eichmann's dated May 30, several transports were planned. A total of 5,000 "previously convicted or asocial elements" were to be taken to Dachau, 4,000 of them from Vienna and the rest from the provinces.[20]

On May 31, the first train with 601 Jewish Austrians left Vienna traveling in the direction of Dachau; on June 3, the second followed with 593 Jews.[21] But then, early in June, Heydrich combined the Hitler operation with a raid by the Reich Criminal Police Office planned Reich-wide for mid-June, with the goal of sending so-called asocials to concentration camps.[22] On June 25, the next transports arrived at Dachau Concentration Camp with 589 Austrian Jews, but also with 744 Austrian non-Jews, almost half of them classified as "Reich forced labor" (*Arbeitszwang Reich*).[23] Just as in Austria, a disproportionately large number of Jews were arrested throughout the Reich during the so-called Asozialen-Aktion. In the concentration camps they then regularly fell victim to special harassment.[24]

SEGREGATED LABOR DEPLOYMENT: AN IDEA FROM VIENNA, FALL 1938

Harassment and internment in concentration camps could force departure, but could not resolve the basic contradiction in the anti-Jewish policy – in other words that due to persecution, Jews increasingly did not have the money to leave the country. The social situation of Austrian Jews soon deteriorated rapidly. Added to the plundering, Aryanization, clearing of residences, and arrests in the first weeks were dismissals of numbers of Jewish employees from newspapers, theaters, public institutions, city administrations, and then, in summer, from private businesses.[25] In April or May – not in Octo-

---

[19] YV Jerusalem, 030/ No. 36, Fols. 4–5, Gestapo decree, May 24, 1938.

[20] YV Jerusalem, 051/OSOBI, No. 88 (Moscow 500/1/261), Fol. 33, Note of Eichmann, May 30, 1938.

[21] Jonny Moser, "Österreich," in *Dimension des Völkermords. Die Zahl der jüdischen Opfer des Nationalsozialismus*, edited by Wolfgang Benz (Munich, 1991), 67–93, here 88.

[22] See Chapter 1 and Gruner, *Der geschlossene Arbeitseinsatz*, 41–45.

[23] On June 15 and 17, 24 and 96 Jews, respectively, and at the same time, 414 non-Jews arrived. On June 24, 330 Austrian Jews were delivered, and on June 25, 155 Austrian Jews and 314 Austrians categorized as "Reich forced labor." These figures were made available to me by the Archiv der KZ-Gedenkstätte Dachau, for which I thank Dr. Barbara Distel.

[24] See Chapter 1 and Gruner, *Der geschlossene Arbeitseinsatz*, 41–45.

[25] Jonny Moser, "Die Katastrophe der Juden in Österreich 1938–1945," in *Voll Leben*, edited by Wolfgang Plat, 233–243; *Sopade*, Vol. 5, 732–735, No. 7, July 1938; Safrian and Witek, *Und keiner war dabei*, 61–65; Rosenkranz, *Verfolgung*, 127 and 151.

ber as is usually assumed – the process of forcibly concentrating the Jews from the province in Vienna had also begun, by order of the Reichsführer SS and Chief of the German Police, even more drastically aggravating mass poverty.[26] Soon, 60,000 of an estimated 180,000 Viennese Jews, essentially one in every three, were regarded as socially needy. In Germany at this point in time, poverty affected "only" one in every eight.[27] Many Austrian Jews thus lacked the money to flee persecution. To speed expulsion, Eichmann and the SS Security Service established the Central Office for Jewish Emigration (*Zentralstelle für jüdische Auswanderung*). In addition to organizing expulsion, the functions of the Central Office included monitoring Jewish organizations and "supervising retraining sites."[28] But even Eichmann's new system of plundering rich Jews to finance the emigration of impoverished Jews, which was being tested in the Central Office, did nothing to change the basic situation.

The Viennese labor administration first reacted in late summer 1938 to growing Jewish unemployment and poverty, and to the resulting dependency on the Nazi state, at a time of general labor shortages. Friedrich Gärtner,[29] President of the Austrian branch office of the Reich Institute for Labor Placement and Unemployment Insurance, wrote on September 20, 1938, to Reich Commissar Josef Bürckel, about "forced labor as a means of handling" unemployed Austrian Jews, who in the meantime numbered more than 10,000 and some of whom received unemployment assistance: "It just won't do that these Jews are granted support from public funds, while at the same time laborers are urgently needed. . . . I have therefore already made arrangements to employ Jews supported by public means in excavation work, quarry work, etc., until they are able to emigrate."[30]

On October 11, 1938, Gärtner was already able to report to Bürckel that 200 Austrian Jews were being utilized for public projects in the Vienna

---

[26] Michael Wildt (ed.), *Die Judenpolitik des SD 1935–1938. Eine Dokumentation* (Munich, 1995), 188, Doc. No. 29, SD II 112 Report for April–May 1938. The October date appears in H. G. Adler, *Der verwaltete Mensch. Studien zur Deportation der Juden aus Deutschland* (Tübingen, 1974), 8; and still in Saul Friedländer, *Nazi Germany and the Jews. Vol. 1: The Years of Persecution, 1933–1939* (New York, 1997), 245.

[27] Figures are according to Wildt, *Die Judenpolitik*, 200, Doc. No. 32, Situation report of the SD II 112 for 1938.

[28] Österreichisches Staatsarchiv/Archiv der Republik (ÖStA/AdR) Vienna, Bürckel Materials, No. 1762/2, Fols. 45–47, Circular decree of Bürckel, August 8, 1938. On the founding, see Gabriele Anderl, "Die 'Zentralstelle für jüdische Auswanderung' in Wien, Berlin und Prag – ein Vergleich," in *Tel Aviver Jahrbuch für deutsche Geschichte*, 23 (1994): 276.

[29] Born on September 30, 1882, in Ahaus; was President of the Westphalian regional labor office in 1927–34; was director of the Austrian branch office of the Reich Ministry of Labor in 1938–40; and was Reich Inspector for Labor Utilization in 1943–45.

[30] ÖStA/AdR Vienna, Bürckel Materials, No. 1762/2, Fols. 40–41, Excerpt quoted by Rosenkranz, *Verfolgung*, 173–174.

regional labor office district in "segregated groups working apart." Gärtner appealed to the Reich Commissar to exert pressure on public builders to make separate work sites available, whether inside or outside Vienna. Initial experience was good, in Gärtner's view, because both office employees and over 1,000 laborers and craftsmen were unemployed.[31] Bürckel was pleased that "unemployed Jews" were being "enlisted for work." In addition, he demanded of the labor administration that the Jews be strictly segregated in the workplace and called for their use preferably "in segregated columns for large-scale projects."[32] In short order, "exclusively single, unemployed Jews" were to go to work "at several Reich Autobahn work sites" as "a temporary relief measure,"[33] and later, hundreds of Jewish forced laborers were to work on dam and power plant construction projects.

In an initiative parallel to that of the labor administration, the President of the Viennese Property Transfer Office (*Vermögensverkehrsstelle*),[34] Walter Rafelsberger, worked in constant contact with Reich Commissar Bürckel's office on "proposals for the effective removal of all Jews (*Entjudung*)" from Austria.[35] His plans included the construction of mass barracks camps. "To simplify start-up," he first wanted to establish "a camp for male inmates only" in order to simultaneously facilitate "urgent removal" of about 10,000 unemployed Jews. At the end of October 1938, the construction of a first camp[36] was started in the Marchfeld area on Bürckel's instructions.[37]

Although this project could never be put into effect to the extent intended, the Viennese labor administration nevertheless systematically expanded utilization of unemployed Jews. The Austrian branch office of the Reich Institute for Labor Placement and Unemployment Insurance proposed to Reich Commissar Bürckel on November 30, 1938, that unemployed Jewish men and women, who in the meantime numbered over 11,000, be put to work "at special construction sites (street sewers, drainage systems, and also stone and gravel extraction), as well as in production operations (internal work

---

[31] Ibid., No. 2160/7, Fol. 55, Bürckel to Gärtner, October 11, 1938.

[32] Ibid., Fol. 54, Bürckel to Gärtner, October 21, 1938.

[33] Ibid., No. 2160/00/1, Fols. 35–36, Rafelsberger to Vice-President Barth, October 27, 1938, Attachment, "Third Supplement to the Proposals for Removal of Jews."

[34] On the mission and history of the Viennese property transfer office, see Susanne Heim and Götz Aly, "Die Ökonomie der 'Endlösung,'" in *Beiträge zur Nationalsozialistischen Gesundheits- und Sozialpolitik*, Vol. 5 (Berlin, 1987), 27–30.

[35] On this project already, see Rosenkranz, *Verfolgung*, 208–210; Götz Aly and Susanne Heim, *Vordenker der Vernichtung* (Hamburg, 1991), 40–41.

[36] Lists with dates and source citations for all camps with Austrian Jews confirmed to date in Austria and Germany are printed in Gruner, *Zwangsarbeit und Verfolgung*, Appendix.

[37] ÖStA/AdR Vienna, Bürckel Materials, No. 2160/00/1, Fols. 32–33, Rafelsberger to Bürckel, October 25, 1938, Attachment, "Second Supplement to the Proposals for Effectively Carrying Out the Removal of Jews"; ibid., Fols. 35–36, Rafelsberger to Barth, October 27, 1938, "Third Supplement to the Proposals for the Removal of Jews." For details, see Gruner, *Zwangsarbeit und Verfolgung*, Excursus III and IV.

halls, for example, in the electrical industry)." The latter option, in the Reich Institute's view, was particularly suitable for Jewish women. But as too few such work sites for columns were available in Austria, the Viennese branch office had already "started negotiations with offices in the Old Reich to arrange placement of Jews outside Austria." The transfer of 500 to 700 Jews for water control projects had been arranged with the Hanover Waterways Directorate (*Wasserstraßendirektion*).[38] After the November pogrom, the Austrian prototype was to serve as the model for compulsory employment of Jews throughout the Reich.

THE BEGINNING OF FORCED LABOR, END OF 1938–SPRING 1939

After the November pogrom in 1938, the Nazi leadership agreed on a two-pronged strategy: expulsion, and strict segregation of the persons left behind. This policy was to be directed centrally but implemented with a division of labor among various agencies. A policy of this kind, although uncoordinated, had already been put into practice in Austria months earlier by the NSDAP, the Reich Commissar, the SD Central Office for Jewish Emigration, and the municipalities.[39] A basic element of the forced-community plan was revised control over access to the labor market. In a concerted action of labor offices, local authorities, and local Party offices, all unemployed Jews were to be put to work expeditiously as unskilled laborers for state and municipal construction and projects, as well as in private enterprises or divisions of enterprises.

To ensure effective organization of compulsory employment, the Viennese labor office established an office for the placement of Jews (*Judenvermittlungsstelle*) as comparable big cities such as Berlin did in Germany. In January 1939, the office for the placement of Jews already estimated the number of unemployed Jews at 13,000. Even though thousands escaped registration by relinquishing their support, there were not enough suitable workplaces available for segregated labor in columns. For that reason, Reich Commissar Bürckel held discussions on January 24 in Vienna with the chief of the labor administration, Gärtner, on forced labor of unemployed Jews. At that point, 100 men were working on construction of the Liesing Canal in Vienna, but the first fifty men had already been sent to Emsland in northern Germany.[40] Gärtner continued to negotiate further with the Viennese

---

[38] ÖStA/AdR Vienna, Bürckel Materials, No. 2160/7, Fols. 46–49, Letter of the Reich Institute for Labor Placement and Unemployment Insurance, November 30, 1938, and Attachment, Statistics on "Unemployed Jews – Country of Austria, Status as of October 25, 1938."

[39] See Gruner, *Zwangsarbeit und Verfolgung*, Chapter 1.

[40] ÖStA/AdR Vienna, Bürckel Materials, No. 2160/7, Fol. 41, Note of Bürckel, January 26, 1939.

magistrate: "In Gärtner's view, utilization of Jewish workers in agriculture for cultivation and harvesting work could not be considered, mainly because the farming population could not be expected to take the Jewish workers into their households. He did anticipate, however, that utilization of Jewish workers for road construction projects, drainage work, and the like would be successful even within the Vienna Gau, because it would be possible there to take the laborers to the work site early in the morning with privately owned transportation and to transport them back from the site into the city in the evening."[41]

Two months later, Jewish men constituted almost a third of all the available unemployed persons in Austria, because in the meantime many Aryan unemployed workers had been placed in Germany or in Austria itself.[42] Against this background, Reich Commissar Bürckel demanded a report from the labor administration about its efforts to use Jews.[43] Gärtner reported proudly at the end of March 1939 that thanks to his direct collaboration with the president of the Lower Saxony regional labor office, 400 unemployed Jews had been successfully placed in that region. Agreement also had been reached, he continued, on assignment of an additional 1,500 Jews to construction of the Rappbode Dam and other projects. The Vienna municipal administration then employed 170 Jews for garbage leveling, at the time a common practice of the municipalities in the Old Reich.[44] In addition, a number of Viennese brickworks began to exploit small numbers of Jews. On April 15, the labor administration received the following report: "In the meantime, the brickworks in Vienna have acted on our ideas and are attempting to comply with the wishes of the Gauleiter regarding employment of Jews as laborers in the brickworks. Yesterday morning, fifty of the approximately 150 to 200 Jews who reported to the labor office in Herbst Street were selected for work in the Wienerberger Ziegelei AG, the Ziag,[45] and the Wiener Ziegelwerke AG."[46]

[41] Wiener Stadt- und Landesarchiv, MA 212, Carton 24, R 30, no folio numbers, Note of the head of Office Group III, February 2, 1939.

[42] In January, Jews were still 10 percent of the unemployed males, but in March, they constituted a third of the unemployed males, whose number had now fallen to 42,284; ÖStA/AdR Vienna, Federal Ministry for Social Administration, Carton 379, no folio numbers, Statistics on Unemployed Males in the Ostmark, January 31, February 28, and March 15, 1939.

[43] ÖStA/AdR Vienna, Bürckel Materials, No. 2160/7, Fol. 40, Bürckel to Gärtner on March 4, 1939.

[44] Ibid., Fols. 39 and verso, Reich Ministry of Labor, Vienna branch office (Gärtner) to Bürckel, March 25, 1939.

[45] Ziegelindustrie AG "Ziag" Wien.

[46] ÖStA/AdR Vienna, Bürckel Materials, No. 2225/6, Vol. I, no folio numbers, Trade group for the brick industry, the Ostmark, to the Reich Ministry of Labor, Vienna branch office, April 15, 1939. See ibid., No. 2160/7, Fols. 35 and verso, Reich Ministry of Labor, Vienna branch office, to Bürckel, May 19, 1939.

VIENNESE JEWS FOR DIKE CONSTRUCTION IN LEER, EAST FRIESLAND

The Austrian labor administration had already arranged with the Lower Saxony labor administration in March 1939 to utilize Viennese Jews for flood control construction in the Leda-Jümme region.[47] After the plan to use convicts had failed,[48] local authorities heard about allocation of Jews throughout the Reich and immediately threw in their lot with this new option. Government Building Surveyor Krause from the Leda-Jümme construction department of the Leer hydraulic construction office (*Wasserbauamt*) had already paid a visit on February 1, 1939, to the Hanover regional labor office. He declared himself willing to engage Jewish unemployed persons from Vienna. The regional labor office recommended that all of the not-yet-completed work be reported as urgent emergency work. "No mixed columns" were allowed "to be formed"– only completely separate groups. Two hundred fifty Jewish workers and 150 non-Jewish workers were to dam up the Leda and to expand dikes and banks.[49] The Leer construction department for building up the Ems dikes (*Bauabteilung Emsdeicherhöhung*) had also been negotiating since January with the president of the Aurich administrative district about allocation of 200 Austrian Jews for an expedited labor project.[50]

On March 16, 1939, the Reich Minister of Labor authorized an assistance subsidy of RM 3 per workday for every job in which unemployed Austrian Jews were utilized. On March 23, the Hanover regional labor office warned the responsible officials in Leer and Aurich that, if they did not get the work program on track fast enough, the Jews would be sent to other parts of the Reich.[51] Representatives of the Leda-Jümme construction department, the department for building up the Ems dikes, and the labor office of the Aurich administrative district met for that reason on March 27.[52] The Leer hydraulic construction office then negotiated at the beginning of April with

---

[47] Ibid., No. 2160/7, Fol. 39 and verso, Gärtner to Bürckel, March 25, 1939.

[48] Niedersächsisches Staatsarchiv (StA) Aurich, Rep. 16/3, No. 196, no folio numbers, Leer district administrator to the president of the Aurich administrative district, September 18, 1938.

[49] Ibid., Hydraulic construction office, Leda-Jümme construction department in Leer (Krause) to the president of the Aurich administrative district, February 16, 1939, and Request of the president of the Aurich administrative district to the Lower Saxony regional labor office, February 25, 1939.

[50] Ibid., Rep. 32, No. 2237, no folio numbers, Leer construction department for building up the Ems dikes in Leer to the president of the Aurich administrative district, February 11, 1939, with the Attachment, "Request for Assistance to the Lower Saxony Regional Labor Office," February 10, 1939.

[51] Ibid., Hanover regional labor office to the Leer dike judge, March 23, 1939; ibid., Rep. 16/3, No. 196, no folio numbers, Hanover regional labor office to the president of the Aurich administrative district on March 23, 1939.

[52] Ibid., Rep. 32, No. 2237, no folio numbers, Note of Giencke (president of the administrative district), March 27, 1939.

two construction companies, which agreed to use Jews. At the beginning of May the persons responsible for construction traveled with one of the building contractors to Vienna, in order to select Jews.[53]

The first transport arrived in Leer on May 13,[54] but with far fewer than half of the planned workers. Sixty-three Jews were assigned to the contractors Firma Wurpts-Loga and Firma De Boer Emden for the Leda-Jümme construction department, and the remaining sixty to the construction department for building up the Ems dikes.[55] The Viennese Jews were housed in groups of fifty men in barracks, where they had to sleep on straw matresses.[56] Of course, they usually had no experience with heavy excavation work.[57] Because of the workers' inadequate performance, the Leda-Jümme Construction Department, after only two weeks, launched discussions with the German Labor Front and the Trustee of Labor about introduction of a "wage scale for Jews."[58] The Trustee of Labor refused to take that step, but approved the elimination of social benefits such as free housing. The Jews, if they did not improve their performance by June 20, were threatened with "more severe measures."[59] After the deadline had passed, the president of the administrative district reached agreement with the construction department that payments guaranteed contractually, such as compensation for family separation during stays in outside camps, could be taken away from individual Jews.[60]

Although the president of the district administration had once again requested more Austrian Jews from the regional labor office in June 1939, the request produced no result.[61] While in other parts of Lower Saxony, new labor camps were established – for example, for 150 Jews in Hölingen near Wildeshausen by the Prussian Department for Land Development (*Preußische Kulturbauabteilung*) in Diepholz[62] – transfers from Vienna stopped there.[63] Despite the problems, in the final effect the Leer public

---

[53] Ibid., Rep. 16/3, No. 196, no folio numbers, Note of the Leer labor office and the Leda-Jümme construction department in Leer, April 24, 1939.

[54] Ibid., Rep. 32, No. 2249, no folio numbers, Leda-Jümme construction department in Leer to the president of the Aurich administrative district, June 1, 1939.

[55] Ibid.

[56] Ibid., No. 2237, no folio numbers, Leer construction department for building up the Ems dikes, "Statement of Costs for the Employment of Jews," undated.

[57] Ibid., Rep. 16/3, No. 196, no folio numbers, Statement of costs of the hydraulic construction office, June 20, 1939.

[58] Ibid., Rep. 32, No. 2249, no folio numbers, Leda-Jümme construction department in Leer (Krause) to the president of the Aurich administrative district, June 1, 1939.

[59] Ibid., Rep. 16/3, No. 196, no folio numbers, Handwritten note of the president of the Aurich administrative district, June 8, 1939.

[60] Ibid., Note of the president of the Aurich administrative district, June 26, 1939.

[61] Ibid., Handwritten draft for a letter of the president of the Aurich administrative district to the president of the Lower Saxony regional labor office, June 8, 1939.

[62] Werner Meiners, *Geschichte der Juden in Wildeshausen* (Oldenburg, 1988), 304.

[63] Niedersächsisches StA Aurich, Rep. 16/3, No. 196, no folio numbers, Note of the president of the Aurich administrative district, June 26, 1939, for Leda-Jümme enterprises.

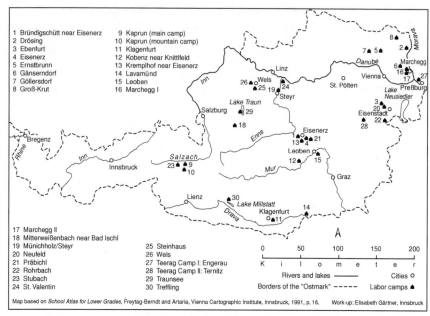

1 Bründigschütt near Eisenerz
2 Drösing
3 Ebenfurt
4 Eisenerz
5 Ernstbrunn
6 Gänserndorf
7 Göllersdorf
8 Groß-Krut
9 Kaprun (main camp)
10 Kaprun (mountain camp)
11 Klagenfurt
12 Kobenz near Knittlfeld
13 Kremplhof near Eisenerz
14 Lavamünd
15 Leoben
16 Marchegg I

17 Marchegg II
18 Mitterweißenbach near Bad Ischl
19 Münichholz/Steyr
20 Neufeld
21 Präbichl
22 Rohrbach
23 Stubach
24 St. Valentin
25 Steinhaus
26 Wels
27 Teerag Camp I: Engerau
28 Teerag Camp II: Ternitz
29 Traunsee
30 Treffling

0　50　100　150　200
K　i　l　o　m　e　t　e　r
Rivers and lakes ——— Cities o
Borders of the "Ostmark" - - - - Labor camps ▲

Map based on *School Atlas for Lower Grades*, Freytag-Berndt and Artaria, Vienna Cartographic Institute, Innsbruck, 1991, p. 16.　　Work-up: Elisabeth Gärtner, Innsbruck

Map 5. Labor Camps for Austrian Jews in the "Ostmark," 1939–42

administration and private enterprises were only able to undertake construction projects because of unemployed Jews recruited involuntarily; otherwise, the projects would long since have been halted for lack of workers. The example of the two labor camps in Leer not only demonstrates the conflict-free collaboration of private companies and public builders with the labor administration and regional offices in allocating forced labor, but also the early consent of most of the participants to discrimination against Jews in terms of labor law.[64]

LABOR CAMPS FOR AUSTRIAN JEWS IN GERMANY, 1939–43[65]

Aschersleben (Saxony-Anhalt)
Denzburg (Upper Silesia)

[64] For the discussion and practice of special law, see Gruner, *Der geschlossene Arbeitseinsatz*, 97–101.
[65] List of camps with source citations and additional details in Wolf Gruner, "Die Arbeitslager für den Zwangseinsatz deutscher und nichtdeutscher Juden im Dritten Reich. Einleitung und 1. Kapitel: Zu den Arbeitslagern für den Zwangseinsatz deutscher und österreichischer Juden im Altreich (1938–1943)," in *Gedenkstättenrundbrief*, published by the Foundation for the Topography of Terror, 78 (1997), 1–17. For additional entries of camps for Austrian Jews, see Gruner, *Zwangsarbeit und Verfolgung*, 312–314.

Gleidingen near Sarstedt (Lower Saxony)
Haldensleben (Saxony-Anhalt)
Hohegaste (East Friesland)
Hölingen near Wildeshausen, Oldenburg Kreis
Kobbensen, Stadthagen Kreis (Schaumburg-Lippe)
Leer I and Leer II (East Friesland)
Nordhausen (Thuringia)
Osterburg (Saxony-Anhalt)
Pogum, Leer Kreis (East Friesland)
Potzhausen, Leer Kreis (East Friesland)
Siems near Mieste (Saxony-Anhalt)
Stendal (Saxony-Anhalt)
Tangermünde (Saxony-Anhalt)
Wendefurt near Blankenburg, Jewish camp II (Harz Mountains)
Werlte Construction Camp II, Rastdorf (Lower Saxony)

FORCED LABOR AND CAMP PLANS, SUMMER 1939

To remedy initial organizational difficulties associated with forced employment, the Reich Ministry of Labor issued a new decree on May 19, 1939. According to the decree, the number of Jews registered as unemployed in many places was too small for deployment in a column; in other places, enough Jews were available but a corresponding number of slots in segregated labor columns were not. Deployments sharply focused on local interests were therefore to be eliminated in favor of supraregional cooperation of the regional labor offices, as demonstrated by the example of Austria with Lower Saxony. According to information of the Ministry, the Ostmark, Saxony, and Silesia ostensibly had a sufficiently large Jewish labor force available that they could send workers to construction projects in other regions.[66]

At that time, 1,000 Viennese Jews were already engaged in road, dam, and dike construction work in Germany, about 700 in Lower Saxony alone. The labor offices in Austria were using Jews primarily away from home for Reich Autobahn and road construction, and for power plant construction. Five thousand two hundred seventy-one unemployed Jews were still registered in Austria, but the capacity for supraregional transfer was thought internally to be exhausted. Not the number, but the physical suitability of the Jews recruited for forced employment was the problem. Of 600 Jews examined by medical officers, only 27 were fit for excavation work. The chief of

[66] Bundesarchiv (BA) Berlin, R 11 RWK, Vol. 1220, Fols. 259–260, Circular decree of the Reich Ministry of Labor, May 19, 1939; see an excerpt in Dieter Maier, *Arbeitseinsatz und Deportation. Die Mitwirkung der Arbeitsverwaltung bei der nationalsozialistischen Judenverfolgung in den Jahren 1938–1945* (Berlin, 1994), 115.

the Austrian labor administration, Gärtner, wanted to proceed more vigorously. On May 19, 1939, he ordered new medical examinations for all Jews registered with the labor office. As this approach had only dim prospects for success in terms of numbers, he ordered that all Austrian Jews who had been supported by the labor office at some time earlier and had ceased to report – there were known to be several thousand – "be summoned to the labor office and examined there so that they could, if appropriate, be obligated to perform labor . . . and directed to suitable jobs."[67] In the planned obligation of persons not receiving support, the Austrian labor administration was once again ahead of the general policies.

In the summer months, the labor offices expanded utilization of unemployed Jews throughout Germany and Austria. Thus, in Vienna, hundreds of Jews were once again recruited for construction projects in the Old Reich, as well as for the Reich Autobahn and the Tauern power plant in Austria itself. A total of around 20,000 Jews were in the segregated labor deployment program of the Reich labor administration. About 2,500 Austrian Jews were employed as forced labor, over a thousand of them in Germany and several hundred in Vienna and in Austrian provincial areas.[68]

About a thousand mostly young people in the camps controlled by the Central Office for Jewish Emigration were also affected by work programs. The SD Central Office in Vienna had developed its own forced-labor system parallel to that of the labor administration. As in Germany, the programs for professional retraining in agriculture, until 1938 organized by Jewish organizations and communities, were now transformed into a system of sealed camps where Jewish young people were concentrated and ostensibly prepared for emigration. The SS placed the old camps and the newly established ones under the protection of the Viennese Jewish Religious Community (*Israelitische Kultusgemeinde*, IKG), not unlike the Reichsvereinigung camps in the Old Reich. At the end of July, there were already fifteen retraining camps and three nurseries in Austria with a total of 947 trainees.[69] In reality, however, the Jews were mostly utilized for work in agriculture and forestry. Four camps, Aggsbach, Aggstein, Landersdorf, and Walpersdorf, were even established under direct control of local forestry administrations. The inmates did not receive wages and were often completely isolated from the outside world.[70]

---

[67] ÖStA/AdR Vienna, Bürckel Materials, No. 2160/7, Fols. 35 and verso, Reich Ministry of Labor, Vienna branch office, to Bürckel on May 19, 1939.

[68] See Gruner, *Zwangsarbeit und Verfolgung*, Chapter II, 3.

[69] YV Jerusalem, 051/OSOBI, No. 111 (500–1–692), Fol. 29, Weekly report of the Viennese IKG, July 25, 1939, 2.

[70] Ibid., Fol. 61, Weekly report of the IKG in Vienna, June 13, 1939. See ibid., Fol. 40, Weekly report of the IKG in Vienna, June 27, 1939; ibid, Fol. 52, Weekly report of the IKG in Vienna, June 20, 1939.

SO-CALLED RETRAINING CAMPS OF THE VIENNESE JEWISH RELIGIOUS COMMUNITY, 1939–41[71]

Absdorf (estate administration, Hechaluz)
Aggsbach (forestry administration, Hechaluz)
Aggstein (forestry administration, Hechaluz)
Fischamend Kafka (estate administration, Hechaluz)
Fischamend Pecina (estate administration, Hechaluz)
Gerolding
Kottingbrunn
Landersdorf (forestry administration, Hechaluz)
Markhof (estate administration, Hechaluz)
Moosbrunn (estate administration)
Nieder-Absdorf
Ottertal – Hammerhof Estate (Alijah Youth)
Schwadorf (estate administration, Hechaluz)
St. Andrä Wördern (retraining for the Viennese Jewish community)
Thalheim (estate administration, Hechaluz)
Walpersdorf (forestry administration, Hechaluz)

The potential of the Viennese Jewish labor force had now been for the most part exhausted. In June 1939, the labor administration had therefore involved Eichmann's Central Office in recruiting men for road construction in the Old Reich. At the request of the Central Office, the Viennese Jewish community was forced to send several thousand letters to its members. However, as former protective detention prisoners and other deported persons were not supposed to be included, it was possible on June 30, 1939, to provide only a "list of 304 persons." After further registration, the Jewish community supplied another list with 103 names on July 3.[72] Hence, the "very limited capacity" of the remaining unemployed Jews "for work and compensation" prevented the orders already on hand for over 500 Jewish workers from being filled. For that reason, Gärtner intensified his forced recruitment in mid-July 1939. The Viennese labor office in Vienna, together with the Gestapo, now carried out an "operation to register unemployed Jews who no longer, or had never, reported to the Labor Office."[73] That meant that in Vienna, Jews who had never been socially dependent on the Nazi state and still had their own means available were now also to be forced into service.

[71] List of camps with source citations and additional details in Gruner, *Zwangsarbeit und Verfolgung*, 312–314.
[72] United States Holocaust Memorial Museum Archives (USHMMA) Washington, DC, RG-11.001M, Reel 8 (OSOBI 500-1-626), no folio numbers, Twenty-sixth weekly report, at the same time sixth monthly report of the IKG in Vienna, July 4, 1939, 2.
[73] ÖStA/AdR Vienna, Bürckel Materials, No. 2160/7, Fols. 10–11 verso, Reich Ministry of Labor, Viennese branch office, to the Reich Ministry of Labor, July 18, 1939.

The radical cooperation of the Viennese labor administration with the Gestapo was connected to a growing number of new persecutory measures for segregation of the Viennese Jews. While Eichmann's Central Office continued to discuss the option of expulsion, the staff of the Reich Commissar and the municipal administration was planning internment of Jews in forced-labor camps. Reich Commissar Bürckel asked Göring personally for support because he wanted finally to implement his old plans, and especially to isolate the impoverished Viennese Jews in a yet-to-be-built "barracks city."[74]

WAR, DEPORTATION, AND FORCED LABOR, FALL 1939

As the war began, the perception prevailed in Vienna that the moment had come for Bürckel's plans to be put into effect throughout the Reich by concerted action. In the first week of September, Göring learned of the joint proposal of the NSDAP Gau leadership, the Bürgermeister, and the *Reichsstatthalter* (Reich Governor) in Vienna to intern all the Viennese Jews in forced-labor camps distributed throughout Reich territory. The Jews were to be guarded and employed as separate units on road construction projects, in brickworks, and in large businesses of many different types.[75] Within the Nazi leadership itself, there had also been some discussion before, if in very vague terms, about introducing forced labor for all Jews in the event of war. But in Berlin, a different decision was made after the rapid conquest of Poland: to deport all German and Austrian Jews to that country.[76]

The decision precluded introduction of general forced labor for Jews in the Reich and obviated establishment of new, expensive camp systems. Nevertheless, Reich Commissar Bürckel persisted at the end of September 1939 in his plan to intern the Jews in massive camps.[77] A first test in Vienna, however, demonstrated that enormous costs would be incurred in "setting up labor camps modeled on the concentration camps (self-sustaining camps)." The best opportunities for utilizing forced labor "without any danger to the labor market" were thought in Vienna to lie in brickworks, the export

---

[74] Ibid., No. 2315/7, Fol. 11, Letter, July 8, 1939.

[75] Ibid., No. 2160/7, Fol. 6–7, Rafelsberger (property transfer office) to Göring's staff (to the attention of Ministerial Director Dr. Gritzbach) on September 5, 1939; see Aly and Heim, *Vordenker*, 31.

[76] See more details on the first deportations in Wolf Gruner, "Von der Kollektivausweisung zur Deportation der Juden aus Deutschland. Neue Perspektiven und Dokumente (1938–1945)," in *Beiträge zur Geschichte des Nationalsozialismus, Bd. 20: Deportationen der Juden aus Deutschland. Pläne, Praxis, Reaktionen 1938–1945* (Göttingen, 2004), 21–62.

[77] ÖStA/AdR Vienna, Bürckel Materials, No. 2315/6, Fol. 192, Bürckel to Neubacher on September 25, 1939. Reproduced in Gerhard Botz, *Wohnungspolitik und Judendeportation in Wien 1938 bis 1945. Zur Funktion des Antisemitismus als Ersatz nationalsozialistischer Sozialpolitik* (Vienna and Salzburg, 1975), 149, Doc. III in the Appendix.

industry, and army production, but not in industry, agriculture and forestry, or garbage disposal sites.[78]

After the basic decision about deportation, the Nazi leadership initially intended to begin by resettling the Jewish population of several annexed territories. Reichsführer SS (RFSS) Heinrich Himmler wanted to submit to Hitler a report on experience gained in the first deportations from the Kattowitz and Mährisch-Ostrau regions, which were to be organized by Eichmann. Hitler then ordered as the first step "relocation of 300,000 Jews without means away from the Old Reich and away from the Ostmark," that is, almost the entire Jewish population.[79] In view of this unexpected perspective, which was communicated to Bürckel on October 10, the plans for internment of Viennese Jews were put on hold.[80] Internally, the information had in fact already been received in Vienna that Eichmann, "in keeping with the express intention of the Führer to cleanse the Ostmark of Jews," had managed to arrange in Berlin that "the Viennese Jews, who almost all were to be considered poor, would be resettled."[81] The first transport from Vienna to Nisko in the General Gouvernement left on October 20, 1939, with 920 persons.[82] Then instructions were even given in Berlin not to involve the Protectorate for the time being in the evacuation operation so that "first and foremost all the Jews can be removed from Vienna as quickly as possible."[83] The priorities were thus redefined, but the entire operation in October was not discontinued completely, as previously assumed.[84] After more than 2,000 people

---

[78] ÖStA/AdR Vienna, Bürckel Materials, No. 2315/6, Fols. 255 and verso, "Data on housing and resettlement of Jews in Vienna," September 30, 1939.

[79] YV Jerusalem, 051/No. 91, no folio numbers, Meeting of Eichmann with the chief of the Gau office, Roden, in Kattowitz (Katowice) on October 9, 1939. See Seev Goshen, "Eichmann und die Nisko-Aktion im Oktober 1939," in *Vierteljahrshefte für Zeitgeschichte*, 29, 1 (1981): 74–96, here 84; Hans Safrian, *Die Eichmann-Männer* (Vienna and Zurich, 1993), 75–78. Goshen believes that this Führer order with the number 300,000 was an invention of Eichmann designed to get the transports in Kattowitz started; Goshen, "Eichmann und die Nisko-Aktion," 85. However, the order, when taken as the concrete result of the plans, fits in with the course of events. The same formulation appears in the memorandum of the Bürckel staff on future persecution in Vienna which was written a few days later. That fact indicates the reality inherent in the formulation; after all, why should Eichmann circulate it at the same time in Vienna; see ÖStA/AdR Vienna, Bürckel Materials, No. 2315/6, Fols. 99–100, "Resettlement of Jews and the Demand for Housing in Vienna," October 11, 1939. Also quoted in Botz, *Wohnungspolitik*, 105.

[80] ÖStA/AdR Vienna, Bürckel Materials, No. 2315/6, Fol. 23, Letter, October 11, 1939; ibid., Fol. 99, "Resettlement of Jews and the Demand for Housing in Vienna," October 11, 1939.

[81] Ibid., Fols. 99–100. Also quoted in Botz, *Wohnungspolitik*, 105.

[82] For general information on the operation, see Botz, *Wohnungspolitik*, 106–107.

[83] ÖStA/AdR Vienna, Bürckel Materials, No. 2315/6, Fol. 22, Note for president of the administrative district Barth, October 25, 1939.

[84] See Gruner, "Von der Kollektivausweisung zur Deportation der Juden aus Deutschland," 31–35. According to Goshen, the operation was halted by Müller's intervention on October 24, so as not to provoke chaos during the deportations of the Jews with haphazard special

had been deported from Vienna alone,[85] Himmler stopped the "expulsion of Jews" at the beginning of November 1939 – until February 1940 – because of "technical difficulties."[86]

CONTINUATION AND EXPANSION OF SEGREGATED LABOR DEPLOYMENT

About a month after the first decision on future deportations, on October 20, 1939, the Reich Ministry of Labor officially informed the regional labor offices that a "reorganization of the Jewish forced labor" had not taken place. In other words, general forced labor had not been introduced in Germany and Austria. At the same time, the Ministry criticized faltering utilization. On the one hand, the Ministry claimed, there were again numerous unemployed Jews in the districts of Brandenburg-Berlin, Silesia, Rhineland, and Austria; on the other hand, local projects had failed in some regions because of the apparent lack of available labor.[87] In the last quarter of 1939, the Austrian labor administration strongly backed dispatch of laborers to camps within Austria, for example to Kaprun for construction of dams, rather than to Germany, as happened previously. In Austria, dam, road, and railway construction projects were considered infrastructure modernization that was important for armament. For that reason, stoppages of construction projects on which Jews were working remained under control, in sharp contrast to the situation in Germany, where camps were closed.[88]

The forced laborers were generally paid at minimum wage levels of unskilled workers. In violation of Reich regulations, Austrian Jewish laborers were not given the supplements that had been granted to workers in the Reich in physically demanding jobs as part of food rationing since the

operations. Nevertheless, according to his own statements, two more transports from Mährisch-Ostrau, one from Kattowitz, and one from Vienna left on October 26; Goshen, "Eichmann," 92. For the two transports from Kattowitz on October 20 and 26, see Sybille Steinbacher, *"Musterstadt" Auschwitz. Germanisierungspolitik und Judenmord in Ostoberschlesien* (Munich, 2000), 114. According to Aly, the reason for stopping on October 20 was that all the Germans from the Baltic, Galicia, and Volhynia were supposed to get resettled first; Götz Aly, *"Endlösung" – Völkerverschiebung und der Mord an den europäischen Juden* (Frankfurt am Main, 1995), 64. Somewhat more refined in his approach, Safrian also speaks of stoppage on October 20 by the RSHA but holds that that did not preclude local transports, if the railway capacity was adequate; Safrian, *Die Eichmann-Männer*, 78–80.

[85] ÖStA/AdR Vienna, Bürckel Materials, Bürckel Office, Red Carton 30, no folio numbers, Office meeting of the Bürgermeister with the deputy Bürgermeister and the office leaders subordinate to the Reich Commissar, November 9, 1939, 8.

[86] ÖStA/AdR Vienna, Bürckel Materials, No. 2315/6, Fol. 25, Himmler to Bürckel on November 9, 1939. More details in Gruner, "Von der Kollektivausweisung zur Deportation der Juden aus Deutschland," 34–35.

[87] Gruner, *Der geschlossene Arbeitseinsatz*, 115.

[88] Gruner, *Zwangsarbeit und Verfolgung*, Chapter III, 3.

beginning of the war.[89] In November 1939, without the authority of any official regulation, the Reich Ministry of Labor telephoned the Central Trade Inspector responsible for distribution of ration cards in Vienna to inform him that supplements for workers performing heavy and very heavy labor were not to be authorized for Jews.[90] The Viennese Jewish community had to intervene with assistance for the hard-working Austrian Jews; it supported many of the Jews ordered to go to labor camps, and not only with food. The fifty Viennese Jews in the camp at Hölingen in the Old Reich required clothing, underwear, shoes, and money.[91]

When in spring 1940 deportations did not resume as announced, the Reich Ministry of Labor took advantage of the change in plans. In Germany, the labor offices everywhere began to obligate Jews who received neither unemployment nor welfare support, a practise already common in Austria. In a departure from previous practice, the labor offices in Germany for the first time sent Jews in massive numbers to industry as unskilled laborers.[92]

In contrast to the Old Reich, however, Austria above all lacked unskilled construction laborers for road and railway construction projects that were important as infrastructure improvements for the armaments industry and the war.[93] In a new wave in May, the Viennese labor office therefore sent 1,000 Jews from Vienna to camps in Carinthia and Styria.[94] (See map 5, p. 116.) In June 1940, still more were sent to labor camps, for example, 248 Jews to Traunsee for construction of Reich roads and Reich Autobahnen.[95] At the same time, however, the labor administration pulled Jewish forced laborers off Autobahn work and passed them surreptitiously to the Reich railway in Vienna for work on railway projects that were important for the war.[96]

---

[89] Thus, in the system of food rationing introduced since the beginning of the war for heavy work, work for long hours, and night work, supplementary food was given out in addition to wages. In the Old Reich, the Leipzig Oberbürgermeister and the Reich Trustee of Labor for Wesphalia – Lower Rhine were successful in their initiatives to cut off partially or completely these supplements to Jewish forced laborers; Gruner, *Der geschlossene Arbeitseinsatz*, 119.

[90] ÖStA/AdR Vienna, Bürckel Materials, Legal Office, ZR No. 1495/1947, no folio numbers, Note on "Treatment of Jews since the Beginning of Food Management," April 15, 1940 (A. Werner), 1.

[91] Rosenkranz, *Verfolgung*, 234.   [92] See Chapter 1.

[93] Bundesarchiv – Militärarchiv (BA-MA) Freiburg im Breisgau, RW 20–18, No. 6, no folio numbers, Situation in the area of the armaments inspection office XVIII, June 22, 1940.

[94] ÖStA/AdR Vienna, Bürckel Materials, Carton 160, Binder 313a, no folio numbers, Weekly report of the Vienna Gau economic advisor, May 15, 1940, 6.

[95] CZA Jerusalem, S 26, No. 1191g, no folio numbers, Report of the IKG in Vienna, 1938–1944/45 (Löwenherz Report), 25.

[96] ÖStA/AdR Vienna, Bürckel Materials, Carton 160, Binder 313a, no folio numbers, Weekly report of the Vienna Gau economic advisor, July 18, 1940, 9; ibid., Reich Railway Collection I, Carton 7, no folio numbers, Draft of an agenda for a meeting with the President of the Reich Railway Directorate in Vienna (Töpfer) on June 11, 1940, with

AUSTRIAN LABOR CAMPS FOR AUSTRIAN JEWS, 1938–42[97]

Bründlgschütt near Eisenerz (Styria)
Drösing near Marchegg (Lower Danube)
Ebenfurth (Lower Danube)
Eisenerz (Styria)
Ernstbrunn (Lower Danube)
Gänserndorf, "Emigrant Retraining Camp" (Lower Danube)
Göllersdorf (Lower Danube)
Groß-Krut (Lower Danube)
Kaprun main camp (Salzburg region)
Kaprun mountain camp, Ebmatten – Limberg Dam (Salzburg region)
Klagenfurt (Carinthia)
Kobenz near Knittlfeld, Judenburg rural Kreis (Styria)
Kremplhof near Eisenerz (Styria)
Lavamünd (Carinthia)
Leoben near Eisenerz (Styria)
Marchegg I (Lower Danube)
Marchegg II (Lower Danube)
Mitterweißenbach, Ebensee camp, Bad Ischl
Münichholz near Steyr, subcamp of Sandhof Estate in Waidhofen
Neufeld an der Leitha (Burgenland)
Präbichl near Eisenerz (Styria)
Rohrbach, Doppl subcamp
Stubach, Hohe Tauern (Salzburg)
St. Valentin (Lower Danube)
Steinhaus near Wels (Upper Danube)
Wels (Upper Danube)
Teerag camp I, Engerau building site (Lower Danube)
Teerag camp II, Ternitz building site (Lower Danube)
Traunsee (Lake Traun), Traunkirchen post office (Upper Danube)
Treffling (Carinthia)

SS LABOR CAMPS IN AUSTRIA

Doppl near Altenfelden, Linz, so-called retraining camp
Sandhof Estate in Waidhofen on the Ybbs, also Windhag retraining camp

---

handwritten comments; ibid., Note for the Senior Reich Railway Councillor Jezdinsky, June 8, 1940.

[97] List of the camps with source citations and additional details in Gruner, *Zwangsarbeit und Verfolgung*, 312–314.

CONDITIONS IN THE LABOR CAMPS, SUMMER 1940

The more than 600 Jewish forced laborers sent to the labor camps in Eisenerz in early summer 1940 were stigmatized from the very beginning with markings and were forbidden to have any contact with local residents, first by the road construction management running the building projects under contract to Styria and then by orders of the Bürgermeister in the towns where the camps were located, Kobenz and Eisenerz.[98] Although weeks later a first order of the Labor Office in Berlin to mark all Jewish forced laborers was blocked by the Reich Security Main Office (RSHA) because it was illegal,[99] Gestapo Chief Heinrich Müller authorized the "measures taken" in the Eisenerz camps in a letter dated May 31 to the Reichsstatthalter of Styria. In Müller's view, marking Jews in no way represented "defamation of Jewish employees." It was necessary, he continued, to prohibit Jews from leaving the camp during certain hours. He could see no limitation on freedom of movement in that.[100]

Gestapo Chief Müller also wrote to the Reichsstatthalter of Styria, however, that the provisions on minimum wage rates and social benefits for forced laborers were to be observed.[101] His intervention did not prevent private companies from reducing the wages of Jews living in the Eisenerz and Präbichl camps by two-thirds.[102] The forced laborers in the camp at Eisenerz worked for Teerag-Asdag AG.[103] Dr. Walter Opitz, president of the Graz regional labor office and at the same time Reich Trustee of Labor, defended the companies to the Reichsstatthalter with a long-familiar argument: Because of poor performance, he had authorized that the enterprises pay forced laborers at the enterprises' own rates.[104] Such random reductions in wages were probably the rule rather than the exception in Austria. In the Traunsee labor camp as well, Jewish forced laborers earned

---

[98] Steirisches Landesarchiv (SteiLA) Graz, I A Pol 386, Ju, 1, 1940, no folio numbers, Judenburg district administrator to the Reichsstatthalter on May 28, 1940. For these documents I am grateful to Florian Freund, Vienna. For detailed information on these labor camps and the conditions for the inmates, see Gruner, *Zwangsarbeit und Verfolgung*, Excursus.

[99] For the events in Berlin, see Gruner, *Der geschlossene Arbeitseinsatz*, Chapter III, 3.

[100] SteiLA Graz, I A Pol 386, Ju, 1, 1940, no folio numbers, Express letter of the the Chief of the Security Police and SD /IV A 5 b (Müller) to the Reich Trustee of Styria, May 31, 1940.

[101] Ibid.

[102] "Thus the companies supposedly promised the Jews an hourly wage of about 60 Pfennig and for the most part only pay 20 Pfennig"; ibid., no folio numbers, Leoben district administrator to the Reichsstatthalter's Office (I A Pol), August 15, 1940.

[103] Central Archives for the History of the Jewish People (CAHJP) Jerusalem, A/W, 426, no folio numbers, Establishment of labor service camps, October 2, 1941. For forced labor and this company, see Stefan August Lütgenau and Alexander Schröck, *Zwangsarbeit in der österreichischen Bauindustrie. Die Teerag Asdag AG 1938–1945* (Innsbruck and Vienna, 2001).

[104] SteiLA Graz, I A Pol 386, Ju, 1, 1940, no folio numbers, Reich Trustee of Labor for Styria-Carinthia to the Reichsstatthalter (I A Pol), October 4, 1940.

so little that their board was just covered. In many cases, they owed money, "contributions for food," to the camp leadership or the construction companies.[105]

In addition to the labor and retraining camps subordinated to the Viennese Jewish community, there were two sites, Sandhof Estate in Waidhofen and Doppl near Altenfelden, which were also called "retraining camps." These camps were in reality operated by the Central Office for Jewish Emigration, and thus by the SS.[106] Since spring 1940, the number of people sent to both camps by the SD Central Office had increased. There was no training at all, only work on roads or railways or in quarries. The recruits evidently received RM 3 every ten days for the heaviest labor.[107] SS men from the 89th Standarte guarded Jewish inmates. Harassment and abuse were nothing out of the ordinary.[108] Recruits were told initially that they would only be in the camp for three months. In reality, most of them had to work there for years, until they were finally deported in 1942.[109]

RENEWED DEPLETION OF THE FORCED-LABOR POOL, SUMMER AND FALL 1940

The victories in the west of Europe once again fortified the basic factors underlying anti-Jewish policies. Eichmann openly informed the functionaries of the Viennese Jewish community at the end of July 1940 "that after the end of the war a total solution of the European Jewish problem will presumably have to be sought."[110] However, the fundamental problem for all the anti-Jewish measures, whether expulsion or deportation, was more than ever the social situation; at that point more than 86 percent of all 50,000

---

[105] CAHJP Jerusalem, A/W, No. 165/6, Fol. 258, Traunsee camp leader to the IKG in Vienna, July 1, 1940.

[106] For the camp Doppl in detail, see Gruner, *Zwangsarbeit und Verfolgung*, Excursus VI.

[107] CZA Jerusalem, S 26, No. 1191g, no folio numbers, Report of the IKG in Vienna, 1938–1944/45 (Löwenherz Report), 26–27; The Jewish Black Book Committee, *The Black Book* (New York, 1943), 175.

[108] SS Camp Leader Robert Walcher was sentenced in 1946 in Austria to ten years incarceration and loss of property because of abuses in both camps and because of appropriation for person gain. There were also proceedings against SS Camp Leader Alfred Slawik in 1948 before the Viennese regional court. For more details, see Gabriele Anderl, "Zwangsarbeit, jüdische 'Auswanderung' und Deportation in Österreich. Geschichte der SS-Lager Doppl und Sandhof sowie der Wiener Leergutsammelstelle," in *Neue Zürcher Zeitung*, August 31, 1999, 40.

[109] YV Jerusalem, 030/No. 62, Fols. 1 and 8, Report on Alijah and Histadruth Noar in Vienna on September 19 and 20, 1942. For Sandhof in more detail, see Anderl, "Zwangsarbeit," 40.

[110] CZA Jerusalem, S 26, No. 1191g, no folio numbers, Report of the IKG in Vienna 1938–1944/45 (Löwenherz Report), 25. See note about summons to Eichmann on July 3, 1940, referenced in Safrian, *Die Eichmann-Männer*, 95.

Jews still living in Vienna received some form of support from the Jewish community.[111]

Eichmann was informed that even "the not inconsiderable number of Jews being used as labor for the public good" did not, as expected, provide relief for the welfare budget of the Jewish community. Many of the men and women called up for labor service, it was said, neither received adequate wages nor had work clothes and appropriate footwear. The reaction of the SD Central Office was cynically to exclude the forced laborers completely from Jewish welfare support. The workers would in the future no longer have any claim either to cash or to food.[112]

In the meantime, the Viennese labor administration had started to use men over sixty-five years old for heavy construction work because the labor pool was once again depleted – despite the new expanded recruiting criteria of summer 1940.[113] The labor administration of the Ostmark therefore also increasingly included Jewish women in forced labor. From fall on, many women were obligated to work at various work sites in Vienna and were also sent to camps in the Old Reich.[114] More and more women, because they were sent away, had to leave behind children and relatives requiring care.[115]

Depletion of the labor pool by labor administrations in the Old Reich and in the Ostmark at the same time resulted in the failure of a special forced-laborer operation. General Inspector Todt had applied to the RSHA several times regarding provision of workers to the Reich Autobahn,[116] so the RSHA demanded in mid-October that the Reichsvereinigung register 10,000 Jewish men eighteen to twenty-five years old in a high-speed operation. The Viennese Jewish community learned that the Austrian Autobahn construction management offices required 2,127 men. However, the number of the men still available was small; most of them were long since working as forced laborers.[117] In Germany, the situation was similar; instead of 10,000,

---

[111] See the extensive excursus in Wolf Gruner, *Öffentliche Wohlfahrt und Judenverfolgung. Wechselwirkungen lokaler und zentraler Politik im NS-Staat (1933–1942)* (Munich, 2002), 283–288.

[112] CZA Jerusalem, S 26, No. 1191g, no folio numbers, Report of the IKG in Vienna 1938–1944/45 (Löwenherz Report), 25.

[113] BA Berlin, R 2 Reich Ministry of Finance, No. 9254 f, Fols. 25–26, Reichsstatthalter in Vienna, State Administration, to the Reich Ministry of Finance, June 20, 1940.

[114] BA Berlin, R 58 (former RSHA PSt. 3), No. 490 Vol. I, no folio numbers, Forty-fourth weekly report of the IKG in Vienna, October 29, 1940, 7.

[115] CAHJP Jerusalem, A/W, No. 591, no folio numbers, Murmelstein (IKG in Vienna) to the Viennese labor office, December 8, 1941, and January 8, 1941; ibid., Löwenherz (IKG in Vienna) to the Viennese labor office, December 10, 1940; ibid., Note of Marie Blechinger, December 8, 1940; ibid., Office director to the research group, December 8, 1940.

[116] BA Berlin, 46.01. General Inspector for German Roadways, No. 1200, Fol. 385, Müller to General Inspector for German Roadways on November 1, 1940. See Chapter 7.

[117] BA Berlin, R 58 (former RSHA PSt. 3), No. 490 Vol. I, no folio numbers, Forty-fourth weekly report of the IKG in Vienna on October 29, 1940, 6–7.

a total of just 1,500 Jews could be sent. Rather than requesting further personnel, the RSHA from then on demanded statistics, on the one hand from the Jewish offices, and on the other from the Gestapo. The statistics encompassed the Jewish men and women capable of working and being used for forced labor Reich-wide since October.[118] The Viennese Gestapo informed the Reichsstatthalter there about these activities. Knowing the situation in the Ostmark, the Gestapo said, there were probably not very many Jews still available. If there were any, however, the Gestapo had no reservations about putting the Jews to work "clearing away destroyed synagogues."[119]

THE STATUS OF FORCED LABOR AND NEW DEPORTATIONS, 1940–41

Massive utilization, in the meantime encompassing tens of thousands, had demanded official definition of the Jews' labor status. Although no consensus was reached, the Reich Ministry of Labor instructed the Trustees of Labor at the beginning of June 1940 to issue regional orders regarding discrimination against Jews under labor law. The orders were to prohibit Jews from receiving contractual or company benefits, bonuses on special holidays, or assistance for births or weddings. As in Germany, local labor offices, private companies, and public builders long since had operated in this manner in Austria. Or, like the responsible Trustee for Labor in Styria, they had already gone far beyond the general guidelines by excluding compulsory employees from the contractual wage scales. The massive utilization of forced labor, encompassing almost 50,000 Jews in Germany and Austria at New Year's 1941, induced further strictures. From that point forward, all Jews in Austria were subject to a special anti-Jewish tax of 15 percent on all income. For the most part, the tax affected forced laborers.[120] Massive allocation fueled discussion in the ministries about the legal definition of forced labor.[121]

The decision regarding "legalization" of the forced-labor system was made against the background of concrete planning for new transports. At the end of 1940, Hitler approved the deportation of 60,000 Viennese Jews into the General Government "while the war was still going on." In the first phase,

---

[118] Gruner, *Der geschlossene Arbeitseinsatz*, 165–167. These Gestapo decrees were also viewed in literature as the beginning of forced labor for Jews; see Adam, *Judenpolitik*, 248.

[119] *Der Prozeß gegen die Hauptkriegsverbrecher vor dem Internationalen Militärgerichtshof (IMT), Nürnberg 14. November 1945–1. Oktober 1946*, Vol. XXIX (Nuremberg, 1948), 174–175, Doc. PS-1948, Note of the Reichsstatthalter in Vienna (I A Pol), November 7, 1940.

[120] "Second Decree for Implementation of the Decree on the Imposition of a Social Compensation Charge," December 24, 1940, *Reichsgesetzblatt*, 1940 I: 1666. See Gruner, *Der geschlossene Arbeitseinsatz*, 194–200.

[121] See Chapter 1.

10,000 were to be taken away in transports in early 1941.[122] The decision was a blatant departure from the interim plan not to conduct deportations until after the war and clearly coincided with instructions to prepare for the attack on the Soviet Union, which again moved an end to the war further out in time.[123] On February 1, the Viennese Jewish community learned about the plan from the Gestapo: "Approximately 1,000 persons are to be processed with each transport; the first transport will depart . . . on February 15. . . . These Jews will be settled in small Kreis city centers." All training courses and the so-called retraining camps now had to be shut down.[124] The Gestapo and the SD Central Office discussed with representatives of the city and the Party the possibility of preferentially deporting individuals without means and giving no consideration to forced employment.[125] The war economy was therefore also informed about the impending "resettlement." The Viennese armaments inspection office (*Rüstungsinspektion*) complained that the transports would enormously aggravate the situation on the Austrian labor market. It was feared that 8,000 Jewish workers potentially would be lost.[126] By March 12, five transports with about a thousand people each were finally taken to the area around Lublin, but then the deportations were again interrupted because of preparations for the attack on the Soviet Union.[127]

After thousands of Austrian Jews had left in transports, Polish Jews suddenly moved to the center of attention of the people responsible for the labor market and the armament economy. Tens of thousands Jews still lived in the annexed Warthegau; they could not be deported for the time being to the General Government for the same reasons as the Austrians. Therefore, in February 1941, the Reichsstatthalter in Posen (Poznán) and the Reich Minister of Labor considered allocating 73,000 Jews from there to serve as forced laborers in the territory of the Reich.[128] The Gau economic advisor in Vienna

[122] IMT, Vol. XXIX, 175, Doc. PS-1950, Letter from Lammers (Chief of the Reich Chancellery) to the Reichsstatthalter in Vienna, Schirach, December 3, 1940; ibid., Letter of the Reich Reichsstatthalter in Vienna to Kaltenbrunner (HSSPF, Military District [*Wehrkreis*] XVII), December 18, 1940.

[123] IMT, Vol. XXVI, 47–52, Doc. PS-446, Directive No. 21, "Barbarossa Case," December 18, 1940.

[124] CZA Jerusalem, S 26, No. 1191g, no folio numbers, Report of the IKG in Vienna 1938–1944/45 (Löwenherz Report), 31–32, Entry on February 1, 1941. Reproduced in Rosenkranz, *Verfolgung*, 258.

[125] YV Jerusalem, 030/No. 84, Fols. 1–3, Note of the Vienna NSDAP Gau leadership, February 12, 1941.

[126] BA-MA Freiburg im Breisgau, RW 20–17, No. 14, no folio numbers, Armaments Inspection Office XVII in Vienna to the economic armaments office, February 12, 1941, Attachment with a situation report, 12. See Schausberger, *Rüstung in Österreich*, 79.

[127] CZA Jerusalem, S 26, No. 1191g, no folio numbers, Report of the IKG in Vienna 1938–1944/45 (Löwenherz Report), 34.

[128] For details, see Gruner, *Der geschlossene Arbeitseinsatz*, 184–186, as well as Chapter 6 in the present study.

informed the armament offices on March 26 that the "Jews from Posen were to be used for road construction projects in the Lower Danube region."[129] Some of these workers had already been scheduled to construct a junction line for the Reich Railway directorate in Vienna.[130] Although the plan met with approval in private and public enterprises, the RSHA criticized it sharply for reasons relating to persecutory policy. Then, at the beginning of April 1941, Hitler categorically prohibited utilization of "Jews from the General Government and the Warthegau" in the Reich.[131] After that, the Reich Ministry of Labor instructed the Vienna–Lower Danube regional labor office to utilize either prisoners of war or, once again, "Jewish workers" from their own districts instead of the anticipated Polish Jews.[132]

Against the background of the deportations in February and March 1941, the SD in Vienna, much like the RSHA in the Old Reich, began to collaborate directly with the labor administration. To finance the planned mass deportations, expenditures of Jewish offices were to be reduced by dismissals and cancellations of training courses. Together, the two agencies accelerated use of forced labor. The Central Office helped register still more Jews, especially young people. Several hundred girls and women were thus sent in May 1941 to harvest asparagus in Germany. Various labor camps were established there to house Jewish women. The Magdeburg Gestapo, which had responsibility for the project, prohibited the female forced laborers from attending local events and frequenting restaurants, or from leaving the camp location. The times for going out were limited to a very few hours on weekends. On the other hand, marking the Viennese Jewish women was considered initially and then again rejected because of their total isolation from the local population,[133] even though marking was in the meantime a common practice for forced laborers in Berlin.[134]

The office for the placement of Jews in the Viennese labor office controlled the allocation of 6,000 women and men for forced labor in August 1941.[135]

---

[129] BA-MA Freiburg im Breisgau, RW 20–18, No. 9, no folio numbers, File note on the session of March 26, 1941, Attachment to the situation report of the Armaments Inspection Office XVIII at the end of March, 1941, Salzburg, March 28, 1941, 2.

[130] BA Berlin, R 3901 (former R 41) Reich Ministry of Labor, No. 193, Fol. 106, President of the Vienna – Lower Danube regional labor office to the Reich Ministry of Labor, April 21, 1941.

[131] Ibid., Fol. 97, Express letter of the Reich Ministry of Labor, April 7, 1941, to revoke the decree of March 14, 1941.

[132] Ibid., Fol. 110, Reich Ministry of Labor, Department Va, Labor Utilization (Dr. Letzsch) to the Vienna – Lower Danube regional labor office, May 17, 1941.

[133] Verwaltungsarchiv Landkreis Oschersleben, Registration of Hornhausen, No. 184, Fols. 6–8, Circular of the Magdeburg Gestapo, May 23, 1941. For more detail on this deployment, see Chapter 2, first section, in the present study, and especially, Wolf Gruner, *Zwangsarbeit und Verfolgung*, Excursus VIII, 226–234.

[134] See Gruner, *Der geschlossene Arbeitseinsatz*, 186–190.

[135] YV Jerusalem, 030/No. 34, no folio numbers, Thirty-sixth weekly report of the IKG in Vienna, September 9, 1941, 5–6.

Two thousand people still worked for the Viennese Jewish community.[136] The proportion of people utilized for forced labor and working in Jewish establishments was not even 50 percent of the Jews of working age, but after the transports to Poland this percentage was remarkable.[137] In contrast, exploitation in Germany was in the meantime almost 100 percent. At that point, a total of between 57,000 and 59,000 Jewish Germans and Austrians toiled in the segregated labor deployment program.

THE NEW REICH-WIDE DEPORTATIONS, FALL 1941

As a result of anti-Jewish policies, persecuted persons in both Germany and Austria lived in isolation in a forced community, the basic prerequisite for deportation. And it was just at this point, shortly before new mass transports, that the Nazi state, with the October 3 decree, legalized the long-standing practice of forced labor in the German Reich. The relatively large number of Jewish forced laborers – several tens of thousands – did not, however, prevent the Nazi leadership from deciding to deport the entire Jewish population in the immediate future. Compared to the foreign forced laborers, who numbered in the millions, Jewish forced laborers in Germany, and to an even greater extent those in Austria, were inconsequential in number. As the victory over the Soviet Union was expected to be quick, the decision was made by Hitler in July or August 1941 to initiate new transports, and preparations had reached their critical stage by September 1941. According to Hitler, "the first cities that were to be freed of all Jews (*judenfrei*)" were Berlin, Vienna, and Prague.[138]

The Viennese Jewish community was told at the end of September that families would be "resettled" as separate groups, and Jews capable of working would then be employed in the Warthegau "in defense companies for pay." The first transport would leave on October 15 and the last on November 3. In the first phase, 5,000 Viennese Jews were to be "evacuated" to the Getto Litzmannstadt (Lodz) in the Warthegau.[139] The mass deportations, which began in Vienna on October 15 (that is, three days before deportations in the Old Reich) included many forced laborers. The Security Police assured that there would be exemptions for the Wehrmacht and

---

[136] *Jüdisches Nachrichtenblatt*, Viennese edition, August 1, 1941, p. 1.

[137] CAHJP Jerusalem, A/W, No. 421, no folio numbers, Note of Murmelstein for Löwenherz, August 25, 1941.

[138] *Die Tagebücher von Joseph Goebbels. Teil II: Diktate 1941–1945*, edited by Elke Fröhlich as commissioned by the Institut für Zeitgeschichte and with support of the State Archive Service of Russia, Vol. 1 (Munich and others, 1996), 485, Entry of September 24, 1941. For more details see Gruner, "Von der Kollektivausweisung zur Deportation der Juden aus Deutschland," 46–52.

[139] CAHJP Jerusalem, A/W, No. 3015, Fols. 28–29, Note on visit with Brunner, September 30, 1941. See CZA Jerusalem, S 26, No. 1191g, no folio numbers, Report of the IKG in Vienna 1938–1944/45 (Löwenherz Report), 37.

the labor offices. But this issue was of scarcely any significance in Vienna – compared to the situation in many German big cities – as at this point only a few Viennese Jews were employed in the armaments industry and therefore were protected from transports as workers important for the war effort.[140]

Instead, hundreds of Austrian forced laborers lived in camps and worked for the most part in road and power plant construction. Two years after the shut-downs in Germany, Austrian road projects then also had to be halted in favor of armament projects because of the looming defeat of the Wehrmacht. In a number of camps, work continued anyway, clearly only because of the Jewish forced laborers. As far as the work on the Traunkirchen-Ebensee road was concerned, the president of the Upper Danube regional labor office requested authorization from the Ministry of Labor "to continue until the withdrawal of the Jews." He acknowledged that he had already been informed by the Higher SS and Police Leader in Vienna about the imminent "transfer of these Jews to Litzmannstadt," but no other "allocation of Jews in the Upper Danube" region would be possible.[141]

SPECIAL LABOR ASSIGNMENTS IN VIENNA, FIRST HALF OF 1942

At the beginning of February 1942 about 670 Jewish forced laborers still lived in seventeen Austrian labor camps and about 400 lived in five German camps. In Vienna itself, about 4,500 Jewish women and men were engaged in forced labor.[142] In contrast to the situation in Germany, where in the meantime Jews labored predominantly in industry, just 57 Jews worked in armaments companies in Vienna, together with 4,000 foreigners and 3,500 prisoners of war.[143]

The deportations rendered obsolete the division of labor characteristic of anti-Jewish policy since the 1938 pogrom. Viennese Jews were subjected to special operations that had nothing to do with labor allocation by the labor administration. Possibly on the model of several big German cities, which

---

[140] ÖStA/AdR Vienna, Reichsstatthalter Baldur von Schirach, 1a Pol, 1301, No. 2289/41, no folio numbers, Stapo headquarters in Vienna (II B/ J. Huber) to Reichsstatthalter (Dr. Dellbrügge), October 10, 1941.

[141] BA Berlin, R 3901 (former 41) Reich Labor Ministry, No. 195, Fol. 221–222, President of the Linz regional labor office to Reich Minister of Labor (Dr. Timm), October 23, 1941. According to an inquiry of the Reich Ministry of Labor to the Commissioner for the Four-Year Plan, agreement was reached on November 18; ibid., Fol. 224, Commissioner for the Four-Year Plan and General Commissioner for Administration, construction industry, to the commissioner for the Linz subregion on November 18, 1941.

[142] CAHJP Jerusalem, A/W, No. 413, no folio pages, Statistics of the IKG in Vienna, Status as of February 6, 1942.

[143] BA-MA Freiburg im Breisgau, RW 21–63, No. 4, no folio numbers, Quarterly report on the war diary of the Viennese armaments command, January 1–March 31, 1942.

had assigned Jews to snow removal in the previous winters,[144] the Viennese Gestapo asked on the evening of February 16, 1942, for the Jewish Community to make thousands of Jews available the next morning for snow removal. Despite recruiting difficulties (because most Jews capable of working were being utilized for forced labor), in the following weeks thousands of women and old men had to help remove ice and snow.[145] This special work assignment continued in March. Without involving the labor office, the Gestapo had provided short-term assistance to the Vienna municipal administration in the form of about 3,000 laborers at no cost.[146]

Only a few weeks later, at the end of May 1942, the Gestapo informed the Jewish community of Vienna that workers had to be made available again for a special operation, this time at the request of the NSDAP Gau leadership. On Sundays, wood was to be cut in the Wiener Wald.[147] The only forced laborers excused were those who had to work on Sunday for their companies or were sick. Although many more people had been selected, only 145 men appeared to cut wood on May 31. The Jewish community notified more Jews on every subsequent Sunday, but not even once did the number of people who showed up actually reach 200. Several private enterprises had in the meantime introduced their own Sunday work, for example unloading freight trains.[148] In addition, since May 31, a total of 4,000 people had been deported from Vienna, among them 1,500 men under sixty-five years old. Despite these obstacles, a total of 1,360 Jews performed heavy labor for the wood operation for thirteen Sundays in a row, until August 23, 1942.[149]

ACCELERATION OF DEPORTATIONS AND THE FORCED LABORERS, SECOND HALF OF 1942

At the beginning of June 1942, only 28,000 Jewish women and men still lived in Vienna. The labor administration employed 5,020 Austrian Jews, men and women. One thousand, seven hundred twenty-five women and men worked for the Jewish community. The proportion of forced laborers was over 50 percent of the people capable of working.[150] As the Nazi leadership had decided quickly to deport all the Jews, new mass transports became

---

[144] Gruner, *Der geschlossene Arbeitseinsatz*, 122, 176, and 293.

[145] CAHJP Jerusalem, A/W, No. 424, no folio pages, Note of the IKG office directors (undated, about February 17, 1942).

[146] YV Jerusalem, 030/No. 13, no folio numbers, Activity report of the IKG in Vienna and the council of elders in 1942, 14.

[147] CAHJP Jerusalem, A/W, No. 445, no folio pages, Note about a telephone call of the Gestapo (Krisch), May 28, 1942.

[148] Ibid., Note of the IKG in Vienna, June 1 and 16, 1942.

[149] YV Jerusalem, 030/No. 13, no folio numbers, Activity report of the IKG in Vienna and the council of elders for 1942, 16.

[150] Fifty-one hundred twenty-nine men who were fourteen to sixty-five years old were considered capable of working. However, as persons over sixty-five years old also had to work, the

increasingly common throughout the Reich, but also in Vienna. The male and female Austrian forced laborers were not permitted to leave their camps, even when they wanted to share the fate of their family members in Vienna who had already been put in collection camps. The camp leadership refused to release several Jewish women in Aschersleben because there was no order from Vienna.[151] The forced laborers in Wendefurt Jewish camp near the Rappbodetal Dam in the Harz Mountains shared this experience.[152]

In mid-September, the SD Central Office closed down its own labor camp in Doppl and sent the inmates to Vienna.[153] Doppl's end was a signal. Now the Austrian camps for Jews were closed, with some exceptions, such as the camp for power plant construction in Lavamünd. The Austrian Jewish inmates of German labor camps were also all sent to Vienna. The last sixty women were moved from Nordhausen and Aschersleben, and the last twenty-five men from Wendefurt. Considerably more than 100 inmates from several camps were thus deported on October 5 from Vienna to Minsk.[154] The same fate befell the employees of the Vienna Jewish Religious Community. On November 23, 1942, the Reichsstatthalter liquidated the Jewish community with the following justification: "As the Jewish question in Vienna seems to be for the most part resolved, the basis for the legal existence of the Jewish community in Vienna is gone."[155] Through persecution, expulsion, and deportation, the Nazis had reduced the number of Austrian Jews within four years from 200,000 to only a few thousand, most of them living in mixed marriages.[156]

FORCED LABOR OF JEWISH PARTNERS FROM MIXED MARRIAGES

Forced labor of Jewish men and women living in mixed marriages was reorganized in the Reich in March 1943 on the order of the RHSA; from that point on only unskilled labor could be considered. The Viennese labor office had long since been calling up Jews from mixed marriages for segregated

percentage of persons involved in forced labor can only be estimated; CAHJP Jerusalem, A/W, No. 416, no folio pages, Statistics of the IKG in Vienna, Status as of June 1, 1942.

[151] Ibid., No. 430, no folio numbers, Two teletypes from Aschersleben, June 1, 1942.

[152] Ibid., Letters and teletypes of the Reichsvereinigung, Hanover-Kassel district office to the IKG in Vienna, June 3, 1942.

[153] As their transport was delayed, they again were utilized for forced labor in Vienna; YV Jerusalem, 030/No. 62, Fol. 1, Report on Alijah and Histadruth Noar in Vienna, September 19 and 20, 1942.

[154] From the private archive of Jonny Moser. A copy is in the hands of the author; the document includes handwritten excerpts from the deportation lists.

[155] YV Jerusalem, 030/No. 15, Fol. 9, Circular letter on the disbanding of the IKG in Vienna, November 23, 1942.

[156] LBIA New York, Microfilms, Wiener Library, 500 Series, No. 526, Inspector for statistics with the RFSS, January 1, 1943 (Korherr Report), 5 (also in BA Berlin, NS 19, No. 1570).

labor deployment. At the beginning of 1943, after the deportations were almost complete, SS statistics showed 1,126 Jewish forced laborers in Vienna and seven in Salzburg; hence, the majority consisted of Jews from mixed marriages.[157] In order to expand the forced-labor program, the labor administration registered Jews living in mixed marriages and Mischlinge for the first time in several operations starting at the beginning of 1943.[158]

In contrast to the situation in the Old Reich, in Vienna the labor office apparently followed the RSHA order for reorganization less scrupulously. Dozens of Austrian Jews continued to work in various Viennese industrial sectors such as light industry, the chemical industry, and the metal-working industry. Many Jews were utilized for excavation and garbage management work, as well as for paper production and leather working – that is, decidedly difficult and dirty jobs. Malvine Böck, who lived in a mixed marriage with a Catholic husband, was assigned to work at one of the garbage dumps located on the periphery of Vienna: "There was a giant platform; a train ran up above, loaded with junk, and we all stood below. The doors were then opened, and all the junk fell down. Then we had to sort as follows: rags, metal, glass, paper, and iron. We buried pieces of iron again immediately, because we knew that they would be used to produce cannons. It was often very dangerous; if we had been caught we would have been charged with sabotage. Sabotage was punishable by death." Later the labor office obligated her, and others, to serve as masonry women: "If a bomb had hit somewhere, we had to clear away bricks."[159] The Wehrmacht was at this time the other operation requiring a great deal of labor. By threatening draconian punishments and conducting several recruiting operations, the labor administration increased the number of Jewish forced laborers to over 3,800 by the end of 1943; that was more than 60 percent of the entire remaining Jewish population. At the end of 1944, more than 90 percent of all Jews were then finally being utilized; ability to perform work and illness played no role at all. Even one in every five persons over sixty-five years old was working, and every third person among children and young people.

By the end of the war, the Viennese labor administration had thus pulled the entire population of Jews living in mixed marriages into the forced-labor program, in sharp contrast to the utilization patterns for full Jews in the years 1938 to 1942. With forced labor, ghettoization, and installation of a council of elders, the Nazis established a forced community for the Jews who had previously been protected, that community being the prerequisite for future deportations. The confusion of war prevented the last Reich-wide act of persecution from being fully realized. The RSHA had ordered deportation to Theresienstadt in mid-January 1945. In Vienna, the victims were

---

[157] Ibid, January 1, 1943 (Korherr Report), 17.
[158] For the following discussion in detail, Gruner, *Zwangsarbeit und Verfolgung*.
[159] Report of Malvine Böck, in *Jüdische Schicksale*, 184–185.

to report for "assignment as labor" on February 19, but then the date was moved by a week. A last transport with one thousand people left Vienna for Theresienstadt in March.[160] Then it was over; the Soviet troops were almost there.

SUMMARY

In the development of anti-Jewish policy, Austria, or rather Vienna, gained a special position after the annexation in 1938. In the first weeks, the SA, SS, and Party hatchet men directed the infamous "scouring operations" in Vienna and at other locations as rituals of public humiliation. Scouring groups mutated relatively quickly into cleaning columns, and Jewish Austrians were recruited spontaneously as unpaid labor to clean streets or offices. Scouring operations, just as arrests for forced labor in concentration camps, were among the methods with which the Jewish population was to be expelled. The impoverishment of that group rapidly exceeded all known dimensions. The chief of the Austrian labor administration, Friedrich Gärtner, reacted in September 1938 to the massive dependency on public welfare and unemployment assistance with the novel measure of forcing unemployed Jews to perform excavation work in segregated columns. After the November pogrom, the Austrian prototype became the model for segregated labor deployment of all Jews in the Reich. In Austria, the labor offices now used hundreds of Jews in columns for garbage management work in Vienna, in brickyards, and in gravel pits for the Reich Autobahn, as well as for Reich road construction and power plant construction. Even though in Vienna thousands at first refused to report to the labor office, and therefore relinquished their unemployment assistance, the number of suitable slots available in labor columns was inadequate to accommodate the Jews who did report. Hence, after negotiations with regional labor offices in the Old Reich, over a thousand Viennese Jews were sent in summer 1939 to perform road, dam, and dike construction, especially in Lower Saxony. In addition to the Jews utilized by the labor administration, over thousand mostly young people had to perform agricultural and forestry work in SD-controlled retraining camps without the promised training. In summer 1939, the Viennese labor office, together with the Gestapo, was already preparing to extend forced labor to all Austrian Jews, once again playing the role of a trailblazer for the Nazis. After the beginning of the war, the Viennese labor administration strongly backed sending Jews to camps inside Austria, as many construction projects in Germany had been halted as a result of the war. In Austria, where infrastructure modernization was part of armament preparations, thousands of Jews thus were sent in 1940 to camps for dam and street construction projects.

---

[160] Gruner, "Vonder Kollektivaus Weisung zur Deportation," 59.

The deportations carried out at the beginning and end of 1941 in Vienna included many forced laborers. In contrast to Germany, exemption provisions played no role, because Austrian Jews scarcely ever worked directly in the armaments industry. Of course, many slaved at road and power plant expansion important for the war; consequently, a number of labor camps still remained in existence until spring and summer of 1942, when the inmates were deported. By summer 1939, 1,300 Austrian Jews were in the segregated labor deployment program of the labor offices. At the beginning of 1941, forced labor reached its peak at around 8,000 persons. As a result of the next transports to Poland in February and March, the number sank to 6,000. After renewed recruitment efforts, 5,000 Jews were then performing forced labor in February 1942, despite new, large-scale deportations in fall 1941. Jews performing forced labor were de facto subject to special laws initially unwritten but later successively codified. In contrast to occupied Poland, companies in Austria and Germany formally signed labor contracts with Jewish forced workers for the entire war period. Exceptions were forced labor in SS camps and so-called retraining camps, and special assignments by the Gestapo. As the Austrian Jewish population had been concentrated in Vienna at an early point, a much larger proportion of forced employment involved deployment to outside locations than was the case in Germany. To date, thirty labor camps, two SS camps, and sixteen camps of the Viennese Jewish community have been confirmed in the Ostmark, as well as eighteen labor camps in the Old Reich established or used for mandatory employment of Austrian Jews. Thus, a total of at least sixty-six camps existed fully independently of the concentration camp system. In the SS camps and in the retraining camps, there were no wages but instead only a kind of pocket money. In short, the Ostmark can be described as the regional trailblazer with regard to the ideas, methods, and discriminatory conditions for segregated labor deployment for Jews. This does not, however, apply for the totality of segregated labor deployment: The Viennese labor administration was never able to expand forced labor as completely as the German labor offices, due to early and extensive deportations. The exception to this rule was the forced labor of Jews in mixed marriages almost at the end of the war. The more intensive participation of the Gestapo and the SS in organizing forced labor of Austrian Jews demonstrates the different conditions in the annexed territories, as well as in the Protectorate created from the former Czech state.

THE PROTECTORATE OF BOHEMIA AND MORAVIA

5

After the Failure of Deportation Plans – Forced Labor of Czech Jews, 1939–1945

OCCUPATION: UNEMPLOYMENT AND IMPOVERISHMENT

On March 15, 1939, Germany occupied the territory of the Czech Republic, which had already been reduced after cession of the Sudeten regions. The occupiers installed a Czech government headed by General Alois Eliaš (after April 1939) and President Emil Hácha, as well as a German Protectorate Administration headed by Baron Konstantin von Neurath, the former Foreign Minister of Germany. Karl Hermann Frank, formerly Deputy Chairman of the Sudeten German Party and later HSSPF, became von Neurath's State Secretary. The Office of the Reich Protector included a central administration and four main departments. The administrative office of the Commander of the Security Police, and the SD (*Befehlshaber des Sicherheitspolizei und des SD*, or BdS) and the Order Police, were attached to the office.[1] One hundred eighteen thousand, three hundred ten persons later classified by Nazis as Jews – possibly even more – lived at this point in the remaining Czech territory annexed by Germany.[2]

Because the Nazi leadership actually expected war, the specialist for Jewish Affairs in the Reich Interior Ministry, Ministerial Councillor Bernhard Lösener,[3] held a meeting on "the service of Jews in case of war" immediately before annexation, at the end of February 1939. He invited representatives of the OKW, the main Gestapo offices and the Order Police, and the Chief

---

[1] See Livia Rothkirchen, "The Protectorate Government and the 'Jewish Question,' 1939–1941," in *Yad Vashem Studies XXVII* (Jerusalem, 1999), 331–362, here 336; Jan Björn Potthast, *Das jüdische Zentralmuseum der SS in Prag, Gegnerforschung und Völkermord im Nationalsozialismus* (Frankfurt am Main and New York, 2002), 56–60.

[2] *Deutsche Politik im "Protektorat Böhmen und Mähren" unter Reinhard Heydrich 1941–1942*, edited by Miroslav Kárný (Berlin, 1997), 125, Doc. No. 23, Report of the Central Office, October 2, 1941, Attachment, Table 1. See Miroslav Kárný, "Zur Statistik der jüdischen Bevölkerung im sogenannten Protektorat," in *Judaica Bohemiae*, Vol. XXII (Prague 1986), No. 1, 9–19.

[3] As a precaution, Lösener does not mention the meeting in his statements on his role and on the "narrowly defined responsibilities of Department I" in the Reich Interior Ministry; see Bernhard Lösener, "Das Reichsministerium des Innern und die Judengesetzgebung," in *Vierteljahrshefte für Zeitgeschichte*, 9, 3 (1961): 293.

of the Inspectorate of Concentration Camps. The "service," forced labor, was to affect all Jewish men between eighteen and fifty-five years old. Estimates put their number at about 200,000 of the total of 600,000 Jews in the German Reich and the annexed territories. The meeting participants agreed that "special deployment of Jewish women and children would be out of all proportion to the expenditures required for labor (guards) and equipment." Nevertheless, "total registration of all Jews with a view to special utilization in the war" was essential, not least of all because of the "measures of the Security Police (for example, special guarding) against all Jewry" that might become necessary. The people present rejected establishing a legal basis for imposing forced labor on Jews when the war began; apparently they did not consider that necessary any longer then. The type of work was described as follows: "Ministerial Councillor Lösener explained that the Jews were to be employed in columns, separated from the workers of German blood. They are probably suitable primarily for use on road construction projects and for acquisition of the materials required for such projects (work in quarries). In consequence of the Führer's generous road building program and the special demands on the entire road system during the war, thought should be given to having all Jews capable of working engaged in this type of work." Plans had been made, he continued, to intern the Jews performing forced labor "in special camps." The organizers were undecided whether the Wehrmacht, the Inspectorate of Concentration Camps, or the labor administration should finance, build, and maintain the camps. Regarding possible placement and the type of forced labor, the organizers wanted to consult directly with the Reich labor administration, which had not participated in that important meeting. The Security Police was to assume the dominant role in the planned forced labor.[4] Germany occupied the territory of the Czech Republic without a struggle, however, so Berlin for the time being relegated plans for war-time use of forced labor to the files.

Right after occupation, attacks on Jews ocurred at various locations and the first anti-Jewish measures were imposed. The small city of Iglau banned Jews from the streetcars and forced them to perform snow removal.[5] In the capital, Prague, the authorities immediately made arrests and closed Jewish establishments or placed them under the supervision of Gestapo. Although the latter's power threatened to become even greater than in Austria, several organizations actually carried out persecutory measures: the Office of the Reich Protector, Konstantin von Neurath, the Gestapo, and the Czech government under Eliaš. Hitler had already determined in March 1939 that, as

[4] Konrad Kwiet, "Forced Labor of German Jews in Nazi Germany," in *Leo Baeck Institute Year Book XXXVI* (London, 1991), 408–410, Note of Dr. Best (Chief of the Security Police and SD), March 1, 1939.

[5] Jens Hampel, "Das Schicksal der jüdischen Bevölkerung der Stadt Iglau 1938–1942," in *Theresienstädter Studien und Dokumente 1998* (Prague, 1998), 70–99, here 74.

the course of action in the "Jewish question": "The Jews would be excluded from the public life of the Protectorate." Performing this task was to be the duty of the government of the Protectorate, not of the Reich.[6] Similar to the course of events in Germany and Austria, Czech government regulations quickly cut off Jews from many employment opportunities. As early as March, the practices of Jewish doctors and lawyers were closed down, Jews were removed from leadership positions in industry and in social organizations, and non-Aryan businesses were marked. The Czech side proved committed to the task; it hoped to combat massive unemployment at the expense of the Jewish population.[7] And even before occupation, in January 1939, the Czech Republic had introduced measures against Jewish civil servants.[8]

The policies after establishment of the Protectorate maneuvered the Jewish population into a hopeless situation. Not until three weeks after occupation, on April 6, 1939, was the Jewish Social Institute (*Jüdisches Soziales Institut*) in Prague allowed to reopen and again provide support to poverty-stricken Jews. Many persons dismissed from jobs became support recipients, but so did many refugees from the Old Reich, Austria, and the Sudeten region. A report of the Prague Jewish community (*Jüdische Kultusgemeinde*) stated at the beginning of June, "The number of people in need of support is growing daily. Jewish employees are being dismissed, the Jewish middle class supporting all the social work and the Jewish communities is steadily becoming impoverished, the rich Jews are leaving the country, and the Jews here will very shortly be without any means to satisfy their social needs by themselves. Without substantial help from abroad, our social welfare system will not function in the long term."[9]

After having been shut out of independent professions and government, Jews were allowed to perform almost only manual labor from summer 1939

---

[6] Quoted according to Stuckart at the meeting of the State Secretaries on March 25, 1939, in Jaroslava Milotová, "Die Zentralstelle für jüdische Auswanderung in Prag. Genesis und Tätigkeit bis zum Anfang des Jahres 1940," in *Theresienstädter Studien und Dokumente 1997* (Prague, 1997), 7–30, here 7. For more details on the course of anti-Jewish policies in the period 1939–1941, see Wolf Gruner, "Das Protektorat Böhmen/Mähren und die antijüdische Politik 1939–1941. Lokale Initiativen, regionale Maßnahmen und zentrale Entscheidungen im "Großdeutschen Reich," in *Theresienstädter Studien und Dokumente* (Prague, forthcoming in 2005).

[7] Rothkirchen, "The Protectorate Government," 340.

[8] Mentioned in United States Holocaust Memorial Museum Archive (USHMMA), Washington, DC, RG-48.005M, Reel 5 (Prague State Archive), Carton 387, I 3b-5800, No. 18, no folio numbers, Presidium of the Ministerial Council to the Office of the Reich Protector on July 24, 1940.

[9] Bundesarchiv (BA), Zwischenarchiv (ZwA) Dahlwitz-Hoppegarten, ZB I, No. 600, Fols. 231–234, Letter of Böhme (Prague SD-Central Office) to the Chief of the Reich Security Main Office, June 8, 1939, with a report of the Prague Jewish Religious Community, date June 1, 1939.

on. Twenty-five thousand, four hundred fifty-eight men and 24,028 women were of working age, that is, eighteen to forty-five years old.[10] Orders of the Reich Protector established twenty-three labor offices with eighty-five branch offices at the end of July 1939. They were subordinate to the Ministry for Social and Health Administration (*Ministerium für Soziales und Gesundheitsverwaltung*); the heads of office were appointed with the approval of the Reich Protector.[11] Although unemployment among the Czech Jews increased, the December 20, 1938, decree of the Reich labor administration on segregated labor deployment was not introduced in the Protectorate of Bohemia and Moravia, as it was in Germany and Austria. Nevertheless, some Jewish engineers, chemists, and physicists who had sought emigration papers from the Gestapo were sent to Germany to work in May 1939.[12]

Not only did growing poverty prevent many Jews from emigrating, but – in contrast to expulsion practices in the Reich – so did the Gestapo. In early May 1939, Heydrich provided "as a guideline for the handling of the Jewish question by the special detachment in Prague the instruction . . . that Jewish emigration should be stopped." Thus, in contrast to Austria, the plan at first was not to establish a Central Office for Jewish Emigration.[13] At a May 12 meeting in Prague, the SD decided categorically not to permit further emigration: Only cases of absolute destitution would warrant consent. The objective was to prevent emigration from the Protectorate from counting against the quota for emigration from the Reich.[14] In summer 1939, however, a Central Office for Jewish Emigration was established on the Austrian model, subordinate to the Security Main Office (*Sicherheitshauptamt* or SHA) in Berlin and combining functions of the Gestapo and the SD. The objective of the office was to force emigration and – as a compromise – to use Czech funds to spur German Jews' departure.[15] Founded by order of the Reich Protector's July 15, 1939, decree, it was initially only responsible for Prague and the vicinity. The BdS in Prague, Franz Walther Stahlecker, was

[10] *Deutsche Politik im "Protektorat,"* 125, Doc. No. 23, Report of the Central Office, October 2, 1941, Attachment, Table I.

[11] Wilhelm von Dennler, *Sozialpolitik im Protektorat Böhmen und Mähren* (Berlin, 1940), 4.

[12] The Jewish Black Book Committee, *The Black Book* (New York, 1943), 176–177.

[13] BA, ZwA Dahlwitz-Hoppegarten, ZB I, No. 600, Fol. 260, July 10, 1939, note of the SD II 112, Dannecker, July 10, 1939, according to a May 2, 1939, note of Hagen. For more details on this and the following discussion, see "Gruner, Das Protektorat Böhmen/Mähren."

[14] BA, ZwA Dahlwitz-Hoppegarten, ZB I, No. 600, Fols. 243–245, note of Hagen on the submission to Leader II (Six), June 16, 1939; ibid., Fol. 260, note of the SD II 112, Dannecker, July 10, 1939.

[15] Ibid, Fols. 249–250, Circular of Leader II (Six), June 16, 1939; ibid., Fols. 243–245, note of Hagen on the submission to Leader II (Six), June 16, 1939; ibid., Fol. 261, Note of SD II, June 22, 1939; ibid., Fols. 260 and verso, note of the SD II 112, Dannecker, July 10, 1939. For establishment of the Central Office after July 1939, see the overall view in Milotová, "Die Zentralstelle für jüdische Auswanderung in Prag," 7–30.

put in charge of the office.[16] At this point, establishment of a second Central Office in Brünn (Brno) was already under discussion.[17]

Hitler's initial intention was for the Germans not to interfere significantly with the Czechs regarding the Jewish question.[18] However, when the Czech government was preparing a Jewish law similar to the Nuremberg Laws in May 1939, the Reich Protector for Bohemia and Moravia forestalled the government and issued a decree for "settlement of the Jewish question." This June 21 decree limited Jews' use of their property and obligated them to report what they owned. Theft was thus the most urgent objective.[19] On July 4, the Czech government then issued an order regarding exclusion of Jews from public life – that is, from all judicial and administrative functions, from public corporations, from public service, and from the independent professions.[20] And the Prague Interior Ministry Directorate's August 3, 1939, decree centrally mandated isolation of the Jewish population, ostensibly because of arbitrary actions (for example, attacks with explosives) against inhabitants "of Jewish descent." The local authorities were emboldened to control the use of public establishments (inns, restaurants, coffee houses, and wine rooms) so that visitors did not constantly encounter Jews, to impose segregation in public baths and facilities such as hospitals, hospices, and sanatoriums, and to mark all Jewish operations and businesses.[21]

On August 10, 1939, State Secretary Stuckart instructed the Reich Protector in Bohemia on the current views of the Reich Interior Ministry regarding "handling of Jews in the Protectorate." There were to be further restrictions: (1) revocation of active and passive voting rights; (2) exclusion from public offices; (3) exclusion from press, radio, and other institutions that influenced public opinion; (4) exclusion from Czech associations; and (5) as a

---

[16] USHMMA Washington, DC, RG-48.005M, Reel 5 (Prague State Archive), I 3b-5811, Central Office, No. 1, no folio numbers, Copy of the circular decree of the Reich Protector, Baron von Neurath, with the letter of Neurath to the Minister President in Prague, July 15, 1939, 1–5. See also Potthast, *Das jüdische Zentralmuseum*, 66–69.

[17] USHMMA Washington, DC, RG-48.005M, Reel 1 (Prague State Archive, Interior Ministry, Jewish Regulations), No. 10, no folio numbers, Copy of the Interior Ministry to the Brünn and Prague regional authorities, August 1, 1939.

[18] Potthast, *Das jüdische Zentralmuseum*, 62.

[19] *Deutschland-Berichte der Sozialdemokratischen Partei Deutschlands (Sopade) 1934–1940*, edited by Klaus Behnken, 7th edition, Vol. 7 (Salzhausen and Frankfurt am Main, 1989), 261. See BA, ZwA Dahlwitz-Hoppegarten, ZB I, No. 600, Fol. 255, SD Central Office, Prague B 1 (Böhme) to the Chief of the Security Police and SD, June 23, 1939; Rothkirchen, "The Protectorate Government," 341; Potthast, *Das jüdische Zentralmuseum*, 62–63.

[20] *Hitler's Ten Year War on the Jews*, published by the Institute of Jewish Affairs (New York, 1943), 57.

[21] USHMMA Washington, DC, RG-48.005M, Reel 1 (Prague State Archive, Interior Ministry, Jewish Regulations), No. 11, no folio numbers, Order of the Reich Interior Ministry in Prague, August 3, 1939. See Report of a traveler; *Sopade*, Vol. 7 (1940), April, 262–264.

supplement to (4), a prohibition on owning firearms and on manufacturing and dealing in weapons. "Another interest of the Reich consists in ensuring that the solution to the Jewish question in the Protectorate is not undertaken hastily. Experience in the Old Reich shows in all clarity that expulsion of the Jews, when they are so intimately involved in all phases of life, can only be accomplished without disadvantage to the general public if the method of approach is systematic and not too fast-moving." The goal of Jewish policy, according to Stuckart, was still emigration.[22]

THE TURNING POINT IN PERSECUTORY POLICY AND THE FIRST FORCED-LABOR MEASURES, FALL 1939–END OF 1940

Everything was to change when the war began. After the rapid victory of the Nazis over Poland, an important strategic decision completely changed the persecuted people's situation. Hitler and the Nazi leaders had decided to "resettle" the Jewish population of the entire Greater German Reich to Poland. On September 21, 1939, Heydrich informed the Gestapo that Hitler had authorized the deportation of the Jews to a foreign-language-speaking Gau to be established on Polish territory.[23] As shown in the previous chapters, the die was thus cast regarding the fate of the Jews in the Greater German Reich, including the Protectorate.

On October 6, SS Hauptsturmführer Adolf Eichmann received the order from the Gestapo chief Heinrich Müller to initiate the expulsion of 70,000 to 80,000 Jews from the Kattowitz area as well as Jews from the Mährisch-Ostrau (Moravská Ostrava) region to the other side of the Vistula.[24] Himmler expected an experience report that "probably would be forwarded to the Führer." Then the only option was to wait for the general departure of the transports to be ordered. Hitler first ordered the regrouping of 300,000

[22] BA, ZwA Dahlwitz-Hoppegarten, ZB I, No. 600, Fol. 274–275, Stuckart (Reich Interior Ministry) to the Reich Protector of Bohemia and Moravia, to the attention of district administrator Fuchs, August 10, 1939.

[23] *Europa unterm Hakenkreuz. Die faschistische Okkupationspolitik in Polen (1939–1945)*, document selection and introduction by Werner Röhr with the assistance of Elke Heckert (Berlin, 1989), 119, Doc. No. 12, RSHA note, September 27, 1939, regarding the meeting on September 21, 1939. For this and the following, see Wolf Gruner, "Von der Kollektivausweisung zur Deportation der Juden aus Deutschland. Neue Perspektiven und Dokumente (1938–1945)," in *Beiträge zur Geschichte des Nationalsozialismus, Vol. 20: Die Deportation der Juden aus Deutschland. Pläne, Praxis, Reaktionen 1938–1945* (Göttingen, 2004), 21–62.

[24] Yad Vashem Archive (YV), Jerusalem, 051/ No. 91 (Prague State Archive), Fol. 3, Note, October 6, 1939. See Seev Goshen, "Eichmann und die Nisko-Aktion im Oktober 1939," in *Vierteljahrshefte für Zeitgeschichte*, 29, 1 (1981): 84; H. G. Adler, *Der verwaltete Mensch. Studien zur Deportation der Juden aus Deutschland* (Tübingen, 1974), 128–140; Hans Safrian, *Die Eichmann-Männer* (Vienna and Zurich, 1993), 73–78.

destitute Jews from the Old Reich and from Ostmark.[25] To this end, Jews were registered Reich-wide. On October 1, 1939, 90,147 Jews were counted in the Protectorate, based on lists from the Jewish communities; of that number, 80,139 were practicing Jews. In total, 28,000 fewer people resided there than when the Protectorate was established. Forty-six thousand one hundred seventy Jews lived concentrated in Prague alone.[26]

On October 6, 1939, Eichmann made the following notes regarding his preparatory activities on Berlin: "1. Sort all lists of Jews registered by Old Reich, Protectorate, and the Ostmark. Order these in turn within each group by religious community . . . based on the maps sent in by Jewish organizations. 2. List the property of destitute Jews being deported."[27] On October 12, Eichmann flew to Krakow. Soon after that, he informed Mährisch-Ostrau that Nisko am San was to be the destination of the transports.[28] The first transport left Czech territory with 901 Jews on October 18. It was accompanied by Border Police and SS men of the Vienna and Prague Central Offices for Jewish Emigration.[29] Eichmann personally met the train from Mährisch-Ostrau in Nisko.[30] However, Berlin then gave orders that "the Protectorate [was] not to be brought into the evacuation operation for the moment so that the removal of all Jews from Vienna [could] be carried out as quickly as possible."[31] It is still unclear why two more transports left Mährisch-Ostrau.[32] The second, a freight train that had pulled out of Prague on October 28 loaded with over 300 Jews designated "prisoners" by the SD, departed on November 1. But the transport, accompanied by the Gestapo and Municipal Police (*Schutzpolizei*), only got as far as Sosnowitz in eastern Upper Silesia.[33] As of early November 1939 – after about 5,000

---

[25] YV Jerusalem, 051/ No. 91 (Prague State Archive), Fol. 5, Note, October 11, 1939, regarding the meeting of Eichmann and Günther with Gauamtsleiter Roden in Kattowitz (Katowice) on October 9, 1939. Reproduced in Adler, *Der verwaltete Mensch*, 129.

[26] *Hitler's Ten Year War*, 55. See the slightly different numbers (80,391 Jewish persons, and 9,828 non-Jews) in Alena Hájková, "Erfassung der jüdischen Bevölkerung des Protektorats," in *Theresienstädter Studien und Dokumente 1997*, 50–62, here 53.

[27] YV Jerusalem, 051/ No. 91 (Prague State Archive), Fol. 4, Note, October 6, 1939.

[28] Safrian, *Die Eichmann-Männer*, 75–76.

[29] The train included twenty-two passenger cars and twenty-nine freight cars with building materials, tools, and food products; YV Jerusalem, 051/ No. 91 (Prague State Archive), Fol. 22, Note for Eichmann, October 18, 1939; see also ibid., Daily report of the Mährisch-Ostrau SD office (Dr. Heinrich), October 18, 1939.

[30] Goshen, "Eichmann," 90.

[31] Österreichisches Staatsarchiv/Archiv der Republik (ÖStA/AdR) Vienna, Bürckel Materials, No. 2315/6, Fol. 22, Note of Eichmann for the president of the district administration Barth, October 25, 1939. For more detail on the following section, see Wolf Gruner, *Zwangsarbeit und Verfolgung. Österreichische Juden im NS-Staat 1938–45* (Innsbruck, Vienna, and Munich, 2000), 137–142.

[32] Goshen, "Eichmann," 92.

[33] YV Jerusalem, 051/ No. 91 (Prague State Archive), Fol. 38, November 3, 1939, teletype with a daily report (Dannecker) to the Viennese Central Office, November 1 and 2, 1939.

persons from Upper Silesia Austria and from Prague, Brünn, and Mährisch-Ostrau in the Protectorate had been deported to the Lublin area – Himmler discontinued the deportations "until further notice" because of "technical difficulties."[34]

Nevertheless, plans for total deportation stayed on the table. In spring 1940 transports were expected to resume. In preparation, the BdS expanded the jurisdiction of the Prague Central Office for Jewish Emigration to the entire territory of the Protectorate on January 29.[35] On March 5, 1940, an order of the Reich Protector announced the centralization of internal Jewish matters in the Prague Central Office. The Jewish communities, as well as all the Jewish organizations and foundations, were henceforth placed under the supervision of the Central Office.[36] In addition, the Jewish population's freedom of movement was restricted. In February 1940, the Gestapo forbade the Jews from being in public places, on streets, and in squares after 8:00 p.m. In the Interior Ministry's view, the problem of Jews' going out in the evening for entertainment (to the theater or cinema, for example) was solved. As to afternoon visits, the regional authorities were to order that signs announcing appropriate prohibitions be posted wherever they were not yet present.[37] On order of the Reich Protector, persons who were considered Jews under the Nuremberg Laws had to report starting in March 1940 to the Jewish communities, even though they were not members.[38] He ordered at the same time that for Jews, the citizen identification papers introduced in 1939 as a substitute for the passport were to be marked with a red "J."[39]

On January 26, 1940, the Protector in Bohemia and Moravia issued another order regarding exclusion from economic life. Among other things, Jews were prohibited from management of enterprises.[40] Thus, Jewish Czechs increasingly found themselves without any chance for employment and income because of vocational and trade prohibitions and because of

---

[34] Quoted according to Gruner, *Zwangsarbeit und Verfolgung*, 142.

[35] USHMMA Washington, DC, RG-48.005M, Reel 4 (Prague State Archive), I 3b-5811 Central Office, No. 2, no folio numbers, Circular decree of the Reich Protector and the BdS II 308/40, January 29, 1940. It is not accurate that this did not happen until mid-February, as Potthast writes; Potthast, *Das jüdische Zentralmuseum*, 76.

[36] *Deutsche Politik im "Protektorat,"* 123–124, Doc. No. 23, Report of the Central Office, October 2, 1941; *Hitler's Ten Year War*, 57; and Potthast, *Das jüdische Zentralmuseum*, 92–93.

[37] Mentioned in USHMMA Washington, DC, RG-48.005M, Reel 1 (Prague State Archive, Interior Ministry, Jewish Regulations), No. 25, no folio numbers, Order of the Prague Interior Minister, February 20, 1940. See ibid., No. 1, no folio numbers, List of the legal provisions issued by the Prague Interior Ministry, September 25, 1940, 1.

[38] Hájková, "Erfassung der jüdischen Bevölkerung des Protektorats," 54.

[39] Ibid., 52.

[40] Excerpt in *Europa unterm Hakenkreuz. Die faschistische Okkupationspolitik in Österreich und der Tschoslowakei (1938–1945)* (Berlin, 1988), 139. See *Sopade*, Vol. 7 (1940), April, 261; *Hitler's Ten Year War*, 57.

dismissals from public and private enterprises.[41] On March 19, a government order reorganized unemployment assistance: The labor offices – not the Czech labor unions anymore – would be responsible for this support,[42] with the result that the new offices increasingly recruited Jews who reported that they were unemployed. The first large group of Jews who received public unemployment assistance was forced to work at a municipal trash burning site in Prague in 1940.[43]

Still, in contrast to the situation in Germany, Austria, or Poland, neither the SS nor the labor administration centrally introduced compulsory labor for Jews in the Protectorate. In the course of the general radicalization of anti-Jewish policies, however, local administrations resorted to their own measures. The city councilman (*Stadtrat*) in Holleschau decided at the beginning of July 1940 to seek authorization from district authorities to introduce "mandatory labor for Jews." At the same time, the town's Jews were prohibited from using the swimming pool. The decision of the city administration was the subject of an article in the newspaper *Neuer Tag* with the title "Work Obligation for Jews in Holleschau."[44] The headline encouraged imitation of the local practice. When the city councilman went to the district authorities for authorization, the authorities submitted the request to the Moravian regional authorities in Brünn because "normative regulation of Jewish conditions" was involved. The responsible chief district administrator in Zlín, Bayerl, not wanting to reprimand Holleschau for the unauthorized solution "to the basic questions of Jewry," asked the Office of the Reich Protector, which had been alerted by the newspaper article, for instructions that would "settle such questions immediately" by opposing local initiatives and providing central guidance.[45]

Despite the lack of central regulations, a compulsory work program comparable to that in Germany or Austria thus developed on the local level. In early July 1940, about 60 percent of Czech Jewish men had already been singled out for forced labor; the rest worked in the independent professions still allowed, in trade, in commerce, or in Jewish institutions.[46] Although the pay was just as bad, the fundamental elements of segregated labor deployment

[41] *Deutsche Politik im "Protektorat,"* 127, Doc. No. 23, Report of the Central Office, October 2, 1941, Attachment, Table 2.

[42] Dennler, *Sozialpolitik,* 9.

[43] Helena Krejčová, Jana Svobodová, and Anna Hyndráková (eds.), *Židé v Protektorátu. Hlášení Židovské náboženské obce v roce 1942. Dokumenty* (Prague, 1997), 112, Doc. 5, Report of the Prague Jewish community, "Arbeit," undated (mid-1942).

[44] Article of July 5, 1940, quoted in USHMMA Washington, DC, RG-48.005M, Reel 4 (Prague State Archive), Carton 389, I 3b-5850, No. 28, no folio numbers, Reich Protector to the chief district administrator in Zlín on July 10, 1940.

[45] Ibid, No. 31, no folio numbers, Chief district administrator in Zlín to the Reich Protector, August 30, 1940.

[46] *Deutsche Politik im "Protektorat,"* 127, Doc. No. 23, Report of the Central Office, October 2, 1941, Attachment, Table 2.

were slightly different in the Protectorate; for example, segregation in work groups was at first not strictly enforced because Czechs and Jews were considered equally "inferior." The survivor Max Manheimer described his situation near the Slovak border in 1940 as follows: "Now I am working in road construction. . . . My housing during the week is a board shack behind the equipment shed. . . . My work colleagues, exclusively Czechs, are friendly to me and I am acknowledged by them as completely their equal. . . . Road construction alone cannot feed the family. Their reserves are long since used up."[47]

In the course of 1940, however, the number of initiatives designed to separate Jews from the rest of the population grew. The Reich Protector received petitions demanding introduction of a mark for Jews. Individuals proposed, for example, a Star of David on clothing; the National Aryan Cultural Association (*Narodni Arijeká Kulturni Jednotav*) in Prague suggested a yellow strip of fabric with the inscription "Jew."[48] This stoked discussion within government agencies regarding introduction of a mark. However, as in the territory of the Reich and in contrast to Poland, the Gestapo stated that in 1940 marking Jews was not yet desired by people in high places.[49] In the month of June, the Olmütz NSDAP Kreis leaders proposed that limited shopping hours be set for Jews, that the Jews be marked with arm bands, and that a ghetto be established; the chief district administrator notified the Reich Protector of the proposals.[50] The Czech Interior Minister's July 9 decree then restricted Jews' time for shopping to a few hours of the day. Local authorities were to announce the restriction, and the shopping times were to be adapted to the local circumstances in cooperation with the trade associations. If possible, the times were to fall between 10:30 a.m. to 1:00 p.m. and 3:00 p.m. to 5:00 p.m. and appropriate signs were to be posted on the businesses.[51]

Because of the increasing number of local initiatives to limit Jews' freedom of movement, the Prague BdS sent a circular to all chief district administrators on August 17, 1940. It contained the following critical remarks: "Because such orders often only take into consideration purely local interests and are not attuned to the interests of the rest of the Reich territory, not only does the consistency in orientation of such measures suffer but they also often entail

[47] Max Manheimer, "Von Neutitschen nach Dachau (1969)," 15, Memoir Collection, Leo Baeck Institute Archive (LBIA), New York.

[48] USHMMA Washington, DC, RG-48.005M, Reel 4 (Prague State Archive), Carton 389, I 3b-5851, No. 1, no folio numbers, Handwritten petition (Rudolf Pitzak) to the Reich Protektor's Office (February 1940); ibid., No. 6, Narodni Arijeká Kulturni Jednotav Prag to Reich Protector von Neurath on June 12, 1940.

[49] Ibid., No. 3, no folio numbers, Reich Protector/Commander of the Security Police and SD to Group I/3 at the Reich Protector's Office on March 5, 1940.

[50] Ibid., No. 4, no folio numbers, Olmütz chief district administrator to the Reich Protector on June 13, 1940.

[51] Ibid., Reel 1 (Prague State Archive, Interior Ministry, Jewish Regulations), No. 44, no folio numbers, Circular decree of the Prague Interior Minister to regional authorities, July 9, 1940.

increased expenditures to care for the Jews affected and thus a great burden to the resources of the emigration fund." The chief district administrators were called upon to carry out anti-Jewish measures only after consultation with the Central Office for Jewish Emigration. The BdS, for whom State Secretary Frank signed, had prompted the government of the Protectorate to issue the additional limitations on Jews' freedom of movement: a prohibition on going to parks and sporting events and on using dining and sleeping cars on trains, regulation of streetcar use and shopping hours, and an end to mixed restaurants with special rooms for Jews. According to the circular, marking Jews as demanded by the chief district administrators and establishing ghettos or concentrating Jews in certain buildings or sectors could "not be considered at this time."[52] That was also soon to change, however. In October 1940, an order of the Reich Protector on evicting renters to gain building space afforded the opportunity to begin concentrating the Jewish population in certain dwellings and buildings.[53]

In the meantime, on August 7, 1940, the Czech government had also ordered Jewish children's exclusion from public schools.[54] As a result of this action, many young people then ended up in forced labor. Ruth Felix, who lived in the small city of Stráznice in Moravia, had to leave her *Gymnasium* at fifteen and do farm work on German estates until the end of 1940. She toiled in the fields and on the harvest and cleaned manure from stalls.[55] In this phase, labor camps supported by Jewish communities and similar to those of the German Reichsvereinigung had evidently also been established. Increased "integration of Jews into agriculture" began in spring 1939 as preparation for emigration. By the end of August, the number of mostly young people was 550, but it fell again because of the seasonal nature of the work. In spring 1940, many new and for the most part small groups were established. There were apparently more than 100 such groups in which 1,500 people were retrained, even though the opportunities for emigration had diminished drastically since the beginning of the war.[56] For the most part, the groups were intended for forced labor, as in the Reich.

According to the administrative report of the chief district administrator of Mährisch-Ostrau, the Klein-Kuntschitz Jewish community in Freideck

---

[52] Ibid., Reel 3 (Prague State Archive), No. 60, no folio numbers, Circular decree of Reich Protector/Commander of the Security Police and SD II 1305–6/40 (signed Frank), August 17, 1940.

[53] *Hitler's Ten Year War*, 57. Ghettoization was simplified by the general reporting obligation imposed requiring house owners to report all persons living in the houses and the changes in their lives; Hájková, "Erfassung der jüdischen Bevölkerung des Protektorats," 50–51.

[54] *Hitler's Ten Year War*, 58.

[55] Ruth Felix, *Diese Hölle überlebt. Ein jüdisches Familienschicksal aus Mähren 1924–1994. Mit einer Dokumentation*, edited by Erhard Roy Wiehn (Constance, 1995), 18.

[56] Krejčová, Svobodová, and Hyndráková (eds.), *Židé v Protektorátu*, 111, Doc. 5, Report of the Prague Jewish community.

district set up a labor camp where fifty-two Jews were staying.[57] The twenty men in the Hluboš labor group formed in June 1940 had to perform forestry work, ostensibly as preparation for emigration to San Domingo. In July 1940, the Prague Jewish community received a request from the Central Office for Jewish Emigration to provide a labor detail for the Linden training estate. On July 15, an advance detail of thirty Jewish workers, led by two construction specialists, arrived at Linden estate in Deutsch Brod. In short order, three barracks for 400 men were erected. By the end of August, the number of trainees had already risen to 200, and then in October, to 340. In contrast to all the other retraining camps, a representative of the Prague Central Office for Jewish Emigration was in charge of the camp, similar to the Viennese Central Office running Doppl and Sandhof camps. From the time the workers got up in the morning to their lunch break, evening roll call, and bed time, their daily regimen was subject to strict rules that also extended to after-work activities. Camp inmates worked on the estate, performing work in the fields, garden, stalls, and estate workshops. The work force was also assigned to so-called special tasks: railway construction and snow and ice removal.[58]

After another order, on September 14, 1940, regarding eviction of Jewish employees,[59] the Office of the Reich Protector in Bohemia and Moravia finally, in early December 1940, issued the first labor regulations in keeping with the situation of German Jewish forced laborers: the prohibition on paying Jews for the New Year's holidays.[60] In contrast, the special tax introduced in Germany and Austria at the end of 1940 (the "social equalization tax for Jews") was not effected in the Protectorate of Bohemia and Moravia, apparently because Jews received reduced wages anyway.[61]

THE SYSTEMATIZATION OF FORCED LABOR IN 1941

By the beginning of 1941, in the Protectorate – even without any central order – most Jewish men under forty-five years old were already under

---

[57] Excerpt from the administrative report of the chief district administrator, in USHMMA Washington, DC, RG-48.005M, Reel 4 (Prague State Archive), Carton 389, I 3b-5850, No. 8, no folio numbers, Reich Protector I 1 a to Group I 3 b, Dr. Mokry, undated.

[58] Krejčová, Svobodová, and Hyndráková (eds.), *Židé v Protektorátu*, 110–116, Doc. 5, Report of the Prague Jewish community.

[59] *Hitler's Ten Year War*, 57.

[60] BA Berlin, R 8150, No. 12, Fol. 158, Lists of legal regulations, here Order of the Reich Protector, December 9, 1940.

[61] "Second Decree for Implementation of the Decree on the Imposition of a Social Compensation Charge (Sozialausgleichsabgabe)," December 24, 1940, *Reichsgesetzblatt*, 1940 I: 1666. See Chapter 1 and Gruner, *Der geschlossene Arbeitseinsatz*, 194–200. For the purview, Hessisches Hauptstaatsarchiv (HHStA) Wiesbaden, Dep. 483, No. 10036, no folio numbers, Information sheet No. 39 of the Frankfurt am Main Gau chairman, January 24, 1941, Fol. 3.

obligation to work as unskilled laborers in construction, road construction, or private companies,[62] the demand for labor in the German Reich was climbing,[63] and the deportations announced for the Protectorate were repeatedly being delayed. Hence, regulations requiring work finally seemed necessary. First, Czech Jews were prohibited beginning on January 10, 1941, from engaging in any independent economic activity.[64] The first government decree with forced-labor measures affecting the population of the Protectorate, especially Jews, then was issued on January 23, 1941. The obligation to perform labor applied to everyone between eighteen and fifty years old. All Jewish men, by no means only those who received public support, had to be registered at a Jewish labor placement office.[65] The decree stated, "It is neither desirable nor justifiable for Jews capable of utilization as labor to be supported by unemployment assistance and for them to become long-term support recipients. It is therefore necessary for all Jews who report that they are unemployed to be put to work as soon as possible. The main jobs to be considered are road construction, excavation work, surface area lay-out (parks), and the like. Such jobs are suitable because individuals from any occupation can perform them, and because physical labor for Jews is altogether desirable."[66] With that in mind, the labor offices began systematically deploying Jews who reported that they were unemployed. In February 1941, unemployed Prague Jews were put together in a group that had to perform tasks beneficial to the community in the municipal trash-burning facility. During the winter months, 350 men per four-hour shift removed snow from the airfield of the Prague-Rusin air base headquarters. Two hundred sixteen Jewish men worked in the same time period on a project to construct an embankment to protect against high water.[67]

As of April 1, 1941, 70 percent of the registered male Jewish population between eighteen and fifty years old and capable of working were recorded as engaged in forced labor, 10 percent performed odd jobs, and the rest were employed in the few professions still permitted.[68] The Prague Jewish community then received instructions from the Reich Protector of Bohemia and Moravia to expand the segregated labor deployment program for Jews

---

[62] Manheimer, "Von Neutitschen nach Dachau (1969)," 17.

[63] *Deutsche Politik im "Protektorat,"* 123, Doc. No. 23, Report of the Central Office, October 2, 1941.

[64] Potthast, *Das jüdische Zentralmuseum,* 112.

[65] BA Berlin R 8150, No. 12, Fol. 158, Collection of regulations. See *The Black Book,* 177.

[66] The decree is cited in: Krejčová, Svobodová, and Hyndráková (eds.), *Židé v Protektorátu,* 105, Doc. 5, Report of the Prague Jewish community.

[67] Ibid., 105–111.

[68] Central Archives for the History of the Jewish People (CAHJP), Jerusalem, A/W, No. 421, no folio numbers, Anonymous report on the "Utilization of Jewish Labor," undated, 3. See *Deutsche Politik im "Protektorat,"* 123, Doc. No. 23, Report of Central Office, October 2, 1941; and ibid., 127, Attachment, Table 2.

and "to perform fitness examinations for Jewish men eighteen to fifty years old."[69] That obviously meant that categorically all Jews, even those not previously registered at the labor offices, were to be included. On April 17, the Reich Protector informed the Ministry for Social and Health Administration in Prague about these instructions and about the procedure that he had defined and filed under the same reference number, 5431, used in Germany since the end of 1938 for Jewish forced labor: According to the Reich Protector, he had instructed the Jewish community that "all Jews were to be examined to determine their fitness for work." The examinations prospectively would be concluded by April 25. Until a complete overview was available, no one was to be placed, except for persons who had already been put to work the previous year. "To ensure that the systematic use of Jews as forced labor [was] not disrupted," the Ministry was to instruct the labor offices to proceed according to the following guidelines: (1) Only the labor offices were to select suitable workplaces. (2) All male Jews could be deployed only in groups. During work, they had to be separated from the Aryan workers. The enterprises were responsible for segregation and were to be monitored by the labor offices. (3) Male Jews could be employed in agriculture, but only in groups of at least ten. (4) Jewish girls were to be employed as household helpers in Jewish households or for farm work in groups. (5) Placement of Jews was exclusively a matter for the labor offices. The forced-labor section of the Jewish community was to apprise the labor office of the number of Jewish workers available. (6) The "Jewish foremen selected by the Jewish community were to lead Jewish work groups."[70] In order to arrange for the "systematic use of Jews as labor," the Ministry for Social and Health Administration in Prague then issued relevant guidelines to the labor offices.[71]

On May 9, 1941, the Ministry for Social and Health Administration distributed further instructions for segregated labor deployment to the Prague Jewish community. Joint instructions of the Office of the Reich Protector, the Central Office for Jewish Emigration, and the Ministry for Social and Health Administration ordered that recruitment and conditions were to conform to the following procedures in the future: (1) The enterprises would report their needs and furnish proof of special workplaces, housing, and provisions for the Jews requested. (2) The labor offices would examine work projects in their district as to suitability for Jewish forced labor. The labor offices would place Jews in the enterprises based on the Jews' qualifications and fitness. The labor offices were to exercise placement authority. (3) The Jewish

---

[69] CAHJP, Jerusalem, A/W, No. 421, no folio numbers, Anonymous report on the "Utilization of Jewish Labor," undated, 1.

[70] USHMMA Washington, DC, RG-48.005M, Reel 4 (Prague State Archive), Carton 389, I 3b-5813, Treatment of Jews under labor law, No. 2, no folio numbers, Copy of Dr. Bertsch (Reich Protector/II 4 a 543/41) to the ministry on April 17, 1941, 1–2.

[71] CAHJP, Jerusalem, A/W, No. 421, no folio numbers, Anonymous report on the "Utilization of Jewish Labor," undated, 1.

community would keep a card file of vocations and deployments to "facilitate rapid and orderly selection at any time of workers suitable for the various labor projects in terms of specialty, health, and social factors"; the community would report fit Jews to the labor office and assist the labor office in selecting Jews for deployment. The Jewish community was not allowed to accept direct requests; placement was a matter for the government labor offices alone. However, the Jewish community had to care for the labor columns. (4) The Central Office for Jewish Emigration (SD-Gestapo) would authorize allocation and would exercise its right to supervise.[72] This last point was a decided change from the guidelines of the Reich Protectorate issued in April 1941. In contrast to the situation in the Old Reich and in Austria, the SD and Gestapo had the right to supervise both Jewish organizations and segregated labor deployment.

Examination to determine fitness for work established that 4,897 of 17,447 Jews in the eighteen-to-fifty age group were suitable for heavy labor, 5,010, for middle-range labor, 5,419, for light labor, and 2,121, unsuitable for labor.[73] At the end of July 1941, the Ministry for Social and Health Administration planned to publish more precise guidelines for forced labor. According to its May 9 decree, Jews could only be sent to ministry-approved sites because no forced-labor overview existed yet and disruption by special measures was to be avoided. After the medical examinations had been completed and all the labor offices had experience with forced labor, rigid central control could be relaxed. Open slots for Jewish labor were to be reported to the labor offices. The enterprises were to describe their projects' wage and labor conditions and guarantee separate lodgings. The Jewish community was to have all Jews between eighteen and fifty years old examined. "Initially, only unemployed Jews" were to be candidates. The decree transferred to the labor offices responsibility for "putting Jews in their districts to work." Only Jews who had previous agricultural experience, who were coming from reorientation programs, or who had volunteered were to be assigned to farm labor, which also required groups of at least four persons. Of course, Jews were to be used only if no other labor was available. Use in industry and trade also required segregation and groups of at least four. Placement in the armaments industry was not to occur. "Jews generally can be used for road work, underground construction, quarries, brickworks, mining operations, sandpits, and clay pits, if the work projects are considered important." Special guidelines were to apply for forced labor in industry and trade. The labor offices were supposed first to procure work for the Jews living in their districts. If further need should arise, Jews could be requested through the Prague ministry. In this case the group had to include at least ten men. The

---

[72] Ibid., 1–3; see BA Berlin R 8150, No. 12, Fol. 158, Collection of regulations.
[73] CAHJP, Jerusalem, A/W, No. 421, no folio numbers, Anonymous report on the "Utilization of Jewish Labor," undated, 1.

ministry would then have the labor offices provide workers. Compensation was to be according to the wage scale. Substandard productivity clauses imposing wage reductions were to be applied for poor performance. Jews were to be withdrawn from jobs not compensated according to the wage scale and from unpaid compulsory labor so that the Jewish communities would not have to support the workers, because "all Jewish property" had to be saved "for emigration." These statements clearly indicate the influence of the Security Police, which in Germany at this point were also attempting to prepare for anticipated deportations by minimizing the expenditures of Jewish organizations. The guidelines stated further that the Jews were always to be housed separately. When housing was mixed, the barracks for Jews had to be constructed at the outer edge of the camp. As a rule, the Central Office's authorization was to be required for Jews in camps to change location. Permission was to be granted only for groups of more than ten persons. The Jewish community was to assign special trusted persons to the labor offices as liaisons. The decree applied for all "unemployed Jews"; a special decree was to be issued for the Jews employed at the time. Jews were to be removed from individual jobs in agriculture, but not yet from industry.[74]

The Office of Reich Protector discussed the draft of the ministry's guidelines and forwarded it to the BdS, the Central Office, and the Gestapo for their comments. Group I 3 in the Office of the Reich Protector complained about not being directly involved even though the document related to a matter "the resolution of which" clearly fell "in the Jewish policy area." The group continued that it had no objection to the guidelines, but efforts should be made to ensure both that Jews were housed separately and that they were strictly segregated from other workers. Otherwise, "very close relationships" could develop, accompanied by the danger of whispered propaganda.[75]

A debate subsequently arose within the Office of the Reich Protector about which interests should take priority in organizing the forced-labor system – those of persecutory policy or those of the economy. The Prague Jewish community had submitted a list of names of previously employed skilled workers and asked that they be placed in professionally appropriate jobs working independently. According to the Office's Department II 4, however, the current situation was that most persons fit for heavy or mid-level labor in the meantime were working in construction or agriculture. Individual placements occurred almost only in agriculture, with the ministry's approval. But in those cases there had been sham employment relationships

---

[74] USHMMA Washington, DC, RG-48.005M, Reel 4 (Prague State Archive), Carton 389, I 3b-5813, Treatment of Jews under labor law, No. 3–4, no folio numbers, Circular of the Reich Protector/ Leader of Group II 4 with a copy of the draft of the ministry, July 21, 1941, 1–8.

[75] Ibid., No. 3–4, no folio numbers, Note of the Reich Protector/ I 3 b and draft of a letter to II 4, July 29, 1941.

to evade excavation and road work. Experiences in the construction trade were generally good, Department II 4 reported. After a period of adjustment necessary because most Jews were "unaccustomed to working," they "achieved credible performance levels." On the other hand, a number of Jews had to be removed from underground labor because they were not up to it physically. Without employment, they then had to be supported by the Jewish community. The need to protect the Jewish community's assets intended for emigration and the great demand for skilled workers raised the question of whether and how Jewish skilled workers were to be utilized. Most specialists had not been dismissed after the October 1939 order, anyway. In Department II 4's view, if businesses were unable to find any other workers after a reasonable search, they would have to be allowed to hire such Jews even under the present circumstances. Since the number of such searches was increasing with the growing shortage of skilled labor, special guidelines were necessary. Labor offices were not allowed to place Jewish physicians; their deployment to non-Jewish institutes was "naturally" out of the question. However, an order containing special guidelines would reintegrate into professional life a number of persons dismissed in October 1939. After all, putting them to work was better than their receiving unemployment assistance.[76]

Group I 1 in the Office of the Reich Protector categorically rejected these views: "Because of fundamental political misgivings," it was considered "urgently necessary to deny Jews any relief or improvement in their use as labor." Further, "certain work advantages" should be avoided and the principle of "regularly assigning Jews manual labor" should be upheld. Only "with careful adherence to this approach" and with strict controls would Group I 1 agree to limited use of Jews as skilled workers. According to this view, a general employment authorization for Jews would have to be introduced so that Czechs "friendly to Jews" would not circumvent the labor office. Deviation from the principle of group allocation was permissible only in exceptional cases. And Jews working independently were also to be isolated. Their use in defense-industry businesses was prohibited.[77] Although clearly advocating persecution initially, the factions within the agency nevertheless deigned to compromise in the interest of the labor market.

By the end of August, 1941, the labor offices had obligated further thousands of Jews, mainly to perform high-rise, underground, and railway construction, regulating work, and unskilled labor in businesses, agriculture, forestry, and trade operations.[78] Of over 17,600 male Jews eighteen to fifty

---

[76] Ibid., No. 5, no folio numbers, Reich Protector II 4 to Group I 3 b, July 31, 1941.

[77] Ibid., No. 6, no folio numbers, Copy of a draft of the Reich Protector I 1 to Group II 4, August 1941.

[78] CAHJP, Jerusalem, A/W, No. 421, no folio numbers, Report on the "Utilization of Jewish Labor," undated, 3. See *Deutsche Politik im "Protektorat,"* 123, Doc. No. 23, Report of Central Office, October 2, 1941; and ibid., 127, Attachment, Table 2.

years old who had been examined for fitness to work, more than 15,000 were registered as suitable for heavy to light labor and only about 2,000 as unable to work. A total of 11,700 already were in forced labor; 2,332 in agricultural groups and 4,560 in building enterprises, a total of 6,892. Just under 5,000 worked in industry and businesses, where they had already been employed earlier. For example, in Brünn district, the labor office used as forced labor 866 of the 2,038 Jews registered there, 667 in large groups for construction companies.[79] Jewish workers both from the province and from Prague were assigned to many construction projects. In either case, that meant deploying Jewish workers in large groups outside their permanent places of residence and thus establishing camps that are for the most part forgotten today. In 1941, columns of Jewish forced laborers constructed, among other things, a film studio in Barrandow, an airport in Letnian, the express highway in Strielek, the electrical power plant in Srnojed, and the Mas company's factory in Alt Tabor. They were engaged in railway construction in Sassau-Grosse, Losenitz, Neuhof, Retschowits, Malmeritz, Zinsendorf, and Neudorf. Groups of forced laborers regulated the Ostrawitza (Ostravice) River near Kunzendorf, the Elbe River near Pardubitz, and the Moldova (Vltava) River near Baurowitz; and they constructed the port in Kolin, the Stiechowitz Dam, and the lock at Gross Ossek. They labored in mines for the Ober Birken Kaolinwerke (clay works), the Kaolinwerke Ledetz (clay works), the Südböhmische Elektrizitätswerke (electrical power plant), the Kohlenbergwerk Midlowar (coal mine), the Kohlenbergwerk Gaya (coal mine), the Prager Eisen AG (iron) in Kladno, and for industrial operations such as the Landwirtschaftliche Maschinenfabrik Hofherr-Schrans (agricultural equipment factory), Firma Holzverarbeitung Hrdlička (woodworking), Firma Kunststoffe Baklax (synthetics), Firma Kartonagen Kos (cardboard), Buchdruckerei Pleva (printers), Firma Optische Apparate Matuška (optical equipment), Firma Mann Lederwaren Wildner (men's leather products), Kaolinfabrik Chlumpschau (clay factory), Kofferfabrik Singer (luggage factory) in Klattau, Zuckerfabrik Hatschein (sugar factory), Radiofabrik Jiskra (radio factory) in Pardubitz, Dachpappenfabrik Žaček (tar paper factory), Keramische Fabrik Tschemoschau (ceramics factory), and the Zementwerke Malmeritz (cement works).[80]

The Ministry for Social and Health Administration expanded the obligation to perform compulsory labor to Jews between sixteen and sixty years old with a decree on August 29, 1941. They were all to be examined for fitness. Point 5 of the decree emphasized that Jews were to receive adequate compensation so that subsidies from the Jewish community would not be

---

[79] USHMMA Washington, DC, RG-48.005M, Reel 2 (Prague State Archive), Carton 859, II 4–4055, no folio numbers, Statistics on labor utilization, Status as of September 1, 1941.
[80] Krejčová, Svobodová, and Hyndráková (eds.), *Židé v Protektorátu*, 112–114, Doc. 5, Report of the Prague Jewish community.

necessary, all of which suggests that at that time the practice was just the opposite. The Protectorate's Labor Utilization Department II, the Czech ministry that had issued the decree, and the SD Central Office bore responsibility for forced labor.[81]

ISOLATION, MARKING, AND DEPORTATIONS

At this point, exclusion of Czech Jews from the wage-earning world was far-ranging; their property was controlled or was in frozen accounts. Visiting public establishments and changing residences were prohibited.[82] Since spring 1941, the process of concentrating the Prague Jewish population in "Jewish houses" had begun; simultaneously, the authorities arranged systematic resettlement of the Jewish population from the small towns of the separate chief district administrators' districts to individual cities. The Jews were thus forced to move from Gaya, Kostel, and Holleschau in Zlín district to Hungarian Brod.[83] A prohibition on emigrating that particularly affected Jewish men fit to work was extended to Germany and Austria in summer 1941.[84]

The Protectorate was also the starting point for the revival of the often-postponed marking debate in the Reich. After the Reich Protector's agencies circulated a report early in July 1941 that complaints about the Jews' impertinent behavior were piling up in all parts of the Protectorate and that the German population demanded marking Jews with armbands,[85] the State Secretary of the Protectorate, Karl Hermann Frank, took action in mid-month. Frank wrote to the Chief of the Reich Chancellery in Berlin (Reich Minister Hans Heinrich Lammers) that in his opinion the moment had come for introduction of armbands for Jews. The "impertinent and provocative behavior of the Jews in connection with the war against the Soviet Union" was on the rise, and "from the standpoint of policy and police, Czech contact with Jews"

---

[81] CAHJP, Jerusalem, A/W, No. 421, no folio numbers, Report on the "Utilization of Jewish Labor," undated, 3–6. See *Deutsche Politik im "Protektorat,"* 123–124, Doc. No. 23, Report of Central Office, October 2, 1941.

[82] Ibid.

[83] USHMMA Washington, DC, RG-11.001M.23, Reel 91 (OSOBI [Center for the Preservation of the Historical Documentary Collection, Moscow]1488-1-150), Fol. 7, Copy of the Prague SD Main District March 1941 monthly report, 57; ibid., RG-11.001M.15, Reel 83 (OSOBI 1322-2-391), Fol. 49, Copy of the Prague SD Main District May 1941 monthly report, June 1, 1941, 46.

[84] See *Widerstand und Verfolgung in Wien 1934–1945, Bd. 3: 1938–1945*, edited by Documentation Archive of the Austrian Resistance, 2nd printing (Vienna, 1984), 276, Doc. No. 145, File note of the leader of the IKG in Vienna, August 5, 1941.

[85] USHMMA Washington, DC, RG-48.005M, Reel 4 (Prague State Archive), Carton 389, I 3b-5851, No. 13, no folio numbers, Protectorate Group I to Group 1 3, to the attention of Ministerial Councillor Dr. Mokry, July 2, 1941.

must "be made more difficult in every possible way."[86] Lammers brought
in the Reich Interior Ministry. At the end of July, Frank pressured Lammers
to take the question "to the Führer for resolution" if necessary.[87] Lammers
conveyed these ideas on August 10, 1941, to the Reich Interior Ministry
because it had the "leading role in handling the entire Jewish question."[88]
The State Secretary Stuckart – based on changes in the situation since 1938
and 1940 – believed that the time had come to introduce a system for marking
Jews in the Protectorate. Foreign policy considerations should be ignored, in
Stuckart's view; marking had existed in the General Government for a long
time. Of course, consideration should be given to "whether marking Jews
could be expected to increase Jewish workers' departures from businesses in
the Protectorate," departures that could not be offset with other workers.[89]
Minister Wilhelm Frick also commented positively on August 14, but he
wanted to wait for the Foreign Office to state its opinion and for the results
of studies on whether marking would affect forced labor.[90] The discussion
soon also extended to German territory. After Goebbels finally had obtained
Hitler's consent directly, the RSHA drafted a police order.[91] The introduction
of a Jewish mark signaled to the public at home and abroad the completion
of the forced community in the Greater German Reich. The limitation on
individual freedom of movement contained in the order simultaneously put
in place the last technical condition for mass deportation of the Jewish population for which preparations were in full swing. The order introducing the
Star of David took effect on September 19, 1941, in Germany, Austria, and
the Protectorate of Bohemia and Moravia.[92]

From this time on, Jews in the Protectorate had to wear the stigmatizing
mark. On September 17, 1941, the BdS, Horst Böhme, sent out a circular
in which he reserved implementation of all measures to his agency in order

---

[86] Kurt Pätzold (ed.), *Verfolgung, Vertreibung, Vernichtung. Dokumente des faschistischen
Antisemitismus 1933–1942* (Leipzig, 1983), 294, Doc. No. 269, State Secretary Karl Hermann Frank to Lammers, July 16, 1941.

[87] USHMMA Washington, DC, RG-48.005M, Reel 4 (Prague State Archive), Carton 389, I
3b-5851, No. 8, no folio numbers, State Secretary Frank to Lammers on July 30, 1941.

[88] BA Berlin, Case XI, No. 371, Fols. 70–71, Lammers to the Reich Interior Minister on August
10, 1941, as well as Lammers to Frank (NG-1111).

[89] Ibid., Fols. 72–73, Stuckart to Lammers, August 14, 1941 (NG-1111); see excerpt in Pätzold,
Verfolgung, 302–303, Doc. No. 276.

[90] BA Berlin, Case XI, No. 371, Fol. 74, Note of Ficker on the position of the minister, undated
(NG-1111).

[91] *Die Tagebücher von Joseph Goebbels. Teil II: Diktate 1941–1945*, edited by Elke Fröhlich
as commissioned by the Institut für Zeitgeschichte and with support of the State Archive
Service of Russia, Vol. 1 (Munich and others, 1996), 278, Entry of August 20, 1941; see
Lösener, "Das Reichsministerium," 305, Note of Lösener, August 20, 1941.

[92] *Reichsgesetzblatt*, 1941 I: 547; see *Jüdisches Nachrichtenblatt* (JNBl), 61 (September 12,
1941): 1.

to centralize the Protectorate's anti-Jewish policies.[93] And on September 25, Heydrich was appointed Deputy Reich Protector. A few days later Heydrich removed Premier Eliaš.[94] The German personnel change, against the background of new deportation plans, brought with it more extreme anti-Jewish policies. On September 29, in one of his first official acts, Heydrich placed the Jewish partners of "privileged mixed marriages" in the Protectorate on the same footing as Jews. All restrictions thus applied to this group, including the obligation to wear a Star of David. In the same decree, he closed all synagogues because of ostensible whispered propaganda and threatened "Jewish sympathizers with severe penalties."[95]

The Jewish population had to be registered again by October 1, 1941. The Prague Central Office surprisingly reported on October 2, even before re-registration had gotten underway, that approximately 88,000 Jews still lived in the Protectorate.[96] The Czech government and the German Protectorate administration continued to work hand in hand. In this period, Hácha proposed isolation of Jews in closed-off residential districts – de facto ghettos – but this approach was rejected internally because the deportations were already underway.[97] Hitler himself ordered on October 6, 1941, that all the Protectorate Jews were to be deported directly to the East, not first to Poland. However, at that moment the military's demand for transportation was still great.[98] The Czech Jews not transported quickly were therefore supposed to be brought together in Czech ghettos – as in Poland – and to perform forced labor there, as is evident from an October 10, 1941, meeting of Heydrich in Prague with Frank, Böhme, Eichmann, and others. For the moment, 5,000 Jews would be "evacuated" from Prague. The persons remaining were to be concentrated initially in three large cities of the Protectorate. For practical reasons, however, the plan was to establish only two ghettos, one in Bohemia and one in Moravia, each of which would be subdivided into a work camp and a supply depot. "The Jews can be well provided for with work (in the

---

[93] Jaroslava Milotová, "Der Okkupationsapparat und die Vorbereitung der Transporte nach Lodz," in *Theresienstädter Studien und Dokumente 1998*, 40–69, here 41; Potthast, *Das jüdische Zentralmuseum*, 133.

[94] Rothkirchen, "The Protectorate Government," 353.

[95] USHMMA Washington, DC, RG-48.005M, Reel 4 (Prague State Archive), Carton 389, I 3b-5851, No. 21, no folio numbers, Circular decree of the Reich Protector/BdS on September 29, 1941. See *Deutsche Politik im "Protektorat,"* 97, Doc. No. 14. See Milotová, "Der Okkupationsapparat," 57.

[96] *Deutsche Politik im "Protektorat,"* 125, Doc. No. 23, Report of the Central Office, October 2, 1941, Attachment, Table I. This number was possibly not the result of a new round of registrations, but rather of calculations based on emigration and earlier numbers, according to Milotová, "Der Okkupationsapparat," 48.

[97] *Deutsche Politik im "Protektorat,"* 128, Doc. No. 24. See Milotová, "Der Okkupationsapparat," 41.

[98] *Deutsche Politik im "Protektorat,"* 130, Doc. No. 25, Record of the table talks of Hitler on the treatment of the Czechs, October 6, 1941.

camp by production of small objects without the expense of machines, for example, wooden shoes, woven straw for Wehrmacht units in the north, etc.). The council of elders is to collect these objects and to receive in return the bare minimum amount of food with the calculated minimum of vitamins, etc. (under control of the Security Police). In part, small details also can work outside the ghetto under guard; this is especially the case for the special workers needed." In Moravia the ghetto was to be established in a small village, in Bohemia, either in the Alt Ratibor Hussite castle, or better yet, in the Theresienstadt fortress after its take-over by the Central Office. Following evacuation of the Jews from Theresienstadt to the East, the town could later become an exemplary German settlement. Resettlement of the Czech Jews in ghettos within the Protectorate was to proceed according to the principles of deportation, meaning that all possessions had to be left behind.[99]

Only two days after the meeting, Heydrich officially ordered the "migration" of Jewish property during evacuation. An order of the Reich Protector to appear shortly would transfer this task to the Central Office for Jewish Emigration.[100] The Jews scheduled for evacuation had been assembled in the Prague exposition palace since October 10. German Order Police and Czech policemen accompanied them from there to the railway station. The first train of five planned transports left Prague for the Lodz ghetto in the Warthegau on October 16, and the second, on October 21.[101]

As the mass deportations began, the BdS, Horst Böhme, once again emphasized to the Czech Interior Minister, Josef Jezek, that all future measures against Jews were the business of the BdS.[102] The German measures encountered little resistance from the Czechs, but the potential for supply problems in the period after transport out of the cities caused concern. For that reason, Národní Souručenství, for example, proposed to the Czech government in mid-October 1941 that a better alternative was "to collect all the Jews in one part of the city or somewhere near the city, and to control, monitor, and manage every aspect of their lives while they worked for the common good."[103]

THE EXPANSION OF FORCED LABOR BY THE LABOR ADMINISTRATION

Since the decree at the end of August that extended age limits, the Protectorate's labor administration had been able to expand the forced-labor

[99] Ibid., 137–141, Doc. No. 29. Notes from the meeting, October 10, 1941.

[100] USHMMA Washington, DC, RG-48.005M, Reel 3 (Prague State Archive), No. 9, no folio numbers, Circular decree of the Reich Protector/BdS I 2776/41, October 12, 1941.

[101] Milotová, "Der Okkupationsapparat," 60–61.

[102] *Deutsche Politik im "Protektorat,"* 174, Doc. No. 44, Eleventh meeting of Jezek with Böhme on November 3, 1941. See Milotová, "Der Okkupationsapparat," 42; Potthast, *Das jüdische Zentralmuseum,* 133.

[103] Quoted in Milotová, "Der Okkupationsapparat," 56.

program a second time. In August, the Olmütz labor office had 333 of 741 registered men eighteen to fifty years old performing forced labor. One month later, 472 of 1,079 Jews sixteen to sixty years old were engaged in compulsory labor, and in October, the number had risen to 531.[104] In the Zlín labor office district, 366 of 525 registered men worked as forced laborers during August, and 415 of 579 during September.[105] The non-Aryan department of the Prague labor office registered 10,106 men in August; 574 of them worked in agriculture and 2,206 in construction. In September, 15,710 men had been registered in Prague.[106] Despite the ground rules given against it, Jews also worked in the armaments industry, for example, 215 men in war production at the Avia Flugzeugwerke (airplane factory).[107]

On September 9, 1941, the Ministry for Social and Health Administration added another decree for the labor administration. Besides extending the age limits, the decree forbade individual allocation, and pressed for separate Jewish columns and for their preferred assignment to heavy labor in construction or in companies critical to the war.[108] Parallel to this development, the Reich Protector transferred to the Jewish community the obligation of providing public welfare to the poor. The welfare practices for needy Jews in the Protectorate were thus aligned with the provisions in effect since the end of 1938 in Germany and Austria.[109]

The Iglau labor office reported to the ministry for September 1941 that 284 of the 303 Jewish men in forced labor were working in groups, 208 of them in railway construction and 76 in agriculture.[110] At this time, seventy-three Jews worked in Klattau district, twelve of them women engaged in

---

104 USHMMA Washington, DC, RG-48.005M, Reel 2 (Prague State Archive), Carton 859, II 4–4055, no Doc. No., no folio numbers, Statistics on utilization of Jews as labor in the Protectorate, Status as of September 1, 1941; ibid., No. 1, no folio numbers, Olmütz labor office statistics for October 1941, October 31, 1941.

105 Ibid., no Doc. No., no folio numbers, Statistics on labor utilization, Status as of September 1, 1941; ibid., No. 2, no folio numbers, Zlín labor office Statistics for September 1941.

106 Ibid., no Doc. No., no folio numbers, Statistics on labor utilization, Status as of September 1, 1941; ibid., No. 9, no folio numbers, Prague labor office statistics for September 1941.

107 *Deutsche Politik im "Protektorat,"* 101, Doc. No. 18, Monthly report of the Prague Stapo central office, September 30, 1941.

108 Mentioned in USHMMA Washington, DC, RG-48.005M, Reel 2 (Prague State Archive), Carton 859, II 4–4055, No. 21, no folio numbers, Klattau Labor Office to the Ministry for Social and Health Administration, October 6, 1941.

109 The August 5, 1941, decree of the Reich Protector took effect on September 1, 1941, after being publicly announced on August 22, 1941; ibid., Reel 4 (Prague State Archive), I 3b-5812, Welfare for Jews, Nos. 2–3, no folio numbers, Handwritten note on the draft of the Reich Protector's June 1941 decree. On public welfare and the Jews in Germany and Austria, see Wolf Gruner, *Öffentliche Wohlfahrt und Judenverfolgung. Wechselwirkungen lokaler und zentraler Politik im NS-Staat (1933–1942)* (Munich, 2002).

110 USHMMA Washington, DC, RG-48.005M, Reel 2 (Prague State Archive), Carton 859, II 4–4055, No. 3, no folio numbers, Iglau labor office to the Ministry for Social and Health Administration on October 2, 1941.

leather goods production at the Firma Gottlieb Singer. The Westböhmische Kaolinwerke (clay works) in Klumtschau employed thirty-nine forced laborers, and the Sägewerk Kusy (sawmill) in Klattau, four men; the carpenter Kufner in Neugedein had four for construction of military barracks, as did the quarry of the Firma Pokorny in Schüttenhofen. The Klattau labor office had assigned further columns to river regulation in Schüttenhofen and to construction of a new road between Schüttenhofen and Rabi, as well as to work in agriculture and forestry. A total of 74 men labored for construction companies, and 124 in agriculture.[111]

In several labor office districts, including in Mährisch-Ostrau, however, the fitness examinations of the Jews were not yet complete, which impeded full implementation of forced labor.[112] In September 1941, Jewish women still had not been examined in any district. Nevertheless, many already worked in the forced-labor program "as volunteers," such as forty-one women in Olmütz for the beet harvest.[113] In order to protect Jews from heavy labor, especially the elderly and the very young, the Jewish side suggested to the authorities assignments to light work, for example, cardboard box manufacture, hand-looming, jewelry making, bookbinding, electric appliance manufacture, and so forth. To meet the requirements for forced labor and thus convince the authorities, the plan was to employ Jews in special Jewish departments, working at home or in separate rooms supervised and organized by the Jewish community.[114]

In October 1941, the labor offices expanded use of forced labor still further, primarily by placement of male Jews in construction enterprises. In the Kolín district, the number of registered unemployed Jews sixteen to sixty years old and fit to work was reduced in this manner from 215 to 150.[115] Only a few labor office districts, such as Königgrätz, had not yet completed the examinations for the sixteen-to-eighteen-year-old and fifty-to-sixty-year-old age groups. But in Königgrätz the pool of eighteen-to-fifty-year-olds was entirely depleted after forty-seven men were sent to work in forestry.[116] In several labor office districts (for example, in Pilsen, Beneschau, Pardubitz,

[111] Ibid., No. 21, no folio numbers, Klattau labor office to Dr. Fleischer, Ministry for Social and Health Administration on October 6, 1941.

[112] Ibid., No. 22, no folio numbers, Statistics on utilization of Jews as labor in the Protectorate for October 1941 (undated).

[113] Ibid., No. 7, no folio numbers, Olmütz labor office statistics for October 1941, October 31, 1941.

[114] CAHJP, Jerusalem, A/W, No. 421, no folio numbers, Report on "Utilization of Jewish Labor," undated, 4–6.

[115] USHMMA Washington, DC, RG-48.005M, Reel 2 (Prague State Archive), Carton 859, II 4–4055, No. 14, no folio numbers, Kolín labor office statistics for October 1941, October 24, 1941.

[116] Ibid., No. 15, no folio numbers, Königgrätz labor office to the Ministry for Social and Health Administration on October 24, 1941; ibid., Königgrätz labor office statistics for October 1941, October 31, 1941.

and Strakonitz) officials had already pressed almost the entire local contingent of sixteen-to-sixty-year-old men into forced-labor service.[117] In contrast, women had been spared from the forced-labor measures in most districts. That fact, however, drove the Tabor labor office to distraction. The rabbi, as the local Jewish community's representative, had assured the office that Jewish women were not subject to the labor obligation. The labor office asked the ministry in Prague for clear guidelines.[118]

The balance sheet of the Protectorate's labor administration for October 1941 shows that almost all Jewish men sixteen to sixty years old finally had been examined for fitness and were registered at the labor offices; in contrast, this was only the case for women in Jungbunzlau, Klattau, Kolín, Pilsen, and Mährisch-Ostrau districts. In Königgrätz, Tabor, Iglau, and Zlín districts, not even the number of potential female workers was known. In the Protectorate, where 17,600 men had been registered in August, the number in October was already up to 25,857 men and 26,612 women, a total of 52,469 persons. As of the beginning of the month, 3,963 men and 425 women were still classified as unemployed and thus available. In the course of the month, the labor offices committed 504 men to construction, as well as 409 men and 98 women to other economic sectors. The number of Jewish forced laborers at the end of October encompassed 11,949 men and 307 women, a total of 12,256.[119] That was only slightly more than in August, but in the meantime there were scarcely any individual placements. Thus, from the end of August to the end of October the number of Jews performing forced labor had risen from just under 7,000 to 12,000 despite the fact that mass deportations had begun in October.[120]

On October 23, 1941, the newspaper *Neuer Tag* publicized the use of Jews for forced labor in Mährisch-Ostrau. In a report about the forced-labor unit there utilized for constructing roads and collecting garbage, the article maintained that the unit was known as the "Jewish punishment column" because many concentration camp prisoners worked in it. In light of the evidence presented here, that can hardly have been the truth, and must necessarily be viewed as denunciation.[121]

---

[117] Ibid., No. 17, no folio numbers, Pilsen labor office statistics for October 1941, October 27, 1941; ibid., No. 18, Beneschau labor office statistics for October 1941, November 1, 1941; ibid., No. 19, Pardubitz labor office statistics for October 1941, October 27, 1941; ibid., No. 20, Strakonitz labor office statistics for October, 1941, October 27, 1941.

[118] Ibid., No. 21, no folio numbers, Tabor labor office to the Ministry for Social and Health Administration on November 1, 1941.

[119] Ibid., No. 22, no folio numbers, Statistics on the utilization of Jews as labor in the Protectorate for October 1941 (undated).

[120] See also the statement that in this time frame over 6,300 persons more were recruited; CAHJP, Jerusalem, A/W, No. 421, no folio numbers, Report on the "Utilization of Jewish Labor," undated, 3–6; *Deutsche Politik im "Protektorat,"* 123–124, Doc. No. 23, Report of the Central Office, October 2, 1941.

[121] *The Black Book,* 177.

In the course of November as well, the number of forced laborers increased steadily in all districts. In many places, more women were now affected, too.[122] In a few labor office districts, the Jewish community (which performed the fitness examinations) at least was able to delay, and even for a long time to block, forced labor for sixteen- to-eighteen-year-olds and fifty-to-sixty-year-olds.[123] In other places, such as the Pardubitz, Strakonitz, Tabor, Mährisch-Ostrau, and Zlín districts, the labor offices had in the meantime called up all available Jewish men for utilization as labor.[124] In Mährisch-Ostrau, the labor office recorded no more unemployed men and reported that 233 of 466 men allocated as forced laborers performed excavation work and 7 were employed in Aryan companies. One hundred seventy Jews were ostensibly still active in trade, as physicians, or in Jewish organizations.[125]

While the Prague labor administration had over 15,710 Jewish men sixteen to sixty years old in their card file as of September 1941, only a few more than 13,800 remained in November, after the first mass transports from the city to Litzmannstadt (Lodz). Obviously, 1,500 men fit for work had been among the thousands of persons deported. Besides sending Jews to agriculture and construction in November, the labor office also sent 300 Prague Jews to other economic sectors, probably to industry. At the end of November, 6,300 persons, 175 of them women, were thus being used as forced labor in the former Czech capital. Amazingly, that was almost 1,000 more than at the end of September, despite the transports.[126]

In December, 1941, only 43,000 Jewish men and women sixteen to sixty years old were still registered at the labor offices. Nevertheless, 12,071 men and 959 women, a total of 13,030 persons, were forced laborers. Despite the ongoing deportations, there were once again a thousand more performing forced labor than in the previous month. The labor offices now considered 4,267 Jews unemployed and available for utilization. Of that number, 1,927 were women, which confirms that in the meantime more women had been examined to determine fitness for forced labor.[127]

During the winter months, various construction projects on which Jews had worked as forced laborers had to be shut down for a time. In the

---

[122] USHMMA Washington, DC, RG-48.005M, Reel 2 (Prague State Archive), Carton 859, II 4–4055, Nos. 25–39, no folio numbers, Deutsch-Brod, Jitschin, Jungbunzlau, Kladno, Klattau, Beneschau, and Brünn labor office statistics for November 1941.

[123] Ibid., No. 31, no folio numbers, Königgrätz labor office to the Ministry for Social and Health Administration on December 2, 1941.

[124] Ibid., Nos. 32, 36, 37, 40, and 42, no folio numbers, Pardubitz, Strakonitz, Tabor, Mährisch-Ostrau, and Zlín labor office statistics for November 1941.

[125] Ibid., No. 40, no folio numbers, Mährisch-Ostrau labor office statistics for November 1941, explanation regarding column 9.

[126] Ibid., No. 9, no folio numbers, Prague labor office statistics for September 1941; Ibid., No. 35, no folio numbers, Prague labor office statistics for November 1941.

[127] Ibid., No. 64, no folio numbers, Statistics on the utilization of Jews as labor in the Protectorate for December 1941 (undated).

Königgrätz labor office district, 299 of 343 registered Jews were working as forced laborers in January 1942. For the seven workers dismissed because of the season from the Firma Ingenieur Kindl (engineering) in Predmeritz, the labor office was able to find work as unskilled laborers for the Königgrätz municipal administration.[128] Königgrätz was one of the last labor office districts in which, even in February 1942, neither men aged sixteen to eighteen and fifty to sixty nor women of any age had been examined to determine fitness.[129] In February 1942, the Protectorate labor offices only recorded 18,709 men and 19,486 women, totaling 38,195. Of these, 13,567 men and 754 women were reportedly working, once again more than at the end of 1941, despite further deportations. While there were obviously scarcely any placements in agriculture and construction because of the season, more than 2,000 new persons were sent to other economic sectors, evidently to industry.[130] In the winter months of 1941–42, 1,372 Jews were engaged every day at seventeen sites clearing snow for the Prague municipal administration, just as in Vienna. At the same time, separate clearing columns were employed again at the Prague-Rusin airfield, a total of 929 men.[131]

In March 1942 the last fitness examinations took place in Jitschin district. A number of large landholders there had already submitted requests to the labor office for Jewish forced-labor columns to perform spring tasks. In Pardubitz district, Jewish columns were withdrawn from civilian sectors (for example, the toy industry, construction, food production, and the leather, wood, and metal industries) so that they could be assigned to work important for the war. In Iglau district, the local labor office planned to send all able-bodied Jews to two camps for railway construction between Brünn and Deutsch Brod after April, as in previous years. When winter weather interrupted railway construction activities, the forced laborers had worked in cities and towns, usually clearing snow. In Brünn, too, over 2,000 Jews were employed in winter jobs for the regional capital's administration, on average about 100 Jews a day. After new deportations, however, these assignments were cancelled. Still, the Brünn labor office, according to its own statements, succeeded in having at least the Jews working in mining released "from transports until further notice" by calling attention to the "extraordinary importance of coal output in the Rossitz mining area." Deportations also considerably reduced the number of employed Jews in the Pilsen area.

---

[128] Ibid., No. 74, no folio numbers, Königgrätz labor office to the Ministry for Social and Health Administration on February 2, 1942.

[129] Ibid., No. 96, no folio numbers, Königgrätz labor office to the Ministry for Social and Health Administration on March 2, 1942.

[130] Ibid., No. 108, no folio numbers, Statistics on the utilization of Jews as labor in the Protectorate for February 1942 (undated).

[131] Krejčová, Svobodová, and Hyndráková (eds.), *Židé v Protektorátu*, 111, Doc. 5, Report of the Prague Jewish community.

Nevertheless, the labor office there planned to put together a large suprare-gional work group of 4,000 Jews to remove a windbreak in the Kammwald. In Strakonitz district, various columns of Jews already performed forest tasks for the forestry offices. The Kladno labor office, on the other hand, had diffi-culty placing Jews in agriculture because farmers blocked their employment and because segregated housing for groups of twenty-five workers was not readily available. The small number of Jews not yet deported, mostly those in mixed marriages, were to be used in mining. Likewise, plans were made in Kladno to dispatch 1,000 Jewish women for reforesting. Housing and guards had been secured. But the Kladno labor office was particularly interested in local mining. The performance of the Jewish workers employed before now had been satisfactory, the labor office maintained, and although "use of Jews seemed undesirable for the long term," the lack of any other workers left no recourse but to set aside all misgivings and fall back on Jewish labor. The office in the meantime had obtained 250 men from Theresienstadt through the Prague ministry; the men were housed separately. Another 160 were expected.[132]

Jewish Forced Laborers in the Protectorate

	Jewish Population	Forced Laborers
September 1941	88,105	7,000
October 1941		12,256
November 1941		
December 1941	74,190	13,030
January 1942		
February 1942		14,321
March 1942	61,320	14,453
April 1942		15,747
May 1942	Approx. 50,000	More than 16,000

GHETTOIZATION AND DEPORTATIONS

Meanwhile, a ghetto for Jews had been established in Theresienstadt.[133] At the beginning of November 1941, the BdS had ordered construction on instructions of the Reich Protector and had invited all groups, the Central Office (SS Hauptsturmführer Hans Günther), and the Kladno chief district administrator to a meeting with the Reich Protector.[134]

[132] Ibid., No. 129, no folio numbers, Copy of the situation reports from the labor offices for March 1942.
[133] On the following section, also see Potthast, *Das jüdische Zentralmuseum*, 136–139.
[134] USHMMA Washington, DC, RG-48.005M, Reel 3 (Prague State Archive), No. 11, no folio numbers, Circular decree of the BdS (Böhme) I 498/41, November 4, 1941.

When the preparations in Theresienstadt were far enough along that transports could be sent there, on December 8 the BdS issued guidelines for "evacuating the Jews" to the chief district administrators in the Protectorate.[135] Heydrich himself then signed a circular decree "on evacuating the Jews" on December 15, 1941. Parallel to the "transports of Jews to the Litzmannstadt, Minsk, and Riga ghettos," dispatch of "large transports" to the Theresienstadt ghetto began at this point. The BdS was to determine the territories and sequence of the transports "because only central control" would guarantee that "the requirements of the economy, commerce, and labor deployment, and protection of other general interests [would be] taken into consideration appropriately." The Central Office for Jewish Emigration was to take responsibility for putting together collective transports and also for taking charge of property. The basis for the latter was to be the property declaration provided by the victims immediately before deportation.[136] The fortifications in Theresienstadt were not adequate, however, so the Reich Protector dissolved the municipality on February 16, 1942, because of "measures having to do with housing Jews in segregated settlements."[137] Thus, the entire city of Terezin became a ghetto.[138] The German population was supposed to leave the city. The emigration fund covered reimbursement for expropriation with the Jewish property seized.[139] Ten thousand Czech Jews supposedly had been taken to Terezin by mid-1942.[140] Ghetto inmates had to perform forced labor, but not only in Theresienstadt. Beginning in spring 1942, hundreds of inmates were sent to different regions of the Protectorate, for example, to Kladno. In April, over 1,000 women were taken to Rakovnik district to plant trees. Some of these prisoner details existed until fall 1943.[141]

In the first half of 1942, the Nazi leadership selected Theresienstadt as the transit ghetto for German Jews, and the Czech Jews were therefore deported at an early point from the fortress to the East.[142] On March 6, Eichmann announced in a meeting at the RSHA that another 20,000 persons soon would be "evacuated" from Prague.[143] After the March and April deportations that followed, the labor offices in the Protectorate only had about

---

[135] Mentioned in ibid., No. 3, no folio numbers, Note of Grouup I 3 b in the Office of the Reich Protector, December 10, 1941.

[136] Ibid., No. 10, no folio numbers, Circular decree of the Reich Protector/BdS I 3098/41, December 15, 1941.

[137] Official gazette of the Reich Protector, No. 7 (1942), February 28, 1942, Facsimile in *Europa unterm Hakenkreuz. Österreich und Tschechoslowakei*, Illustration 22.

[138] *Deutsche Politik im "Protektorat,"* 237, Doc. No. 82, Heydrich to Frick, February 16, 1942, decree; see *Hitler's Ten Year War*, 57.

[139] *Europa unterm Hakenkreuz. Österreich und Tschechoslowakei*, Illustration 22.

[140] *Hitler's Ten Year War*, 60.

[141] Kárný, "Zur Statistik der jüdischen Bevölkerung," 9–19, here 16.

[142] *Hitler's Ten Year War*, 60.

[143] *Kennzeichen J. Bilder, Dokumente, Berichte zur Geschichte der Verbrechen des Hitlerfaschismus an den deutschen Juden 1933–1945*, edited by Helmut Eschwege (Berlin, 1981),

35,000 Jews sixteen to sixty years old at their disposal. Those offices increasingly sent hundreds of workers to agriculture and construction. At the end of April, 1,868 persons examined and declared capable of working were still unemployed. Meanwhile, 14,809 men and 938 women performed forced labor, a total of 15,747.[144] Despite further transports carrying 4,000 persons, the reports of the labor offices for May 1942 still recorded increases in forced labor to over 16,000 Czech Jews.[145] (See map 6, p. 171.) As in Germany and Austria, forced labor in agriculture and forestry organized by the Prague Jewish community reached its highest level. While in 1941 the peak number was still 1,650 (including 300 men at the Central Offices's Linden estate), after a seasonal drop, the number rose in May 1942 to more than 1,900 men (including 300 on the Linden estate) who in 110 groups performed spring seasonal tasks on estates and in forestry districts. The largest group consisted of 200 men employed at the Wischau army forestry administration in Scherowitz.[146] At this point, Jewish forced labor used in the Protectorate had peaked, and the pool of Jews between sixteen and sixty capable of working was finally virtually depleted.

While massive use of forced labor already declined in Germany, a delayed high point in the Protectorate during spring 1942 prompted consideration of establishing special labor laws for Jews there in keeping with conditions in the Old Reich. At the beginning of May, 1942, a draft by the Ministry for the Economy and Labor (*Ministerium für Wirtschaft und Arbeit*) circulated within the Office of the Reich Protector; the proposed decree was to replicate the German regulations of October, 1941. In contrast to the legislation in Germany, the draft for the Protectorate also provided for partial discrimination against Jews in mixed marriages.[147] Group I 3 of the Office of the Reich Protector, "from the viewpoint of the general policy on Jews," spoke adamantly in favor of generally treating the privileged Czech Jews in mixed marriages the same as the rest of the Jewish forced laborers and referred to the September 29, 1941, Heydrich decree.[148] The "government

---

Report of the Düssedorf Gestapo, March 9, 1942, on the March 6, 1942, meeting in Office IV B 4; *Deutsche Politik im "Protektorat,"* 241, Doc. No. 85.

[144] USHMMA Washington, DC, RG-48.005M, Reel 2 (Prague State Archive), Carton 859, II 4–4055, No. 150, no folio numbers, Statistics on the utilization of Jews as labor in the Protectorate for April 1942 (undated).

[145] Ibid., No. 171, no folio numbers, Statistics on the utilization of Jews as labor in the Protectorate for May 1942 (undated). (Some numbers are hard to read in original.)

[146] Krejčová, Svobodová, and Hyndráková (eds.), *Židé v Protektorátu*, 111, Doc. 5, Report of the Prague Jewish community.

[147] For example, Jewish women were not to receive any maternity benefits; USHMMA Washington, DC, RG-48.005M, Reel 4 (Prague State Archive), Carton 389, I 3b-5813, Treatment of Jews under labor law, Nos. 8–9, no folio numbers, Circular of the Reich Protector II 4 to Groups in the Office, BdS, and to the Party liaison office in the Reich Protector's office II 4, May 8, 1942.

[148] Ibid., Reich Protector I 3 b to Group II 4, May 21, 1942.

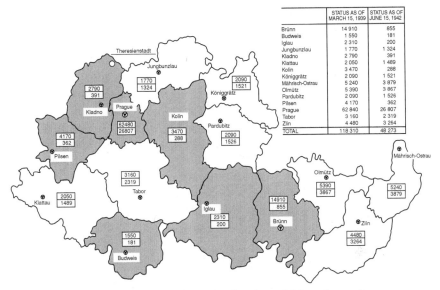

	STATUS AS OF MARCH 15, 1939	STATUS AS OF JUNE 15, 1942
Brünn	14 910	855
Budweis	1 550	181
Iglau	2 310	200
Jungbunzlau	1 770	1 324
Kladno	2 790	391
Klattau	2 050	1 489
Kolin	3 470	288
Königgrätz	2 090	1 521
Mährisch-Ostrau	5 240	3 879
Olmütz	5 390	3 867
Pardubitz	2 090	1 526
Pilsen	4 170	362
Prague	62 840	26 807
Tabor	3 160	2 319
Zlin	4 480	3 264
TOTAL	118 310	48 273

Map 6. The Jews in the Protectorate of Bohemia and Moravia, on June 15, 1942

order on treatment of Jews under labor law in the Protectorate of Bohemia and Moravia" was finally issued on July 17, 1942, and took effect on August 1, 1942. There were no exception provisions for "privileged" Jews.[149] Jews lost the right to social insurance, overtime wages, vacations, and other benefits available to the other Czech laborers.[150]

In August 1942, 12,000 Jews were sent for forced labor to the Moravska and Kamienna coal mines. There they toiled twelve hours a day for 15 percent of the usual wages and received only food and government share certificates, to be redeemed after the war.[151] Soon, however, because of deportations, hardly any Czech Jews remained for forced labor in the Protectorate. By the end of 1942, the Security Police had "evacuated" 69,677 Jewish men and women from the Protectorate. Only 15,530 Jews were then left in that area, 13 percent of the original number.[152]

Many of these people lived in mixed marriages. They were also used as forced labor. In Prague, Jews in mixed marriages had to report to the competent Gestapo office in the beginning of March 1943; the Gestapo then designated them "full Jews" and assigned them to compulsory employment, as Berta Landré reported. In Prague male and female Jews worked in book

---

[149] Ibid., Reich Protector II 4 b to Group I 3 b, October 16, 1942.
[150] *Hitler's Ten Year War*, 58.   [151] *The Black Book*, 178.
[152] LBIA New York, Microfilms, Wiener Library, 500 Series, No. 526, Inspector for statistics with the RFSS, January 1, 1943 (Korherr Report), 5 (also in BA Berlin, NS 19, Nr. 1570). See *The Black Book*, 178.

warehouses cataloging and sorting. Forced laborers were used to clean out and renovate residences of the Jews deported shortly before. Female forced laborers were taken from Czech provincial areas to a Prague barracks camp at a former sports field of the Jewish Hagibor organization; there they had to spend twelve-hour shifts with Jewish women from Prague splitting mica into small, paper-thin wafers. Then transports to Theresienstadt ghetto ended this chapter as well.[153] Far more than 100 men from mixed marriages were shipped from Prague to two special labor camps in the Komotau area (Sudeten) in December 1944. They lived in wooden barracks in Kalek. Two local inns housed sixty Prague Mischlinge, who had to work for the Rothenhaus forestry administration.[154] They all were luckily liberated there at the end of the war.

SUMMARY

After establishment of the Protectorate of Bohemia and Moravia on the territory of the Czech state, a systematic anti-Jewish policy developed there beginning in March 1939, advanced both by the Germans and by the Czech government. The Gestapo's Prague Central Office for Jewish Emigration, established in summer 1939, was to gain more influence at an early point than its sister organization in Vienna. At first the progressive exclusion of Jews from employment in administration and business by the Czech government led rapidly to impoverishment, just as in the Reich. As the odds favored deportation of the Jewish population in the near future, no central regulations governed forced labor at first. Nevertheless, in 1939 labor offices began preferentially assigning Jews registered as unemployed, and then in 1940, individual Bürgermeister commenced obligating all Jewish residents to labor. Then, after April 1941, a number of successive decrees of the Czech government based on agreements with the Reich Protector and the SD Central Office established a forced-labor system for Jews. While in May the system usually affected unemployed men eighteen to fifty years old, recruiting was extended at the end of August to all men sixteen to sixty years old. Initially, women had scarcely any role, but in fall 1941, after examinations to determine fitness, the forced-labor system finally included the majority of all Jews fit to work. That meant that in the Protectorate, the Czech government and the German Protectorate government jointly set compulsory allocation in motion. The labor offices first placed the Jews mostly in agriculture and construction, then later in industry and forestry. Segregation was initially not as strict as in the Reich, as the Czechs were also viewed as inferior. However,

---

[153] Berta Landré, "Jüdische Zwangsarbeit in Prag," in *Zeitgeschichte*, 9, 11/12 (Vienna, 1982): 365–377.

[154] Ludomír Kocourek, "Das Schicksal der Juden im Sudetengau im Licht der erhaltenen Quellen," in *Theresienstädter Studien und Dokumente 1997*, 86–104, here 96.

Jews' wages were reduced first informally, then in 1941 formally, to levels below Czechs' wages, often so far below that the Jewish community had to intervene with additional assistance. While on the one hand tens of thousands of men and women were deported after October from the Protectorate to the East, on the other hand the labor administration expanded the forced-labor program. At the peak in spring 1942, more than 16,000 persons were involved. In July 1942, Jews in the Protectorate were made subject to special labor laws, as in most countries under German rule. The labor administration directed and organized forced labor in the Protectorate, but in contrast to Reich territory, some control was in the hands of the Prague SD Central Office after May 1941. Thus, the Protectorate of Bohemia and Moravia possessed transitory significance for the form of forced labor introduced in the occupied parts of Poland that formed the General Government.

Jewish Population in the Greater German Reich and Occupied Poland[155]

Territory	May 17, 1939	December 31, 1942
Old Reich	233,973	51,327
Sudeten	2,649	–
Austria	94,270	8,102
Bohemia and Moravia	110,000	15,550
Annexed Polish Territories (e.g., Warthegau)	790,000	233,210
General Government	2,000,000	297,914
Total	3,230,892	606,103

[155] LBIA New York, Microfilms, Wiener Library, 500 Series, No. 526, Inspector for statistics with the RFSS, April 1, 1943 (Korherr Report), 3 (also in BA Berlin, NS 19, Nr. 1570).

THE OCCUPIED TERRITORIES
OF POLAND

6

Camps and Ghettos – Forced Labor in the Reich Gau Wartheland, 1939–1944

EXPULSION PLANS AND FORCED LABOR AS AN INTERMEDIATE SOLUTION

Forced labor had been a basic component of Jewish policy in the Reich before the war, and it was to become an element of war and occupation thinking as well. In September 1939, the Nazi state started the war with Poland. After the quick defeat of the Polish state, it became clear that the forced-labor plans discussed at the end of February could not be implemented as projected in Germany, Austria, or the Protectorate: The Nazi leadership had very hastily made a new, fundamental decision to deport all the Reich's Jews to Poland in the near future. On September 14, 1939, Heydrich announced that Himmler would put forward proposals shortly that "only the Führer could approve because they would have significant implications for foreign policy."[1] On September 19, the Council of Ministers for Reich Defense, including Göring, Heydrich, Frick, and State Secretary Syrup from the Reich Ministry of Labor, conferred on the "population of the future Polish Protectorate and accommodation of the Jews living in Germany."[2]

On September 21, 1939, at a meeting with the Security Police office chiefs and Einsatzgruppe leaders, Heydrich provided an overview of the planned course of events in Poland. The former German provinces were to become German Gaue, and a Gau for speakers of foreign languages would be created on the remaining Polish territory. According to Heydrich, Hitler had authorized the Jews' deportation to the latter Gau. "However, the entire process should be spread over a year. . . . Jewry is to be concentrated in

---

[1] Quoted in Dieter Pohl, Von der *"Judenpolitik" zum Judenmord. Der Distrikt Lublin des Generalgouvernements 1939–1944* (Frankfurt am Main, Berlin, and Bern, 1993), 26.

[2] *Der Prozeß gegen die Hauptkriegsverbrecher vor dem Internationalen Militärgerichtshof (IMT), Nürnberg 14. November 1945–1. Oktober 1946*, Vol. XXXI (Nuremberg, 1948), 231–232, Doc. PS- 2852, Protocol of the meeting on September 19, 1939; see Hans Safrian, *Die Eichmann-Männer* (Vienna and Zurich, 1993), 71. Pohl also reaches the conclusion on the basis of other documents that the decision was made on September 19; Pohl, *Judenpolitik*, 26. For the variants and the difficulties in implementing them – as well as the causal context for resettling ethnic Germans – see Götz Aly, *"Endlösung" – Völkerverschiebung und der Mord an den europäischen Juden* (Frankfurt am Main, 1995).

city ghettos to facilitate control and later removal." Summarizing, Heydrich ordered: "1. Jews out of the cities as fast as possible, 2. Jews out of the Reich to Poland, 3. the remaining 30,000 Gypsies to Poland, too, [and] 4. systematic dispatch of Jews out of German territory with freight trains."[3] For the overall plan, Heydrich differentiated between the "final objective" and the "steps for reaching that objective (which would be taken in the short term)." The first step was to deport Jews from the newly annexed territories of Danzig, West Prussia, Posen, and eastern Upper Silesia, as well as to concentrate the Jews in the other occupied territories of Poland in cities along railway lines. Jewish councils of elders were to be established everywhere; they would be responsible for registration of Jews and then for their removal from the countryside or for deportation preparations in the cities. For security reasons, Jews would probably be banned from "certain sectors" of the city or ordered not to leave the ghettos. However, expulsion of the Jews was to "take into consideration the interests of the German economy." That applied not only to support for companies critical to the war effort, but also – with the advent of the newly established German labor offices – to Jewish labor. Copies of this decree went to the SS, the Wehrmacht High Command (OKW), the Reich Interior Ministry, and the chiefs of the civilian administrations of the occupied territories.[4] Heydrich's decree did not refer to the territories east of Krakow because as Heydrich explained in a September 22, 1939, conversation with the Army High Commander, Walther von Brauchitsch, plans called for a "German-administered Jewish state near Krakow."[5]

On October 30, 1939, Himmler again categorically demanded removal of all Jews from "formerly Polish, presently Reich German provinces" by February 1940.[6] However, after a meeting with the General Governor in Krakow, he scaled back the plan. To "cleanse and secure the new German territories," an "initial operation" from mid-November 1939 to the end of February 1940 would first deport 100,000 Jews from the new Reich Gau Wartheland to the area around Lublin and south of Warsaw (see map 7, p. 179). The rural *Kreise* (county-size units of government) and the cities of Posen, Gnesen, and Hohensalza would have to be totally cleansed first, while

[3] *Europa unterm Hakenkreuz. Die faschistische Okkupationspolitik in Polen (1939–1945)*, document selection and introduction by Werner Röhr with the assistance of Elke Heckert, et al. (Berlin, 1989), 119, Doc. No. 12, RSHA file note, September 27, 1939, regarding the September 21, 1939, meeting.

[4] Ibid., 120–122, Doc. No. 13, Commander of the Security Police express letter, September 21, 1939; *Kennzeichnen J. Bilder, Dokumente, Berichte zur Geschichte der Verbrechen des Hitlerfaschismus an den deutschen Juden 1933–1945*, edited by Helmut Eschwege (Berlin, 1981), 161–164; and *Eksterminacja Żydów na ziemiach polskich w okresie okupacji hitlerowskiej. Zbiór dokumentów*, edited by Tatiana Berenstein, et al. (Warsaw, 1957), Doc. No. 1, 21–25.

[5] Quoted in Safrian, *Die Eichmann-Männer*, 72.

[6] *Eksterminacja Żydów*, Doc. No. 2, 29, RFSS Himmler order, October 30, 1939.

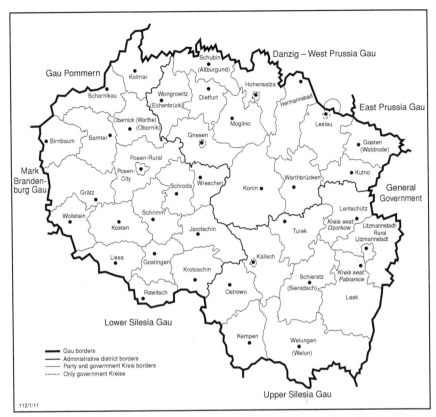

Map 7. The Warthegau – its State and Party Districts, on February 15, 1942

part of the Jewish population (30,000 persons) was to be removed from Lodz (Litzmannstadt).[7] In the part of western Poland annexed to Reich territory and now called the "Warthegau," preparatory measures took effect. For example, the authorities in various cities established the first ghettos in fall 1939. In mid-November, Jews were prohibited from changing residences.[8] On November 14, the newly appointed President of the Kalisch Administrative District, Friedrich Uebelhör, ordered that Jews in the Kalisch district, including Lodz, be marked with yellow armbands and prohibited from leaving their residences between 5:00 p.m. and 8:00 a.m. without special

---

[7] *Eksterminacja Zydów*, Doc. No. 3, 30–32, HSSPF circular (Koppe), November 12, 1939; reproduced in *Herrschaftsalltag im Dritten Reich. Studien und Texte*, edited by Hans Mommsen and Susanne Willems (Düsseldorf, 1988), 456–457, Doc. No. 18. See also Aly, *Endlösung*, 59–71.

[8] For the order to mark the Jews, see Gerald Reitlinger, *Die Endlösung. Hitlers Versuch der Ausrottung der Juden Europas 1939–1945*, 4th reworked and expanded edition (Berlin 1961), 52. For the November 13, 1939, prohibition on changing residence, see Aly, *Endlösung*, 69.

authorization.[9] Then, on December 11, 1939, the Reichsstatthalter of the Warthegau, Arthur Greiser, ordered that all Jews in his territory be marked on the chest and back with a Star of David, the first such measure within the Greater German Reich.[10] But the deportations could not be implemented as quickly and as totally as planned (although by spring 1940 more than 87,000 Jewish and non-Jewish Poles had been removed from the Warthegau), which left room for forced-labor measures.

Various occupation authorities – for example, the civilian administration of the Lodz *Wehrkreis* (military area) commander – already had drafted Jewish men and women for forced labor during the campaign.[11] A general order instituted forced labor for Jews for the first time on October 6 or 7, 1939.[12] In Petrikau, previously Piotrków, Oberbürgermeister Drechsel not only established a ghetto, but also proclaimed on December 1 that the Jewish community would have to provide 1,000 men a day for "mandatory jobs"; the work orders could be picked up at the municipal construction office.[13] As shortly before in Germany, the newly constituted Jewish councils in Warthegau soon had to register all potential workers in card files. The December 1938 decree on segregated labor deployment did not apply to the annexed territories and forced labor for Jews was only instituted officially by the October 1941 order for the entire Reich; consequently, the Warthegau lacked appropriate regulation. However, at this point all the authorities expected rapid deportation of the Jewish population living in the annexed territories.

On December 10, 1939, District President Uebelhör ordered creation of a ghetto in Lodz, where the majority of the Warthegau Jews lived, and specified the following details: A Jewish elder and a community committee were to head the ghetto's self-government. They were to take charge of food, health, security, inhabitants' housing, accounting, and registration. The nutrition office (*Ernährungsamt*) of the Lodz city administration would supply food and fuel to the ghetto's administration. Workers from the ghetto would build a wall to enclose the Jewish residential district. Thus, from the outset the labor potential of the victims was the focus of interest. The instruction states, "When the other city sectors are combed for Jews fit to work and the Jews removed to the ghetto at the time of or shortly after its

[9] *Eksterminacja Żydów*, Doc. No. 30, 72.

[10] Florian Freund, Bertrand Perz, and Karl Stuhlpfarrer, "Das Getto in Litzmannstadt (Lódz)," in *"Unser einziger Weg ist Arbeit". Das Getto in Lódz 1940–1944. Eine Ausstellung des Jüdischen Museums in Zusammenarbeit mit Yad Vashem u. a.*, edited by Hanno Loewy and Gerhard Schoenberner (Frankfurt am Main and Vienna, 1990), 17–31, here 18.

[11] *Faschismus-Getto-Massenmord. Dokumentation über Ausrottung und Widerstand der Juden in Polen während des zweiten Weltkrieges* (Berlin [GDR], 1960), 199, Doc. No. 147, Letter to the Jewish rabbinate, October 13, 1939.

[12] Freund, Perz, and Stuhlpfarrer, "Das Getto in Litzmannstadt," 17–18.

[13] *Eksterminacja Żydów*, Doc. No. 32, 75.

creation, the Jews fit to work living there are to be taken into custody. They are to be put together in work units, housed in barracks set up by the city administration and the Security Police, and guarded there. These Jews are intended for labor deployment in segregated units [*"für einen geschlossenen Arbeitseinsatz"*]. The work will consist initially in the units razing buildings ready for demolition in the city center." According to the instructions, able-bodied Jews were to be put to work outside the ghetto, and as they lived in the ghetto, they were also to take care of any work there. Uebelhör's order concluded, "I will determine later whether Jews capable of working will be taken from the ghetto and placed in labor barracks. Providing the ghetto is only a temporary measure. . . . The final objective must be in any case to cauterize this plague canker completely."[14] According to the central plan, the entire Warthegau was in the future to be purely German territory "free of Jews" (*judenfrei*). The Lodz ghetto was from the outset a way station before the Jews were shoved across the border. The deportations were repeatedly postponed, however, so in February 1940 construction of the ghetto began, and on May 10, 1940, the ghetto was sealed off from the outside world.[15]

GHETTOIZATION AND FORCED LABOR

The areas of responsibility for the Lodz ghetto were already clearly defined in April 1940. The municipal administration assumed general supervisory control of the ghetto and was to regulate its internal affairs and economy, while the local police chief (*Polizeipräsident*) was to focus exclusively on keeping the peace and order.[16] The ghetto was thus under the authority of the Oberbürgermeister of Lodz, in the future called Litzmannstadt by the Germans; the Municipal Police, the Gestapo, and the Criminal Police were only responsible for police supervision. Oberbürgermeister Schiffer then transferred limited authority for self-government in the ghetto to the Jewish elder Mordechai Chaim Rumkowski. The liaison office between the ghetto Jewish council and the Litzmannstadt authorities was the city administration's ghetto food and economic office (*Ernährungs- und Wirtschaftsamt "Ghetto"*), which was called the "ghetto administration" after October 1940. The Bremen coffee importer Hans Biebow headed this office. His agency, which employed about 400 people, later

---

[14] Document reproduced in *Unser einziger Weg ist Arbeit*, 153–154.

[15] Wolfgang Scheffler, "Das Getto Lódz in der nationalsozialistischen Judenpolitik," in *Unser einziger Weg ist Arbeit*, 12–16; Helge Grabitz and Wolfgang Scheffler, *Letzte Spuren. Ghetto Warschau. SS-Arbeitslager Trawniki. Aktion Erntefest. Fotos und Dokumente über Opfer des Endlösungswahns im Spiegel der historischen Ereignisse* (Berlin, 1988), 280–281; Freund, Perz, and Stuhlpfarrer, "Das Getto in Litzmannstadt," 19.

[16] Czeslaw Madajczyk, *Die Okkupationspolitik Nazideutschlands in Polen 1939–1945* (Berlin [GDR], 1987), 156–157.

oversaw labor camps outside the ghetto where its inmates performed forced labor.[17]

Exploitation of Jewish workers thus played a role in planning for persecution in the Warthegau from the outset. In contrast, Christopher Browning believes that in light of the anticipated deadline for total expulsion (summer 1940) there were initially no plans to assign Jews to forced labor, despite initiatives of the ghetto's Jewish elders. Only when deportation plans failed and the ghetto's mortality rates climbed did the German ghetto administration reassess the situation. All efforts for self-preservation were undertaken at this point, including work arrangements.[18] However, registration of workers in the Warthegau, in Lodz, and in the ghetto was a significant factor already in the first planning stages. Thus, the work of building a tailor shop in the ghetto began in May 1940.[19]

CENTRALIZATION OF FORCED LABOR AND MASS TRANSFER OF WORKERS

On July 27, 1940, Reichsstatthalter Greiser issued an order that employers in the Warthegau had to pay Jews standard schedule wages. This measure could only mean that previously, because no official regulations existed, large numbers of Jews had been employed as forced laborers and frequently were compensated inadequately or not at all. However, even with the new order, the individual situations of the compulsory employees improved little. Jews only received 35 percent of the schedule wages paid; the other 65 percent flowed into special accounts set up by the district administrators. The Bürgermeister of the Warthegau were ordered to report on their experiences with forced labor, and more specifically, on the relationship between food and performance, the satisfaction level of companies employing Jews, and the support costs for Jews.[20] All these circumstances indicate that forced labor was planned centrally in the Warthegau and that consideration was being given to expanding the program further. In the course of 1940, the

---

[17] Madajczyk, *Okkupationspolitik*, 156–157; Freund, Perz, and Stuhlpfarrer, "Das Getto in Litzmannstadt," 20–21.

[18] Christopher Browning, "Jewish Workers in Poland. Self-Maintenance, Exploitation, Destruction," in *Nazi Policy, Jewish Workers, German Killers* (Cambridge, New York, and Melbourne, 2000), 66.

[19] Freund, Perz, and Stuhlpfarrer, "Das Getto in Litzmannstadt," 25.

[20] Mentioned in the June 18, 1941, circular order of the district administrator of Kempen and the Litzmannstadt administrative district, reproduced in facsimile in Diemut Majer, *"Fremdvölkische" im Dritten Reich. Ein Beitrag zur nationalsozialistischen Rechtssetzung und Rechtspraxis in Verwaltung und Justiz unter besonderer Berücksichtigung der eingegliederten Ostgebiete und des Generalgouvernements* (Boppard am Rhein, 1981), appended illustrations (English translation published by John Hopkins University Press, 2003).

first labor camps were constructed for Jews in the Warthegau, in Pabianitz and Löwenstadt, for example.[21]

As the SS leadership was still unable to realize the planned deportations to the General Government to the extent desired in 1940, ghettos were established in the Warthegau's small towns. For example, the non-Jewish Poles were driven out of eighteen villages in Turek Kreis, and 4,000 Jewish Poles were concentrated there.[22] At the same time, exploitation of Jewish labor intensified, because in the meantime tens of thousands of unemployed Jews lived in the Warthegau as the result of all the persecutory measures. Labor shortages continued to grow in the Reich; as a consequence, Fritz Todt received special authorization in October 1940 to use Polish Jews from the Warthegau in constructing the Reich highway system. Beginning at the end of 1940, thousands of Jews were sent from the ghetto to the camps along the Berlin–Frankfurt an der Oder–Posen Autobahn, as we will see in Chapter 7.

A few months later, efforts were initiated to transfer a large number of Jews to the Old Reich. After Reichsstatthalter Greiser had offered workers to the Reich Minister of Labor, both agencies arranged to send 73,000 Polish Jews to the Old Reich in February 1941 for forced labor, believing that the consent of Himmler and Göring was assured.[23] The regional labor offices in Germany and Austria were informed about the undertaking while the Ministry of Labor was still drafting the official instructions for the planned project." At the beginning of March 1941, the Hermann Göring Reichswerke enterprise in Watenstedt was discussing the offer of the Lower Saxony regional labor office to employ 2,000 Polish Jewish forced laborers.[24] Other enterprises also immediately ordered large contingents; the Reich Autobahn directorate (*Reichsautobahn-Direktion*) ordered 8,000, and the Siemens-Schuckert Werke AG, in Berlin, 1,200. The Labor Ministry sent the requests right on to the Reichsstatthalter in Warthegau.[25] On March 14, the ministry informed the regional labor offices of the procedure

---

[21] Raul Hilberg, *Die Vernichtung der europäischen Juden*, new and expanded edition of the translation into German of 1982 edition, Vol. 1 (Frankfurt am Main, 1990), 265.

[22] Madajczyk, *Okkupationspolitik*, 259.

[23] On February 4, 1941, Greiser offered Reich Labor Ministry 42,187 male and 30,936 female Jewish workers for the Old Reich; BA Berlin, R 3901 (former R 41) Reich Labor Ministry, No. 193, Fol. 98, March 7, 1941, note of Letzsch as an attachment to the March 14, 1941, decree of the Reich Labor Ministry.

[24] Use of Jews was supposed to free up "persons of German blood." The "loyal supporters' leadership, main labor office" (*Gefolgschaftsführung Hauptarbeitseinsatz*), negotiated with the construction and camp service of the enterprise; BA Berlin, 80 Re 15 FC Hermann Göring Reichswerke, Film 44 263, Letter of March 5, 1941 (NI-4283); ibid., Meeting record, March 13, 1941 (NI-4285); see H. G. Adler, *Der verwaltete Mensch. Studien zur Deportation der Juden aus Deutschland* (Tübingen, 1974), 210–211.

[25] BA Berlin, R 3901 (former R 41) Reich Labor Ministry, No. 193, Fol. 98, March 7, 1941, note of Letzsch as an attachment to the March 14, 1941, decree of the Reich Labor Ministry.

for directly reserving the workers in Posen and allocated to each district 2,000 Jewish men and 1,500 Jewish women. The ministry demanded that the regional labor offices make available suitable work places in cooperation with all "participating and interested offices and large businesses" and house workers in special labor camps, thereby preventing contact with the general population.[26]

The Reich Ministry of Labor notified the East Prussian regional labor office in Königsberg regarding some special concerns on March 14, 1941. The Army High Command (OKH) had informed the ministry that, despite the withdrawal of 10,000 prisoners of war, the workers required for the so-called Otto Program to expand the railway and street networks in the occupied territories and to prepare for the attack on the Soviet Union still had to be provided. If prisoners of war were no longer available, the ministry asked the regional labor office "to use Jews from the Warthegau if necessary."[27] The ministry wrote much more emphatic comments on a parallel copy of the letter sent to the OKH: "With regard to the situation resulting from withdrawal of large numbers of POWs in Wehrkreis I . . . the projects of the Otto Program must rely on Jews from the Warthegau. I request that possible misgivings be set aside." An additional sentence in the draft says, "The situation regarding the danger of sabotage and separate housing is not significantly different from using prisoners of war."[28] The Brandenburg and Silesian regional labor offices received notification to the same effect.[29] The OKW then informed the homeland transport department (*Heimattransportabteilung*) on March 20, 1941, that Königsberg headquarters I had requested yet another 2,400 prisoners of war for the Otto Program. As prisoners of war could not be brought in from other labor offices, the Ministry of Labor "had already dispatched 7,000 Jewish civilian workers from the Warthegau to Wehrmacht

---

[26] Ibid., Fols. 98 verso – 99 verso, Reich Labor Ministry express letter, March 14, 1941; Nordrheinwestfälisches Staatsarchiv (StA) Münster, Central Presidium (*Oberpräsidium*), No. 5138, Fols. 4 and verso, March 26, 1941, decree of the Rhineland regional labor office; or Paul Sauer (ed.), *Dokumente über die Verfolgung der jüdischen Bürger in Baden-Württemberg durch das nationalsozialistische Regime 1933–1943*, Part II (Stuttgart, 1966), 203–204, Doc. No. 421, March 25, 1941, decree of the southwestern German regional labor office. The Hessian regional labor office intended to use its laborers for improvements. The Hesse-Nassau German Labor Front informed its district administrations regarding the approval of a contingent "from Litzmannstadt" that was not in any case to be employed in the food industry; Hessisches Hauptstaatsarchiv (HHStA) Wiesbaden, Dep. 483, No. 10036, no folio numbers, Frankfurt am Main German Labor Front – Gau circular, March 27, 1941.

[27] BA Berlin, R 3901 (former R 41) Reich Labor Ministry, No. 193, Fol. 64, Reich Labor Ministry, Department Va, Labor Utilization, to the East Prussian regional labor office, March 14, 1941.

[28] Ibid., Reich Labor Ministry, Department Va, Labor Utilization, to the OKH in Berlin, March 14, 1941.

[29] Fol. 64 verso, Reich Labor Ministry, Department Va, Labor Utilization, to the Silesian regional labor office, March 14, 1941; ibid., Fol. 64 verso, Reich Labor Ministry, Department Va, Labor Utilization, to the Brandenburg regional labor office, March 14, 1941.

Headquarters I.[30] On March 28, the Reich Ministry of Labor noted that the Reich Ministry of Transportation required yet another 2,000 laborers to lay cable on the stretch from Berlin to Krakow. The regional labor office there reported that the Breslau Reich Railway directorate needed 400 more prisoners of war but rejected Jews "for security reasons."[31] The Ministry of Labor informed the Reich Ministry of Transportation of this situation and pressed for review of doubts about security related to Jews with the argument that the chief of the OKW's transportation planning department also had agreed to the deployment.[32] Likewise on March 28, the Reich Ministry of Labor had supposedly asked the president of the East Prussian regional labor office to assess whether Jews from the Warthegau could be put to work for the railway department.[33] According to East Prussia's April 8, 1941, reply to the Reich Minister of Labor, the proposal supposedly had been made to the Königsberg (East Prussia) Reich Railway directorate that Jews from the Posen area be employed at the Otto Program's building sites in place of prisoners of war. After several consultations, the Reich railway directorate finally, on April 4, telephoned the regional labor office's president with the number of Jews needed, a total of 1,010. The President of the East Prussian regional labor office had that very day contacted the Reichsstatthalter in Posen and requested transfer of another transport of Jews.[34] But the planned transfer of tens of thousands of Jews did not meet with approval. The RSHA objected vigorously, and in April 1941 Hitler himself personally prohibited transfer of Jewish forced laborers out of the Warthegau to the Old Reich.[35]

THE LODZ GHETTO – A LARGE-SCALE OPERATION AND LEGALIZATION OF FORCED LABOR

Although the Greiser transfer project failed, the exceptional authorization allowing use of Polish Jews in Autobahn construction endured. In spring 1941, Jews were recruited intensively in the Lodz ghetto, which had been declared a permanent facility in October 1940. As hunger and death already held sway over life there, 7,000 people reported for forced labor in the Old

---

[30] Ibid., Fol. 72, OKW to the home transport department, May 20, 1941.

[31] Ibid., Fol. 78 and verso, Note of the Reich Labor Ministry, Department Va, Labor Utilization, March 28, 1941.

[32] Ibid., Fol. 78 verso – 79, Reich Labor Ministry, Department Va, Labor Utilization, to the Reich Transportation Ministry (Ministerial councillor Dobmeyer), March 28, 1941, with a handwritten addition.

[33] Ibid., Fol. 94, Reich Labor Ministry, Department Va, Labor Utilization, to the East Prussian regional labor office, March 28, 1941.

[34] Ibid., Fols. 84 and verso, President of the East Prussian regional labor office to the Reich Labor Ministry (Ministerial Councillor Dr. Richter), April 9, 1941.

[35] Ibid., Fol. 97, Reich Labor Ministry express letter of April 7, 1941, rescinding the March 14, 1941, decree. See also Chapter 7.

Photo 5. Jewish children working in a locksmith's workshop in the Lodz ghetto,
1940–44

Reich.[36] When the terrible circumstances threatened to affect the working
inmates in the ghetto, the people in charge changed the rules for supplying
food. After July 1941, the rations distributed to working Jews were to be
the same as for non-working Poles; rations for non-working Jews would be
the same as for Polish prisoners.[37] After all, 40,000 of the 160,000 inmates
labored in the ghetto's own workshops. That made the city of Lodz one of the
largest enterprises in the Warthegau. Bürgermeister Kar Marder called the
ghetto a "large-scale operation sui generis."[38] The inmates' work was organized by the Jewish council but controlled by the municipal ghetto administration. As the ghetto was located within Reich territory, it was hermetically
sealed from the outside world. On the one hand, food hardly could be smug-
gled into the ghetto; on the other – in contrast to the Warsaw ghetto – no
private companies managed to penetrate the ghetto walls in order to employ
Jews.[39]

In September 1941, after the Nazi leadership's decision about resuming
deportations of Jews from the Old Reich, Austria, and the Protectorate, the

---

[36] Lucjan Dobroszycki (ed.), *The Chronicle of the Lodz Ghetto 1941–1944* (New Haven and
London, 1984), 46, Entry of April 11, 1941.
[37] Madajczyk, *Okkupationspolitik*, 370.
[38] Quoted in Scheffler, "Das Getto Lódz," 13–14. See Browning, "Jewish Workers," 70.
[39] Scheffler, "Das Getto Lódz," 14.

responsible officials in the Warthegau had to accept that 20,000 Jews would be brought to the overcrowded ghetto. Additionally, in October 1941 Germany issued the first regulations on segregated labor deployment since 1938. The October 3 order defined the relationship of Jews to forced labor; the execution order issued shortly thereafter set down a detailed special labor law. While the former order also took effect in the Warthegau, the special labor law was not introduced in the annexed eastern territories. The Reich Ministry of Labor earlier had agreed directly with the Reichsstatthalter to remove "Jews working in the Jewish residential districts themselves or for businesses in the Jewish residential district from the effective scope of all legally defined social-support regulations." That applied to the ghetto inmates' forced labor. Thus, the Litzmannstadt Jews assigned in 1940–41 to the Frankfurt an der Oder–Posen stretch of Autobahn received only 10 Pfennig per day in pay. As Chapter 7 will describe, 80 percent of the wages left after deducting camp housing, taxes, and fees regularly flowed into a Litzmannstadt ghetto account. The Reich Ministry of Labor wanted to apply the new special law at least to the Polish Jews in the annexed territories employed outside the ghetto in private or public enterprises.[40] At a "heavily attended" meeting in the Berlin ministry, however, the participants agreed at the end of November 1941 that, given the "special circumstances" in the formerly Polish territories annexed to the German Reich, there was no need anywhere to introduce a detailed special labor law for Jews. Agencies' representatives from the Warthegau, Upper Silesia, and Ziechenau administrative districts made it unmistakably clear that the Jews living there had been forced for a long time already to work under much harsher conditions. Introduction of the Old Reich's regulations would thus be a step backwards.[41]

ACCELERATION OF FORCED LABOR BY THE LABOR OFFICES IN LATE 1941

At this point, the labor administration in the Warthegau intensified the use of forced labor and recruited tens of thousands of Jews for road and improvement projects. Labor shortages were acute in this area. In fall 1941, not enough laborers were available to help with the harvest "despite allocation of prisoners of war, convicts, and several hundred Jews." Overall, however, the labor offices gained hundreds of additional workplaces where Jewish men

---

[40] *Akten der Parteikanzlei der NSDAP*, Part III, Vol. 4, No. 044775–76, Reich Labor Ministry express letter of October 31, 1941, to Reich Governor in Posen, with an invitation to the November 28, 1941, meeting.

[41] Ibid., No. 044778–79, Reich Justice Ministry note regarding the November 28, 1941, meeting; see an excerpt in Kurt Pätzold (ed.), *Verfolgung, Vertreibung, Vernichtung. Dokumente des faschistischen Antisemitismus 1933–1942* (Leipzig, 1983), 322, Doc. No. 300.

and women could be put to work in groups. The labor office thus considered the "operation to employ Jews in groups for the first time to be complete." However, planning for further mandatory commitment was already underway.[42] In October 1941, the Warthegau labor offices placed 2,490 Jews, men and women equally, in forced-labor jobs, distributed across the various districts as shown below.

Statistics on New Forced Laborers Recruited by Warthegau Labor Offices in October 1941[43]

Labor Office District	Jewish Men	Jewish Women
Hohensalza	166	609
Leslau	55	48
Lissa	152	0
Litzmannstadt	0	168
Posen	243	0
Samter	0	63
Schieratz	95	14
Warthbrücken	553	324
Total for October 1941	1,264	1,226

In November, the Warthegau labor administration recruited an additional 2,674 Jews, and in December, 531.[44] Regarding "utilization of prisoners of war, convicts, and Jews for compulsory labor," a report of the labor administration at the end of 1941 stated, "In Leslau administrative district, all working Jews were housed in camps and therefore taken out of the ghetto. In Gnesen administrative district, the prisoners of war and Jews utilized continued to work despite the weather conditions. The Reich Autobahn employs 1,500 Jews at the moment in Samter administrative district. In Kolmar administrative district, the number of sick among the Jews utilized has increased to twenty per hundred. The Welungen labor office again used Jews for emergency work, so that 603 Jews are now employed there. . . . In Kutno administrative district, collection of data on work capabilities of Jews is complete; 758 Jews were transferred to labor ["*in den Ausgleich*

---

[42] "Die Lage des Arbeitseinsatzes im Reichsgau Wartheland im Monat Oktober 1941 (The Status of Forced Labor in Reich Gau Wartheland for October 1941)," in "Der Arbeitseinsatz im Reichs-Gau Wartheland, Mitteilungsblatt der Abteilung Arbeit beim Reichsstatthalter in Posen, Fachgebiet Landesarbeitsamt, Posen 1941–42," No. 1, 1 verso to 3 verso.

[43] Statistics on managing forced labor by workers for October 1941, in "Der Arbeitseinsatz im Reichs-Gau Wartheland," No. 1, Appendix.

[44] Statistics of the Reich Labor Ministry on managing forced labor for November 1941, in "Der Arbeitseinsatz im Reichs-Gau Wartheland," No. 2, Appendix; Statistics of the Reich Labor Ministry on managing forced labor for December 1941, in "Der Arbeitseinsatz im Reichs-Gau Wartheland," No. 3, Appendix.

vermittelt"]. The Posen labor office reported further demand for prisoners of war and Jews."[45] In spring, allocations were to increase further.

Assignment to Forced Labor by Warthegau Labor Offices, 1941–42[46]

Labor Utilization	Jewish Men	Jewish Women	Total
1941			
October	1,264	1,226	2,490
November	1,962	712	2,674
December	509	22	531
1942			
January	242	22	264
February	648	32	680
March	1,062	23	1,085
April	2,299	22	2,321
May	2,983	605	3,588
Total	10,969	2,664	13,633

Within eight months the labor offices thus committed far more than 13,000 Polish Jews, mostly men from small cities, to forced labor in the Warthegau. Only in the May 1942 recruitment of over 2,900 men did 2,219 come from the major city Posen alone.[47]

CONFLICTS BETWEEN THE LABOR MARKET AND PERSECUTORY POLICIES

While forced labor of Jews was being expanded throughout the Warthegau, the same process was also in progress in the Lodz ghetto. There, Hans Biebow, the head of the ghetto administration, reported to the Gestapo office on March 4, 1942, that about 53,000 workers were employed in jobs essentially furthering the interests of the war economy. Of course, he continued, there were considerable problems because for a year the rations in the ghetto had been even below the usual dietary allowances for convicts. The mortality rates among the inmates were therefore extremely high. In only four days, 307 people had died of starvation; "Anyone familiar with the conditions in the ghetto knows that workshop employees literally collapse at their workbenches from debilitation." But Biebow immediately qualified this criticism

---

[45] Statistics of the Reich Labor Ministry on managing forced labor for December 1941, in "Der Arbeitseinsatz im Reichs-Gau Wartheland," No. 3, Appendix.

[46] Statistics of the Reich Labor Ministry on managing forced labor by labor office for October 1941–May 1942, in "Der Arbeitseinsatz im Reichs-Gau Wartheland," Nos. 1–8, Appendix.

[47] Statistics of the Reich Labor Ministry on managing forced labor by labor office for May 1942, in "Der Arbeitseinsatz im Reichs-Gau Wartheland," No. 8, Appendix.

of the Gestapo, with the emphatic statement, "The ghetto administration would never allot more food to the Jews than is absolutely justifiable."[48]

As in other occupied territories, the forced-labor objectives clashed with the interests of persecutory policy. This conflict became especially acute when the anti-Jewish murder program began in the Warthegau, replacing previous deportation plans at the end of 1941. Most of the victims were then killed with gas vans in Kulmhof (Chelmno). The Litzmannstadt State Police office described the mass murder of Polish and non-Polish Jews from the ghetto in June 1942: "On instructions from the Gauleiter, all Jews unable to work were to be evacuated and the persons able to work from the entire Gau concentrated in the Litzmannstadt ghetto. . . . In creating the Gau ghetto, it first proved necessary to make space for the Jews to be settled there. To this end, a large number of the people unable to work were evacuated from the ghetto and taken to the Sonderkommando. Since January 16, 1942, 44,152 Polish Jews have been removed. Ten thousand, nine hundred and ninety-three of the 19,848 Jews sent in October 1941 to the ghetto here from the Old Reich, the Ostmark, and the Protectorate of Bohemia and Moravia were evacuated; thus, space in the ghetto has now been freed up for around 55,000 Jews."[49] So after the ghetto inhabitants from the Greater German Reich had been included in the murder process in May 1942, Polish Jews from rural areas of the Warthegau were moved into the ghetto to replace them.[50] In the course of these deportations from rural Kreise, 60 percent of the forced-labor camps in the Posen area closed during summer 1942.[51]

At this point, about 70,000 of the 103,000 ghetto inmates were still working as laborers and about 15,000 as employees of the Jewish council. To increase productivity, the workers received additional bread rations;[52] intervention of the Wehrmacht offices interested in the inmates' contribution to war production was clearly successful. At the same time, efforts were made to increase the number of forced laborers. The Litzmannstadt Gestapo reported to the inspector of the Secret Police on July 2, 1942, "As the ability of the Jews to resist has waned, their productivity has fallen off. For that reason, the Jewish elder has put all children over ten years old to work."[53] (See photo 5, p. 186.) In addition, repressive measures for poor performance became more severe. After a few weeks, there were signs of improvement: "Despite very bad food and nutrition for the Jews – a daily rate of nineteen

[48] *Europa unterm Hakenkreuz: Polen*, 217, Doc. No. 104, Hans Biebow report, March 4, 1942, also reproduced in *Unser einziger Weg ist Arbeit*, 9.

[49] *Europa unterm Hakenkreuz: Polen*, 217, Doc. No. 111, Stapo situation report of June 9, 1942.

[50] *Unser einziger Weg ist Arbeit*, 200.   [51] Madajczyk, *Okkupationspolitik*, 230.

[52] Dobroszycki (ed.), *The Chronicle of the Lodz Ghetto*, 195 and 199, Entries of June 2 and 4, 1942.

[53] *Faschismus-Getto-Massenmord*, 292.

Pfennig per head – production has risen from the previous month, which can be attributed more or less to the continuous 'pressure' exerted on Jews or individual work leaders."[54]

THE NEW RENTAL SYSTEM OF THE LABOR OFFICES AND THE SITUATION OF FORCED LABORERS, 1942–43

While in summer 1942 the SS resumed control of forced labor in the General Government as the mass murder program was progressing, that did not occur in the Warthegau. As in Germany, the labor administration continued to play a decisive role reinforced by the new June 25, 1942, "Order regarding Employment of Jewish Workers in the Wartheland Reich Gau." The labor department of the Reichsstatthalter in Posen emphasized in the order that "employment of Jewish workers . . . [was] only allowed with consent of the Reichsstatthalter's labor department"; from that point forward, the same also applied to ghetto inmates. Jews would have to be ordered from the responsible labor office. They were to receive free room and board, but both together were not to exceed one Reich Mark. The forced laborers, who had to work ten hours a day, received no wages, but the employers could pay bonuses up to RM 1.50 per week as an incentive to increase productivity. Every day the amount of RM 0.70 per forced laborer was to be paid to the account of the Oberbürgermeister of the Litzmannstadt ghetto administration at the city savings bank to cover subsistence of "Jews incapable of working." The ghetto was to provide clothing; maintaining the strength to work was absolutely necessary.[55] This order meant that forced laborers in the Warthegau, unlike their counterparts in the Old Reich, no longer even received minimum wages for unskilled labor. The Warthegau labor-office-controlled system for renting out forced laborers used methods resembling those developed in parallel by the SS.

With its order, however, the Reichsstatthalter's labor department also transferred responsibility for maintaining productivity of the borrowed workers to the enterprises and agencies using them. Exploitation of the Jews to the point of total exhaustion had clearly exceeded the level tolerable to the labor administration, which was striving for cost-effective use of Jewish labor. As Jewish forced laborers had no official protection, neither private companies nor public builders felt responsible for them.[56] In spite of the order, the following months brought little change in the victims' situation. At

---

[54] Gestapo situation report of July 27, 1942, in *Unser einziger Weg ist Arbeit*, 87.

[55] *Dokumenty i Materialy*, Vol. 1: *Obozy*, edited by Nachman Blumental (Lodz, 1946), 302–303, "Order on Employment of Jewish Workers in the Wartheland Reich Gau," June 26, 1942.

[56] See *Dokumenty i Materialy*, Vol. 1, 304–305, Reich Governor, labor department, to the Posen Oberbürgermeister, main construction office, December 21, 1942.

the beginning of October 1942, Altburgund District Commissar in Schubin complained to the municipal administration of the Litzmannstadt ghetto that on June 9 the Hinterwalden camp that he ran received 100 Jews, 86 of whom were incapable of working from the outset. By mid-September, seven forced laborers had died. After a number of requests by the district commissar, the Gestapo had picked up the remaining Jews, who were completely incapable of working, on September 21. For that reason, the district commissar said, he would only pay the rental fee for the laborers capable of working. Referring to the June 1942 order, he requested clothing and footwear for his forced laborers.[57]

At the end of September 1942, the compulsory employees in the Litzmannstadt ghetto were working a twelve-hour day.[58] The head of the ghetto administration had lengthened the work week from fifty-four hours in the beginning to sixty and then to seventy-two hours.[59] Because of its importance for production, the Litzmannstadt ghetto was not closed down, as were so many other Polish ghettos at this point, but instead was declared an SS-controlled labor camp. The Jewish council thus lost its responsibilities, and from that point the Germans exercised direct control over the forced-labor in the ghetto.[60] At year's end, 73,782 people worked in over 90 ghetto factories and workshops, 85 percent of them for the German war economy.[61] In addition to the forced laborers inhabiting the ghetto, at this time 21,000 more forced laborers lived in camps and in other cities. Overall, at New Year's 1943, 95,112 Jewish men and women were performing forced labor in the Warthegau.[62]

Deportations for the purpose of murdering the ghetto inmates continued; the people remaining were mostly forced laborers. Himmler's new plan to relocate the ghetto to Lublin, thereby rendering the Warthegau *judenfrei*, failed.[63] In spring 1943, the ghetto held more forced laborers than ever, 80,000.[64] During the following months, small groups returned from outside deployments. For example, on July 1, fifty totally exhausted men arrived from Jedrzejow labor camp; some of them had to be sent immediately to the ghetto hospital. In August 1943, sixteen Jews in relatively good condition arrived from Klomna labor camp near Lask, where they had worked

---

[57] *Dokumenty i Materialy*, Vol. 1, 314 and 316, Subdistrict commissar for Altburgund – Rural to the Oberbürgermeister (ghetto administration) of Litzmannstadt, December 5, 10, and 19, 1942.

[58] Dobroszycki (ed.), *The Chronicle of the Lodz Ghetto*, 265, Entry of September 30, 1942.

[59] Browning, "Jewish Workers," 70.

[60] Madajczyk, *Okkupationspolitik*, 158; Dobroszycki (ed.), *The Chronicle of the Lodz Ghetto*, 298, Entry of December 8, 1942.

[61] Freund, Perz, and Stuhlpfarrer, "Das Getto in Litzmannstadt," 25.

[62] Leo Baeck Institute Archive (LBIA) New York, Microfilms, Wiener Library, 500 Series, No. 526, Inspector for statistics with the RFSS, January 1, 1943 (Korherr Report), 17.

[63] Freund, Perz, and Stuhlpfarrer, "Das Getto in Litzmannstadt," 29–30.

[64] Browning, "Jewish Workers," 70.

since 1942.[65] The conditions in the labor camps had not basically changed, despite the previous year's order by the labor administration. Most labor camp inmates suffered from a severe lack of food and clothing, regardless of whether the camps were run by municipal administrations, district administrations, or private enterprises.

In July 1943, Rudolf Lautrich, who operated an engineering and construction enterprise for hydraulic construction and water supply in Hohensalza, wrote to the Oberbürgermeister of Litzmannstadt (ghetto administration) that "the rags" of most of his Jewish forced laborers were "literally falling off their bodies." At his building site, Lautrich employed 211 men and 157 women. He reported to the ghetto administration that he had "succeeded with unrelenting harshness" in converting the men to "halfway decent" workers but that the women were another story. The businessman complained that last winter he had had to pay the "rental fee" for the Jews without actually being able to employ the forced laborers for construction. When the weather got warmer, the Hohensalza district administrator's office had taken most of the Jews away. The same thing had happened in July 1942: The Kreis construction administration had withdrawn thirty Jews who were not sent back until November. Lautrich asked the ghetto administration to officially allocate the Jews to him so that he could conserve his resources for construction measures that he was to undertake for the Reich water resources office in Hohensalza. However, the labor office was still responsible for labor assignments and clearly set other priorities: It had ordered seventeen of Lautrich's forced laborers back to the Litzmannstadt ghetto-labor camp in mid-June 1943.[66]

FORCED LABOR AND THE LAST STAGE OF MASS MURDER, MID-1943–44

At the end of August 1943 the Posen Gestapo central office ordered that all municipal Jewish camps in Posen be liquidated. The forced laborers were deported, and the Posen city administration, including its main construction office, lost all of its Jewish forced laborers. In summer and fall 1943, the Security Police closed other labor camps, among them Wolsztyn camp in Posen district. Hundreds of inmates were taken to Auschwitz, and many of them were immediately murdered there.[67] In January 1944, after various

---

[65] Dobroszycki (ed.), *The Chronicle of the Lodz Ghetto*, 352 and 373, Entries of August 1, 7, and 21, 1943.

[66] *Dokumenty i Materialy*, Vol. 1, 310–313, Lautrich to the Oberbürgermeister (ghetto administration) of Litzmannstadt, on July 13 and 17, 1943.

[67] *Dokumenty i Materialy*, Vol. 1, 319, Posen Oberbürgermeister, main construction office, to the Oberbürgermeister (ghetto administration) of Litzmannstadt, August 31, 1943; and Danuta Czech, *Kalendarium der Ereignisse im Konzentrationslager Auschwitz-Birkenau 1939–1945* (Reinbek near Hamburg, 1989), 513, 585, and 629.

new deportations, only 60,000 people lived in the Litzmannstadt ghetto. Of course, 78 percent of the ghetto inmates worked in companies and 17 percent in the ghetto administration; only 5 percent were classified as unemployed ghetto residents. The persecutors were at that point discussing a plan to transform the ghetto/labor camp into a regular concentration camp, the approach taken in a number of SS camps in other Polish areas. But after a long break, the killing facilities in Chelmno were reactivated.[68]

While the murder program intensified, neither local nor central employers wanted to give up their most important forced laborers. According to a March 1944 plan, 1,700 Jews were to be moved from the ghetto to labor camps, for example, to the Jewish camp of Hugo Schneider AG (HASAG), in Częstochowa,[69] today considered one of the worst companies employing forced laborers.[70] At the beginning of June 1944, Himmler personally ordered that the Litzmannstadt ghetto be closed – in other words, that all the inmates be murdered. For economic reasons, however, this order met with the resistance of other parts of the Nazi leadership. Reichsstatthalter Greiser wrote to Himmler on June 9, "The armaments inspection office has undertaken significant countermeasures in opposition to your order to clear the Litzmannstadt ghetto. On June 5, Reich Minister Speer requested figures from the duty officer of the armaments inspection office showing the number of persons employed in the ghetto's various production operations, their weekly work times, and the weekly production of the various branches, ostensibly so that the figures could be presented to the Führer."[71] Himmler still had his way; in June and July transports left the ghetto every three days; each carried 700 people to their deaths in Chelmno.[72] Complete liquidation of the Litzmannstadt ghetto followed, and the remaining inmates were deported to Auschwitz. Two thousand of the people were put in forced labor, and the others were murdered. In the ghetto itself, a horrifying number of people, 43,000, had died of hunger, disease, or debilitation between 1940 and 1944. Seven hundred to 880 Jews remained in Lodz to perform clean-up tasks.[73]

SUMMARY

The comparatively long survival of the Litzmannstadt ghetto, which originally was meant only as a transit station, was primarily the result of the work

---

[68] Madajczyk, *Okkupationspolitik*, 258; Freund, Perz, and Stuhlpfarrer, "Das Getto in Litzmannstadt," 31; Scheffler, "Das Getto Lódz," 16.

[69] Dobroszycki (ed.), *The Chronicle of the Lodz Ghetto*, 466–469, entries of March 4 and 6, 1944.

[70] For details, see Felicja Karay, *Death Comes in Yellow. Skarzysko-Kamienna Slave Labor Camp* (Amsterdam, 1996).

[71] *Europa unterm Hakenkreuz: Polen*, 300, Doc. No. 179, Greiser to Himmler, June 9, 1944.

[72] Dobroszycki (ed.), *The Chronicle of the Lodz Ghetto*, 481–527.

[73] Scheffler, "Das Getto Lódz," 16; Freund, Perz, and Stuhlpfarrer, "Das Getto in Litzmannstadt," 31; Czech, *Kalendarium*, 850–851.

important to the war performed by the inmates. The ghetto had transformed itself into a significant production factor and was able in that way to hold off liquidation until summer 1944. That was truly impressive because Lodz was in the Warthegau, which as an annex to the Reich was to be Germanized as quickly as possible. Not the SS, but the labor administration (and in the case of the ghettos, the municipal administrations) organized forced labor of the Jews in the Warthegau until the very end. Overall, the work and living conditions of the victims in the annexed Polish territories were much more brutal than in the Old Reich. In practice, social benefits were eliminated and wages reduced in 1941 without any central regulations to that effect. Finally, from mid-1942 on, the labor administration itself officially conducted a rental operation that placed Jews (mostly ghetto residents) with government agencies and private enterprises in the Warthegau; the system functioned in much the same manner as the parallel system introduced by the SS in the General Government at the same time. Because of 1939 plans to deport the Jews rapidly from the Warthegau, the labor administration accelerated use of forced labor here relatively late. Then, when in 1940 a significant labor pool was going to waste, mass transfers were used to remedy situations such as the need for Reich Autobahn construction in the Old Reich.

7

On the "Führer's Road" – Polish Jews in Germany, 1940–1943[1]

TEN THOUSAND GERMAN JEWS FOR THE AUTOBAHN: A PLAN OF THE SS AND FRITZ TODT

In mid-October 1940, Arthur Greiser, the Reichsstatthalter in Posen, announced to journalists that he "had received permission to construct a Reich Autobahn from Frankfurt an der Oder to Posen that would provide work for a large number of unemployed Warthegau Jews."[2] Against the background of years-long persecution of Jews on the one hand, and on the other the forced labor introduced since the beginning of the war in the occupied Polish territories for the Jews living there, this announcement of a special forced-labor project to develop the east–west connection critical to the war was nothing spectacular. Buried in this news, however, was an ideologically explosive problem: Part of the stretch of road was located on Old Reich territory, the region that all the efforts of the National Socialists had sought since 1933 to "cleanse" of Jews – whatever their nationality. From the Nazi perspective, establishing dozens of labor camps for Polish Jews in this sector was out of the question.

The responsible officials therefore initially intended to employ German Jewish forced laborers for this segment. For this, they actually could have relied on the help of the Reich labor administration, which had been arranging segregated labor deployment since the beginning of 1939. Nevertheless, the General Inspector for the German Roadway System (*Generalinspektor für das Deutsche Straßenwesen*, or GIS), Fritz Todt, at the beginning of October 1940 pressed the Reich Security Main Office (RSHA), not the labor administration, to supply laborers quickly to the highway construction sites important for the war. Obviously he expected faster and more friction-free results from this contact than by going through the strictly regulated

---

[1] Chapters 7 and 8 are based on the following article of the author, here considerably expanded, updated, and reworked: "Juden bauen die 'Straßen des Führers.' Zwangsarbeit und Zwangsarbeitslager für nichtdeutsche Juden im Altreich 1940 bis 1943–44," in *Zeitschrift für Geschichtswissenschaft*, 44, 9 (1996): 789–808.

[2] Leo Baeck Institute Archives (LBIA) New York, Microfilms, Wiener Library, Reel 156, No. 2 B 2, Thurgauer Zeitung, No. 242, October 14, 1940.

labor market.[3] Utilizing Jews on a large scale broke with the principle established by Todt himself a year and a half earlier, never to employ Jews on the "Führer's Road." In mid-March 1939, Todt instructed the Reich Autobahn Directorate, "Using Jews on Reich Autobahn construction sites is out of the question. On the other hand, there can be no objection to placing Jewish laborers at work locations only indirectly connected to construction of the Reich Autobahn system, and located apart, for example, gravel pits, quarries, etc. With that approach, German workers can be released to employers directly involved in construction of the highways."[4]

After a year of war, however, the situation had changed completely: Workers were scarce commodities. Preparations for the planned conflict with the Soviet Union required quick solutions, which Todt expected in this case from the RSHA. So far the SS had had almost no influence on Jewish forced labor in the Old Reich, as we have seen. As a result of the General Inspector's unreasonable request, the RSHA interfered for the first time in the forced-labor program organized until then autonomously by the labor offices. On October 17, 1940, the Chief of the Security Police and the Security Service (SD) called upon the Reichsvereinigung out of the clear blue sky to provide within five days 10,000 German Jewish men between eighteen and fifty-five years old for highway construction. But both agencies had made their calculations without consulting the key figures involved. Most Jews already were in forced labor, so the Jewish organization could offer only disappointing results. Just 1,590 people were found,[5] even though the RSHA most exceptionally allowed concentration camp prisoners to be designated for this forced-labor program.[6] The RSHA and General Inspector Todt were

---

[3] Bundesarchiv (BA) Berlin, 46.01 General Inspector for German Roadways, No. 1200, Fol. 385, Commander of the Security Police and the SD (Müller) to the General Inspector for German Roadways, November 1, 1940.

[4] Ibid., Fol. 323, Reich Autobahn directorate (*Reichsautobahn-Direktion*, or RABD) to the construction management headquarters of the Reich Autobahn system (*Oberste Bauleitung der Reichsautobahnen*, or OBR) on March 13, 1939. The local building management offices also immediately received instructions; Brandenburgisches Landeshauptarchiv Potsdam (BLHA), Pr. Br. Rep. 47, No. 4, no folio numbers, Breslau OBR at locations in the district, March 20, 1939. See Paul Sauer (ed.), *Dokumente über die Verfolgung der jüdischen Bürger in Baden-Württemberg durch das nationalsozialistische Regime 1933–1943*, Part II (Stuttgart, 1966), 77, No. 334, GIS to Reich Labor Ministry on June 22, 1939.

[5] These Jews were to be assigned to the labor offices in Brandenburg, Silesia, Pomerania, and Austria; BA Berlin, R 8150, No. 2, Fol. 83, Protocol of the Reichsvereinigung board meeting, October 21, 1940; ibid., Fol. 79, Protocol of the Reichsvereinigung board meeting, October 4, 1940.

[6] Of course it was clear to the Reichsvereinigung board, informed by Polish sources, that SS forced labor differed little from that of concentration camps. An attempt was made to keep open the option of placing new labor camps under Jewish supervision; BA Berlin, R 8150, No. 2, Fols. 83 and verso, Protocol of the Reichsvereinigung board meeting, October 21, 1940.

astonished at the low number of unemployed Jews.[7] The RSHA was not willing to accept this and on October 31 ordered the State Police offices to determine the number of able-bodied Jewish men and women, as well as the number of persons already assigned to forced labor.[8] This special registration sometimes has been misinterpreted as the beginning of Jewish forced labor in the Old Reich.[9]

THE ALTERNATIVE: JEWS FROM THE WARTHEGAU IN REICH AUTOBAHN CONSTRUCTION

While conducting its own operation, the Gestapo at last asked the labor offices for their data.[10] Without waiting for answers that were very likely to be negative, the Chief of the Security Police and the SD finally authorized General Inspector Todt on November 1 to bring non-German Jews into the Old Reich for forced labor in this special case. His letter stated, "After reexamination of the matter, I have completely dispelled my doubts about using Jews from the Warthegau for the Reich Autobahn construction segment from Frankfurt an der Oder to the former Reich border, as long as those Jews are kept separate from the other workers both in their housing and in the workplace, and as long as their return to the Warthegau after the work's end appears assured."[11] Depletion of the labor pool of Jewish Germans by the labor administration after 1939 and the consequent failure of the special operation of the general inspector and of the RSHA led to abandonment of all ideological principles.

Before now, scholars knew as little about forced labor of thousands of Polish Jews in Germany (for which the Reich Autobahn authorities assumed responsibility and which lasted about two and a half years) as they did about the forced-labor camp system developed specifically for this purpose. At the

---

[7] Ibid., Fol. 80, Reichsvereinigung board meeting on October 28, 1940; ibid., No. 45, Fols. 135 and 124, Notes of Dr. Hirsch on summons to RHSA on October 23, 1940 and to the Gestapa on November 11, 1940.

[8] BLHA Potsdam, Pr. Br. Rep. 41 Klausiushof, No. 15, Fols. 1 and verso, April 11, 1940, decree of the Potsdam Gestapo referring to the October 31, 1940, RHSA teletype. See Stadtarchiv Bad Salzuflen, Schötmar, No. 104, Fol. 69, Circular order of the Bielefeld Gestapo, November 2, 1940.

[9] See Uwe-Dietrich Adam, *Judenpolitik im Dritten Reich* (Düsseldorf, 1972), 248.

[10] Munich Gestapo to Munich regional labor office on November 2, 1940, in *Erinnerungszeichen. Die Tagebücher von Elisabeth Block*, edited by House of Bavarian History and by the Rosenheim Historical Society (Rosenheim, 1993), 333 (Appendix). See November 11, 1940, circular memo of the southwest Germany regional labor office, facsimile in Dieter Maier, *Arbeitseinsatz und Deportation. Die Mitwirkung der Arbeitsverwaltung bei der national-sozialistischen Judenverfolgung in den Jahren 1938–1945* (Berlin, 1994), 83.

[11] BA Berlin, 46.01 General Inspector for German Roadways, No. 1200, Fol. 385, Commander of the Security Police and the SD (Müller) to the General Inspector for German Roadways, November 1, 1940.

end of December 1940, the Litzmannstadt ghetto administration furnished the first 1,300 men and women to the segment of highway from Frankfurt an der Oder to Posen.[12] Transports left the ghetto on December 10, 13, and 16, 1940, and on January 16, 1941.[13] The construction management headquarters of the Reich Autobahn system (*Oberste Bauleitung der Reichsautobahnen*, or OBR) in Berlin had ensured that ghetto inmates could be used without having first awarded contracts to construction companies; the OBR therefore had to establish and run the necessary camps alone in the beginning. This procedure was soon considered so advantageous that – instead of leaving the camps to the private companies performing construction in the future – the construction management got authorization from the Reich Autobahn Directorate to keep the camps under its own control.[14]

In January 1941, the construction management headquarters in Berlin set down the conditions for use of Polish Jews on the segment of road from Frankfurt an der Oder to Posen in camp regulations: "The Jews will be housed in separate, fenced-in residential camps. . . . The residential camps intended for Jews will be equipped appropriately. Every Jew will receive, depending on the supplies available, one straw mattress with a pillow, two blankets, one wash basin, one towel, and one set of tableware. The food fees are uniformly RM 1.00. Lighting and heat are included in the additional overnight fee of RM 0.20. The responsible police or Gestapo office is to handle guarding."[15] According to the regulations, the Reich Autobahn authorities were to assume the costs for travel from the ghetto to the camps; private companies were to pay for transportation to work. Local construction departments distributed the forced laborers to the private companies performing projects; the private companies had to use them eight hours a day for at least four weeks. Although the Jews were to be reported to all "social institutions," the "Jewish community" was responsible – contrary to the usual practice – for the costs of room, board, and camp money for sick workers. In addition to taxes withheld and "social charges," a total amount of RM 2 per day was taken out for room, board, and camp maintenance. Eighty percent of the remaining gross wages had to be paid into a ghetto account at the Litzmannstadt city savings bank. Half of the remaining

---

[12] "Record of the Commissioner of the Accounting Offices of the German Reich on the local audit of the ghetto food and economic office of the Litzmannstadt Oberbürgermeister . . ." (January 1941), in *Beiträge zur Nationalsozialistischen Gesundheits- und Sozialpolitik*, Vol. 9, *Bevölkerungsstruktur und Massenmord* (Berlin, 1991), 56, Doc. No. 4.

[13] Lucjan Dobroszycki (ed.), *The Chronicle of the Lodz Ghetto 1941–1944* (New Haven and London, 1984), 46–47, Entry of April 11, 1941.

[14] BA Berlin, R 65 II General Inspector for German Roadways, Binder 10, no folio numbers, OBR Berlin to the RABD, January 18, 1941.

[15] Ibid., OBR Berlin to RABD, January 18, 1941, Appendix entitled "Utilization of Jews for construction projects in the region of the OBR Berlin," 1–2.

20 percent was withheld for a camp collective fund to cover sick costs and additional expenses such as delousing. According to a sample of calculations prepared by Berlin construction management headquarters, exactly 10 Pfennig a day remained for the Jewish workers from the Warthegau,[16] which quite adequately satisfied Himmler's demand before deployment that compensation be kept as low as possible.[17] The Polish Jews forced to work for the German highway authorities thus found themselves completely excluded from the labor laws in force in the German Reich, even though the labor administration obviously controlled and directed their employment. The conditions under which they performed forced labor for the Reich Autobahn authorities on German soil were far more repressive than those of the German Jews in the segregated labor deployment program.

Work on the stretch of road from Frankfurt an der Oder to Posen did not get underway for the workers sent there until the beginning of March 1941. In March and April, further contingents of Polish Jews were obligated to perform highway work. Transports left the Litzmannstadt ghetto on March 27 and 28 and on April 8 and 11. Jewish physicians in the ghetto selected forced laborers whom the German authorities examined again to verify their fitness to work. Between the beginning and the end of April, a total of 2,700 men and 230 women were to be sent.[18] As a then-contemporary diary relates, on April 11, 1941, another proclamation appeared in the Litzmannstadt ghetto "on voluntary registration of men eighteen to forty-five years old and women twenty to thirty years old for work in Germany. From Saturday on, all those who had previously registered for work but had not yet left received notification requiring them to report immediately for departure. A few thousand people have already left."[19]

Compared to their situation in Litzmannstadt up to then, many of those shipped off considered their situation advantageous. As hunger and death prevailed over life in the ghetto, 7,000 people had reported for forced labor in the Old Reich.[20] In the ghetto, Dawid Sierakowiak commented about the persons sent to Germany that "they seem to be the lucky ones who have won new opportunities not existing previously in the ghetto to survive the war. All the letters coming in from individuals sent to work promise a degree

[16] Ibid., 1–2.

[17] On Himmler's instructions, the RHSA appealed at the very beginning to the Reich Labor Ministry "for reduction of the wages and social benefits" of these Jews and advised Todt to follow suit; BA Berlin, 46.01, General Inspector for German Roadways, No. 1200, Fol. 385, Note of the General Inspector for German Roadways, November 2, 1940.

[18] Dobroszycki (ed.), *The Chronicle of the Lodz Ghetto*, 46–47, Entry of April 11, 1941.

[19] Diary entry on April 16, 1941, reproduced in *"Unser einziger Weg ist Arbeit". Das Getto in Lódz 1940–1944. Eine Ausstellung des Jüdischen Museums in Zusammenarbeit mit Yad Vashem u. a.*, edited by Hanno Loewy and Gerhard Schoenberner (Frankfurt am Main and Vienna, 1990), 163.

[20] Dobroszycki (ed.), *The Chronicle of the Lodz Ghetto*, 46, Entry of April 11, 1941.

of satisfaction no longer known in the ghetto: 'We can eat, eat, and eat again.'"[21]

NEW PLANS FOR MASS TRANSFERS IN THE INTERESTS OF THE ECONOMY

The construction management offices of the Reich Autobahn required an ever-growing number of laborers, as did the entire industry. The Nazi leadership chose no longer to allow themselves the luxury of ideological resentment against forced labor of "foreign nationals" at the time of immediate preparations for war on the Soviet Union. In that context, Göring exhorted all Nazis in positions of responsibility on February 18, 1941, to pursue a temporarily pragmatic labor policy: "In other cases, taking in laborers of foreign ancestry or races (for example, Poles or Jews), or allowing them to stay, will cause difficulties from the standpoint of racial or national policy. . . . These considerations are in themselves correct. However, . . . they must come second to the exigencies of the armaments economy during the war."[22]

Despite this course change, the large-scale project developed by the Reichsstatthalter in Posen, Greiser, and the Reich Labor Ministry in the same month failed; as described in Chapter 6, the plan had sought to bring 73,000 Polish Jews from the Warthegau to the Old Reich. Polish Jewish forced laborers were to go to armaments companies, but also 1,000 of them to the Reich Autobahn project in the Frankfurt an der Oder area and 7,000 to the Autobahn in the Danzig region.[23] The plan had encountered vigorous objections, not least of all because of its sheer size – implementation would have meant a 40 percent increase in the number Jews living in the Old Reich: "For years the intent of the Reich Security Main Office has been to cleanse Reich territory of Jews. The difficulties associated with this task are known there. It is simply unacceptable to move Jews out by exerting extraordinary force on one side, only to let them back in again on the other. Until now only one exception has been made, that is, for construction of the strategically important Autobahn between Frankfurt an der Oder and Posen. . . . Any further shift of Jewish workers from the eastern territories, particularly into Old Reich territory, is not justifiable."[24] The RHSA was not alone in that view.

---

[21] Diary entry on April 16, 1941, reproduced in *Unser einziger Weg ist Arbeit*, 163.

[22] BA Berlin, R 3901 (former R 41) Reich Labor Ministry, No. 281, Fol. 44, Circular to the Reich Governor, etc., February 18, 1941.

[23] On February 4, 1941, Greiser offered the Reich Labor Ministry 42,187 male and 30,936 female Jewish workers for the Old Reich; ibid., No. 193, Fol. 98, March 7, 1941, note of Letzsch as an attachment to the Reich Labor Ministry's March 14, 1941, decree.

[24] The RSHA's point of view was reflected in the April 16, 1941, letter of the Hermann Göring Reich Works, main labor utilization department, to the Watenstedt labor office; BA Berlin, 80 Re 15 FC, H. Göring Reich Works, Microfilm 3963 P, Frame 3448159. The Gestapo, too,

Hitler himself categorically prohibited "Jews from the General Government and the Warthegau" from being used in Germany.[25]

The Polish Jewish forced laborers already working on highway segments were not sent back, but after mid-April further transports from Litzmannstadt ghetto were initially stopped. The April 15, 1941, transport that was to carry 347 men to Germany was held for two days in the vicinity of Lodz, and in the end two-thirds of the laborers were returned to the ghetto.[26] As a result, the Reich Autobahn directorates feared that it would have difficulty completing the east–west connection important for the war. At the end of April 1941, Ministerial Councillor Edvard Schönleben informed the Reich Ministry of Labor that the construction management offices for the Berlin–Posen and Stettin–Posen segments had in the meantime signed contracts with construction companies, transported machines to the building sites, and resolved the problematic acquisition of camp barracks for the large labor force of 20,000 Jews (3,000 for the OBR in Berlin, 5,000 in Danzig, 10,000 in Stettin, and 2,000 in Königsberg). If the promised forced laborers were cancelled and no prisoners of war were supplied as substitutes, only the workers already present, who were estimated to be totally inadequate, could be deployed.[27]

ECONOMY VERSUS IDEOLOGY: ACCELERATED UTILIZATION

In violation of Hitler's clear order, the Reich Autobahn employed more than 7,000 Polish Jews in May 1941, not only on the excepted stretch from Frankfurt an der Oder to Posen and Litzmannstadt, but also on the segments from Stettin to Danzig and from Breslau to Krakow. Large sections of all three segments were located in Old Reich territory.[28] At the beginning of August, the Berlin construction management headquarters alone had a total of 5,147 construction laborers, 2,027 of them Jews and 1,411 foreigners and convicts, for the Frankfurt an der Oder–Posen segment.[29] Allocation of forced laborers was supraregional; local offices had no access to these resources.[30]

---

for example, in Constance, opposed "moving Jews in," especially as months before Jews has been expelled to France; Sauer, *Dokumente*, Part II, 204, Doc. No. 421 b), Report of the Karlsruhe labor office to the southwestern Germany regional labor office, April 2, 1941.

[25] BA Berlin, R 3901 (former R 41) Reich Labor Ministry, No. 193, Fol. 97, Reich Labor Ministry express letter, April 7, 1941.

[26] Dobroszycki (ed.), *The Chronicle of the Lodz Ghetto*, 48, Entry of April 17, 1941.

[27] BA Berlin, R 3901 (former R 41), No. 166, Fols. 176–178, Express letter of the General Inspector of German Railways, RABD to Letzsch (Reich Labor Ministry), April 30, 1941.

[28] In addition to the Jewish forced laborers, 12,000 foreigners and 26,000 prisoners of war worked on Autobahn construction projects in Germany; BA Berlin, 46.02 RABD, No. 5826, Fol. 150, June 10, 1941, note of the Reich Accounting Office about the Reich Autobahn advisory board meeting on May 27, 1941.

[29] Ibid., No. 98, Fols. 1 and verso, Note of the RABD, August 6, 1941.

[30] Not the district administrator, the president of the administrative district, or the labor office was able to get "a Jewish column working on the Autobahn" in Weststernberg district

The regulations drafted by the construction management headquarters in Berlin for use of Polish Jews in camps had been blessed in mid-May 1941 by the Reich Autobahn directorate.[31] On that basis, at least seventeen labor camps had been constructed directly on the Berlin–Frankfurt an der Oder–Posen segment by 1942. Nine of the camps were located in Old Reich territory, including Brätz, Beelitz, Grunow near Wutschdorf, Kreuzsee near Reppen, Liebenau I near Schwiebus, Pinnow near Reppen, Selchow, Spiegelberg, and Sternberg.[32] In addition, hundreds of Polish Jews worked in other highway construction camps in the Mark Brandenburg.[33]

The project organized first by the Berlin and later by the Danzig construction management headquarters to complete the Stettin–Danzig segment provides insight into the conditions of Polish Jews exploited in Autobahn camps. Two thousand Jewish forced laborers lived in labor camps in Sdroien, Borowosee, and Thurmberg along the former Danzig Corridor.[34] "The SS performed guard duty in the camps at the expense of the Reich Autobahn, and the companies did the same at the construction sites. The SS men only made checks at the building sites during the day. In the camp, the guard force consisted of one guard duty officer and three or four guards who relieved each other for day and night shifts. The camp was also guarded during the day, as it was continuously occupied by Jews. The need for perpetual guarding arose from the many and various escape attempts undertaken by the Jews."[35] The Danzig Autobahn authorities already had transferred these labor camps to private construction enterprises for management in spring 1941. However, control at the building sites seemed shaky, because

---

"released for the potato harvest"; *Meldungen aus dem Reich 1938–1945. Die geheimen Lageberichte des Sicherheitsdienstes der SS*, edited, and with an introduction, by Heinz Boberach, Vol. 8 (Herrsching, 1984), 2984, Report no. 37, November 13, 1941.

[31] BA Berlin, R 65 II General Inspector for German Roadways, Binder 10, no folio numbers, Draft of a RABD letter to the Berlin OBR, May 13, 1941.

[32] BA Berlin, 46.02 RABD, No. 394, Fols. 49–50, Monthly confirmation of the existing residential camps and quarters of the Berlin OBR, around April 1942.

[33] There were at least ten Autobahn camps: Deutschhöhe, Finkenheerd, Küstrin, Liebenau II, Leimnitz, Rogsen, Stentsch, Topper, Wutschdorf, and Züllichau; see *Verzeichnis der Haftstätten unter dem Reichsführer SS 1933–1945. Konzentrationslager und deren Außenkommandos sowie andere Haftstätten unter dem Reichsführer SS in Deutschland und deutschbesetzten Gebieten*, edited by the International Tracing Service (ITS) of the Red Cross (Arolsen, 1979). See camp lists with source references in Wolf Gruner, "Die Arbeitslager für den Zwangseinsatz deutscher und nichtdeutscher Juden im Dritten Reich, 4. Kapitel, Zu den Arbeitslagern für nichtdeutsche Juden im Altreich (außer Schlesien) (1939–1943/1944)," in *Gedenkstättenrundbrief*, published by the Foundation for the Topography of Terror, 82 (1998): 12–20.

[34] In 1942, over 500 Jews were still housed in barracks in the three camps of the Berent construction management company; BA Berlin, 46.02 RABD, No. 394, Fol. 23, Monthly confirmation of the Reich Autobahn construction management in Danzig, April 1942.

[35] BA Berlin, 23.01 Reich Accounting Office, No. 7177, Fols. 265–268, Record of the local audit of the Danzig OBR by the Reich Accounting Office, October 21 to November 7, 1941.

the "employers' personnel," who were to be selected by the foremen and to be sworn in as auxiliary police by the responsible district administrator, caused problems. The Autobahn authorities therefore soon assumed responsibility for guarding the Polish Jews at the work sites. Amounts withheld from the forced laborers' compensation and earnings were comparable to those set by the Berlin construction management headquarters in its regulations. The social service commissioner of the Danzig construction management headquarters, the private enterprises, and the leaders of the camps in question had the balances from the food accounts at their disposal. The local Autobahn construction management had use of the balances from the camp maintenance accounts and the camp community collective fund. By November 1941, the Borowosee camp alone had realized a profit of RM 20,500 under management of the Firma Wilhelm Goebel Golzow.[36]

Jews from the Warthegau were not the sole means used to resolve the extreme labor shortages in highway construction. Between March and June 1941, over 3,500 Polish Jews were transported from annexed eastern Upper Silesia to the Silesian Autobahn construction management camps, as Chapter 8 will describe.[37] At the end of June, the Autobahn directorate was discussing the possibility of clearing further camps for mass utilization of eastern Upper Silesian Jews on the Silesian Brieg–Gleiwitz segment of the highway to Krakow.[38] When the Breslau construction management headquarters requested more skilled and unskilled workers in August 1941, the Autobahn directorate even got in touch with the chief of the Slovak labor utilization office. The directorate saw no other alternative – and was certain of the Ministry of Labor's consent – other than "to resort to Jewish workers from Slovakia,"[39] because its hourly wages, at about RM 0.50, were far below the industry norm and therefore unattractive to non-Jews. As interregional transfers and recruitment of Serbian and Spanish skilled workers failed, the Reichsführer SS withdrew the veto that he had already cast against recruiting Slovak Jews for the Silesian construction segment.[40] The proportion of Jewish forced laborers working on Autobahn construction consequently increased rapidly, especially near the Polish border.

[36] Ibid.; and ibid., Fols. 278 and 298–301, Reich Accounting Office commentary on the local audit of the Danzig OBR, October 21 to November 7, 1941.

[37] Sybille Steinbacher, *"Musterstadt" Auschwitz. Germanisierungspolitik und Judenmord in Ostoberschlesien* (Munich, 2000), 146.

[38] BA Berlin, R 65 II General Inspector for German Roadways, Binder 131, no folio numbers, Note of the RABD in Berlin, June 27, 1941.

[39] BA Berlin, 46.02 RABD, No. 98, Fols. 13 and verso, Draft of a letter from the General Inspector of German Roadways, RABD, to the Berlin Reich Labor Ministry, October 2, 1941 (sent on October 3), with a copy to the Breslau OBR.

[40] Ibid., Fols. 18–19, RABD note, October 14, 1941.

Workers at the Reich Autobahn (November 30, 1941)[41]

OBR	Total number	Staff	Germ. assign.	POWs	Convicts	Poles	Czechs	Jews
1. Berlin	6,099	669	–	866	258	624	2	3,552
2. Breslau	13,469	1,164	969	3,347	–	1,246	2,875	3,823
3. Danzig	2,218	200	151	1,158	20	10	–	601
[...]								
9. Hanover	413	220	39	100	4	7	4	1
[...]								
11. Cologne	1,352	350	430	131	91	–	–	35
All OBR's	60,638	8,066	7,918	20,333	3,160	2,942	3,430	8,012

Thus, in late fall 1941, Jewish forced laborers already represented over half of the Berlin construction management headquarters construction personnel and just under one-third of that of the Breslau and Danzig headquarters.[42] It remains uncertain even today, however, whether the Berlin headquarters increase of fifteen hundred men over the August level was based only on new contingents from the Litzmannstadt ghetto, or whether German Jews also were recruited very actively.[43] In contrast, in western Germany there was a significant contingent only in the Cologne construction management headquarters area. This exception was apparently the Greimerath near Wittlich camp for Luxemburg Jews in Trier district.[44]

Although Jews definitely known to have come from the Warthegau (Berlin and Danzig construction management headquarters) or eastern Upper Silesia (Breslau headquarters)[45] were used massively for highway construction only on the old Polish borders, they statistically represented the third-largest worker group after prisoners of war and cadre staff, whom they almost

[41] The table only lists the OBRs that employed Jews in Reich territory. The table is based on the statistics in "Labor Utilization for Reich Highways"; BA Berlin, 46.03 Reich Ministry for Arms and Munitions (*Reichsministerium für Bewaffnung und Munition*), No. 31, Fol. 14.

[42] According to the table, the Breslau region had 16 percent cadre workers and "Germans," but over 28 percent Jews, 25 percent prisoners of war, and 30 percent foreigners.

[43] Requests for over 1,000 men in the ghetto and at least one transport for work in Germany have been confirmed for November 1941; Dobroszycki (ed.), *The Chronicle of the Lodz Ghetto*, 81.

[44] BA Berlin, R 65 I General Inspector for German Roadways, No. 52, Fol. 6, Letter of the camp leader, September 13, 1941; ibid., Fol. 8, List of Jews transferred to RAB on September 4, 1941; ibid., Fol. 9, List of Jews sent to RAB on September 17, 1941.

[45] Some German Jews from Dresden also worked on the Silesian highway segments; Victor Klemperer, *Ich will Zeugnis ablegen bis zum letzten. Tagebücher 1933–1945, Bd. 1: Tagebücher 1933–1941*, edited by Walter Nowojski, with the assistance of Hadwig Klemperer, 2nd Edition (Berlin, 1995), 647, Entry of July 13, 1941.

equaled, at all construction sites. At least half of these more than 8,000 Jewish forced laborers worked in Old Reich areas.[46] The labor shortages thus overcame all ideological reservations and even a Hitler order. The proportion of Jews among workers who constructed the "Führer's roads" was around 13 percent at the end of 1941.[47]

WORSENING OF THE CAMP INMATES' SOCIAL SITUATION

In summer 1941, the Autobahn social service commissioner ordered that the Jews employed at his building sites were no longer to be subject to mandatory health insurance and had the appropriate premium payments halted.[48] Obviously the Reich Autobahn authority wanted to eliminate the contradictions resulting from their own orders: On the one hand, forced laborers were required to report to all "social institutions," and on the other, the "Jewish community" was obligated to pay for sick care. Exclusion from insurance hit Polish Jews working in the Old Reich doubly hard. According to a decision of the Reichsführer SS, these Jews were not members of the Reichsvereinigung (the compulsory organization for German Jews) and therefore not entitled to receive support from Jewish welfare offices in Germany.[49] On October 31, 1941, the Reich Insurance Agency (*Reichsversicherungsamt*) classified "the Jewish laborers from the eastern territories in the Autobahn camps" as "not free," in other words, involuntary, and thus not covered by insurance protection.[50] At the beginning of March 1942, the Reich Ministry of Labor finally excluded Jews as a group from the Reich's mandatory insurance, even though they were working because the government compelled them to do so.[51]

Nevertheless, forced laborers from the Brandenburg highway camps subordinate to the Berlin construction management headquarters were taken as

[46] As of the beginning of April 1942, an estimated 2,500 Jews were in Old Reich camps of the Breslau OBR and over 1,400 in Old Reich camps of the Berlin OBR; BA Berlin, 46.02 RABD, No. 394, Fols. 7–8, Confirmation of existing residential camps in the Breslau OBR region, April 1942; and ibid., Fol. 49–50, Monthly confirmation of the existing residential camps Berlin OBR, around April 1942.

[47] At the end of November, 1941, the proportion was 13.2 percent. At the end of December, 7,739 Jews worked there; that was 12.7 percent. The Berlin OBR employed 3,499 Jews, the Breslau OBR, 3,629, and the Danzig OBR, 601, as before. One Jew worked in the Hanover region and nine in the Cologne region; BA Berlin, 46.03 Reich Ministry for Arms and Munitions, No. 31, Fol. 15, Laborer status as of December 31, 1941.

[48] BA Berlin, R 8150, No. 759, Fol. 217, General Local Health Insurance in Weststernberg district to the Jewish Hospital, September 1, 1941.

[49] Ibid., Fol. 161, Berlin Jewish Religious Association, Health administration, to the insurance office headquarters in Frankfurt an der Oder, Draft for RSHA, November 7, 1942.

[50] Ibid., Fol. 202, Underground engineering professional society to the Berlin Jewish Religious Association, September 15, 1942.

[51] *Reichsarbeitsblatt*, I (1942): 120, Decree of March 4, 1942.

emergency cases to the Berlin Jewish Hospital after accidents, or when debilitated or very sick. The Berlin religious association responsible for the hospital found itself faced with a growing number of unpaid patient bills, because the General Local Health Insurance Provider in the Weststernberg Kreis, ostensibly the health insurer for the camps in Kreuzsee, Pinnow, Beelitz, and Reppen, cited the new order of the Autobahn authorities as justification for denying claims.[52] In April 1942, the Weststernberg AOK again refused to assume such costs, because a separate infirmary camp was to be provided for Jewish forced laborers.[53] Aside from court disputes regarding old cases,[54] the controversy ended in December 1942 with an express RSHA prohibition on admitting Jewish forced laborers to the Berlin Jewish Hospital.[55] This prohibition placed the Jewish officials with responsibility in an intolerable situation. On the suggestion of Walter Lustig, the Berlin Jewish community and the Reichsvereinigung appealed to the RSHA at least to allow persons with life-threatening injuries or those who had been infected during epidemics to be admitted to the Berlin hospital.[56]

The Autobahn camp at Kreuzsee near Reppen was to be retrofitted as a sick camp for Polish patients.[57] The camp had already existed since 1940 and continued on at least until September 1943.[58] According to statements of the Autobahn authorities, 386 Polish Jews lived there at the end of April 1942.[59] (See photo 6, p. 211.) When and how the transformation to a sick camp occurred is still unclear. After the war, the Gestapo chief responsible for the

[52] BA Berlin, R 8150, No. 759, Fol. 219 verso, Berlin Jewish Religious Association to the Reppen insurance office on April 8, 1942, regarding the September 1, 1941, communication of the leader of the Reppen General Local Health Insurance Provider.

[53] The sick persons had ostensibly been admitted to the Berlin hospital at their own request; ibid., Fol. 220 verso, Berlin OBR to the Berlin Jewish Religious Association on April 22, 1942.

[54] The Reppen insurance office decided that the General Local Health Insurance Provider would be responsible for the old disputes from the RAB camps. The insurance office headquarters in Frankfurt an der Oder set aside the decision, claiming that the Reppen office was not the responsible authority; ibid., Fols. 164 and verso, Decision of the Reppen insurance office, July 1, 1942; ibid., Fols. 146–147, Decision of the insurance office headquarters in Frankfurt an der Oder, December 22, 1942.

[55] Ibid., Fol. 43, December 28, 1942, letter of the Berlin Jewish Religious Association, health administration, with a transfer note regarding completion according to December 29, 1942, instructions of the RSHA.

[56] Ibid.; and ibid., No. 3, no folio numbers, Protocol 1/43 of the Reichsvereinigung board meeting on January 4, 1943, 2.

[57] November 14, 1945, statement in lieu of oath in Oberursel by Reinhard Wolff, head of the responsible Frankfurt an der Oder State Police central office from April 1941 to March 1943; I owe thanks for the copy to the Viadrina Museum, Frankfurt an der Oder.

[58] See Gruner, "Arbeitslager," Chapter 4, 19.

[59] BA Berlin, 46.02 RABD, No. 394, Fol. 50, Monthly confirmation by the Berlin OBR (April 1942). Around 500 Jews were ostensibly there; Martin Weinmann (ed.), *Das Nationalsozialistische Lagersystem (CCP)* (Frankfurt am Main, 1990), 647.

region, Reinhard Wolff, testified that a gas van was used in Kreuzsee camp to murder sick people, which still has to be confirmed by researchers: "I heard about this gas van when it was reported to me that, once [when] the van broke down, the Jews whom the SS had herded into the van tried in vain to get out. Their cries could be heard for hours. I do not know how many Jews that gas van killed. I sent a report about the event to the RSHA saying that the gas van was being used without my knowledge in that area.... According to an order of the RSHA the Kreuzsee labor camp apparently was converted to a hospital for sick Jews and the individuals from the camp who were fit for work were allocated to industry."[60]

FROM HIGHWAY CONSTRUCTION TO UTILIZATION IN INDUSTRY

Not only the Autobahn authorities and the camps subordinate to it had been informed of the new legal position regarding care and insurance for the sick: The Kurmärkische Zellwolle und Zellulose AG (Phrix-Werke) spun rayon and cellulose) in Wittenberge and the Deutsche Sprengchemie GmbH (explosive chemistry) in Dreetz near Neustadt an der Dosse, where similar problems had occurred with Polish Jews in the factories' own labor camps,[61] had been informed as well. In the Wittenberge factory camp, the inmates even had retroactively to scrape together treatment costs of RM 2,961 from their pennies in wages.[62] Eight such factory camps have been confirmed to date. Seven were located in the Mark Brandenburg: Britz near Eberswalde, Dreetz near Neustadt an der Dosse, Fürstenberg, Küstrin near Neustadt, Lautawerk near Senftenberg, Schwiebus, and Wittenberge. The Christianstadt camp was located in Niederlausitz area. When most of the highway camps were closed unexpectedly in the course of 1942, some Jewish inmates were moved out of the Autobahn camps into camps near industrial operations.

In winter 1941–42, the Autobahn directorate had not released the majority of its Jewish forced laborers, the usual practice for auxiliary personnel during the cold season. The Jewish laborers were kept busy maintaining roads or felling trees so that an adequate labor pool would be available in spring 1942. However, this calculation came to naught, because after the defeat of the German army at the gates of Moscow, an order from the highest levels directed that all workers were to be integrated into armaments production.

[60] November 14, 1945, statement in lieu of oath in Oberursel by Reinhard Wolff, leader of the responsible Frankfurt an der Oder State Police office from April 1941 to March 1943; copy in Viadrina Museum, Frankfurt an der Oder.

[61] BA Berlin, R 8150, No. 759, Fol. 153, Letter of the Berlin Jewish Religious Association, health administration, December 28, 1942.

[62] Ibid., Fol. 151, Note of the Jewish Religious Association, health administration, for Dr. Eppstein (Reichsvereinigung), January 4, 1943.

The Autobahn directorate consequently had to halt extension of the east–west stretch, which really was important for the war, and pass the Jewish workers to more important armaments projects.[63] By August 1942 only "work relating to safety and clean-up tasks" was permitted on the highways in the Old Reich, Austria, and in the Protectorate, and only a fraction of the previous workforce was authorized to perform the work.[64] Of the nine Jewish camps located inside the Old Reich on the Berlin–Frankfurt an der Oder–Posen segment, Beelitz and Selchow had already been dismantled by spring and then reassembled at Markstädt in Upper Silesia for armaments projects, and at Berlin Wannsee. One thousand, six hundred forty-six Jews still lived in the remaining camps at the end of April 1942.[65]

Many of these forced laborers from the Autobahn camps were re-employed in industrial operations, for example, 200 inmates of the Finkenheerd camp at the Märkische Elektrizitätswerke AG (power plant).[66] Other Jews were moved to camps newly established in Brandenburg by industrial and armaments companies. The opening of a Jewish camp at the end of February 1942 for construction of a yeast factory of the Phrix Werke in Wittenberge belongs in this context.[67] Oswald Pohl, chief of the SS Economic and Administrative Main Office (*Wirtschafts- und Verwaltungshauptamt*, or WVHA), personally promised the enterprise head to make available 300 to 500 Polish Jews and 150 concentration camp prisoners.[68] By the beginning of May 1942, however, only 250 of the 400 workers promised by the Berlin OBR after mediation by the SS had arrived.[69] When the company lodged protests with the SS, the labor administration, and the Commissioner for the Four Year Plan, it learned that the Brandenburg regional labor office had halted deployment of Polish Jews. The regional labor office had agreed with the SS WVHA

---

[63] BA Berlin, 23.01 Reich Accounting Office, No. 5827, no folio numbers, Reich Accounting Office report on the audit of the RABs for 1942, 3 and 12.

[64] BA Berlin, 46.02 RABD, No. 689, no folio numbers, Statistics on RAB worker requirements, around April 1942.

[65] Ibid., No. 394, Fols. 49–50, Confirmation of existing residential camps in the Berlin OBR region, around April 1942.

[66] See BA Berlin, R 8150, No. 759, Fol. 223, Reichsvereinigung to Brandenburg construction site, July 29, 1942; and ITS, Arolsen, 1979, 382.

[67] For the history of this company, see Hermann Kaienburg, "Zwangsarbeit für das 'deutsche Rohstoffwunder.' – Das Phrix-Werk Wittenberge im zweiten Weltkrieg," in *1999. Zeitschrift für Sozialgeschichte des 20. und 21. Jahrhunderts*, 9, 3 (1993): 12–41.

[68] In exchange, the company assumed all barracks and work expenses, expressed thanks for Pohl's "valuable assistance," and promised to supply 7,000 tons of yeast to the Reichsführer SS; BLHA Potsdam, Pr. Br. Rep. 75 *Kurmärkische Zellwolle AG* (Kurmark Spun Rayon, Inc.), No. 49, Fols. 91 and verso, Pohl to Dörr, February 24, 1942; Ibid, Fols. 98–99, Dörr to Pohl, March 7, 1942. See Kaienburg, "Phrix-Werke," 20–21. For the general developments, see Jan Erik Schulte, *Zwangsarbeit und Vernichtung: Das Wirtschaftsimperium der SS. Oswald Pohl und das SS-Wirtschafts-Verwaltungshauptamt 1933–1945* (Paderborn, 2001).

[69] BLHA Potsdam, Pr. Br. Rep. 75 Kurmärkische Zellwolle AG, No. 61, Fol. 184, Kurmärkische Zellwolle AG, to the Wittenberge labor office, May 9, 1942.

to support factory construction in the future only with concentration camp prisoners. Only the Polish Jews who had already arrived remained at the Phrix Werke.[70] They were not permitted to leave the camp guarded by the industrial protective service (*Werkschutz*). Money, food, and clothing sent were kept from the addressees. The company wanted to avoid withholding food because of poor performance, but according to internal "Service Instructions for Utilization of Jews," treatment of forced laborers was to be "extremely strict" and to involve "corporal punishment."[71] Under these conditions, twelve of the 300 Polish Jews died within a very short time. In summer 1942, the Phrix Werke sent back 160 totally exhausted forced laborers.[72]

Other camps in the Old Reich returned Jewish forced laborers to Litzmannstadt, not only Polish Jews recruited there previously, but also those from small cities in the Warthegau. In August 1942, 77 Jews from a highway camp and 88 from Eberswalde camp arrived in the ghetto, then in September, another 151 men.[73] The forced laborers who returned from Kreuzsee near Reppen (probably the sick camp) in February 1943 were so exhausted that fifteen had to be hospitalized and the rest had to be cared for by the ghetto.[74] At the same time "fresh" forced laborers were transferred out. In August 1942 another group of seventy-five men left the ghetto for Reich Autobahn work.[75]

As deportations in the Old Reich reached their last peak in February and March 1943, after a year and a half, the few Jewish camps still located there were removed, at least on paper. The decree ordering the Gestapo's infamous Fabrik-Aktion in Frankfurt an der Oder stated, "Jews employed in companies, as long as they are housed. . .in separate camps, are not to be seized in this operation. Polish Jews working separately. . .in various businesses and housed in segregated camps are not to be seized, either."[76] But the Gestapo deported the last German Jews from the Brandenburg camps in April 1943, and the exception made for Polish Jews was soon reversed. Himmler ordered that by June 30, 1943, the last "Jews housed in camps (including the Jews formerly with Polish citizenship brought to the Old Reich for segregated labor deployment)" be transported out of Reich territory "to the East and to

---

[70] Ibid., Fols. 177–178, Executive board of Kurmärkische Zellwolle AG, to the Brandenburg regional labor office, April 11, 1942; ibid., Fols. 176 and verso, Note of Phrix liaison office in Berlin, April 11, 1942; ibid., Fol. 181, Teletype of Phrixwerke, April 16, 1942.

[71] Service instructions for utilization of Jews; reproduced in Kaienburg, "Phrix-Werke," 38–39.

[72] Ibid., 27–28.

[73] Dobroszycki (ed.), *The Chronicle of the Lodz Ghetto*, 247 and 260, Entries of September 1 and 23, 1942.

[74] Ibid., 318, Entry of February 7, 1942.   [75] Ibid., 247, Entry of September 1, 1942.

[76] BLHA Potsdam, Pr. Br. Rep. 41 Großräschen, No. 272, Fol. 84, February 24, 1943, decree of the Frankfurt an der Oder Gestapo. For more details, see Wolf Gruner, *Widerstand in der Rosenstraße. Die Fabrik-Aktion und die Verfolgung der "Mischehen" 1943* (Frankfurt am Main, 2005).

Photo 6. Jewish laborers (probably recruited from the Lodz Ghetto) from the Kreuzsee Autobahn camp, 1940–43

Theresienstadt."[77] In summer, the Gestapo therefore shut down the camps for Polish Jews and deported them to death camps. On August 21, 1943, a transport with 500 Jews from a Pomeranian Autobahn camp pulled into Auschwitz. Only sixty-six men were selected for the camp; the rest were immediately murdered. On August 27, a transport with 205 Jews from the Märkische Stahlform-Werke Eberswalde (steel castings factory) reached the extermination site. All the forced laborers were murdered. Eight hundred men from Küstrin labor camp arrived the next day; from this transport, "only" 133 Jews were killed immediately.[78]

In contrast to the situation in the Brandenburg camps of the Reich Autobahn, 1,256 Jewish forced laborers were still performing excavation work and 568 doing construction work for the Silesian Breslau–Gleiwitz highway segment in April 1942.[79] An itemized statement of the Breslau construction management headquarters estimated that at that point there were in

[77] Teletype of the RSHA, May 21, 1943, excerpt in ITS Arolsen, 1979, LXII.
[78] Danuta Czech, *Kalendarium der Ereignisse im Konzentrationslager Auschwitz-Birkenau 1939–1945* (Reinbek near Hamburg, 1989), 580–587.
[79] In columns of ten to twenty men under the supervision of two or three "Germans," forced laborers had to build embankments for structures or perform concrete work. One hundred fifty Jews dug out gravel; BA Berlin, 46.02 RABD, No. 689, no folio numbers, Compilation of safety work and remaining tasks still to be performed at the OBR, Attachment to letter

Lower Silesia over 1,100 Jewish inmates in six camps and in Upper Silesia (Old Reich territory) 1,300 Jewish inmates in another six camps. The Klein–Mangersdorf Autobahn camp was hopelessly overcrowded, with 398 Jews for 288 slots, as was the Sakrau camp, with 553 Jews for 395 slots. While the situation in Lower Silesia had "normalized" somewhat by the end of April (the total number of forced laborers in the six Lower Silesian Autobahn camps had dropped by half), the number of inmates in the Upper Silesian camps increased slightly.[80]

These contradictory developments were the result of the shift of workers to armaments construction sites. In May 1942, the Reich Autobahn directorate only granted the Breslau construction management headquarters 568 Jewish workers, and that number was to be reduced to 298 by July.[81] Unlike in Brandenburg, where the labor administration monitored and directed the transfer of the Polish Jewish highway workers to the armaments companies, in Silesia control of the shift was in the hands of a special arm of the SS. The SS Special Commissioner for Forced Labor in Upper Silesia already had begun to exploit the new situation, housing thousands of Jews from eastern Upper Silesia in the Breslau Autobahn camps for Jews and breaking them in for construction of an expanding armaments industry.[82]

SUMMARY

Thousands of Polish Jews thus had to perform forced labor in Germany, constructing the "Führer's roads" from the end of 1940 to mid-1942. Many of them came from the Lodz ghetto. The Reich Autobahn authorities created a special camp system for this forced deployment and drafted its own discriminatory camp regulations. For extension of the east–west highways, most of the ideological slogans were unceremoniously abandoned. Labor shortages overrode the doctrine of not bringing Jews into the Reich at any time for any reason. In Old Reich territory, the Reich Autobahn authorities managed at least nine camps in Brandenburg, twelve more in Silesia, and one camp in the Trier area. And in addition, the Autobahn authorities also could avail themselves of inmates from camps maintained by private construction companies.

---

of April 28, 1942; ibid., Compilation by military *Wehrkreis* (military district), status as of April 1, 1942.

[80] The Autobahn camps were Groß-Sarne, Klein-Mangersdorf, Brande, Geppersdorf, Johannsdorf, Eichtal, Ottmuth, Gogolin, Sakrau, St. Annaberg, Niederkirch, and Grünheide; BA Berlin, 46.02 RABD, No. 394, Fols. 6–8, Confirmation of the existing residential camps of the Breslau OBR as of April 4, 1942.

[81] For May 1942, a total of only 6,470 workers in the Old Reich, Protectorate, and Upper Silesia, and by July, only 1,429 workers; ibid., No. 689, no folio numbers, Compilation of the RABD worker requirements, about April 1942.

[82] BA Berlin, 23.01 Reich Accounting Office, No. 5827, no folio numbers, Report of the Reich Accounting Office on the audit of the Reich Autobahn for 1942, 3 and 12.

Thus, Autobahn construction projects had at their disposal Jews from twenty Brandenburg camps and thirty Silesian Jewish forced-labor camps in the Old Reich. In contrast to the German Jews in camps, the Polish Jews assigned to Autobahn projects only worked under group contract arrangements set up without their input, their net earnings amounted to pennies, and their living circumstances were dominated by repressive camp regimes. In spring 1942, the highway projects were cancelled in favor of armaments activities. Several Reich Autobahn camps were closed, while others remained, supplying their inmates to industry. The labor administration continued to be involved decisively in the organization of forced labor until the end. Between 1940 and 1943, Germany maintained at least forty forced-labor camps for Polish Jews, the majority in Brandenburg, several in East Prussia, and a few in western Germany, not including dozens of camps in Silesia, where a special regime prevailed.

8

The SS *Organisation Schmelt* and the Jews from Eastern Upper Silesia, 1940–1944[1]

ESTABLISHMENT OF AN UNUSUAL FORCED-LABOR AGENCY

Little more is known about the forced labor of Polish Jews in Silesia than about the use of Jews from the Warthegau in the Old Reich. The forced labor and camps predominantly for Jews from eastern Upper Silesia differ more in structure and control from the camps opened in connection with segregated labor deployment than do the camps of the Reich Autobahn authorities, because in Silesia the SS took over control from the labor administration.[2]

In eastern Upper Silesia (occupied after the attack on Poland and later to become part of the restructured province of Upper Silesia[3]) the German authorities quickly shut Jews out of the economy and trade. (See map 8, p. 215.) The number of people without earnings or means grew rapidly.[4] Initially, the plan was to deport the Jewish population out of the region expeditiously, but despite transports to Nisko during the fall, this objective for the most part had not been achieved by summer 1940. Himmler therefore ordered, most likely on September 12, 1940, that an SS agency be established to intern the Jews of eastern Upper Silesia "energetically" in

---

[1] See Chapter 7, note 1.
[2] See H. G. Adler, *Der verwaltete Mensch. Studien zur Deportation der Juden aus Deutschland* (Tübingen, 1974), 229–231; Alfred Konieczny, "Die Zwangsarbeit der Juden in Schlesien im Rahmen der 'Organisation Schmelt,'" in *Beiträge zur nationalsozialistischen Gesundheits- und Sozialpolitik*, Vol. 5 (Berlin, 1987), 91–110; – , "'Organizacja Schmelt' i jej obozy pracy dla Zydow na slasku w latach 1940–1944," in *Acta Universitatis Wratislaviensis*, No. 1207 (Wroclaw, 1992): 281–314. More recently Sybille Steinbacher, *"Musterstadt" Auschwitz. Germanisierungspolitik und Judenmord in Ostoberschlesien* (Munich, 2000), 138–153.
[3] Shortly after the occupation of Poland, eastern Upper Silesia was added to Reich territory and merged with several pieces of territory to form the Kattowitz administrative district. At the beginning of 1941, the Upper Silesian portion of the NSDAP Gau Silesia was combined on Hitler's instructions with the annexed eastern Upper Silesian to form the Gau of Upper Silesia (Oppeln and Kattowitz administrative districts). The new Prussian province of Upper Silesia was accordingly created; Instructions of January 28, 1941, in Max Domarus, *Hitler. Reden und Proklamationen 1932–1945, Bd. 2: Untergang; 2. Halbband 1941–1945*, new printing (Wiesbaden, 1973), 1656. For the administrative reorganization, see Steinbacher, *"Musterstadt" Auschwitz*, 124–125.
[4] Konieczny, "Die Zwangsarbeit," 91–97.

A

Gleiwitz Municipal Kreis
Tarnowitz Municipal Kreis
Beuthen Municipal Kreis
Hindenburg Municipal Kreis
Königshutte Municipal Kreis
Sosnowitz Municipal Kreis
Beuthen-Tarnowitz Rural Kreis

—·—·— Borders of the German Reich
and the Free City of Danzing
in 1937
———— Reich borders since 1941
———— Borders between Prussia, the Reich
Gaue, the General Government, and
the Bialystok Region under the
Chief of the Civilian Administration
———— Borders between the
administrative districts
———— Borders between the Kreise

Map 8. The Annexed and Occupied Territories of Poland, 1941–42

"separate camps" and to force them to work "in quarries and on streets."[5] He appointed SS Brigadeführer Albrecht Schmelt[6] to the position of "Special Commissioner of the Reichsführer SS for Utilization of Foreign Nationals as Labor in Upper Silesia" (*Sonderbeauftrager des Reichsführers der SS für fremdvölkischen Arbeitseinsatz in Oberschlesien*) and personally installed him in his new office. As head of the labor department of the Higher SS and Police Leader, Albrecht Schmelt had gained experience with forced labor since 1939 in the General Government. His new Upper Silesian agency, consisting initially of eight workers (which grew to forty), most of them SS members, was located in Sosnowitz. His agency later organized the forced labor of Jews from eastern Upper Silesia for the entire Wehrkreis VII, or the SS Southeast district – that is, in all of Upper and Lower Silesia as well as parts of the Sudetengau.[7]

The Gestapo linked announcement of the new agency with a broad campaign to register the Jewish labor pool in Upper and eastern Upper Silesia, conducted parallel to but independent of the registration of able-bodied Jews at the end of October 1940 in the Old Reich.[8] All Silesian businesses that employed Jews had to disclose their number and the nature of the labor contract with them to the SS special commissioner by November 10.[9] Because of a review that was in his eyes unsatisfactory, Schmelt ordered the Jewish community in eastern Upper Silesia on November 15 to register all the Jews fit to work.[10] Schmelt obligated the council of elders of the Jews in eastern Upper Silesia to institute a department especially for labor utilization. This measure was modeled on examples from the large Jewish communities in Germany, Austria, and even the General Government.[11]

---

[5] Quoted in Steinbacher, *"Musterstadt" Auschwitz*, 139.

[6] Albrecht Schmelt was born in Breslau in 1899 and educated as a farmer and then for a career as a mid-level official. After 1930, he was a member of the NSDAP and after 1932 a representative in the Silesian Landestag and the Reichstag for the NSDAP. In 1933 he was a government councillor at the Breslau Presidium headquarters (Oberpräsidium); in 1934, Breslau police president; after 1939, SS member and head of the labor department in the office of the Higher SS and Police Leader in the General Government; and from 1941 to 1944, president of the Oppeln administrative district.

[7] Steinbacher, *"Musterstadt" Auschwitz*, 139–140.

[8] Konieczny, "Organizacja Schmelt," 308, Doc. No. I, Circular letter No. 9 of the Kattowitz State Police central office, October 31, 1940. See *Verzeichnis der Haftstätten unter dem Reichsführer SS 1933–1945. Konzentrationslager und deren Außenkommandos sowie andere Haftstätten unter dem Reichsführer SS in Deutschland und deutschbesetzten Gebieten*, edited by the International Tracing Service (ITS) of the Red Cross (Arolsen, 1979), LVII; Steinbacher, *"Musterstadt" Auschwitz*, 140.

[9] Konieczny, "Organizacja Schmelt," 308, Doc. No. I, Circular letter No. 9 of the Kattowitz State Police central office, October 31, 1940.

[10] Ibid., 309–312, Doc. No. III. For this measure, he secured the support of the president of the Kattowitz administrative district. The latter obligated district administrators and local police offices to assist; ibid., 311–312, Doc. No. IV, Schmelt to the president of the Kattowitz administrative district, November 15, 1940. See Konieczny, "Die Zwangsarbeit," 99.

[11] Steinbacher, *"Musterstadt" Auschwitz*, 143.

Just at this time the Army High Command (Oberkommando des Heeres, or OKH) had asked the Reich Ministry of Labor for an additional 1,800 Jewish workers to expand the infrastructure in Silesia. However, this operation petered out after a few months with no tangible results because the Silesian labor administration appeared to be increasingly impotent in the face of the recruiting efforts of the SS Organisation Schmelt.[12] After the first raids, considerably more than a thousand Jews were transported in the period before November 1940 from the Sosnowitz and Auschwitz districts to the Reich Autobahn camps in Silesia, apparently by Schmelt. Thousands more were to follow in 1941, because the highway from Breslau to Upper Silesia had gained great strategic importance with the attack on the Soviet Union, and expansion of the highway consequently was to be accelerated in summer.[13] It was subsequently extended in 1941 as *Durchgangstraße 4*, the so-called "SS superhighway" in Galicia, the supply route for the southern section of the eastern front; the SS established another forced-labor camp system along this road, as can be seen in Chapter 9.[14]

After March 1, 1941, neither private enterprises nor government agencies were allowed to employ Jews without authorization by the SS special commissioner.[15] This date marked the complete transfer of the power of disposition over most of the Jewish workers in Upper and eastern Upper Silesia, including Old Reich regions, from the labor administration to the SS Organisation Schmelt; control extended to the unannexed "eastern strip," with the cities Sosnowice (Sosnowitz), Bendzin (Bendsburg), and Oswiecim (Auschwitz). The Jews residing in Auschwitz, who were affected by "population policy measures for I. G. Farben's Buna" and the associated construction of the concentration and extermination camp, were placed under the SS special commissioner.[16] The Ministry of Labor pressed to have these

---

[12] Nine hundred Jews were requested for the Oppeln Reich Railway directorate, 600 for Breslau, and 300 for the Lublin railway directorate; according to PS-1589 in Adler, *Der verwaltete Mensch*, 210. This fact is often cited in literature out of context. At the end of November 1940, the OKH requested workers from the Labor Ministry for the "Otto Program" (expansion of the war infrastructure in the east); in mid-December, the ministry ordered the Silesian regional labor office and the labor department of the Krakow General Government to meet the requests. As no Jews were present, the OKH then considered utilizing prisoners of war; BA Berlin, R 3901 (former R 41) Reich Labor Ministry, No. 193, Fol. 51, OKH to the Reich Labor Ministry, November 26, 1940; ibid., Fols. 50 and verso, Reich Labor Ministry to the Silesian regional labor office and the labor department in the General Government, December 11, 1940; ibid., Fols. 56 and verso, Reich labor ministry to the OKH and the Silesian regional labor office, January 21, 1941. See also Chapter 9.

[13] According to Schmelt to Meinecke on July 25, 1941, in Steinbacher, *"Musterstadt" Auschwitz*, 147.

[14] More details in Chapter 9.

[15] See Schmelt authorities to Henig company, February 28, 1941, reproduced in ITS, Arolsen, 1979, LIX, Decree of the senior president of Kattowitz, February 23, 1941; reproduced in ibid., LVIII. See Konieczny, "Die Zwangsarbeit," 100.

[16] Quoted according to BA Berlin, R 3901 (former R 41), Reich Labor Ministry, No. 194, Fol. 292, Note of the Reich Labor Ministry, February 28, 1941 (NI-14188). According

able-bodied Jews immediately integrated into the forced-labor program.[17] In the first week of April 1941, 3,000 Jews left Auschwitz for Sosnowitz and 2,000 for Bendsburg. The Jews capable of working were subordinated to the Schmelt office and entered forced-labor camps.[18]

THE CAMP SYSTEM

The SS Organisation Schmelt had begun constructing its own labor camps throughout Silesia. For these camps, tens of thousands of men had been recruited from Jewish residential districts in eastern Upper Silesia.[19] Almost 100 labor camps for Jews later existed in the province of Upper Silesia alone. However, it is doubtful for several reasons that (as has always been maintained[20]) they were all under the control of the special commissioner: At least three Upper Silesian camps established in 1939 and twenty-eight set up before the Schmelt organization was founded in 1940 were obviously built for the segregated labor deployment program organized by the labor administration. Most of them, or perhaps only the inmates, then came under the control of the special commissioner by spring 1941. The same applies to nine of the fifty Jewish labor camps in Lower Silesia; one of them was established in 1939, and the other eight, before fall 1940.[21] By no means all the Silesian Jewish forced laborers had been placed under the Schmelt system by 1941, as demonstrated by the labor office's independently organized compulsory employment of German Jews, with 2,451 persons still in Breslau in 1943, and by utilization of German Jewish families in several Gestapo-controlled Silesian labor and residential camps erected after 1941, for example in Riebnig.[22]

to Krauch's letter (I. G. Farben) to Ambros (I. G. Farben), March 4, 1941, Himmler had the Jews deported to Auschwitz in 1941 on the order of Göring; Dietrich Eichholtz and Wolfgang Schumann (eds.), *Anatomie des Krieges. Neue Dokumente über die Rolle des deutschen Monopolkapitals bei der Vorbereitung und Durchführung des zweiten Weltkrieges* (Berlin [GDR], 1969), 320. See Dieter Maier, "Die Mitwirkung der Arbeitsverwaltung beim Bau der IG-Farben Auschwitz, in *Beiträge zur Nationalsozialistischen Gesundheits- und Sozialpolitik*, Vol. 8 (Berlin, 1990), 175–182.

[17] BA Berlin, R 3901 (former R 41), Reich Labor Ministry, No. 194 a, Fol. 292 and verso, Note of the Reich Labor Ministry and express letter draft, March 12, 1941 (NI-14187), reproduced in Maier, "Die Mitwirkung der Arbeitsverwaltung," 180.

[18] Steinbacher, *"Musterstadt" Auschwitz*, 218.

[19] *Faschismus-Getto-Massenmord. Dokumentation über Ausrottung und Widerstand der Juden in Polen während des zweiten Weltkrieges* (Berlin [GDR], 1960), 226, Doc. No. 173, Testimony of Rudolf Höß, 1946.

[20] For example, in Konieczny, "Die Zwangsarbeit." Steinbacher also leaves the question unanswered; see Steinbacher, *"Musterstadt" Auschwitz*.

[21] See list at ITS, Arolsen, 1979. See Konieczny, "Die Zwangsarbeit," 103.

[22] Leo Baeck Institute Archive (LBIA) New York, Microfilms, Wiener Library, 500 Series, No. 526, Inspector for statistics with the RFSS, January 1, 1943 (Korherr Report), 17 (also in BA Berlin, NS 19, No. 1570). See Chapter 2.

The assumption that the SS authorities established all forced-labor camps themselves and operated them alone appears just as unlikely. As shown above, a significant portion of the Jewish camps built in Silesia after fall 1940 definitely belonged to the Autobahn authorities, and another part to the Organisation Todt (OT).[23] At the end of 1941, the Reich Autobahn employed about 8,000 Jews who – according to statements of a Gau representative from Upper Silesia at a meeting in the Reich Ministry of Labor – lived in fenced-in camps guarded by the police and SS because "otherwise in our experience orderly and purposeful utilization cannot be achieved."[24] (See photo 7, p. 221.)

REICH AUTOBAHN CAMPS IN LOWER SILESIA

Altenhain
Faulbrück
Gräditz
Hermannsdorf
Klein Mangersdorf
Klettendorf
Markstädt-Fünfteichen
Obernigk
Wiesau

REICH AUTOBAHN CAMPS IN UPPER SILESIA

Anhalt
Annaberg
Auenrode
Brande
Eichtal
Flössingen
Geppersdorf
Gogolin
Groß Sarne
Grünheide
Johannsdorf
Lindenhain
Mechtal

[23] For the Organisation Todt and the camps, see Hans Werner Wollenberg, " . . . *und der Alptraum wurde zum Alltag." Autobiographischer Bericht eines jüdischen Arztes über NS-Zwangsarbeiterlager in Schlesien (1942–1945)* (Pfaffenweiler, 1992), 59.

[24] Kurt Pätzold (ed.), *Verfolgung, Vertreibung, Vernichtung. Dokumente des faschistischen Antisemitismus 1933–1942* (Leipzig, 1983), 322–323, Doc. No. 300, Note on a meeting on November 28, 1941.

Niederkirch
Ornontowitz
Ottmuth
Rogau
Rostiz
Sackenhoym
Sakrau
St. Annaberg

At that time the Breslau construction management headquarters alone was exploiting around 3,600 Jews.[25] A memoir said of the Silesian Autobahn camps for "Polish Jewish volunteers" that every Jewish community had received the order "to provide x number of Jews," and then had to designate the victims themselves. It was still "possible to buy one's way out by supplying replacements." In the camps, mail, package, and money traffic flowed, canteens provided for shopping possibilities, and there were some possibilities for recovery.[26] To appearances, as in the workshops and factories under Schmelt, the compulsory workers for the Autobahn initially earned 70 percent of the wages of non-Jewish workers.[27] In reality, however, they received only RM 0.50 pocket money; the rest went to the SS organization, which used it to finance the ghettos in eastern Upper Silesia.[28] The special commissioner thus carried on an active rental business with the Jews under his control; primarily the Autobahn authorities and OT profited from it. The two latter institutions made the labor arrangements and ran the camps.

Besides the camps, there were workshops in the cities of the "eastern strip" beyond annexed Upper Silesia. Thousands of Jewish men, women, children, and older persons worked from spring 1941 on in Wehrmacht production shops, workshops of private companies, and former Jewish businesses with German trustees located in Bendsburg, Sosnowitz, and other localities. They apparently received only half the wages of comparable Aryan workers but at the same time had to divert an additional 30 percent of their compensation to the Schmelt office. The main utilization areas were armaments and Wehrmacht clothing, collection and evaluation of old materials, and repairs.[29]

In addition, Himmler had already ordered in spring 1941 that the forced workers under Schmelt increasingly be put to work for armaments projects. In response, the notorious Blechhammer camp was built for construction of the Oberschlesische Hydrierwerke (hydrogenation factory) – called by the victims "Ohne Hoffnung Weiter," that is, "go on without hope." The camp set up in Markstädt for the Bertha Werke of Krupp AG in Essen was expanded. The two camps supplemented the long list of the facilities already

---

[25] See table in Chapter 7.
[26] Wollenberg, *Alptraum*, 59. For practices in the Brandenburg camps, see Chapter 7.
[27] According to the July 12, 1941, report of Wisliceny in Hilberg, *Vernichtung*, Vol. 1, 264.
[28] Wollenberg, *Alptraum*, 59.
[29] Steinbacher, *"Musterstadt" Auschwitz*, 147–151.

Photo 7. Eastern Upper Silesian Jews from Klettendorf labor camp at Autobahn construction in Silesia, 1942

existing for Reich Railway and Reich Autobahn projects. These camps were located either directly on the grounds of the companies or nearby.[30]

In fall 1941 Schmelt controlled a total of 17,000 Jewish forced laborers in Upper and Lower Silesia and in the Sudetengau.[31] The number of women employed in the Reich Autobahn camps was often small. In Brande, where several hundred men worked for four construction companies (Grün & Bilfinger AG, Firma Hoffmann, Firma Brockmann, and Firma Moll), only twenty women had jobs in the kitchen or camp. At the same time, Schmelt maintained several large women's camps, especially for textile production and manufacture for the Wehrmacht. Other Jewish forced-labor camps had separate departments for women.[32]

FROM HIGHWAY CONSTRUCTION TO UTILIZATION IN INDUSTRY

In spring 1942 the construction activities for Reich Autobahn largely ceased and all the Jewish forced laborers and the Russian prisoners of war employed there were transferred to armaments construction sites. At the same time, "several thousand Jewish forced laborers from eastern Upper Silesia" were sent to the Breslau construction management headquarters camps under a Schmelt "special order" (Sonderauftrag) for "expansion of the armaments industry"; the workers were broken in at the associated construction sites for later use in armaments construction activities. The Autobahn authorities paid for the housing and use of the newly recruited Schmelt workers in advance with about RM 800,000, as a report of the Reich Accounting Office (*Reichsrechnungshof*) shows. In order to recover their advance payments, the Autobahn authorities claimed a RM 0.50 share of the future daily lump sums that would have to be paid by the companies to the SS Organisation Schmelt for forced laborers.[33] Instead of the previous wage payments, this "daily remuneration" for skilled laborers rented as a group amounted to RM 6, and for unskilled laborers, RM 4.50.[34] As a matter of fact, the SS Economic

---

[30] For the conditions in Blechhammer and the name of the OHW; Wollenberg, *Alptraum*, 115–131. For Markstädt, see Konieczny, "Die Zwangsarbeit," 102–103; Benjamin Ferencz, *Lohn des Grauens. Die Entschädigung jüdischer Zwangsarbeiter – Ein offenes Kapitel deutscher Nachkriegsgeschichte* (Frankfurt am Main and New York, 1986), 124–126 (Benjamin Ferencz, *Less than slaves. Jewish forced labor and the quest for compensation* [Cambridge: Harvard University Press, 1979]).

[31] Steinbacher, *"Musterstadt" Auschwitz*, 149.

[32] See the camp list at ITS, Arolsen, 1979. In contrast, Steinbacher assumes that there were no women in the RAB camps, Steinbacher, *"Musterstadt" Auschwitz*, 148.

[33] BA Berlin, 23.01 Reich Accounting Office, No. 5827, Fol. 3 and 7 verso – 8, Reich Accounting Office report on the audit of the RABs' financial statements for 1942. For the history of the Reich Accounting Office in the Nazi era, see Rainer Weinert, '*Die Sauberkeit der Verwaltung im Kriege." Der Rechnungshof des Deutschen Reiches 1938–1946* (Opladen, 1993).

[34] ITS, Arolsen, 1979, LX.

and Administrative Main Office (WVHA) soon charged the same rate for the rental of concentration camp prisoners.[35] The Schmelt organization then arranged for active transfer of workers among cities in eastern Upper Silesia, the Autobahn camps, and its own forced-labor camps (*Zwangsarbeitslager*, or ZAL). Many forced laborers passed through several camps in those years, some even more than eight.[36]

Only with the war-related change in course in spring 1942 did the special commissioner gain complete control over the Reich Autobahn camps and inmates, at least twenty-two of them in Upper Silesia and at least eight in Lower Silesia. Then the SS ruled without restriction.[37] The redesignation of the Autobahn camps as Zwangsarbeitslager symbolized the change; as a result, the inmates lost any and all wages and vacation and mail privileges were cancelled. Only camp staff were given bed linens, as one survivor recalls. At the beginning of November 1942, the special commissioner tightened regulations still more, confiscating any money, the last of the valuables, and later even "superfluous underwear and articles of clothing."[38]

Rudolf Schönberg bore witness after the war to the miserable conditions that prevailed in Schmelt camps. He was first taken at the end of 1942 to the Sakrau Reich Autobahn camp with 350 Jews from Krenau in Upper Silesia. From there, he began an odyssey through the camps in Mechtal, Markstädt, Klettendorf, Langbielau, Faulbrück, Reichenbach, and Annaberg: "The same conditions prevailed in all those camps. [You had to perform] the hardest work with the least food in the form of 200–400 grams of bread a day and a watery soup." Very occasionally, 20–25 grams of margarine were added. Yet the camp company received RM 0.90 a day per inmate for food. Twelve-hour work days were the rule. The forced laborers had to accomplish the most difficult tasks, often "without adequate clothing" in winter, and while suffering steady abuse from guards and many of the foremen and master craftsmen.[39]

---

[35] While the WVHA first charged the companies RM 4 for skilled prisoner workers and RM 2 to 3 for unskilled workers, those rental fees were increased to RM 6 and RM 4 in fall 1942 after intercession of the Reich Accounting Office; Ulrich Herbert, "Arbeit und Vernichtung," in *Europa und der "Reichseinsatz". Ausländische Zivilarbeiter, Kriegsgefangene und KZ-Häftlinge in Deutschland 1938–1945*, edited by Ulrich Herbert (Essen, 1991), 409. See Weinert, *Rechnungshof des Deutschen Reiches*, 114.

[36] Wollenberg, *Alptraum*, 67–69; Steinbacher, *"Musterstadt" Auschwitz*, 149. See in contrast the one-sided thesis of Weinmann that Jews generally came from the Schmelt camps to the Autobahn camps; Weinmann, *Lagersystem*, 63.

[37] The Reich Ministry of Economics wrote to the Armaments Ministry that only if the SS Special Commissioner "left 150 Jewish forced laborers at the construction site again in 1943," would the demand for workers at the Breslau-Herrenprotsch mineral oil conversion camp be met; BA Berlin, 46.03 Reich Ministry for Arms and Munitions, No. 30, Fol. 156, Reich Ministry of Economics to the Reich Ministry for Armaments and Munitions, February 2, 1943; ibid., Fol. 157, Reich Ministry for Arms and Munitions to the General Commissioner for Construction (*Generalbauvollmächtigter*, or GBB), February 11, 1943.

[38] Wollenberg, *Alptraum*, 59 and 87.

[39] *Der Prozeß gegen die Hauptkriegsverbrecher vor dem Internationalen Militärgerichtshof (IMT), Nürnberg 14. November 1945–1. Oktober 1946*, Vol. XXXIV (Nuremberg, 1948),

The Order Police, SA, or SS, but also Wehrmacht soldiers and OT construction workers unsuitable for the front, usually served as guards in the Silesian forced-labor camps.[40] In Dyhernfurt, a guard force consisting of auxiliary police, one person for every forty Jewish workers, guarded the camp of the I. G. Farben Luranil Baugesellschaft GmbH (construction).[41] The "camp leader" (*der Lagerführende*), who attended to financial matters, and the "guard duty officer" (*der Wachhabende*), who controlled "internal order" and arranged labor allocation, ran the forced-labor camp. A Jewish elder (*Judenältester*) headed a Jewish sub-hierarchy; he had to "answer to the camp leadership for everything." The smallest camp held about 100 forced laborers, the largest, up to 1,000 or more. When more than 800 inmates were present, a Jewish supervisor (*Judenordner*) was appointed. According to this system, the Jewish formation elders (*Kolonnen-Ältester*) came next in the sub-hierarchy, followed by the "overseers" (*Schieber*), not unlike the kapo system in concentration camps. Roll calls were frequently held. The forced laborers had to wear a white star on the chest and back of their clothing – to contrast with the yellow mark for the Old Reich. Some wore black laborers' uniforms, but many only had overalls and straw shoes.[42] "Similar facilities" were supposed to be created soon in Slovakia modeled on the Schmelt system.[43]

With the transition in 1942 to systematic murder of Polish Jews, the Schmelt camps moved into the sights of the deportation planners. But amazingly, these camps were not to be shut down until 1943, and then only

---

Doc. No. PS-4071, 143–144, Statement in lieu of oath, July 22, 1946. For the terrible living conditions in Johannsdorf, Brandes, Blechhammer-Ehrenforst, and Faulbrück forced labor camps, see Wollenberg, *Alptraum*, 58–155. Also see ITS, Arolsen, 1979, LX; Konieczny, "Die Zwangsarbeit," 100–101.

[40] *Faschismus-Getto-Massenmord*, 226; Kurt Pätzold, *Verfolgung*, 322, Doc. No. 300, Meeting in the Reich Labor Ministry, November 28, 1941; Wollenberg, *Alptraum*, 118 and 123; Karla Wolf, *Ich blieb zurück* (Heppenheim, 1990), 34; BA Berlin, 46.03 Reich Ministry for Arms and Munitions, No. 30, Fol. 206–208 verso, December 4, 1942, draft letter of the Reich Ministry of Armaments and Munitions, armaments expansion department, to the Reich Ministry of Armaments and Munitions, Breslau construction commissioner, and Note of the Reich Ministry, February 11, 1943; IMT, Vol. XXXIV, Doc. No. PS-4071, 143.

[41] ITS, Arolsen, 1979, LX; see Konieczny, "Die Zwangsarbeit," 100–101.

[42] The somewhat "privileged" persons included the Jewish camp physician, the cobbler, and the tailor; Wollenberg, *Alptraum*, 64, 102, and 123; Wolf, *Ich blieb zurück*, 33; Summarized according to the camp lists based on survivor statements in ITS, Arolsen, LXI. See Steinbacher, "*Musterstadt" Auschwitz*, 147–148.

[43] The NSDAP Gauleiter invited a Slovak government delegation that included the German advisor for social policy, Albert Smagon, and the advisor for Jewish issues, Dieter Wisliceny, to inspect the Upper Silesian Jewish labor camps; Institut für Zeitgeschichte (IfZ) – Archiv Munich, Eich 1267, Teletype of the German Embassy in Pressburg to the Berlin Foreign Office, July 2, 1941. See Hilberg, *Vernichtung*, Vol. 1, 264. See also S. Fauck, "Jüdischer Arbeitsdienst in der Slowakei 1939–1941," in *Gutachten des Instituts für Zeitgeschichte*, Vol. II (Stuttgart, 1966), 59–60.

partially, despite their location within the Old Reich. In spring 1942, Schmelt employed 30,000 to 40,000 Jews.[44] The men from the forced-labor camps worked constructing armaments factories and in sugar factories, brickworks, and armaments production directly. They manufactured barracks, dummy airplanes, and light-bulbs for U-boats and airplanes; they even manufactured ammunition.[45] In addition, newly constructed factories for Wehrmacht clothing, for example in Sosnowitz and Bendsburg, employed thousands of Jewish men and women. In fall 1942 around 20,000 Jews labored in the workshops, 8,750 of them in the textile industry.[46]

The forced laborers had been trained at an early point. Especially the men who had been taught special concrete and construction skills since the end of 1940 in "intensive training courses" were sometimes considered irreplaceable.[47] For example, the contract for the construction of an I. G. Farben factory to produce combat gas classified 130 of 180 Jews as underground construction specialists and only 50 as trainees.[48] In January 1943 the construction commissioner of the Ministry of War responsible for Silesia still was requesting new workers so that thousands more Jews could be certified.[49] Sixty-five hundred forced laborers working directly on large-scale armaments projects were considered essential, at least for the short term.[50] Additionally, since the end of 1941 thousands of Jewish women had been trained for massive deployment to flax spinning mills in Silesia and the Sudetenland; there they were to take over the second shifts.[51] Later, more than ten women's camps operated in Silesia in the vicinity of textile mills.[52]

FORCED LABOR AND DEPORTATIONS

Even more than the deportation plans, the extremely high mortality rates in camps placed training measures in jeopardy. According to witness statements, twelve or more persons died every day in the Markstädt and

---

[44] Steinbacher, *"Musterstadt" Auschwitz*, 275.

[45] Summarized according to the camps lists based on survivor statements in ITS, Arolsen, 1979.

[46] One operation alone employed 1,500 Jews; Bundesarchiv – Militärarchiv (BA-MA) Freiburg im Breisgau, RW, 20–8, No. 21, Fol. 150, Situation report of Armaments Inspection Office VIII, October 14, 1941; Steinbacher, *"Musterstadt" Auschwitz*, 151.

[47] See the letter of the Upper Silesian HSSPF to Himmler, April 20, 1942, quoted in Adler, *Der verwaltete Mensch*, 230.

[48] Konieczny, "Die Zwangsarbeit," 100–101.

[49] Only later was the transition to be made to "more significant, more comprehensive, and more permanent training of the eastern workers"; BA Berlin, 46.01 General Inspector for German Roadways, No. 1576, Fol. 41, Report of the Breslau construction commissioner (Armaments Inspection Office VIII), January 18, 1943.

[50] Hilberg, *Vernichtung*, Vol. 2, 551.

[51] BA-MA Freiburg im Breisgau, RW 20–8, No. 21, Fol. 163–164, Situation report of Armaments Inspection Office VIII, November 14, 1941.

[52] Summarized according to the lists based on survivor statements in ITS, Arolsen, 1979.

Faulbrück labor camps, and the situation was similar in Johannsdorf and Blechhammer-Ehrenforst. In Brande camp, over 100 Jews died between October 1942 and August 1943 of beatings, debilitation, or outright murder.[53] Between May and August 1943, sixteen inmates from the camps at Masselwitz, Neukirch, and Hundsfeld were buried at the Breslau cemetery on Flughafen Street, among them Dutch and Polish Jews; in January 1944 there were ten, and in February, twenty-four.[54]

Since late fall 1941, the Schmelt office had performed first sporadic then systematic selections in the forced-labor camps. Persons unable to work later were sent to Auschwitz and murdered there.[55] To replace those who had died or been taken away, the Jews in eastern Upper Silesia were pressed into forced-labor service with threats of draconian repressive measures such as punishment camps, withdrawal of food ration cards, or deportation of entire families.[56] But the number of people recruited in this manner was soon no longer sufficient to meet the demands of the armaments projects. In addition, systematic deportations from the cities of eastern Upper Silesia began in early summer 1942. During large-scale raids in August, only persons working in collective workshops were excepted from the Auschwitz transports. In the course of this operation, 9,000 young men from private businesses were now taken to Schmelt camps. In fall 1942, the Jews remaining in the cities of eastern Upper Silesia were finally concentrated in sealed ghettos.[57]

Because of the acute labor shortages, Special Commissioner Schmelt, after the Armaments Ministry had exerted pressure on the Reichsführer SS, received extraordinary permission to muster an additional 10,000 Jews from among those aboard deportation trains from western Europe to fill up his camps.[58] Commissioner Schmelt stopped the trains on the way to Auschwitz

---

[53] IMT, Vol. XXXIV, Doc. No. PS-4071, 143–144, Statement in lieu of oath, July 22, 1946. See Wollenberg, *Alptraum*, 58–155; Wolf, *Ich blieb zurück*, 34. Summary of statements by Jewish survivors; ITS, Arolsen, 1969, XXVI; Andreas Reinke, "Stufen der Zerstörung. Das Breslauer Jüdische Krankenhaus während des Nationalsozialismus," in *Menora. Jahrbuch für deutsch-jüdische Geschichte 1994* (Munich and Zurich, 1994), 406–407.

[54] See lists in Archiwum Panstwowe (AP) we Wrocław, Senior president for finance in Lower Silesia, No. 1395, Fol. 301; BA Berlin, R 8150, No. 780, Fols. 102 and 94.

[55] Wollenberg, *Alptraum*, 94 and 125; Steinbacher, *"Musterstadt" Auschwitz*, 280–282. At the beginning of 1942, "sick transports" containing debilitated forced laborers were sent from Mechtal camp to Heidebreck, Upper Silesia, where the workers were killed by the methods used for *Aktion T4*, the murder operation for the disabled and ill; IMT, Vol. XXXIV, Doc. No. PS-4071, 143–144, Statement in lieu of oath, July 22, 1946.

[56] *Faschismus-Getto-Massenmord*, 232, Doc. No. 178, Letter from Schmelt, January 15, 1942. Furthermore, May 31, 1942, request (on orders from the special commissioner) through the council of elders of the Bendsburg Jewish Religious community for laborers, quoted in Konieczny, "Die Zwangsarbeit," 102.

[57] Steinbacher, *"Musterstadt" Auschwitz*, 287–291.

[58] According to Höß, quoted in Danuta Czech, *Kalendarium der Ereignisse im Konzentrationslager Auschwitz-Birkenau 1939–1945* (Reinbek near Hamburg, 1989), 289 and note.

at the Kosel railway station in Upper Silesia. His subordinates selected male Jews between sixteen and forty-five years old – other sources say fifty years old – who seemed to be capable of working. By November 9, at least fifteen trains had been searched; they carried Dutch and French Jews and German Jews who had fled to western Europe.[59] At the end of 1942, 8,188 Jewish foreign nationals not from Poland were performing compulsory labor in the Schmelt system.[60]

At the beginning of 1943, the SS special commissioner had at his disposal a total of over 50,570 male and female Jewish forced laborers, probably the zenith of Schmelt forced labor.[61] Mid-1943 marked the beginning both of ghetto liquidations and of mass deportations of forced laborers in Upper Silesia. The over 800 artisans' workshops in the cities of eastern Upper Silesia were closed and the workers deported to Auschwitz.[62] Thus, on June 25, 1943, a transport with 2,500 people from the Bendsburg ghetto reached the extermination camp. All the inmates on the train went to their deaths. In August, further transports from Sosnowitz and Bendsburg with over 30,000 people followed.[63]

Under SS control in the course of 1943, many Jews were removed from the Schmelt camps – even from armaments production operations such as the Adolf Hitler tank construction program – and deported; then the camps were closed.[64] On August 24, 1,000 sick Jews transferred from the Markstädt labor camp were killed in the extermination facilities at Auschwitz. On November 12, a transport of Jewish women from a Silesian forced-labor camp arrived there. The SS placed 191 of them in the concentration camp, while the rest were murdered. At New Year's 1944, further transports with thousands of people from the ghettos of eastern Upper Silesia reached Auschwitz.[65]

[59] *Die Ermordung der europäischen Juden, Eine umfassende Dokumentation des Holocaust 1945–1945*, edited by Peter Longerich (Munich and Zurich, 1989), 267, Doc. No. 110, Affidavit of Gutmacher, "From Malines camp to Auschwitz, October 27, 1960." See Wollenberg, *Alptraum*, 56 and note 46 (196).

[60] LBIA New York, Microfilms, Wiener Library, 500 Series, No. 526, Inspector for statistics with the RFSS, January 1, 1943 (Korherr Report), 17. (also in BA Berlin, NS 19, No. 1570) There were also Bulgarians, Greeks, and Romanians in Blechhammer; Wollenberg, *Alptraum*, 119–120.

[61] LBIA New York, Microfilms, Wiener Library, 500 Series, No. 526, Inspector for statistics with the RFSS, January 1, 1943 (Korherr Report), 17.

[62] Steinbacher, *"Musterstadt" Auschwitz*, 300–301.

[63] Czech, *Kalendarium*, 529. There were further transports in June and August 1943; ibid., 527 and 561–572.

[64] *Faschismus-Getto-Massenmord*, 226, Doc. No. 173, Statement of Rudolf Höß, 1946. Hilberg dates the beginning of the deportations of forced laborers to August; Hilberg, *Vernichtung*, Vol. 2, 551. See also the years 1943–44 in Czech, *Kalendarium*; and Konieczny, "Die Zwangsarbeit," 105–106.

[65] Czech, *Kalendarium*, 582, 652, 682, and 705.

But even the SS had to respect overall economic interests. Hence, the forced-labor camps most important for war production, a total of forty-three, were taken away from Special Commissioner Schmelt on instructions from Himmler, and placed together with their inmates under the supervision of the SS WVHA in Berlin. After that, the camps functioned as outside detachments of the Auschwitz or Groß-Rosen concentration camps.[66] Thus, in December 1943, Auschwitz controlled new subcamps at Neu-Dachs, Jawischowitz, Eintrachthütte, Lagischa, Fürstengrube, Golleschau, Janinagrube, Sosnowitz, and Brünn. In April 1944, Auschwitz III took over Blechhammer forced-labor camp with 3,056 male and 150 female prisoners working on Oberschlesische Hydrierwerke projects. A short time later, Auschwitz also acquired the Bobrek, Gleiwitz I, II, and III, Günthergrube, and Laurahütte subcamps.[67] As a result of this transaction, many companies were able to continue uninterruptedly exploiting their forced laborers as concentration camp prisoners.

In September 1943, Schmelt moved his office to Annaberg; from there, he directed his considerably reduced forced-labor camp system into which he had apparently begun drafting non-Jewish Poles.[68] Schmelt transferred to special funds part of the profits that the SS organization garnered by renting out the eastern Upper Silesian forced laborers; one such fund of the NSDAP Gauleiter supported ethnic German resettlement projects, and another sponsored by the Higher SS and Police Leader provided social services for the families of SS men who had died in battle. However, Schmelt also pocketed RM 100,000, for which he had to answer to an SS court in 1944.[69]

SUMMARY

Thus ended Schmelt's career, which had begun in fall 1940 with his appointment as SS special commissioner and with the assignment of implementing forced labor in Upper Silesia. By 1941, the SS Organisation Schmelt had built its own network of forced-labor camps, and – assuming the functions of the labor office, with a few exceptions – placed Polish Jewish men and women in private enterprises and government agencies. The conditions in the Silesian camps of the Organisation Schmelt at first were similar to those in Reich Autobahn camps. The inmates were handed over every day to enterprises under a group contract for a work day of up to twelve hours in exchange for collective wages. Then, after the beginning of 1942, the Schmelt agency

---

[66] The Auschwitz administration took over at least fifteen Upper Silesian camps in 1943 and 1944, and in 1944 Groß-Rosen took over at least twenty-three Jewish forced labor camps in Lower Silesia and five in the Sudeten region; see ITS, Arolsen, 1979. On the actual process, see Wollenberg, *Alptraum*, 132–186.

[67] Czech, *Kalendarium*, 682, 747, and 759.   [68] Steinbacher, *"Musterstadt" Auschwitz*, 305.

[69] Steinbacher, *"Musterstadt" Auschwitz*, 152–153.

rented them to interested parties for a per-person charge. The regime of the SS Organisation Schmelt affected tens of thousands of mostly Polish Jews in at least 158 Silesian and 19 Sudeten forced-labor camps.[70] In the Silesian camps, which were guarded around the clock, starvation, abuse, and death prevailed. Nevertheless, for economic reasons, the camps often offered the inmates a better chance for survival than did the cities. The labor and living conditions in the Silesian camps, despite the fact that they were mostly located in the Old Reich, closely resembled those in Jewish forced-labor camps of the General Government.

[70] According to my research. Konieczny was still assuming a total of 162 labor camps; Konieczny, "Die Zwangsarbeit," 104.

9

The Labor Office versus the SS – Forced Labor in the General Government, 1939–1944

EARLY INTRODUCTION OF FORCED LABOR UNDER SS CONTROL

During the campaign in September 1939, Wehrmacht units in occupied Polish territory obligated Jews to perform auxiliary tasks.[1] In the period that followed, military and civilian offices forced men and women to clear away ruins, to fill in tank trenches, or to shovel snow. Under unsanctioned compulsory measures at Biała Podlaska in October, 300 Jewish men and women had to perform cleaning tasks in public buildings and caserns for four weeks. In Zamość, between 500 and 600 people a day were recruited in raids.[2] In Oświęcim, Jews had to "report in columns to sweep the streets for purposes of education and punishment." Abel Gimpel, at the time a young man barely twenty years old, describes how he was humiliated by a German soldier: "He said, 'You have to wash the car. . . .' I said, 'Give me a bucket and a cloth.' He said, 'No.' I had on a coat that I had owned for less than two weeks. He said: 'Take your coat and wash the car with it.' When I was finished, he screamed: 'Get lost.' I wanted to take my coat with me. But he wouldn't let me have it. – I stood there in winter without a coat."[3] The brutal behavior of the occupiers – in occupied Poland the Einsatzgruppen began murdering at various places in the very first weeks – threw its dark shadow on future policies regarding Polish Jews.[4]

[1] Dieter Pohl, "Die großen Zwangsarbeitslager der SS- und Polizeiführer für Juden im Generalgouvernement 1942–1945," in *Die nationalsozialistischen Konzentrationslager. Entwicklung und Struktur*, edited by Ulrich Herbert, Karin Orth, and Christoph Dieckmann, Vol. 1 (Göttingen, 1998), 415–438, here 416.

[2] Raul Hilberg, *Die Vernichtung der europäischen Juden*, Vol. 1, 261; *Verzeichnis der Haftstätten unter dem Reichsführer SS 1933–1945. Konzentrationslager und deren Außenkommandos sowie andere Haftstätten unter dem Reichsführer SS in Deutschland und deutschbesetzten Gebieten*, edited by the International Tracing Service (ITS) of the Red Cross (Arolsen, 1979), XXII; Bogdan Musial, *Deutsche Zivilverwaltung und Judenverfolgung im Generalgouvernement. Eine Fallstudie zum Distrikt Lublin 1939–1944* (Wiesbaden, 1999), 115–117.

[3] Quoted in Sybille Steinbacher, *"Musterstadt" Auschwitz. Germanisierungspolitik und Judenmord in Ostoberschlesien* (Munich, 2000), 57.

[4] For the murders, see Michael Wildt, *Generation des Unbedingten. Das Führungskorps des Reichssicherheitshauptamtes* (Hamburg, 2002), 447–468; and recently with extensive details,

After the end of the military administration and establishment of the so-called General Government, the situation in the rest of Poland differed from that in western Polish territories annexed to the Reich. The General Government had its own administrative structure independent of the Reich. It consisted first of four parts, the Warsaw, the Krakow, the Radom, and the Lublin districts. (See map 8, p. 215.) The General Government was initially envisaged as the holding space for all Jews from the Reich and the annexed territories. For that reason, in contrast to the Warthegau and eastern Upper Silesia, the anti-Jewish regime established there was not regarded as an intermediate solution. The new General Governor, Hans Frank,[5] as one of his early official acts, issued the first regular order concerning Jewish forced labor: "1. Compulsory labor is introduced for Jews residing in the General Government, effective immediately. For that reason, Jews are to be put together in forced laborer groups. 2. The Higher SS and Police Leader will issue the regulations required to carry out this order. . . ."[6] The new features of the October 26, 1939, order compared to previous approaches in the Old Reich lay in using a public order instead of a non-published decree, in officially sanctioning forced labor itself, and in establishing for the first time the SS's influence on the development of the policy.

The HSSPF in the General Government, Friedrich Krüger, promptly pushed for implementation of the order: "It is especially urgent that forced labor be established for Jews. The Jewish population must be taken from the cities as soon as possible, and put to work performing road jobs."[7] A first problem was registering the workers; it was still usually spontaneous. Many places formed work columns for a day. HSSPF Krüger therefore issued an order on December 2, 1939, empowering the so-called Jewish

Alexander B. Rossino, *Hitler Strikes Poland: Blitzkrieg, Ideology, and Atrocity* (Lawrence, Kansas, 2003).

[5] Hitler's decree of October 19, 1939, in *"Führer-Erlasse" 1939–1945. Edition sämtlicher überlieferter, nicht im Reichsgesetzblatt abgedruckter, von Hitler während des Zweiten Weltkrieges schriftlich erteilter Direktiven aus den Bereichen Staat, Partei, Wirtschaft, Besatzungspolitik und Militärverwaltung*, compiled and with an introduction by Martin Moll (Stuttgart, 1997), Doc. No. 14, 103–105.

[6] *Verordnungsblatt des Generalgouverneurs*, 1939: 6; reproduced in *Eksterminacja Żydów na ziemiach polskich w okresie okupacji hitlerowskiej. Zbiór dokumentów*, edited by Tatiana Berenstein, et al. (Warsaw, 1957), 202–203, Doc. No. 100; and *Faschismus-Getto-Massenmord. Dokumentation über Ausrottung und Widerstand der Juden in Polen während des zweiten Weltkrieges* (Berlin [GDR], 1960), 203, Doc. No. 152; see Diemut Majer, *"Fremdvölkische" im Dritten Reich. Ein Beitrag zur nationalsozialistischen Rechtssetzung und Rechtspraxis in Verwaltung und Justiz unter besonderer Berücksichtigung der eingegliederten Ostgebiete und des Generalgouvernements* (Boppard am Rhein, 1981), 554 (English version published by the Johns Hopkins University Press, in association with the United States Holocaust Memorial Museum, 2003).

[7] Statement of November 8, 1939, quoted in Dieter Pohl, *Von der "Judenpolitik" zum Judenmord. Der Distrikt Lublin des Generalgouvernements 1939–1944* (Frankfurt am Main, Berlin, and Bern, 1993), 81.

councils created since November to set up forced-laborer columns themselves.[8] In practice, that was already happening in some places. The Warsaw Jewish council already had relevant experience before the forced-labor decree appeared. Under an agreement with the local Gestapo, the council had already been supplying workers to "German and municipal offices" since October 21. While it was a matter of several hundred Jews in October, almost 2,400 were involved by mid-December 1939, and later more than 10,000 Jews a day.[9]

To moderate the practice of hunting people outright, which was spreading through Poland like a disease, the SS and the General Government authorities held discussions on December 8, 1939, in Krakow regarding future "useful" employment of Polish Jews, many of whom formerly had worked as artisans. They agreed that systematic registration of the Jews between fourteen and fifty years old was essential. However, the participants had to acknowledge that "Thorough planning is required for that. For the time being, the Jews will have to be formed into columns and put to use wherever there is urgent need."[10] At that stage, the SS, too, had in mind an organized approach to forced labor. Thus, the Jews were to be deported from the Polish territories annexed to the Reich, but in Heydrich's view, not placed in a reserve, as first planned, but distributed across the entire General Government. And, "if the possibilities presented themselves," the "male Jews from about eighteen to sixty years old" would then "be put together in work details and utilized appropriately."[11]

Marking of the Jewish population – delayed in Germany for various reasons – was introduced first in the occupied Polish territories, on November 23 in the General Government and a short time later in the whole Warthegau. From December 1939 on, this action visibly separated the Jewish minority from the rest of the Polish population.[12] Additionally, based on the September 1939 plans, an order regarding establishment of Jewish councils was

---

[8] *Verordnungsblatt des Generalgouverneurs*, 1939: 246–248; Hilberg, *Vernichtung*, Vol. 1, 262.

[9] *Eksterminacja Żydów*, Doc. No. 99, 202, Report for the period from October 7, 1939, to December 31, 1940.

[10] *Eksterminacja Żydów*, Doc. No. 101, 203–204, Meeting of department heads of the government of the General Government in Krakow, December 8, 1939; also in *Faschismus-Getto-Massenmord*, 203, Doc. No. 153. See Christopher Browning, "Nazi Germany's Initial Attempt to Exploit Jewish Labor in the General Government: The Early Jewish Work Camps 1940–1941," in *Die Normalität des Verbrechens. Festschrift für Wolfgang Scheffler zum 65. Geburtstag* (Berlin, 1994), 171. See also Christopher R. Browning, *Die Entfesselung der "Endlösung". Nationalsozialistische Judenpolitik 1939–1942*, with an essay by Jürgen Matthäus (Berlin, 2003), 214–228.

[11] Quoted according to the Heydrich plan; Götz Aly, *"Endlösung" – Völkerverschiebung und der Mord an den europäischen Juden* (Frankfurt am Main, 1995), 74.

[12] Order of November 23, 1939, which applied to all Jews over ten years old; *Eksterminacja Żydów*, Doc. No. 23, 70. See Pohl, *Von der "Judenpolitik" zum Judenmord*, 66.

issued.[13] The December 11, 1939, regulations of the occupation administration to implement the forced-labor order prohibited Jews from leaving their town of residence and set a curfew. For violations, the threat of "intensive, long-lasting forced labor service" loomed.[14] A second implementing order called upon all Jews between twelve and sixty years old to register through the Bürgermeister for two years of obligatory service. In this second order, the occupation powers explicitly stated that Polish Jews were to be "housed in camps and utilized for labor."[15] Forced labor could be extended arbitrarily after two years if within that period the ostensible "educational goals [were] not met." Contrary to the usual practice in the Reich, the Jews in Poland were, "if possible, to be employed in keeping with their professional training," that is, more efficiently from the outset in economic terms.[16] In addition, in January 1940, instructions went to the Jewish council to prepare a card file of workers.[17]

The Jewish Population in the General Government,
First Half of 1940[18]

District	Number of Jews	Percentage of the Population
Krakow	200,000	5.3%
Radom	310,000	10.4%
Warsaw	540,000	17.4%
Lublin	250,000	9.6%
Total	1,300,000	10.4%

FORCED LABOR UNDER THE SS: MEGAPLANS AND REALITY

In a book published in May 1940, *Das Generalgouvernement*, HSSPF Krüger wrote about the new mission of the SS: "The men of the SS and the police had, and have, to perform the rather thankless, but nonetheless important, labor of looking after people. The work-shirking Jewish rabble had to be taken to

[13] Helge Grabitz and Wolfgang Scheffler, *Letzte Spuren. Ghetto Warschau. SS-Arbeitslager Trawniki. Aktion Erntefest. Fotos und Dokumente über Opfer des Endlösungswahns im Spiegel der historischen Ereignisse* (Berlin, 1988), 278.

[14] *Eksterminacja Żydów*, Doc. No. 102, 204–205; see Pohl, *Von der "Judenpolitik" zum Judenmord*, 66.

[15] *Faschismus-Getto-Massenmord*, 205–206, Doc. No. 156. See ITS, Arolsen, 1979, LXIII; Pohl, *Von der "Judenpolitik" zum Judenmord*, 66.

[16] January 15, 1940, report from Krakow, in *Ostdeutscher Beobachter*, Posen, January 16, 1940; WL London, Reel 156, 2 B (2).

[17] Browning, "Nazi Germany's Initial Attempt to Exploit Jewish Labor," 171.

[18] According to a document of July 1940, in *Eksterminacja Żydów*, Doc. No. 36, 86.

Photo 8. Jewish forced laborers digging in a water-filled trench in Poland, circa 1940

the work sites provided. As the result of police forced labor measures, many Jews could be introduced for the first time in their lives to fruitful work for the benefit of the general population, but at the same time it should be kept in mind that thus initiating all Jews into work indirectly meant considerable easing of the police burden in a major task area."[19]

These statements made the process sound well-organized, but the reality of the matter was different. For example, Odilo Globocznik, the SS and Police Leader (SSPF) in Lublin, immediately established an SS section for Jewish forced labor. In December 1939, the first labor camp was set up in Lublin with workshops for the SS. The SS section, however, only covered the city area; in the countryside, the *Kreishauptmänner* (Kreis administrators) made labor arrangements for the Jews because the SS was too short-staffed.[20] Uncoordinated, random recruiting continued to prevail in the General Government, often with fierce competition among various local administrations. Local authorities, the Wehrmacht, and the SS frequently utilized large numbers of

---

[19] Cited by Gerald Reitlinger, *Die Endlösung. Hitlers Versuch der Ausrottung der Juden Europas 1939–1945*, 4th reworked and expanded edition (Berlin, 1961), 76–77. See *Das Generalgouvernement. Im Auftrage und mit einem Vorwort des Generalgouverneurs Reichsminister Dr. Frank*, edited and revised by Dr. and Baron Max von Prel, 2nd edition (Würzburg, 1942), 65.

[20] Musial, *Zivilverwaltung*, 115–117; Czeslaw Madajczyk, *Die Okkupationspolitik Nazideutschlands in Polen 1939–1945* (Berlin [East], 1987), 229; Siegfried Pucher, *". . . in der Bewegung führend tätig". Odilo Globocznik – Kämpfer für den "Anschluß", Vollstrecker des Holocaust*, with a foreword by Karl Stuhlpfarrer (Klagenfurt, 1997), 77.

Jews without pay. From October 21, 1939, to November 15, 1940, 1.44 million of two million work days were not paid.[21] In the case of paid work, the officials in charge argued about whether social insurance contributions had to be paid; the Wehrmacht was opposed.[22] Despite an undiminished, comprehensive obligation to pay for social insurance, Jewish forced laborers only received health insurance benefits.[23]

At the same time, the Wehrmacht and SS outdid each other with planning exercises involving use of hundreds of thousands of Jewish forced laborers on huge building projects at the border with the Soviet Union. The army wanted to construct an eastern wall, a project for a time even approved by Hitler. Himmler instead proposed a vast tank trench, to be constructed by millions of people housed in a future "Jewish reservation." At the end of January 1940, Himmler planned as a first phase to have several hundred thousand Jews in forced-labor camps work on fortifications in the East; the Jews were not to come from the General Government but apparently would be deported from the annexed territories. Their families would be put together with Jewish families living in the General Government.[24] Based on a proposal by Globocznik, 2.5 million Jewish forced laborers would have to construct tank trenches that were about 40 to 50 meters wide.[25] However, during 1940, with the concrete preparations for an attack on the Soviet Union,[26] the authorities gave up the plans for a Jewish reservation and for the trench.

At the same time there was discussion of mass deployment of forced laborers to regulate the rivers between the Vistula and the Bug.[27] With time, coordination improved between the SS and the Security Police on the one hand with the civilian administration on the other. Representatives of the SD and representatives of the Lublin district departments of labor (Dr. Heine), internal administration (party comrade Richard Türk), food and agriculture (SA Sturmbannführer Kaiser), road construction (Construction Councillor Muth), and forests (Chief Forester Krainer) participated in a spring 1940 meeting in Lublin with SSPF Globocznik regarding use of Jewish forced laborers. Globocznik had to acknowledge there that no large work projects could be carried out without systematic preparations. The self-defense corps (*Selbstschutz*) was to take over planning. Snow removal in Lublin was the

---

[21] *Encyclopedia of the Holocaust*, edited by Israel Gutman (New York and London, 1990), Vol. 2, 502.

[22] See Pohl, *Von der "Judenpolitik" zum Judenmord*, 72.

[23] "Continuation and Reorganization of Polish Social Insurance in the General Government," in *Zentralblatt der Reichsversicherung und Reichsversorgung*, 7–8 (April, 1940): 69.

[24] According to Heydrich's letter of January 30, 1940, in Madajczyk, *Okkupationspolitik*, 238.

[25] Pucher, *Globocznik*, 83.

[26] Pohl, *Von der "Judenpolitik" zum Judenmord*, 81; Pohl, "Zwangsarbeitslager," 416.

[27] Madajczyk, *Okkupationspolitik*, 229.

first area of success. The self-defense corps organized daily labor placement inside and outside Lublin. In addition, the departments of the district chiefs and the Kreishauptmänner created labor plans.[28]

The representative of the district administration's road construction department declared that there were 45,000 registered Jewish forced laborers in the Lublin district and that 5,000 new ones would be added "as the first installment on the construction of the border trench." However, he continued, that would deplete the supply of able-bodied Jews in the district. Room and board, as well as family support, created significant problems above everything else: "If the work site is not in the immediate vicinity of the residence, housing in barracks is planned, especially for larger jobs. The costs for food and housing are to be charged to the Jewish community, thus at the same time making available to us Jewish property that otherwise could not be seized. Jewish wenches and Jews no longer capable of heavy labor will provide care and support. Of course, men and women will be strictly separated." The workers would be "completely or almost completely cost-free."[29] As a then-contemporary letter stated, many German Jews deported from Pomerania to Lublin in February 1940 were "snatched" and taken further to the east for forced labor.[30]

Because SS-organized forced labor was not coordinated with the supraregional needs of the General Government's labor market, the civilian administration exerted its influence and demanded that it be given authority. In Poland, the number of unemployed Jews (and thus potential forced laborers), and the proportion of skilled workers among them, was very high. The Jews consequently represented a significant factor on the labor market. Moreover, labor shortages were increasing in 1940, when the massive withdrawal of non-Jewish Poles into the Reich to serve as "foreign workers" had begun.[31] The labor offices, however, had no access to unemployed Jews to remedy the situation. The General Government had introduced support for the unemployed in a December 1939 order, but unemployed Jews were excluded from it and therefore not registered with the labor offices. The labor administration consequently saw no possibility of being able to rely

---

[28] Institut für Zeitgeschichte (IfZ) – Archiv Munich, Fb 84, Fols. 32–36, here 33, Protocol (Hofbauer) of the meeting of April 22, 1940; an excerpt reproduced in *Eksterminacja Zydów*, Doc. No. 103, 207–208.

[29] IfZ – Archiv Munich, Fb 84, Fols. 32–36, here 35, Protocol (Hofbauer) of the meeting of April 22, 1940; this part quoted by Wolfgang Benz, "Die Ausbeutung "fremdvölkischer" Arbeitskräfte," in *Der nationalsozialistische Krieg*, edited by Norbert Frei and Hermann Kling (Frankfurt am Main and New York, 1990), 258–259.

[30] May 30, 1940, letter of Martha Bauchwitz, in *Lebenszeichen aus Piaski, Briefe Deportierter aus dem Distrikt Lublin 1940–1943*, edited by Else Rosenfeld and Gertrud Luckner (Munich, 1968), 50.

[31] Hilberg, *Vernichtung*, Vol. 1, 261; Madajczyk, *Okkupationspolitik*, 222; Browning, "Jewish Workers," 61.

on unemployed Jews.[32] For example, in December 1939 4,500 Jewish and non-Jewish Poles who had been deported from the Warthegau arrived in the Tarnow labor office's district. While the "Poles" were immediately registered by the labor office and considered for assignment to work, the "Jews" were not.[33]

The policy since the beginning of the conquest had led to extreme impoverishment of Polish Jews. Scarcely any income came from independent economic activity. Many of the forced laborers recruited by the SS received no wages. The Jewish councils suffered financial need and could scarcely intervene to help.[34] The situation would become acute for the Jewish population by early summer 1940. During early spring, the Ministry of Labor had discussed the possibility of eliminating all Jews' social and professional wage advantages in the Reich. The planned order was actually also to take effect in the occupied Eastern territories.[35] However, in the General Government, unemployed Jews officially no longer received any health or disability insurance beginning in April, even though they had paid into the plans.[36] In May 1940, responsibility for safeguarding the unemployed who were excluded from the unemployment insurance program in consequence of their mandatory employment, was transferred exclusively to a Jewish social self-help organization,[37] as was that for forced laborers.[38] While non-Jewish Poles were obligated to work but were entitled to unemployment assistance and health insurance benefits, Jews were subject, after October 26, 1939, "to mandatory labor based on a employment situation (*Arbeitsverhältnis*) that was not strictly voluntary and did not include insurance coverage."[39]

The responsible German authorities heard about the drastic situation in Poland from the SS Security Service. In the April 19, 1940, "Report from

---

[32] See General Government, Office of the Chief of Krakow District (ed.), *Abteilung Arbeit. Die Aufbauarbeit im Distrikt Krakau* (Krakow, 1940), 21, in USHMMA Washington, DC, RG-15.041M (Records of the Krakow District Office), Reel 2, no folio numbers; ibid., Unemployment and job-placement statistics from the office of Krakow district, labor department and from the Tarnow labor office, November 1930–April 1940.

[33] Ibid., Report of the Tarnow labor office, December 16–31, 1939.

[34] Hilberg, *Vernichtung*, Vol. 1, 262.

[35] BA Berlin, R 43 II Reich Chancellery, No. 548, Fols. 93–95, April 16, 1940 letter with a draft order attached (NG-1143). Because the order would also take effect in the eastern territories, the OKW also received a draft copy; BA-MA Freiburg im Breisgau, RW, 19, No. 2162, no folio numbers, OKW to the Economic Armaments Office (*Wirtschaftsrüstungsamt*), April 19, 1940.

[36] BA Berlin, R 3901 (former R 41) Reich Labor Ministry, No. 5788, Fols. 8–9, Circular of the chief of the labor department in the General Government, April 30, 1940.

[37] This was not officially formalized until the November 9, 1940, order on granting unemployment assistance; Majer, *"Fremdvölkische,"* 556.

[38] See Pohl, *Von der "Judenpolitik" zum Judenmord*, 72.

[39] *Zentralblatt für Reichsversicherung und Reichsversorgung*, 7–8 (April, 1940): 70.

the Reich" they could read: "The Jews' mood has also worsened because the proletarianization of these elements continues. The National Socialists note that only by implementing the law obligating Jews to work is it possible to feed this segment of the population. Until the obligation to work has been implemented, Jewry cannot be prevented from being heavily involved in dirty dealings to somehow get their hands on money."[40] And even the Commander of the Security Police and the SD was forced to confess to General Government authorities in May, "If the Jewish communities continue to be exploited as they have been, millions of Jews one day will become a burden on the General Government. After all, they cannot just be left to starve. The means at the Jewry's disposal are quite modest; there are no longer any rich Jews in the General Government but for the most part only a Jewish proletariate."[41] A report of the Tarnow *Stadthauptmann* (city administrator) described the local situation: "Because I am increasingly excluding Jews from employment opportunities as part of reorganization in the area of the economy and the food situation, the question of what to do with the Jews in the future constantly arises. Use of the Jews for forced labor only ensures employment and scant food for a portion of the male Jews but not for women and children. The solution of the Jewish problem becomes increasingly urgent as their employment horizon narrows."[42]

Absolute impoverishment was not the only factor prompting changes, however. Another cause was that uneven local and regional handling of forced labor hindered effective use of Jewish labor for the war economy. In Warsaw district, the forced-labor organization was transferred in April 1940 from the SS to the district administration's labor department, while in Lublin district, according to new May police regulations, laborers were still requested at the Security Police offices.[43] In Krakow district, skilled and unskilled workers were withdrawn in an uncoordinated process from Krakow district's private companies and factories in May. The Tarnow Gans und Hochberger company, operating under trusteeship, had workers removed for "the Jewish council's forced labor," even though that company worked for the Reich Labor Service, the construction service, the Polish police, companies important for the war effort, the fire department, and German officers. The Trustee, Walter Tidow, complained to the Tarnow city commissar, Dr. Eckart, with considerable irritation, "For that reason it makes no sense to take away my workers, who are employed in German enterprises, while thousands of unemployed Jews are hanging around on Lemberg Street

[40] *Meldungen aus dem Reich 1938–1945. Die geheimen Lageberichte des Sicherheitsdienstes der SS*, edited and with an introduction by Heinz Boberach, Vol. 4, (Herrsching, 1984), 1031, Report No. 79, April 19, 1940.
[41] According to the official journal (*Diensttagebuch*) of the General Governor, 216, in Musial, *Zivilverwaltung*, 117.
[42] *Eksterminacja Żydów*, Doc. No. 104, 210.   [43] ITS, Arolsen, 1979, LXIII.

or in the ghetto."[44] As Tidow learned, the city commissar and the HSSPF in Krakow had retained "his" forced laborers. The Jewish council had been told that no workers from the company were to be passed to the city administration. In exchange for the workers' "liberation," however – that is, their return to the operation – the company was supposed to pay a certain amount to the Jewish council. And of course, because of a call-up order of the HSSPF, the company would have to go to the Kreishauptmann (Kreis administrator) to get the workers released."[45]

POWER TRANSFER: THE LABOR ADMINISTRATION'S ASSUMPTION OF RESPONSIBILITY FOR FORCED LABOR

To ensure effective allocation of forced laborers in the General Government, a central coordination meeting was held on May 30, 1940. Representatives of the civilian administration called attention to the problem that every possible institution was asking the Jewish councils for forced laborers. As Chief of the Security Police in the General Government, Bruno Streckenbach was in favor of his agency continuing to maintain sole supervisory authority over the Jewish councils. The chief of the Lublin district administration leveled the criticism that too many Jews in his city were unemployed and demanded that sole control of the forced-labor organization be transferred to the civilian administration. In his view, only the latter could effectively force the Jewish councils to mobilize workers. The SD, he insisted, did not have enough personnel.[46] The harsh criticism of the SS did not fall on deaf ears.

Only a week later, on June 6 and 7, the problem was discussed again thoroughly at a government conference. On the first day of the meetings, Dr. Max Frauendorfer, the chief of the General Governor's labor department, proposed a compromise. In the future, the labor offices would handle distribution and employment of the Jewish workers, and the police would handle registration. Frauendorfer also wanted to place Jews in the regular labor market because not all of them could be "stuck" in labor camps, if only for financial reasons. The next day, the participants agreed to a transfer of responsibilities. Deployment of Jews would remain in principle a matter for the police, but in the future, assignment would be arranged by the General Governor's labor department. Jews would be employed within the normal

---

44 USHMMA Washington, DC, RG-15.020M (Polish State Archive, Tarnow), Reel 8, Fol. 117, Trustee to the city commissar on May 31, 1940. (Thanks to Margit Berner, Vienna, for calling my attention to this collection.)

45 Ibid., Fol. 117 verso, Tarnow city commissar to Trustee Tidow, June 4, 1940.

46 *Der Prozeß gegen die Hauptkriegsverbrecher vor dem Internationalen Militärgerichtshof (IMT), Nürnberg 14. November 1945–1. Oktober 1946*, Vol. XXIX (Nuremberg, 1948), 448–456. See Browning, "Nazi Germany's initial attempt to exploit Jewish labor," 172–173; Hilberg, *Vernichtung*, Vol. 1, 263.

labor process, and a special wage scale would be prepared.[47] A short time later, HSSPF Krüger announced, to everyone's surprise, that all the labor utilization competencies would be transferred to the General Governor's labor office, and that "he would only be responsible for security and residence regulation of Jewish forced laborers."[48]

Thus, in mid-June 1940, the SS and the Security Police completely lost authority over this aspect of anti-Jewish policy to the labor administration. The chief of the General Governor's main labor department then directed the Jewish forced-labor program. Obersturmbannführer Frauendorfer was himself an early member of the SS and was considered an "old Party fighter."[49] The labor department heads under the district administration chiefs were subordinate to him. In total, twenty local labor offices with seventy-five branch offices existed in the General Government. The task of the labor administration, as in the Reich, was to "steer deployment of labor."[50] Many places established special Jewish labor offices. Frauendorfer's agencies later (in 1943) had 4,300 employees, 700 of them Germans.[51] Most of them had been ordered there from labor offices in the Reich and thus had information at their disposal, and perhaps even personal experience with segregated labor deployment of Jews. Additionally, the labor offices in the various districts of the General Government preferentially engaged officials from specific regions, thus ensuring their willing collaboration in persecution. In the office of the Krakow district chief's labor department, the labor utilization group employed eleven officials from Austrian labor offices and five from various locations in the Old Reich.[52] (See map 9, p. 241.)

As part of this power transfer, the civilian administration, that is, the Kreishauptmänner and Stadthauptmänner, gained command authority over the Jewish councils.[53] The power shift clearly had immediate effects. A report from Neu-Sandez (Nowy Sacz) indicated on June 29 that Jews increasingly

---

[47] Excerpt of the protocol for both days in ITS, Arolsen, 1979, LXIII. Excerpt from June 7, 1940, in *Eksterminacja Żydów*, Doc. No. 105, 210–211. See Browning, "Nazi Germany's initial attempt to exploit Jewish labor," 173.

[48] According to a statement of June 13, 1940, quoted in Pohl, *Von der "Judenpolitik" zum Judenmord*, 82.

[49] In fall 1943, he was transferred to the Waffen SS after a disagreement with Himmler. Ostensibly they argued about the excessively aggressive registration of Jews. In reality, the problem was probably Frauendorfer's position as chairman of the board for the "General Government's factories," which was a violation of the SS code; see *Reichsführer! . . . Briefe von und an Himmler*, edited by Helmut Heiber (Munich, 1970), 204–205.

[50] *Das Generalgouvernement*, 2nd edition, 136.   [51] Madajczyk, *Okkupationspolitik*, 220.

[52] USHMMA Washington, DC, RG-15.041M (Records of the Krakow District Office), Reel 2, no folio numbers. Personnel list for the Reich German loyal supporters (around 1940). See General Government, Office of the Chief of Krakow District (ed.), *Abteilung Arbeit. Die Aufbauarbeit im Distrikt Krakau* (Krakow, 1940), 21, in ibid, Reel 2, no folio numbers.

[53] After the official meeting of Lublin district and city administrators on June 18, 1940; Pucher, *Globocznik*, 78.

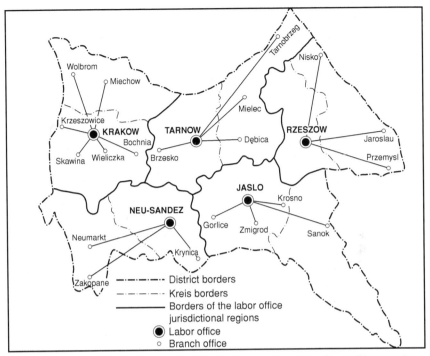

Map 9. Krakow District - Locations and Jurisdictions of the Labor Offices, on June 30, 1940

had been employed as forced laborers. A total of 1,000 Jews were said to have been called up. In Roznow, 300 Jews from Neu-Sandez constructed dams. In the near future, the report continued, the number of Jews engaged in road building was to increase from 100 to 600.[54] The Krakow Stadthauptmann noted similar developments a week later; in fact, the current number of workers could no longer satisfy many requests. In his view, clarification of how the forced laborers were to be paid was urgently needed, as the Jewish councils, previously "enjoined to handle most of this, no longer had sufficient means at their disposal to indemnify the forced laborers themselves. Forced laborers repeatedly collapse at their work sites because of malnutrition because they are unable to purchase adequate food."[55]

Therefore, immediately after the transfer of the forced-labor organization to the labor administration, at the beginning of July 1940, Frauendorfer issued new guidelines for Jewish labor. Based on an agreement with the HSSPF and by consent of the General Governor (the guidelines stated),

---

[54] *Eksterminacja Zydów*, Doc. No. 106, 211, Report of June 29, 1940.
[55] Ibid., Doc. No. 107, 212, Report of July 8, 1940.

the labor administration had gained future authority over registration and placement of Jewish workers in mandatory employment. Jewish laborers were urgently needed to replace the Poles sent to the Reich. The goals of labor utilization were employment of Jews and their maintenance. According to the guidelines, registration of able-bodied Jewish men from twelve to sixty years old was complete. The so-called Jewish card file had been taken over from the HSSPF and distributed to the district's labor administrations. Compulsory employment was to proceed in the future in the following manner: Wages would not be paid for utilization under the forced-labor regulations, especially in camps (so-called forced labor). For obligatory assignments arranged by the labor administration (so-called "free" or voluntary work situations), Jewish workers would receive 80 percent of Polish non-Jewish workers' wages in the form of performance agreement bonuses (*Leistungsakkordprämien*).[56]

On July 25, 1940, the head of the Tarnow labor office in Krakow district informed the Kreishauptmann, the municipal commissar, the army housing administration, the commanders of the SS and police, the Gestapo, the Polish hydraulic construction office, the Reich Railway refurbishment factory (*Reichsbahnausbesserungswerk*), and several private companies that

Implementation of the October 26, 1939, order regarding the introduction of a labor obligation for the General Government's Jewish population, . . . to the extent that registering and controlling the labor forces of the Jewish population both for free labor placement and for application of forced labor provisions are involved, has been transferred to the labor department in the General Governor's office and to its subordinate offices, in this case, the Tarnow labor office for the Tarnow and Dembica *Kreishauptmannschaften* [Kreis administration]. A Jewish labor branch of the Tarnow labor office has been established at Tertil Street No. 11 for registering and allocating able-bodied Jews. The purpose of utilizing Jewish labor is to contribute to eliminating labor shortages in the Government General. The Jews' employment is to be based on the October 26, 1939, order of the General Governor. In all appropriate cases, the attempt will be made to establish a voluntary employment situation. Use of Jews as forced laborers is generally only acceptable for large projects set up to employ large numbers of forced laborers, house them in camps, and have them guarded. *In the future, unauthorized requests for or employment of Jews by any office will not be tolerated.* Jews can only be requested from the Tarnow Jewish council until August 3. From August 5 on, requests for provision of any and all Jewish laborers are to be directed . . . without exception to the Jewish labor utilization office of the labor office. . . . I am directing the Jewish council to forward requests for provision of workers to the labor office from August 5, 1940, on. The labor office will select the workers. To obtain Jewish labor, to ensure that the families are provided for, and to prevent illnesses and epidemics, the head of the labor department has ordered that the employers must compensate their Jewish workers as ordered. Only when workers are housed *in camps* can the employer forgo wages and social benefits (for

---

[56] Ibid., Doc. No. 108, 212–214, Circular letter of the labor department, General Government, July 5, 1940; see Majer, "*Fremdvölkische*," 555.

example, social insurance). In this case, that is a matter for the local Jewish council. Workers not called up for compulsory labor but *placed in jobs* are to be employed, whenever possible, on the basis of an agreement; the pay rate for Jews is to be about twenty percent below comparable wages for Polish workers. If work under an agreement is not feasible, then hourly wages are to be granted, likewise twenty percent below those of Polish workers. A wage scale order to be issued shortly will provide details. Employers are to register Jewish workers who have been *placed* for social insurance.[57]

The different perspective of the labor office and its main interest in supplying the labor market is evident here. The "free" labor classification was of course a euphemism: Since the October 1939 forced-labor order, voluntary employment was no longer possible for Jews. What the term meant was segregated labor deployment, as already familiar from the Reich, but under much worse conditions.

After the Tarnow office for Jewish labor quickly was established,[58] one of its officials complained to the city commissar in a meeting that a number of Jews – in spite of being summoned – had not appeared for registration. They were to be instructed again by the Polish police about their obligation to report and taken "to the labor office, if necessary." The labor office letter stated clearly, "It is absolutely necessary that measures be taken against Jewish elements still believing today that they can ignore orders of the authorities, and this must happen immediately to ensure that the other birth-year contingents do not fail to observe their obligation to report as well."[59] Agreement was reached in Tarnow that the police would render official assistance. On August 1, 1940, the Polish police took seventeen Jews to the labor office. However, that office had requested thirty-one workers. The police were unable to bring another fourteen because they were either dead, deathly ill, confused, or had fled.[60] In the following days and weeks the police continued to carry out searches and to bring people in at the request of the labor office.[61]

The Tarnow labor office sought to enforce with all means the obligation to report. For non-observance, Jews were threatened with fines or imprisonment. While the male Jewish population born between 1880 and 1928 reported almost completely, around 3,000 other unemployed Jews did not appear for the check. The reason, the head of the Tarnow labor office suspected, was that "all the Jews feared my placing them with the new SS construction management in Dembica (Lignose camp)." The latter measure

---

[57] (Emphasis in the original.) USHMMA Washington, DC, RG-15.020M (Polish State Archive, Tarnow), Reel 8, Fol. 635, Circular of the Tarnow labor office, July 25, 1940, 1–2.

[58] Ibid., Fol. 615, Tarnow labor office to Tarnow city commissar, August 1, 1940.

[59] Ibid., Fol. 607, Tarnow labor office to Tarnow city commissar, July 30, 1940.

[60] Ibid., Fol. 637, Polish police commissar to the Tarnow city commissar through Municipal Police headquarters, August 1, 1940.

[61] See ibid., Fol. 609–619 and 733–739, Correspondence among the labor office, the city commissar, the Municipal Police, and the Polish police from July 31 to August 12, 1940.

was important for the war; 800 Jews had already been sent, and others were needed. On September 2, 1940, he therefore requested Polish and German police support for a new raid.[62] When this police operation ("forcible delivery of able-bodied Jews to the labor office") was not particularly successful, the labor office a day later asked the German Order Police for help. To guarantee success, an entire "hundred-man unit" was requested this time.[63] The Lublin labor office also encountered similar Jewish fears before recruitment. There the people who failed to report were immediately threatened with being sent to the notorious SS camp at Belzec.[64]

LABOR OFFICE AND SS: THE EXAMPLE OF LUBLIN

Centrally, agreement had been reached on a division of labor within the administration, but future implementation presented a problem in practice. The labor offices, or rather their Jewish labor sections, standardized the compulsory employment rules inside and outside the ghettos and camps. And they expanded the programs, obligating local Jewish councils to help with registration and provision of contingents. Yet this did not prevent the ethnic German self-defense corps, the SS, or the city administrations from continuing to conduct unauthorized raids for their own purposes. In Lublin district, Globocznik still pursued the plan of fortifying the eastern border. In June 1940, the Wehrmacht gave their consent. As there were apparently no longer enough workers in Lublin district, on July 30 Globocznik ordered from the Krakow Stadthauptmann "30,000 Jews capable of working who would be brought in for excavation work in and out of water." He also needed an additional 1,000 Jews, "craftsmen of various kinds."[65] Globocznik, however, did not wait for the workers from Krakow district, but conducted raids in Lublin for his SS border camps, without informing the labor office.[66]

SSPF Globocznik, and many Kreishauptmänner who behaved like colonial lords, randomly captured Jews already employed in forced labor with the intention of using them for other jobs; this seriously disrupted the authority vested in the Lublin Jewish council so that the Jews' labor obligation would be met. In a memorandum to the Lublin labor office in summer 1940, the Jewish council asked – among many other points – that the size of contingents provided be limited to 500 to 600 men a day and that the raids be stopped. If "the families of the workers" were not to be "sentenced to death

---

[62] Ibid., Fol. 879, Tarnow labor office to general service unit of the Municipal Police, September 2, 1940.

[63] Ibid., Fol. 877, Tarnow labor office to general service unit of the Municipal Police, September 3, 1940.

[64] Announcement of the Lublin labor office, September 20, 1940, in *Lebenszeichen aus Piaski*, 63–64.

[65] Facsimile in *Faschismus-Getto-Massenmord*, 213.

[66] Pohl, *Von der "Judenpolitik" zum Judenmord*, 82 and 85; Browning, "Nazi Germany's Initial Attempt to Exploit Jewish Labor," 175 and 180.

by starvation," the recruited Jews had to be left several days a month to practice their professions and earn money, as the forced labor was usually unpaid. Because of the additional social support required for 1,300 Lublin Jews sent to the camp, the memo continued, the Jewish organization was having difficulties paying. The Jewish council pleaded for stopping the shipment of laborers to camps and for notifying other agencies that only the labor office controlled forced labor.[67]

The ethnic German self-defense corps and the SS serving as guards in the labor camps operated by the SS put the final touch, a reign of terror, on the dreadful conditions that clearly prevailed in all the camps from the outset.[68] Since mid-June 1940 the Lublin Jewish council had only received terrible news, as from Tyszowce camp, where the men were notoriously undernourished, without clothing, often sick, louse-infested, and covered with sores. Sobianowice reported that "a Pole from Pomerania struck the workers without reason. Food is denied, and eating dirt is proposed." Similar news arrived from five other camps. No pay, beatings, and even shootings were part of the normal daily routine. The Jewish council asked the German labor office to switch out the forced laborers as quickly as possible because of their "mental breakdowns" and "physical exhaustion."[69] Besides the camps at the border trench, the Lublin SS ran its own country estates with Jewish forced laborers. Countless workers also toiled for local administrations, the army, and the Luftwaffe.

At an August 6, 1940, General Government-wide meeting presided over by Frauendorfer, representatives of the HHSPF Krüger confirmed the SS border trench plan. As they reported, camps for 15,000 men were already finished. To avoid missing out on the resource allocation, the officials responsible for water and road projects also demanded 7,000 and 12,000 Jews, respectively. The labor administration conceded to the SS that it could conduct further raids in Lublin district, but only in agreement with the labor office. However, the Jews to be seized there had to cover not only the SS demand but also the 2,700 men requested by the water supply and distribution operations. Later on, under an agreement with the Radom and Warsaw districts' labor administrations, additional transports of "single Jews, initially," were to be diverted to the Lublin border projects. But the Krakow district first had to satisfy the demand for workers on the Roznow dam construction project and for road construction. The General Governor's labor department insisted that "uti-

[67] BA Berlin, R 8150, No. 483, Fols. 377–381, Memorandum of the Lublin Jewish council to the Lublin labor office, July 31, 1940.

[68] Browning, "Jewish Workers," 63.

[69] BA Berlin R 8150, No. 483, Fols. 377–381, Memorandum of the Lublin Jewish council to the Lublin labor office, July 31, 1940, Enclosure: Comments on the labor conditions of the Jewish workers in the Tyszowce labor camp and in the tenant farms, July 31, 1940. See similar reports regarding Warsaw Jews in Lublin camps at the end of 1940, in *Faschismus-Getto-Massenmord*, 218–222, Doc. No. 169. For the Lublin Jewish council's list of victims and the SS camps, see Pohl, *Von der "Judenpolitik" zum Judenmord*, 57 and 84.

lization of Jews" had to be shifted strategically from "assistance at agencies and other offices" to mass use for "construction projects of importance from the standpoint of national policy."[70] Only two days later, SS Brigadeführer Globocznik arranged with the Lublin district labor department that it would be "notified promptly before" the planned raids for the border wall and the other construction projects in the next week "so that registration of the Jews in a card file and their allocation by the labor office could be assured."[71]

But the raids produced further conflicts. The Lublin SS drove Jews together without consulting the labor offices and even took away some who had employment assigned by the latter. Often the local labor offices could only record the events but do little about them. At the same time they countered Globocznik in other ways. The raids and transfers from Warsaw and Krakow yielded a total of only 7,000 of the requested 30,000 workers for the SS; the water resources office, on the other hand, received 2,000 of 4,000, and the road construction office, 2,100 for a demand of 2,000.[72] The figures clearly indicate the priorities and the authority of the Lublin labor administration in distributing forced laborers. In November 1940, the parties interested in Jewish forced labor reached new agreements. Any request for workers was to be directed to the labor offices. Only if they could not fill the order were the police allowed to conduct raids. Jews who could produce papers verifying work assigned by the labor office were to be exempted from such operations.[73]

The figures stated by scholars on the number of Jewish labor camp inmates in Lublin district at this time vary from 21,000[74] to 50,000–70,000 in 76 camps.[75] The latter is probably correct. In any case, at the end of 1940, 45 labor camps with approximately 10,000 inmates existed in Lublin district for hydraulic construction projects (such as river regulation and sewerage) alone.[76] In addition, 7,223 Jews were transferred from Radom district in September 1940 and 5,253 from Warsaw district at the end of 1940 to Lublin

---

[70] ITS, Arolsen, 1979, LXIII. See *Eksterminacja Żydów*, Doc. No. 109, 216–217, Excerpt from the protocol of the August 6 meeting, August 9, 1940. See Hilberg, *Vernichtung*, Vol. 1, 264; Browning, "Nazi Germany's initial attempt to exploit Jewish labor," 177.

[71] *Europa unterm Hakenkreuz. Die faschistische Okkupationspolitik in Polen (1939–1945)*, document selection and introduction by Werner Röhr with the assistance of Elke Heckert (Berlin, 1989), 184, Doc. No. 74, Note of the labor department regarding the August 8, 1940, meeting, August 9, 1940.

[72] *Eksterminacja Żydów*, Doc. No. 111, 219, August report for Lublin district, September 7, 1940. See Browning, "Nazi Germany's initial attempt to exploit Jewish labor," 177–178; Browning, "Jewish Workers," 63.

[73] Browning, "Nazi Germany's initial attempt to exploit Jewish labor," 179.

[74] Musial, *Zivilverwaltung*, 167.

[75] Pucher, *Globocznik*, 83; Pohl, *Von der "Judenpolitik" zum Judenmord*, 82 and 85. More details in Browning, "Nazi Germany's initial attempt to exploit Jewish labor," 175–183.

[76] Hilberg, *Vernichtung*, Vol. 1, 265. See the figures of the hydraulic construction inspection office, with 9,300 Jewish forced laborers in thirty-five camps (according to a report of the

district's camps. In 1941 there were supposedly already 24,000 Jews from other regions performing forced labor in Lublin district, 7,000 of them from prisoner-of-war camps.[77]

COMPENSATION AND SPECIAL LAW

At the August 6, 1940, Frauendorfer meeting, representatives of the General Government's administration and officials of the district labor departments complained that under the new orders Jews' wages would be too high.[78] That was rarely the case, however, for despite the labor administration's specific guidelines, forced labor seldom produced earnings. Agencies and offices persisted in their attempts to obtain Jews for personal services. Others suddenly refused to pay wages or to defray the costs for room and board. As this behavior occurred throughout the entire General Government in the first weeks after the new regulations took effect, Frauendorfer informed the heads of the district labor departments and of all labor offices on August 20, 1940, that he had asked the Wehrmacht Commander in Chief East and the HSSPF East on the same day to advise their subordinate offices of the labor administration's sole responsibility for allocation of Jews. Furthermore, he stated, the July 5 decree had given rise to misinterpretations. In their refusal to pay Jews, many offices had referred to Point 7, "Transitional Measures." Others had used the same point as justification for perpetual obligation of Jews to perform personal services and cleaning chores. Frauendorfer therefore set a time limit, August 31, 1940, for all the transitional measures. Jews could only be used further for cleaning and household help if excavation and outside work were physically impossible.[79]

Many district and city administrations soon lost their unpaid Jewish labor. At the same time, some private companies no longer accepted Jews, because at 80 percent of the Poles' wages for road construction they were too badly paid and therefore too malnourished.[80] The Miechów Stadthauptmann demanded a change in the new regulations, allowing Jews to be utilized again without pay, for example, for municipal street cleaning.[81] Other employers cared little about the August central order. In many workplaces

General Government's department of nutrition and agriculture, September 3, 1940); Pohl, *Von der "Judenpolitik" zum Judenmord*, 82.

[77] Musial, *Zivilverwaltung*, 164; Pohl, "Zwangsarbeitslager," 416.

[78] *Eksterminacja Żydów*, Doc. No. 109, 217, Excerpt from the protocol of the August 6 meeting, August 9, 1940. See Hilberg, *Vernichtung*, Vol. 1, 264.

[79] USHMMA Washington, DC, RG-15.020M (Polish State Archive, Tarnow), Reel 8, Fol. 1047b, Copy of an August 20, 1940, circular of the General Government's labor department in the Tarnow Kreishauptmann's office to the city commissar, September 17, 1940,

[80] Browning, "Nazi Germany's initial attempt to exploit Jewish labor," 174.

[81] *Eksterminacja Żydów*, Doc. No. 112, 220, September report of Stadthauptmann Miechow, October 1, 1940.

in the Lublin area, for example, in Piaski, and Bełżyce, Jews continued to receive no money for their compulsory labor.[82] The Krakow city administration passed only modest reimbursement to the Jewish council for the workers that it employed. The Czestochowa Stadthauptmann even had the local Jewish council pay the forced laborers for him.[83] Forced-labor camps were chiefly known for malnourishment, a lack of medical care, poor sanitary conditions, and the brutality of the guard forces. The wages paid were so inadequate that, after room and board had been deducted, the Jews still owed the enterprises money,[84] a situation already familiar from the Styrian labor camps.

Although thus often without a *zloty*, the forced laborers were expected to continue paying for insurance even though, except for health care, they received no services in return. In a draft of the "Third Order on Social Insurance in the General Government" at the beginning of September 1940, the Jews were still mentioned in Paragraph 9: "Even as forced laborers, Jews are obligated to pay for all types of insurance in accordance with the pertinent regulations. They receive benefits from health insurance. They do not receive support from disability or pension insurance."[85] This paragraph no longer reflected what for several months had been the reality in the General Government, and thus it was struck from the published version of the order that appeared two weeks later.[86] From the beginning of October on, the Government General's Jews officially had to work on Jewish holidays.[87] A year later, a December 15, 1941, implementation order officially granted Polish Jews wages only for "work performed." That meant de jure elimination of all social and professional benefits. At that point, the conditions for Polish Jews were similar to those that had been in effect for German Jews since October 1941.[88] However, the uniformity was only on paper, as in the occupied Polish territories many employers in fact paid the Jews no wages at all.

MASS UTILIZATION IN INFRASTRUCTURE PROJECTS

On October 10, 1940, Dr. Gschließer of the General Governor's office, labor department, alerted the Reich Ministry of Labor that the bridge and road construction projects of the Otto Program were short a total of 33,403 workers even though the labor offices had already provided 76,555. The road

---

[82] BA Berlin, R 8150, No. 483, Fols. 387–390, Reichsvereinigung protocol, October 10, 1940.
[83] Hilberg, *Vernichtung*, Vol. 1, 263–264.   [84] Browning, "Jewish Workers," 65.
[85] BA Berlin, R 3901 (former R41) Reich Labor Ministry, No. 5788, Fol. 130.
[86] Order of September 19, 1940, in *Verordnungsblatt des Generalgouverneurs*, Part I (1940): 308.
[87] According to an October 5, 1940, decree of the government of the General Government; Majer, "*Fremdvölkische*," 555.
[88] December 15, 1941, implementation order for the October 31, 1939, order regarding labor conditions; ibid., 555.

construction program required 32,828 workers, 21,114 in Lublin district alone. To this was added the Eastern Railway's requirement for 6,200 workers. The General Government's labor administration was optimistic that after camps had been established all the workers needed could be drawn just from the General Government. Up until then, Gschließer continued, "Jews, and for road construction, women as well," had increasingly been used; it had not been necessary to resort to prisoners of war.[89] At the end of November, the OKH requested 1,800 Jewish workers from the Ministry of Labor for infrastructure expansion under the Otto Program and 300 prisoners of war or Jews to perform excavation tasks for the Lublin railway directorate.[90] In response, the Reich Ministry of Labor instructed the Kattowitz central office of the labor department of the Krakow General Governor's office, to meet the demands quickly. The Ministry of Labor had corrected one point: Instead of prisoners of war, only Jews were to be enlisted.[91] In January 1941, the ministry once again followed up on this correction with the General Governor's office: Only Jewish workers were to be provided to the railway directorate.[92]

The Lublin Labor office had severe difficulties making the necessary workers available. While the labor administration officially controlled the Jewish labor program, it had scarcely any knowledge of some of the SS deployments. The border fortification project was almost finished in October 1940.[93] But Globocznik had made no effort whatsoever to maintain the productive capabilities of his forced laborers and sent completely fatigued Jews from the border camps to other forced-labor camps, where often they were released immediately because of total exhaustion. A letter at the end of October 1940 to the General Government's administration thus criticized "the lack of cooperation on the part of Brigadeführer Globocznik." With completion of the SS border project, Belzec camp was to be shut down and its inmates put to work for the Otto Program. The labor office wanted to move the Jews recruited in Radom and Warsaw districts for SS projects in the Lublin region back to their home regions. Eight trains had been arranged for that purpose, but the SS did not honor the agreements with the labor administration. Four hundred men from a transport of 920 workers bound for Hrubieszów disappeared without trace. "As such a large number could not all have been shot to death," the Lublin district administration suspected that the SS had probably released them after payment of a ransom. This statement reflects that the labor administration had noticed not only the corruption of the

---

[89] BA Berlin, R 3901 (former R 41) Reich Labor Ministry, No. 193, Fols. 36 and verso, General Government's labor department to the Reich Labor Ministry, October 10, 1940.

[90] Ibid., Fol. 51, OKH to the Reich Labor Ministry (Dr. Letzsch), November 26, 1940.

[91] Ibid., Fols. 50 and verso, Reich Labor Ministry (Dr. Letzsch) to the Silesian regional labor office and the General Government's labor department, December 11, 1940.

[92] Ibid., Fol. 56, Reich Labor Ministry to the General Government's labor department, January 21, 1941.

[93] Hilberg, *Vernichtung*, Vol. 1, 265; Pucher, *Globocznik*, 83–84; Reitlinger, *Endlösung*, 77.

Photo 9. Jews obtaining work permits at the Jewish Council in the Krakow ghetto, circa 1941

SS, but also the frequent murders in the SS camps. The second transport, which was to return Jews to Radom as the labor office had intended, even held Lublin Jews randomly placed there by the SS. In an emergency meeting, the lack of cooperation of the SS was labeled a "circus" by the labor administration officials.[94]

By the end of 1940, the forced-labor program in the General Government had registered over 700,000 Jewish men and women who were working for the German economy in ghetto businesses and as labor for projects outside the ghetto;[95] there would be more. In January 1941, the decision was made to conduct further mass deportations of Poles and Jews from the territories annexed to the Reich and from Vienna. Under the third short-term plan, the RSHA intended to deport, between February and April, 238,500 Poles and Jews, and "10,000 Jews to be moved out of Vienna" as the first installment of the 60,000 still living there.[96] Berlin, which was directing the operation centrally, would keep the district chiefs informed, and then receive from them precise information about the departures and arrivals of the transports from

[94] *Dokumenty i Materialy*, Vol. 1: *Obozy*, edited by Nachman Blumental (Lodz, 1946), Vol. 1, 129–131, Lublin district's office for internal administration, demographics, and welfare to the Krakow government's office for internal administration, demographics, and welfare (Dr. Föhl), October 21, 1940.

[95] *Encyclopedia of the Holocaust*, Vol. 2, 501.

[96] IMT, Vol. XXIX, 488–489, Doc. PS-2233, Report on the meeting at the RHSA, January 8, 1941.

Litzmannstadt, Soldau, Gotenhafen, Kattowitz, and Vienna. "Finding work for the able-bodied people evacuated" was said to be "especially important," and in contrast to the first transports in late 1939, that included Jews. At the destination railway stations, the people evacuated were to be mustered immediately and registered by the labor offices. The labor offices were to receive information separately from the district chiefs about arriving transports.[97] In this operation, several thousand Austrian Jews were deported from Vienna to Lublin; 2,000 of them ended up in Opole.[98] The Jews who arrived in Opole had first to construct the barracks for their own camp; then they were sent to perform forced labor in companies. Elias Rei wrote home a card a short time later: "Dear father, . . . I have been working since Thursday in the sugar factory and earn 40 Groschen per hour and cannot even buy four loaves of bread with my daily wages. The food is very bad. From tomorrow on, we will have a ghetto here, although an open one, that is, the Germans and Poles are not allowed into the Jewish sector; they can only pass through. The people who go to work in the factory can pass through the Aryan sector."[99] The occupation administrations created ghettos in the larger cities of the General Government in early spring 1941. After the "Jewish residential districts" had been sealed off, workshops and departments were established there, as were many work sites outside the ghetto. This type of workplace in caserns soon became labor camps.[100] (See photo 9, p. 250.)

The longer the occupation and the war lasted, the worse the conditions became. The number of forced laborers who died from malnourishment rose rapidly. When the SS border trench camps in Lublin closed at the end of 1940, the ethnic German self-defense corps carried out shootings.[101] The years-long occupation gave rise to unbelievable brutality by the SS but also by the civilian administrations. The Reichshof (Rzeszów) Kreishauptmann (Krakow District) demanded in January 1941 that more severe measures be brought for "lazy work performance": "If necessary, Jews were to be hanged."[102] In the next months Jews were shot to death in various forced-labor camps for escaping or as a result of epidemics, for example, in Drevnica in Warsaw district or Ossowa in Lublin district.[103]

[97] USHMMA Washington, DC, RG-11.001M 22, Reel 91 (OSOBI [Center for the Preservation of the Historical Documentary Collection, Moscow], administration in the occupied territories), 1447-1-340, no folio numbers, Circular decree of the government of the General Government, January 17, 1941, 1–8.

[98] Central Zionist Archive (CZA) Jerusalem, S 26, No. 1191g, no folio numbers, Report of the Viennese IKG 1938–1944–45 (Löwenherz Report), 34.

[99] Quoted in Jonny Moser, *Der Gelbe Stern in Österreich. Katalog und Einführung zu einer Dokumentation* (Eisenstadt, 1977), 24.

[100] Grabitz and Scheffler, *Letzte Spuren*, 283; Madajczyk, *Okkupationspolitik*, 238; for more details, see Browning, *Entfesselung*, 209–248.

[101] Pohl, *Von der "Judenpolitik" zum Judenmord*, 84.   [102] Majer, *"Fremdvölkische,"* 555.

[103] Pohl, "Zwangsarbeitslager," 417.

THE SITUATION OF FORCED LABORERS AFTER THE ATTACK ON THE SOVIET UNION

The priorities for utilization of forced labor in the General Government changed after spring 1941 because of concrete preparations for the attack on the Soviet Union. Instead of border fortifications, hydraulic construction projects now took precedence. Many of the camps had closed in fall because of the season, but many of these camps then opened again.[104] A new network of hydraulic construction camps now spread across Warsaw district, where 25,000 Jews were soon employed. By summer 1941, however, problems had grown worse because of the forced laborers' inadequate diet. Their work performance deteriorated drastically.[105]

As was described in a report of the Jewish Social Self-Help organization (*Jüdische Soziale Selbsthilfe*), which gathered information about camp conditions in the General Government, the water resources administration operated fifteen camps in the Warsaw district, nine of which were closed again because of the problems described above. The camp conditions for the forced laborers were characterized by a lack of food, notorious bad treatment by the guards, and the hardest work possible. Improvement work, which usually involved standing in cold water, was not allowed to last for longer than three weeks before the war, even when the food was good. The inadequately nourished Jews, however, had to engage in these activities for months on end. As a consequence, 239 Jews died in these camps. (See photo 8, p. 234.) The remaining six camps were closed in June 1941. Warsaw Jews also had been sent to Krakow district. In Krosno Kreis, several camps were run by Askania Werke AG of the Organisation Todt, which was building roads and sewerage there. In June these camps, too, were closed, but in this case because the work was done. Some of the 1,500 Jews from Warsaw were "released"; the others were sent to Pustkow near Dembica in Tarnow Kreis. They arrived there almost naked, without shoes, and totally exhausted, with the result that another 150 were released. In this camp, administered by an SS office, the 1,155 inmates had to perform road jobs. The work and living conditions were described as bearable in the report. A number of very different reports were circulating about the situation in Radom district's labor camps. The conditions in the quarries near Kielce were said to be passable, but the forced laborers received no compensation because all their wages went for their maintenance. In Zagacie camp, the conditions during improvement work were rumored to have been tragic until a short time before. Most of the inmates had to toil barefoot and almost naked: "Hunger and misery caused large numbers of them to lay down their work." At that point, they had received substantially more food, but the Jewish council had had to intervene

---

[104] Browning, "Nazi Germany's Initial Attempt to Exploit Jewish Labor," 180.
[105] Hilberg, *Vernichtung*, Vol. 1, 265; Browning, "Jewish Workers," 63.

with money because their wages were not sufficient to cover the cost of maintenance. In Staporkow the Jews reportedly received ZL 3.00 a day for "heavy and exhausting forestry work," but no maintenance. In Przyrów the situation was ostensibly terrible. There the forced laborers stood all day long up to their knees in water. "They are often beaten and receive no meals." In Lublin district, there were two camps in Zamość Kreis, Zamość with up to 200 inmates and Plosk, with 350 who were forced to perform unloading. The latter received ZL 5.00 a day, and more for overtime. They were housed in a shed and slept on straw. The meals, it was said, consisted of coffee in the morning, soup at midday and in the evening, with up to 300 grams of bread; for that, ZL 0.60 were deducted. Five camps existed in Radzyn Kreis, and thirteen in Chelm Kreis. In the latter Kreis, 5,500 Jews, some of them from Warsaw, performed forced labor.[106]

The living conditions deteriorated day by day not only in many labor camps, but also in the ghettos.[107] The Warsaw ghetto was formed in October 1940 according to 1939 plans. In May 1941, 500,000 people had to live there. As no food was delivered to the ghetto after January 1941, the responsible Nazi officials had to decide whether they regarded the ghetto as a means of liquidation or as a source of productive labor. From March 1941 on, providing for the Warsaw ghetto was no longer in the hands of the city administration but had been transferred to the Jewish council. Food had to be obtained by the ghetto. Thus, only 336 calories per person could be distributed, a third of the amount in Litzmannstadt.[108] Warsaw therefore decided in favor of self-preservation through work. Christopher Browning believes that this decision was made not because of the importance of the potential of over 100,000 workers but solely on the basis of local viewpoints and ghetto problems, because of malnourishment and the lack of any perspective on persecution.[109] Be that as it may, the labor office estimated that in April 1941, 115,000 men and 60,000 women capable of working lived in the ghetto. At that point only a fraction were employed. The first workshops inside the ghetto were established with up to 7,000 workers. Approximately 12,000 Jews worked outside, in the city of Warsaw proper. Twenty-five thousand were sent to do improvement work, and several thousand found themselves on the way to Lublin district, which had requested 25,000 workers.[110] A first attempt in summer to widen the circle of forced labor failed because the Jews in the ghetto did not register out of fear that

---

[106] *Eksterminacja Żydów*, Doc. No. 116, 225–228, Report of Krakow Jewish Social Self-Help organization, June 30, 1941.
[107] See Browning, "Nazi Germany's Initial Attempt to Exploit Jewish Labor," 182.
[108] Grabitz and Scheffler, *Letzte Spuren*, 9–10; Madajczyk, *Okkupationspolitik*, 369.
[109] Browning, "Jewish Workers," 67–68.
[110] *Eksterminacja Żydów*, Doc. No. 4, 118–119, Protocol of meeting at the office of General Governor Frank, April 19, 1941.

they would be sent to labor camps. Lasting success was only achieved after private companies were allowed into the ghetto.[111] In Germany, the chambers of commerce and trade soon openly publicized the workshops in the Warsaw ghetto as a means of stimulating the German private sector to invest there.[112] In September 1941, 24,000 employees were engaged in the ghetto's own operations, working for the Wehrmacht, police, and SS, and later for the private companies with workshops there. Nine thousand were employed by Jewish institutions.[113]

FORCED LABOR IN THE NEW GALICIA DISTRICT

In summer 1941, after the attack on the Soviet Union and the rapid occupation of vast territories, the new Galicia district was created from parts of the conquered land and annexed to the General Government. On August 1, 1941, the General Government took over the civilian administration in this territory. The labor administration again put in place one of the first functioning agencies. Labor offices and special Jewish labor offices were created, in Lemberg already during July. The Lemberg labor office announced on August 11 that it alone was responsible for organizing Jewish forced labor.[114] It assigned Jews to German agencies, to rail construction, to clearing away ruins from bombing attacks, to airports, and to military camps. Some places paid wages, but the payments went to the labor office, not to the forced laborers.[115] However, the labor office was not the only agency to take an interest in Jewish forced labor at an early point. On August 14, 1941, Oberst Wurm, chief of the Galicia police regiment, ordered police regiments 315, 133, and 254, as well as the Municipal Police detachments in Lemberg, Tarnopol, and Stanislau to investigate "prisoner-of-war camps prepared by the Russians" because they were "well suited for establishing Jewish forced

---

[111] Browning, "Jewish Workers," 70–72.
[112] BA Berlin, R 11 Reich Trade Chamber (*Reichswirtschaftskammer*), No. 1220, Fol. 240, September 15, 1941, circular letter of the Mannheim chamber of commerce and trade, with the September 13, 1941, trade gazette of the Berlin chamber of commerce and trade. (I would like to thank Götz Aly, Berlin, for this document.) See the facsimile of "Jüdischer Arbeitsmarkt im Generalgouvernement" (August, 1940), in Susanne Heim and Götz Aly, "Die Ökonomie der 'Endlösung,'" in *Beiträge zur Nationalsozialistischen Gesundheits- und Sozialpolitik*, Vol. 5 (Berlin, 1987), 77. Regarding the economical reasons for ghetto labor, see ibid., 63–87.
[113] Hilberg, *Vernichtung*, Vol. 1, 268–270.
[114] Dieter Pohl, *Nationalsozialistische Judenverfolgung in Ostgalizien. Organisation und Durchführung eines staatlichen Massenverbrechens* (Munich, 1996), 133.
[115] Eliyahu Yones, *Die Straße nach Lemberg. Zwangsarbeit und Widerstand in Ostgalizien 1941–1944* (Frankfurt am Main, 1999), 25–27.

labor camps." Camps "near especially bad streets" were preferably to be reported for the project.[116]

On August 16, 1941, the Reich Minister of the Occupied Eastern Territories, Arthur Rosenberg, had introduced the "labor obligation" for Jews fourteen to sixty years old in the former Soviet territories.[117] However, as the Galician territory went to the General Government, another new order applied here instead of the one mentioned; the new order was modeled on practice as modified in the meantime in the General Government. The September 20, 1941, order on the labor obligation of Jews fourteen to sixty years old stated that they were to be put to work in a "free," in other words, voluntary, work situation, or by compulsory recruitment.[118] The labor administration, not the SS, was promised authority over shaping the forced-labor program, as is evident from a September 10, 1941, decree of the General Government's main labor department instructing the Galician labor offices to register Jewish workers. At the end of the month, the Lemberg labor office had already registered 45,000 Jews. Just as during Poland's period of occupation, there were unauthorized raids. Or, the police and the SS recruited workers directly from the local Jewish council, bypassing the labor office. In contrast, agencies and companies usually turned to the Jewish utilization section of the labor office for forced laborers. The labor office then routed the requests to the Jewish council's labor utilization department.[119]

Murdering began very early in Galicia district, influenced by events in the nearby Soviet territories. On October 12, 1941, 10,000 Jews were shot to death at the massacre in Stanislawów (Stanislau).[120] On the pretext of taking action against alleged profiteering, the SSPF Friedrich Katzmann, who had experience with a Radom forced-labor camp,[121] became involved at an early point in organizing forced labor. Katzmann later justified this step retrospectively with an entirely different prejudice: "Forceful action had to be taken especially against all the loafers and good-for-nothings lazing about. The best approach was for the SSPF to form forced labor columns. Durchgangsstraße 4 was in catastrophic condition; its extremely important expansion, essential

---

[116] USHMMA Washington, DC, RG-11.001M, Reel 82 (OSOBI – German police in the occupied territories), 1323-2-292b, no folio numbers, Circular letter of the Galicia police regiment, August 14, 1941.

[117] Christian Gerlach, *Kalkulierte Morde. Die deutsche Wirtschafts- und Vernichtungspolitik in Weißrussland 1941 bis 1944* (Hamburg, 1999), 452.

[118] Reproduced in *Faschismus-Getto-Massenmord*, 228; see Pohl, *Judenverfolgung in Ostgalizien*, 133.

[119] Pohl, *Judenverfolgung in Ostgalizien*, 134.

[120] Thomas Sandkühler, "Das Zwangsarbeitslager Lemberg-Janowska 1941–1944," in *Die nationalsozialistischen Konzentrationslager. Entwicklung und Struktur*, edited by Ulrich Herbert, Karin Orth, and Christoph Dieckmann, Vol. 2 (Göttingen, 1998), 608.

[121] Pohl, *Judenverfolgung in Ostgalizien*, 167.

for the entire southern sector, afforded the best work possibility. On October 15, 1941, the expansion of camps along the fast rack (*Rollbahn*) began, and after a few weeks, despite considerable difficulties, seven camps had sprung up, populated with 4,000 Jews."[122] However, because circumstances required that a year earlier than in the rest of the General Government, the SS in Galicia had to find compromises between the murder program and the objective of utilizing forced labor, the SS perspective quickly changed. As Katzmann stated in retrospect, because 90 percent of the craftsmen in Galicia were Jews, destruction of the Jewish population could only proceed step by step, so as not to harm the war economy.[123]

The SS cooperated by organizing their forced-labor program in tandem with the labor administration – in fact, depending on it. The local labor offices issued the work cards with which the Jewish population was sorted into three categories, A, B, and C, on the basis of fitness for work. Using this procedure, the labor office officials performed a preselection, ultimately determining life or death.[124] To put a stop to unauthorized recruiting, District Governor Dr. Karl Lasch ordered on November 28, 1941, that requests for forced laborers could only be directed to the Lemberg labor office. In Galicia district, government offices benefited in the subsequent period: administration, police, Eastern Railway, and Wehrmacht. In Lemberg, the army construction and forestry offices, the army motor pool, the commandants' headquarters, the economic headquarters, and the captured property depot employed Jews. In the countryside, the Kreishauptmänner exploited Jewish forced laborers for road and bridge construction, river regulation, and flood damage recovery. Ukrainian municipal administrations utilized Jews in energy-generation operations and at slaughterhouses. As in the rest of the General Government, compensation was the main problem for the forced laborers. Since even government agencies had no desire to pay their Jewish workers, the labor administration feared a financial fiasco for the Jewish councils, as for example in Drohobycz.[125]

CONFLICTS BETWEEN THE LABOR ADMINISTRATION AND THE SS

In other districts of the General Government, differences of opinion arose between the regional SS and the labor offices in 1941. Local SS authorities still conducted unauthorized raids to supply their own forced-labor camps with workers. In December 1941 a new dispute arose in Lublin, but the labor office retained the upper hand in the end. Without the knowledge of

---

[122] IMT, Vol. XXXVII, Doc. 0–18 L, 391–437, here 392–393, Report of HSSPF Friedrich Katzmann, "The Solution of the Jewish Question in Galicia," June 30, 1943.

[123] Ibid., 394.   [124] Sandkühler, "Lemberg-Janowska," 608–610.

[125] Pohl, *Judenverfolgung in Ostgalizien*, 134–135.

the labor office and the Lublin district labor department, the SS had carried out a raid for the SS company Deutsche Ausrüstungswerke GmbH (armaments factory.). Three hundred twenty Jews were arrested and transported to the Lipowa SS camp. When the Jewish office of the Lublin labor office entered the picture, the labor officials were able to muster the arrestees there, and the SS had to release 170 Jews in possession of valid labor office identification documents. The SS put the rest in prisoners' clothing and took them to the so-called Lublin prisoner-of-war camp, later known as the infamous Majdanek camp.[126] Several of the individuals thus assigned – although they were compulsory laborers – had not been carrying work documents at the time of the raids. The labor office informed the district administration and interceded with the SS, especially in the case of the skilled workers among them. Despite the pledge of SS Hauptsturmführer Hartmann (the camp leader) at a hastily convened meeting, the Jews on a list provided by the labor office were not released. First the SS used the danger of epidemics as a pretext. However, when the labor office promised that the persons in question would be housed in the quarantine facility of the forced-labor camp operated by the labor office, Hartmann stubbornly refused to release them, now giving as an excuse that he required the consent of his superior, Standartenführer Karl Otto Koch.[127] After there had been no release by January 1942, the labor office appealed directly to SSPF Globocznik on behalf of the twenty-four mechanics, carpenters, and clockmakers. Among them were fourteen-year-old youths; some worked for the Eastern Railway, others for the district administrations, and still others directly for the labor office. The labor office even offered replacements for these employees.[128] Only after Globocznik intervened were some of the Jews released, completely exhausted, from the SS camp. The rest had already died within one month.[129]

TRANSITION TO MASS MURDER AND SS TAKEOVER OF THE FORCED-LABOR PROGRAM

After the attack on the Soviet Union, the political framework for persecution of the Polish Jewish population changed. Mass murder of Soviet Jews began in June 1941. Hitler accordingly promised General Governor Frank to remove the Jews from the General Government. The decision to murder the European Jews also passed sentence on the Polish Jewish population. Construction of extermination facilities, such as the one at Belzec,

---

[126] *Dokumenty i Materialy*, Vol. 1, 136, Note of the Lublin labor office, December 23, 1941.
[127] Ibid., 129–131, Note of the Lublin labor office, December 22, 1941.
[128] Ibid., 132–133, Lublin labor office to SSPF, January 6, 1942.
[129] Ibid., 133, Lublin labor office to the General Governor's office, January 14, 1942; ibid., 137, Note of the Lublin labor office, January 22, 1942.

had been underway in the eastern part of the General Government since fall 1941. The notorious *Aktion Reinhard* then set in motion the mass annihilation of Polish Jews in spring 1942. This operation extended not only to annihilation of the Jews and resale of their property, but also – and this has remained unnoticed – to exploitation of Jewish workers.[130] On March 17, 1942, Fritz Reuter, the expert for population and welfare in the Lublin district office, noted regarding a message from SS Hauptsturmführer Hermann Höfle, " . . . 1. It would be useful, at the departure station, to separate the Jewish transports destined for the Lublin district into Jews fit for utilization and those unfit for utilization. . . . 2. Jews unfit for utilization all go to Belzec. . . . 3. Hauptsturmführer Höfle is in the process of building a large camp in which the Jews can be registered according to their vocations and then requested from there. 4. Piaski will be emptied of Jews and will be the collection point for Jews coming from the Reich."[131] As part of getting the extermination program underway in Lublin district, on April 16, 1942, Governor Ernst Zörner passed his authority over anti-Jewish measures to the commander of the Security Police in Lublin; the same was true of forced labor.[132] Höfle therefore called upon the Kreishauptmann of rural Lublin to register all Jews separately by locality and to differentiate between Jews capable of working and those incapable of working. The objective of the census was "to facilitate a uniform plan for utilizing Jewish workers."[133]

A similar course of development was also evident in Galicia district. Since mid-March 1942, around 15,000 persons unfit for labor had been deported to Belzec extermination camp. However, the transports were stopped in April. There was a shift in economic policy. The city and the Jewish council of elders established municipal workshops in Lemberg that carried out the instructions of the city administration and the armaments economy. Soon 3,200 Jews were working in five workshops. By April 20, the Lemberg labor office had distributed 50,000 to 70,000 new identification documents for a total population of 86,000 Jews. In May, HSSPF Katzmann ordered construction of a camp for 10,000 prisoners that would serve on the one hand as a productive labor camp and on the other as a transit camp for Belzec extermination camp. Katzmann requested workers for the camp from the district Kreishauptmänner.[134] The chairman of the Jewish council in Lemberg, Dr. Jozef Parnes, was arrested and murdered because he had opposed taking part in supplying workers.[135]

[130] Madajczyk, *Okkupationspolitik*, 375; Pucher, *Globocznik*, 109.
[131] *Europa unterm Hakenkreuz: Polen*, 218, Doc. No. 105. Also reproduced in Pucher, *Globocznik*, 111.
[132] Musial, *Zivilverwaltung*, 232.   [133] Musial, *Zivilverwaltung*, 243.
[134] Pohl, *Judenverfolgung in Ostgalizien*, 188; Sandkühler, "Lemberg-Janowska," 610–611 and 626.
[135] Madajczyk, *Okkupationspolitik*, 161.

For reasons relating to labor utilization, Heinrich Himmler himself ordered in April 1942 that for the time being sixteen-to-thirty-five-year-olds were to be excepted from the murder operations.[136] In the General Government, the shortages of people for the armaments industry were growing because non-Jewish Poles were being taken in ever-increasing numbers to Germany for forced labor, in part as direct replacements for deported German Jewish forced laborers. Paradoxically, the resulting acute labor shortages in Poland were to be resolved, under an agreement at a May 9, 1942, meeting with the armaments inspection office of the General Government, with 100,000 Polish Jews.[137]

This action was to have foreseeable consequences for the murder program. At a June 22, 1942, meeting, the chief of the General Government's labor administration, Frauendorfer, left little doubt that there was at that moment no other alternative to utilizing Jewish labor. In consequence, the leaders of the General Government and the officers of the Wehrmacht responsible for armaments decided in favor of a compromise: The Jews would "not actually be exempted from SS operations but [would be left] to work for the duration of the war."[138] The General Governor's labor department then confessed, however, that "Jews can only be assigned to labor with the prior consent of the local responsible police leader. Measures to equalize Jews beyond the local level are not to be carried out by the labor offices until further notice." Frauendorfer expected that in the future "the police . . . would be evaluating Jewish laborers to a certain extent themselves, especially for the armaments industry. In those cases, the labor offices would no longer serve as intermediaries." In contrast to the situation in the Old Reich, where the labor administration could autonomously arrange for compulsory labor of German Jews up until the last deportations, in the General Government, the SS and Security Police on June 25, 1942, took back the authority over the forced-labor program that it had ceded almost exactly two years before for the sake of efficient organization.[139]

The consequence was that in the future the army could, and indeed had to, obtain its supply of Jewish workers exclusively through the SS. On July 17, 1942, HSSPF Krüger and Generalleutnant Max Schindler decided on new regulations for "Utilization of Jewish workers," which of course represented a compromise between the murder program and economic interests: "The [previous] agreements with the SS Economic and Administrative Main Office

---

[136] Pohl, "Zwangsarbeitslager," 418.

[137] According to a May 9, 1942, meeting at the armaments inspection office of the General Government; Pohl, *Von der "Judenpolitik" zum Judenmord*, 123.

[138] *Eksterminacja Zydów*, Doc. No. 123, 239, Protocol of the meeting of General Government department heads, June 22, 1942.

[139] *Eksterminacja Zydów*, Doc. No. 124, 240, Circular, June 25, 1942. See Pohl, "Zwangsarbeitslager," 418; *Encyclopedia of the Holocaust*, Vol. 2, 501.

and the armaments inspection office are invalid. [But] the Higher SS and Police Leader is committed to constructing and operating the Jewish forced labor camp according to the wishes of the armaments inspection office." If the Wehrmacht armaments inspection offices determined more of a demand for workers than previously, they would have to request them from the HSSPF. The Security Police would take care of "closing the Jewish ghettos" in cooperation with the responsible Wehrmacht armaments inspection office. The Czestochowa ghetto would not be closed until "the barracks camp for 8,000 Jewish workers" had been completed.[140]

Then Himmler ordered on July 19, 1942 – thus to some extent nullifying the regional compromise reached by the Wehrmacht and the SS in the Government General – that by the end of 1942 all Jewish forced laborers were to be placed in camps and the remaining Polish Jews concentrated in the Warsaw, Krakow, Radom, and Lublin ghettos. He determined that "all other work projects employing Jewish workers are to be terminated by then, or if they cannot be terminated, they are to be moved to a collection camp."[141] That laid to rest the May 1942 plan to replace non-Jewish Polish workers in the Government General with Jewish Polish workers. The SS soon told the Wehrmacht openly that the leadership's thinking was radical in the extreme. Göring considered the Jews dispensable: "The orders given are harsh and clear. They apply not only to the General Government, but to the occupied territories as a whole."[142]

The views on the causes of this rapid transformation vary. Many scholars regard the euphoria after the successful summer offensive against the Soviet Union to be one reason for the decision to eliminate the Jews once and for all.[143] Christian Gerlach identifies the cause as the acute food crisis in the General Government. Thus on August 24, 1942, the General Government's main nutrition department decided to feed only 300,000 forced laborers after January 1943, but not the rest of the 1.2 million members of the Jewish population.[144] Browning considers this an important factor in regional decisions but not for Himmler's central order, because that order only formalized a process set in motion earlier.[145]

---

[140] BA-MA Freiburg im Breisgau, RH 53–23, No. 87, Fol. 51, Results of the meeting with Generalleutnant Schindler, Krakow, July 17, 1942 (signed Krüger); see *Encyclopedia of the Holocaust*, Vol. 2, 501; Pohl, *Von der "Judenpolitik" zum Judenmord*, 127.

[141] Himmler decree in *Faschismus-Getto-Massenmord*, 303, Doc. No. 229.

[142] BA-MA Freiburg im Breisgau, RH 53–23, No. 87, Fols. 47–50, Protocol of a meeting, August 14, 1942.

[143] Pohl, *Judenverfolgung in Ostgalizien*, 235; Browning, *Entfesselung*.

[144] Christian Gerlach, "Die Bedeutung der deutschen Ernährungspolitik für die Beschleunigung des Mordes an den Juden 1942," in Christian Gerlach, *Krieg, Ernährung, Völkermord. Forschungen zur deutschen Vernichtungspolitik im Zweiten Weltkrieg* (Hamburg, 1998), 167–267. Also see Musial, *Zivilverwaltung*, 282.

[145] Browning, "Jewish Workers," 76.

In any case, the influence of economic interests partially gave way to the goals of persecutory policy. It is not without a certain logic that as part of the radicalized murder process the SS and the Security Police would take over control of forced labor. Of course, then the conflict between persecutory intent and war exigencies came along with the control. Interestingly enough, the power transfer did not spell either total abandonment of economic interests in favor of complete annihilation or absolute exclusion of the labor administration from forced labor. At least until fall 1942, the labor offices locally placed Jews in the forced-labor program.[146] Jewish forced labor continued to represent an important factor for the economy and for production in the General Government. The main construction department of the Central Government alone still employed over 18,000 Jews in June 1942. They were "urgently required" to perform "work important for the war on the military supply highways."[147] In the Warsaw ghetto at the same time, 70,000 people had work cards, 22,000 for armaments companies alone and 6,000 for self-contained workshops within the ghetto. Schultz & Co. GmbH (fur finishing), which began production in September 1941 with 150 Jewish workers in the Warsaw ghetto, employed over 4,476 Jews in July 1942, shortly before deportation. And production was expanded still further. In November 1942 there was a total of 95,000 forced laborers in the ghetto.[148]

COOPERATION AND COMPROMISE IN DEPORTATION AND FORCED LABOR

In June 1942 the police and the administration in the General Government discussed the problems for forced labor due to the ongoing deportation of the Jewish population from the ghettos of the large cities. In the city of Krakow there were still 11,000 Jews working for the Wehrmacht and other offices and companies. Eight thousand of the 32,000 Jews in Tarnow performed forced labor. Eighty-five thousand Jews, 45,000 of them forced laborers, still lived in Lemberg (Galicia district).[149] The SS in that city organized a new stamp operation in the second half of July 1942 on Himmler's order to accelerate the extermination process by the end of the year. Companies and businesses had to submit the registration cards of their forced laborers to HSSPF Katzmann's adjutant. The cards were only restamped if the importance of the work for the war was acknowledged.

---

[146] See statements on the cooperation of the labor offices in Pohl, *Von der "Judenpolitik" zum Judenmord*, 279.

[147] Quoted according to the main construction department to the main labor department, June 22, 1942, in Musial, *Zivilverwaltung*, 294.

[148] Madajczyk, *Okkupationspolitik*, 229; Grabitz and Scheffler, *Letzte Spuren*, 24; Hilberg, *Vernichtung*, Vol. 1, 268–270.

[149] *Eksterminacja Zydów*, Doc. No. 150, 285–287, Protocol of a meeting in Krakow, June 18, 1942.

As the businesses then had to request their workers from the SS, the labor office's sections for utilization of Jews were closed.[150] To silence "objections because of the indispensability" of forced laborers, Katzmann announced at a meeting of the district administration that a Jewish camp would be established in every Kreis with well-sorted craftsmen.[151]

In August 1942 a new murder operation took place in Lemberg. Forty thousand victims were sent to Belzec; selections had been performed beforehand in Janowska camp.[152] The labor offices also participated in the deportations in Galicia, as is clear from a report of the Order Police: "The operation scheduled for September 7, 1942, in Kolomea had been prepared well . . . for all participants. The word had been passed to the Jews by the . . . offices and the labor office in Kolomea to appear at the labor office's collection place on September 7 at 5:30 a.m. for registration." Of the approximately 6,900 who showed up, 4,769 were sent to Belzec, and 1,000 were released by the Security Police to serve as workers.[153] After resuming control, the SS eliminated the already reduced wage payments of Jewish forced laborers in September 1942. In the future, enterprises were to pay ZL 5.00 for each Jew in a kind of worker rental system. The SS withheld ZL 2.00 of this amount for maintenance and gave ZL 3.00 to the local Jewish council, which had to support the families of the forced laborers with that money.[154] In Wehrmacht camps, wages were no longer paid in cash because of that arrangement. The army rented the inmates and remitted ZL 5.00 per male worker and ZL 4.00 per female worker, minus ZL 1.60 for maintenance.[155] This rental system was almost identical to the procedure used in Silesia and to the practice of the labor offices in the Warthegau, as well as to the system for transfer of Jewish concentration camp inmates developed by the SS WVHA, all introduced in the same year, 1942. Further research must seek possible central orders and discussion of those rental systems.

To achieve adequate work performance for the army interests, the Wehrmacht armaments inspection office soon had the SS authorize providing their Jewish forced laborers with the better Polish food cards and with clothing. Under a cynical agreement, the Wehrmacht could order underwear directly from the SS, which handed out "clothing left behind by

[150] Sandkühler, "Lemberg-Janowska," 612.

[151] Pohl, *Judenverfolgung in Ostgalizien,* 216.

[152] Sandkühler, "Lemberg-Janowska," 612.

[153] *Europa unterm Hakenkreuz: Polen,* 234, Doc. No. 119, Report of the commander of a police company to the commander of the Galicia Order Police, September 14, 1942.

[154] Circular decree of the Warsaw SSPF, September 14, 1942, facsimile in Grabitz and Scheffler, *Letzte Spuren,* 172.

[155] BA-MA Freiburg im Breisgau, RH 53–23, No. 87, Fols. 176, Circular letter of the military district commander in the General Government (*Wehrkreisbefehlshaber im Generalgouvernement,* or WiG), October 15, 1942.

evacuated Jews."[156] Forced labor itself was organized with armaments interests in mind, as were deportations of forced laborers. On July 22, 1942, a large "resettlement operation" in the Warsaw ghetto began; it lasted until September. Untouched by the deportations, the Schultz and Walter Többens companies were able to retain 16,000 workers.[157]

Only when centrally controlled deportations were conducted without regard for special local circumstances or agreements between the Wehrmacht and the SS did conflicts arise because of loss of local production, just as in Germany. Wehrmacht Senior Quartermaster Forster complained on August 5, 1942, to the General Government's general quartermaster that removal of the Jews had caused disruptions to tasks important for the Wehrmacht in supply camps, for example in the Radom army provisions depot, the Radom army clothing depot, and the Przemysl supply depot camp. Lining 16,000 iron "eastern front ovens" with fire bricks had been impeded, Forster said, adding emphatically, "With the Polish workers completely selected out for the Reich, the Jew is the only worker available."[158]

At this point, Jewish forced laborers were still a significant factor in the General Government's labor market. In mid-September 1942, the authorities there tallied the "total number of commercial workers" at something more that one million. Every third was a Jewish forced laborer. Among these 300,000 Jews, about 100,000 were considered skilled craftsmen.[159] Nevertheless, on September 5 Himmler ordered the Wehrmacht Commander in Chief, Keitel, to replace all Jews in armaments production with Poles.[160] The commander in chief then ordered at mid-month that the Jewish forced laborers in the Wehrmacht offices and in the businesses working for those offices were to be replaced "as quickly as possible by Poles, Ukrainians, etc., without negative effects on the work important for the war."[161] That was not at all easy to do. In the individual businesses making products for the Wehrmacht, the proportion of Jewish forced laborers among the skilled workers was between 25 and 100 percent. All the skilled workers manufacturing winter clothing were Polish Jews. In airplane production, the key workers, the wheelwrights, were Jews. In the companies repairing uniforms, they were 97 percent of the staff. (See photo 10, p. 264.) Sixteen thousand, five hundred of the 22,000 Jewish forced laborers who worked for the army were skilled laborers (textile and leather workers). Because of this

[156] Ibid., Fols. 47–50, Protocol of a meeting, August 14, 1942.
[157] Grabitz and Scheffler, *Letzte Spuren*, 29 and 158–170.
[158] BA-MA Freiburg im Breisgau, RH 53–23, No. 87, Fols. 11.
[159] Ibid., Fol. 117, WiG to the OKW, Armed Forces Operations Staff (*Wehrmachtsführungsstab*), September 18, 1942, Reproduced in *Europa unterm Hakenkreuz: Polen*, 235–236, Doc. No. 120; and *Faschismus-Getto-Massenmord*, 444–446.
[160] Madajczyk, *Okkupationspolitik*, 222; Pohl, *Judenverfolgung in Ostgalizien*, 235.
[161] BA-MA Freiburg im Breisgau, RH 53–23, No. 87, Fols. 130, Reference to September 17, 1942, meeting in Spala in a letter of September 23, 1942.

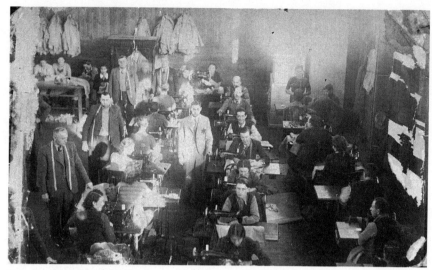

Photo 10. Jews sewing German military uniforms at a factory in the Olkusz ghetto, circa 1942

situation – as in the Old Reich at this point – replacement workers were supposed to be trained promptly: "The guideline is to eliminate the Jews as quickly as possible without negatively affecting the work important for the war."[162] The Eastern Railway was another main employer. In the General Government, 15,383 Jews worked in its track-laying program. The Eastern Railway president, Adolf Gerteis, therefore stated during discussions with HSSPF Krüger in mid-September 1942 that deportation of Jewish forced laborers would only be allowed if replacements could be provided.[163]

In the Reich capital Berlin, the responsible Nazi officers had a completely different perspective. On September 15, 1942, the chief of the SS WVHA, Oswald Pohl, made an agreement with Armaments Minister Speer to transfer some armaments tasks to the concentration camps and to put 50,000 Jews to work for this purpose in "existing separate businesses"; the majority of the workers would come from Auschwitz. Workers for armaments activities were to be selected immediately from deportation transports.[164] The use of non-German Jews in camps was to occur mostly in the Old Reich, to help

---

[162] Ibid., Fol. 117, WiG to the OKW, Armed Forces Operations Staff, September 18, 1942; reproduced in Grabitz and Scheffler, *Letzte Spuren*, 311–312.

[163] Pohl, *Judenverfolgung in Ostgalizien*, 237.

[164] Jan Erik Schulte, "Zwangsarbeit für die SS. Juden in der Ostindustrie GmbH," in *Ausbeutung, Vernichtung, Öffentlichkeit. Neue Studien zur nationalsozialistischen Lagerpolitik*, edited by Norbert Frei, et al. and commissioned by the Institut für Zeitgeschichte (Munich, 2000), 43–74, here 46.

with the labor shortages there for the short term but on a broad scale.[165] Pohl and Speer offered the German armaments industry "foreign Jews" in large numbers, many of them skilled workers. Companies such as Krupp AG in Essen reacted quickly and reported which "works or departments" could be staffed with Jews and "where concentration camps [could] be built to house the Jews." Krupp AG signaled its willingness to employ over 1,000 Jewish skilled workers, after administering their own fitness tests. The company supplied a precise catalogue of the desired qualifications, but demanded that workers be "real skilled craftsmen who have worked for years at machines of the kind generally used for machine building."[166] However, after two weeks, the General Commissioner for Labor Utilization, Fritz Sauckel, officially terminated this operation.[167]

Although the plan for a mass transfer failed, economic interests continued to carry weight in the central decisions regarding anti-Jewish policies. In a September 22, 1942, Führer meeting, Hitler had categorically emphasized "once again the importance of removing Jews from the armaments industry in the Reich," which of course invalidated the Pohl-Speer project. At the same time, Hitler supported Sauckel's proposal that Polish Jewish skilled workers be left for the time being in the General Government working in the compulsory employment program.[168] However, Himmler again diluted this concession to the war interests of the defense industry in the General Government, keeping his focus on the murder program. At the beginning of October, Himmler sent a teletype to Pohl, Krüger, Globocznik, and the RSHA regarding the Jewish armaments workers employed by the Wehrmacht. Compulsory employees working only in tailor, fur, and shoemaking workshops were to be assembled by Krüger and Pohl in concentrations camps at that site, that is, in Warsaw and Lublin. The Wehrmacht were to report their clothing needs to the SS, which would then ensure the continuation of deliveries. "2. The Jews, who located in actual armaments operations, that is, weapons workshops, automobile workshops, etc., are to be removed one at a time. In the first stage, they are to be put together in the businesses' individual halls. In the second stage of this process, the occupants of the individual

---

[165] For the following, see Hilberg, *Vernichtung*, Vol. 2, 464.

[166] BA, Zwischenarchiv Dahlwitz-Hoppegarten, former Archiv des Dokumentationszentrums der Staatlichen Archivverwaltung der DDR (AdZ), Doc/K, No. 560/3, Fols. 46–48, Teletypes, September 17 and 18, 1942 (Nuremberg Case X, NIK-5858–5860).

[167] BA Berlin, R 3901 (former R 41) Reich Labor Ministry, No. 290, Fol. 14, Express letter of the Commissioner for the Four-Year Plan – General Commissioner for Labor Utilization, October 2, 1942.

[168] BA Berlin, R 3 Reich Minister for Armaments and Munitions, No. 1505, Fol. 101, Note of Minister Speer's office, September 28, 1942, regarding the meetings with the Führer on September 20, 21, and 22, 1942; reproduced in Willi Boelcke (ed.), *Deutschlands Rüstung im Zweiten Weltkrieg. Hitlers Konferenzen mit Albert Speer 1942–1945* (Frankfurt am Main, 1969), 189.

halls . . . are to be put together in separate operations, so that we only have a few segregated concentration camp businesses in the General Government. 3. The goal will then be to replace these Jewish workers with Poles and to consolidate the larger number of these Jewish concentration camp businesses into a very few Jewish large-scale concentration camp businesses, if at all possible in the eastern part of the General Government. But even there, the Jews are to disappear one day, in keeping with the wishes of the Führer." The military offices were to coordinate concrete implementation according to these guidelines in cooperation with the responsible SS and Police Leaders.[169]

On October 10, 1942, the OKW informed its economic offices about the Himmler letter.[170] Thus, the Wehrmacht more or less gave in to the pressure of the SS.[171] For practical implementation – if possible, without production disturbances – the two sides agreed a short time later, in conformance with the "Guidelines of the Reichsführer SS," to release individual workers immediately at the military offices and to hand over the Jewish camps maintained by the Wehrmacht offices to the SS. The SS was to consolidate these camps locally if possible and in the future to supply workers from the newly created concentration camps to the Wehrmacht offices.[172] Even the Warsaw ghetto was classified as a labor camp "under police command."[173]

Following the general pattern, the Galicia HSSPF took over control of the ghetto from the Lemberg municipal administration in September 1942. All the Jewish workers had to move into the ghetto; the HSSPF closed down the residential quarter for skilled workers. The SS removed "free" workers from enterprises, delivered them to Janowska, and then, for a price, made them available again to the businesses.[174] An October 23, 1942, letter from Katzmann to the Lemberg armaments headquarters shows that strict SS control over forced labor in the General Government failed, in part as a result of the existing realities. Katzmann wrote that Jewish workers were as a fundamental rule to be housed in barracks; the SS was to have control. As the police did not have its own camps everywhere, the "factory management itself would have to take care of temporarily housing the

---

[169] *Eksterminacja Żydów*, Doc. No. 129, 244–245, Teletype of the RFSS, October 9, 1942. See *Europa unterm Hakenkreuz: Polen*, 236 and note 1.

[170] BA-MA Freiburg im Breisgau, RH 53–23, No. 87, Fols. 173, Teletype of the OKW to the economic office of the military-district commander in the General Government, October 10, 1942; facsimile in Grabitz and Scheffler, *Letzte Spuren*, 179.

[171] See Browning, who believes that Himmler's triumph was almost complete and that the SS was only making temporary concessions to the armed forces; Browning, "Jewish Workers," 79.

[172] BA-MA Freiburg im Breisgau, RH, 53–23, No. 87, Fols. 174, Circular of the WiG, senior quartermaster (Forster), October 14, 1942, referring to a meeting with Krüger on the day before; see Grabitz and Scheffler, *Letzte Spuren*, 314.

[173] Facsimile of a letter of the Warsaw transfer office, October 8, 1942, in Grabitz and Scheffler, *Letzte Spuren*, 175.

[174] Sandkühler, "Lemberg-Janowska," 612.

Jewish workers in barracks. If segregated housing in the works is impossible, the employed Jewish workers are to be housed in certain residential buildings of the Jewish residential districts still present." As in the rest of the General Government, the SS here changed the mode of payment: "From November 1, 1942 on, the Jewish workers will not be paid in cash. The business management offices will pay over to the Galicia SSPF ZL 5.oo per man and ZL 4.oo per women for every calendar day and shift. Wage taxes and contributions for social insurance are to be dropped. The costs for maintenance and management are to be subtracted . . . from the amounts mentioned above."[175] Firma Schwarz & Co. Lemberg (uniform repair), Firma Textilia in Lemberg, Metrawatt AG Feinmechanische und Optische Werke Nürnberg – Lemberg Branch Works (fine mechanical and optical works, products for the Luftwaffe), Ausbildungswerkstätten A. W. (training workshops) in Lemberg, Holzbau AG – Lemberg Branch (wood construction), Fassdaubenfabrik Bolechow (barrel stave factory), Möbelfabrik (furniture) in Bolechow, and Karpathen-Öl AG (Carpathian oil), also received the letter.[176]

Various forced-labor networks thus existed in Galicia simultaneously. Fifteen forced-labor camps existed along Durchgangsstraße 4. The work of 20,000 people had finally completed 160 kilometers of the road in 1943.[177] In addition, the SS operated the Kogsagys farms, around 24 estates with 10,000 forced laborers. Various Jewish forced laborers were also used for the civilian authorities, and after 1942 for the establishment of Wehrmacht camps or for private companies such as Karpathen-Öl AG. Usually, volunteer auxiliaries (Hiwis) – company employees at the labor sites, soldiers in the Wehrmacht workshops, and the railway protective service for railway projects – guarded the inmates.[178] Overall, behavior toward the Jewish workers was more brutal than in many other areas of the General Government. In the SS camps along the Durchgangsstraße 4, where Jews were employed by private construction companies, many Jews incapable of working were simply shot to death.[179]

ACCELERATION OF THE MURDER PROGRAM AND FORCED LABORERS

After fall 1942, close cooperation developed between the SS and the armed forces everywhere. On November 10, the HSSPF for Galicia ordered the

---

[175] Quoted in IMT, Vol. XXXVII, Doc. o–18 L, 398–400, Report of HSSPF Katzmann, June 30, 1943.

[176] Ibid., 401. See Sandkühler, "Lemberg-Janowska," 624–626.

[177] IMT, Vol. XXXVII, Doc. o–18 L, 393, Report of HSSPF Katzmann, June 30, 1943.

[178] Pohl, *Judenverfolgung in Ostgalizien*, 345–346.

[179] Hermann Kaienburg, "Jüdische Arbeitslager an der 'Straße der SS,'" in *1999. Zeitschrift für Sozialgeschichte des 20. und 21. Jahrhunderts*, 11, 1 (1996): 13–39, here 20; Pohl, *Judenverfolgung in Ostgalizien*, 348.

formation of "Jewish residential districts" and accelerated deportation. "With further instructions of the Higher SS and Police Leader to carry out accelerated total resettlement of the Jews, extensive work was once again necessary to register the Jews who would still be permitted for the time being to remain behind in the armaments businesses. . . . The agreement made with the Wehrmacht about the use and treatment of these labor prisoners was committed to paper."[180] In Krakow, SS Obersturmbannführer Specht promised that "operations to resettle Jews working for the military [would] be stopped" until the Wehrmacht had "taken the necessary removal measures." The Wehrmacht was to perform registration and pass to the SS the lists for all locations with more than 100 and all with less than 100 Jewish forced laborers.[181] According to a December 1, 1942, report, the transfer from the Wehrmacht to the SS was proceeding smoothly. The Jewish workers still housed in the Wehrmacht's own camps in the General Government were considered prisoners of the HSSPF.[182]

Concentration of the forced laborers involved expansion of the existing camps, as in Lublin district. In Radom district, new camps were even constructed for HASAG in summer and fall 1942. The largest forced-labor camp in Krakow district, where 12,000 prisoners later lived, was opened on September 28, 1942, on the grounds of the Jewish cemetery in Plaszow, at the same time as the clearing of the Krakow ghetto. At other locations, the ghettos themselves were transformed into labor ghettos – that is, in contrast to the forced-labor camps, the families of the people recruited also remained there. Such ghettos were then renamed "Jewish camps," as was the case in Krakow and Lemberg.[183]

Number of Jews Still Living in the General Government on December 31, 1942[184]

District	Number
Krakow	37,000
Radom	29,400
Lublin	20,000
Warsaw	50,000
Lemberg	161,514
Total	297,914

[180] IMT, Vol. XXXVII, Doc. 0–18 L, 398, Report of HSSPF Katzmann, June 30, 1943.
[181] BA-MA Freiburg im Breisgau, RH 53–23, No. 87, Fols. 178–179, Note of the WiG, October 16, 1942. See ibid., Fol. 193, Circular of the WiG (Forster), October 20, 1942.
[182] Ibid., Fol. 264, War diary, December 1, 1942.
[183] Pohl, "Zwangsarbeitslager," 419–420; Pohl, *Judenverfolgung in Ostgalizien*, 236; Browning, "Jewish Workers," 80.

At the beginning of 1943, Himmler insisted that the remaining Jews also should be murdered. After a visit in Warsaw, he instructed in January that the Jews there be taken to Lublin.[185] On February 16, he ordered the HSSPF in Krakow, Friedrich Wilhelm Krüger, to tear down the Warsaw ghetto after the concentration camp had been moved out. Otherwise, Himmler said, Warsaw would never be peaceful. A plan was to be submitted for destroying the ghetto. The living space for 500,000 "subhumans" would have to disappear and the city of millions, as the center of disintegration and insurrection, would have to be reduced in size.[186] Shut-down of the remaining ghettos and the smaller labor camps in the General Government began in March 1943. Of course, thousands of workers were once again exempted from the murder program. The second wave of ghetto clearings brought with it a second wave of camp construction, mostly for the workers from the ghetto. As the result of the Krakow ghetto liquidation, 14,000 "work Jews" were transported to Plaszow camp on the orders of the SSPF Julian Scherner, but also 3,000 went to Auschwitz.[187]

At this stage, the General Government had more than 120,000 Jews interned in forced-labor camps. In March 1943, 22,000 lived in Radom district, 50,000 in Galicia district, and later in June, 37,000 in Lublin district (where a total of 45,000 Jewish forced laborers were registered). The majority of the labor camps were at that point subordinate to the SS and Police Leaders, but other camps operated by water supply inspection offices or agricultural administrations also continued to exist.[188]

With liquidation of the Warsaw ghetto, several thousand forced laborers, together with the production facilities, were transferred to the still existing Lublin SS forced-labor camps. Warsaw Jews with Többens operations ended up in Poniatowa, and those with Schultz, in Trawniki.[189] Reacting to the unexpected, heroic, April 1943 uprising of the Jewish ghetto fighters who resisted the "clearing" with armed force, the furious Himmler ordered that "evacuation" of the Jews be accelerated to achieve "pacification" (*Befriedung*). In late May, Radom district was likewise "cleansed" and the work Jews placed in camps. Most of the other Jews were murdered. However, at a May 31 labor meeting with General Governor Frank it became clear that the General Government's HSSPF, Krüger, intended to have the Chief of the Berlin RSHA, Kaltenbrunner, sway Himmler to stop the Jewish skilled

[184] LBIA New York, Microfilms, Wiener Library, 500 Series, No. 526, Inspector for statistics with the RFSS, January 1, 1943 (Korherr Report), 14 (also in BA Berlin, NS 19, No. 1570).

[185] Browning, "Jewish Workers," 80.

[186] *Reichsführer! . . . Briefe von und an Himmler*, 239, No. 208.

[187] Browning, "Jewish Workers," 81; Pohl, "Zwangsarbeitslager," 420.

[188] Pohl, "Zwangsarbeitslager," 420–422; Pucher, *Globocznik*, 87.

[189] *Faschismus-Getto-Massenmord*, 349, Doc. No. 271; Pucher, *Globocznik*, 87. On the transfer of a fur company to Trawniki camp, see Grabitz and Scheffler, *Letzte Spuren*, 184–186 and 322.

craftsmen from being withdrawn.[190] However, in this case the regional interests of the General Government were unable to prevail over orders from
Berlin. In Lublin district, the rest of the ghettos was closed down by May.
The SS took part of the able-bodied forced laborers to Majdanek and shipped
the rest off to be murdered in the extermination camps of Sobibor and Treblinka.[191] A wave of camp closings ensued in Galicia district during June; in
the process, the Lemberg "Jewish camp" and a series of Durchgangsstraße 4
camps were brutally liquidated.[192] The Katzmann report states that effective
as of June 23, 1943, all of the Jewish sectors had been shut down because
"resettlement" had been carried out so vigorously. Except for SS camps, Galicia district was then free of Jews. Four hundred thirty-four thousand, three
hundred twenty-nine Jews from there had been "resettled," that is, murdered.
A total of twenty-one SS camps with 21,156 Jews still existed in Lemberg,
Weinbergen, Ostrow, Kurowice, Jaktorow, Lackie, Pluhow, Kosaki, Zborow,
Jezernia, Tarnopol, Hluboczek, Borki Wielki, Kamionki, Drohobycz, Borys-
law, Stryj, Skole, Bolechow, Broschnikow, and Njebielow.[193] In the second
half of July, the SS then liquidated the last forced-labor camps along Durchgangsstraße 4.[194] In summer 1943, the SS in Galicia also transferred a total
of 13.4 million *zlotys*; the lion's share of that was the 11.5 million *zlotys*
withheld from the forced laborers' wages. To that sum was added the 1.2
million *zlotys* taken – that is, stolen – from the forced laborers. In contrast,
the earnings of the SS businesses only amounted to 7.7 million *zlotys*.[195]

By fall 1943 many Jews from the large forced-labor camps in the General
Government had also been murdered. Dozens of camps were then placed
under the concentration camp system organized by the Berlin SS WVHA. In
September 1943, the WVHA chief, Oswald Pohl, took over the ten remaining
labor camps of the SSPF in Lublin district for that organization; the camps
were to continue being run as satellite camps of Lublin-Majdanek concentration camp. Plans had even been made to subordinate all of the local SS
forced-labor camps in Poland to the Berlin WVHA.[196] After several new
uprisings in fall 1943, as during ghetto clearings in Bialystok and at murder
sites such as Treblinka and Sobibor, Himmler ordered that the remaining
forced-labor camps in the eastern General Government were to be closed.[197]

---

[190] Browning, "Jewish Workers," 81–83; Pohl, *Von der "Judenpolitik" zum Judenmord*, 165–
166.
[191] Pohl, *Von der "Judenpolitik" zum Judenmord*, 165–166; Browning, "Jewish Workers," 81.
[192] Pohl, *Judenverfolgung in Ostgalizien*, 347–353.
[193] IMT, Vol. XXXVII, Doc. 0–18 L, 401, Report of HSSPF Katzmann, June 30, 1943.
[194] Pohl, *Judenverfolgung in Ostgalizien*, 347–353.
[195] IMT, Vol. XXXVII, Doc. 0–18 L, 403–404, Report of HSSPF Katzmann, June 30, 1943.
[196] *Eksterminacja Żydów*, Doc. No. 135, 254–255, Note of Oswald Pohl, September 7, 1943.
     See Schulte, "Zwangsarbeit für die SS," 69; Pucher, *Globocznik*, 89.
[197] Pohl, "Zwangsarbeitslager," 428; Browning, "Jewish Workers," 85.

On November 3 and 4, 1943, the SS therefore launched one of the largest murder operations ever against Jewish forced laborers, the notorious *"Aktion Erntefest"* (Operation Harvest Festival). While in Majdanek, Trawniki, Poniatowa, and other forced-labor camps 42,000 to 43,000 Jews were killed, the inmates of five camps for Wehrmacht needs and one SS camp were spared from the wave of murders in the eastern General Government. Twenty-five thousand Jews survived for economic reasons.[198] In Galicia district, the SS and Police Leader removed forced laborers from the Wehrmacht and armaments operations, except for Karpathen-Öl AG. Aktion Erntefest meant death for most of the inmates of Lemberg-Janowska.[199] While massacres likewise took place in mid-November 1943 in Krakow district, for example, in Plaszow (Krakow) and other camps, in Radom district the forced-labor camps remained untouched. Ultimately, the criterion of importance of the forced labor for the war was the critical factor deciding for or against the closure of the camp. In contrast to Lublin, Plaszow, and Upper Silesia, forced-labor camps in Radom district not liquidated also were not placed under the WVHA's control in Berlin. Companies continued to maintain these factory camps that the District SS alone controlled.[200]

After New Year's 1944, the WVHA began transferring concentration camp prisoners to camps not under its control and taking inmates of those camps into the concentration camps. The WVHA also took over other forced-labor camps, even though Oswald Pohl was opposed.[201] This may have been the result of the experience that the chief of the WVHA had had with the so-called Ostindustrie GmbH, or Osti (East Industries). Pohl had founded the enterprise with the Lublin SSPF, Globocznik, in March 1943. Both of them wanted to build it into one of the most important SS-managed armaments operations. Utilization of Jews for the armaments industry in concentration camps had been planned since fall 1942. Then, in February 1943, the planners hit upon the idea of having the enterprise exploit Jewish workers and resell the movable property of murdered Jews. The enterprise profited from the ghetto closings; for example, it received equipment from the Bialystok ghetto, and machines were also to be transferred from Warsaw. The SS was hardly making serious investments, however. After all, the company employed the Jews in a brush factory, in a peat-cutting operation, and in businesses in Warsaw, Radom, and Lublin. The conditions for the inmates in the Osti camps resembled those in other SS camps. The inmates starved; shooting people incapable of working was a normal part of operations. In fall 1943, the Erntefest murder operation created great problems for Ostindustrie GmbH. Without the SS enterprise being informed, all the forced laborers from workshops II, IV,

---

[198] Grabitz and Scheffler, *Letzte Spuren*, 262–263 and 328–330; Pohl, *Von der "Judenpolitik" zum Judenmord*, 172; Browning, "Jewish Workers," 86.
[199] Sandkühler, "Lemberg-Janowska," 615.   [200] Browning, "Jewish Workers," 86.
[201] Pohl, "Zwangsarbeitslager," 427–429; Browning, "Jewish Workers," 86.

Photo 11. Recently liberated Jewish women from the Schatzlar labor camp in the Protectorate, May 1945

V, and VIII, and other workshops as well, were killed. The WVHA finally liquidated the company in November 1943.[202] The remaining workshops and the camps in Lublin, Warsaw, and Radom districts were integrated into the concentration camp system at the beginning of 1944.[203] The high-flying plans for an SS-owned and operated industrial enterprise in the General Government had thus failed. The enterprise never employed more than 10,000 Jewish forced laborers, no more than a local average at this time in Poland. Jan Erik Schulte attributes the failure to the SS giving extermination priority over economic considerations and only using Ostindustrie GmbH to integrate work into the concept of extermination; however, I find this doubtful.[204] The failure was much more likely the result of the diverging goals of different SS agencies, with the WVHA in Berlin and the SSPF in Lublin on one side promoting the war economy and the RSHA on the other directing the murder program. Furthermore, a portion of the forced-labor camps continued to exist as concentration camps.

---

[202] Schulte, "Zwangsarbeit für die SS," 43–74.
[203] Pohl, "Zwangsarbeitslager," 429; Schulte, "Zwangsarbeit für die SS," 71–73.
[204] See these opinions in Schulte, "Zwangsarbeit für die SS," 44 and 74.

After two years of murder, between 70,000 and 100,000 Jews supposedly lived in the General Government's labor camps in summer 1944, actually still an enormous number.[205] And even so, camps were constantly being closed and their inmates deported or transferred. The SS finally liquidated Lemberg camp in July 1944 because of the advance of the Red Army into Galicia. Hundreds of Jews first were shipped to construction jobs and then further west to Plaszow forced-labor camp.[206] In the first days of August 1944 alone, transports arrived in Auschwitz from Kielce, Ostrowiec, Plaszow, and Pustkow.[207] At the same time, the armaments inspection office requested expansion of the forced-labor camps on behalf of the Wehrmacht. A number of the Jews deported from Hungary in summer 1944 were consequently sent to the Warsaw and Plaszow concentration camps. The SS "evacuated" most of the Jewish prisoners westward when the Soviet army advanced in Poland, because their labor was needed. The still existing Lublin camps were also moved. Many of the inmates were taken to Auschwitz, others from Plaszow or Skarzysko-Kamienna to Stutthof, Buchenwald, or Mauthausen concentration camps, and still others from Warsaw to Dachau concentration camp in Bavaria.[208] Thus, the odyssey of thousands of Jewish forced laborers from all parts of Europe ultimately ended for economic reasons on Reich territory, where at least some of them were liberated by the Allies in 1945. (See photo 11, p. 272.)

SUMMARY

The notion dominant today that the SS planned, organized, and implemented forced labor for Polish Jews goes back to the Nazi era. The Nazi newspaper *Das Schwarze Korps* announced in fall 1940 that the HSSPF of Lublin District, Odilo Globocznik, had "given the Jews so much work . . . that they could hardly breathe. . . . Far in the East, over ten thousand Jews [had been] seen working, really working. . . . The Jewish problem [had thus] been solved by work."[209] After the war, the focus of historical research on concentration camps, Auschwitz, and the Lublin SS camps lent further support to this view. The research results presented here are at odds with this traditional view. The Jewish forced-labor programs organized by labor offices throughout the German-occupied Polish territories clearly overshadowed the SS-controlled labor programs, both in size and in significance for the war economy.[210]

---

[205] Pohl, "Zwangsarbeitslager," 429.   [206] Sandkühler, "Lemberg-Janowska," 615.
[207] Czech, *Kalendarium*, 837–843.
[208] Pohl, "Zwangsarbeitslager," 430; Sandkühler, "Lemberg-Janowska," 615.
[209] "Im Generalgouvernement wird gearbeitet," in *Das Schwarze Korps*, 6, 43 (October 24, 1940): 9.
[210] Recently Kaienburg also pointed out that in occupied Poland "forced labor of Jews" was "in the hands of the labor administrations in the first years." However, his very general statement

Certainly, research on Jewish forced labor in Poland must draw distinctions based on territory, war phase, and organizational forms. In the General Government, which was envisioned as the country to receive Jews deported from other territories, the new occupying power introduced (as one of its first persecutory measures) a general forced-labor requirement for Jews in October 1939, and contrary to practice in the German Reich, put the SS in charge. Jewish impoverishment and unemployment resulting from anti-Jewish policies provided the first central impetus for establishment of forced-labor programs. After months of HSSPF-directed organization of forced labor in the General Government – a period marked by chaos and unauthorized raids – the occupation government modified responsibilities in a surprising manner. Beginning in summer 1940, the labor office was granted the task of planning and directing Jewish forced labor to ensure exploitation of the significant labor resources effectively in the interests of the war economy.

The German administration required an enormous number of workers to modernize the infrastructure of the Polish territories, especially for the planned attack on the Soviet Union. As a consequence, exploitation of the Jews was of national importance. By the end of 1940, 700,000 Jews were already engaged in forced labor. In addition to use of tens of thousands of Jews in cities and their surrounding areas, as well as in the ghettos soon established and their workshops, tens of thousands more were placed in newly built camps for water, railway, and road construction. The objective of addressing shortages in the labor market overlapped with the objective of ensuring minimum support to Jewish families. In Lublin district after 1940 and Galicia district after 1941 the SSPFs also maintained their own SS forced-labor camps, which did not pay the forced laborers any wages. Hunger was part of daily life, and many people died of malnutrition. After 1941, people incapable of working were either deported or shot.

In the Polish regions that were annexed to Germany as the Warthegau or Upper Silesia, the Nazi authorities planned rapid deportation of Jews in fall 1939 to Germanize the region. Hence, not central but rather local forced-labor measures were at first predominant. Only when transport plans failed did the authorities begin in 1940 systematically to recruit Jews for forced labor. In the Warthegau, the labor administration thus had sole responsibility for utilization of Jews from the outset. Dozens of labor camps were established in agricultural operations, at improvement sites, and for road building; tens of thousands of Jews had to work in the Lodz ghetto workshops after 1940–41. Thousands of Jews even were transferred at the end of

---

– as shown here – only partially conforms to the reality at that time; see Hermann Kaienburg, "Zwangsarbeit von Juden in Arbeits- und Konzentrationslagern," in *"Arisierung." Volksgemeinschaft, Raub und Gedächtnis,* edited by Irmrud Wojak and Peter Hayes and commissioned by the Fritz Bauer Institute (Frankfurt am Main and New York [Campus], 2000), 224.

1940 into the Reich for economic reasons – in violation of Hitler's express wishes – at first to camps for Reich Autobahn construction, and after 1942 for use in industry. The situation was different in eastern Upper Silesia. There the SS established its own forced-labor regime under Special Commissioner Schmelt at the end of 1940; the associated camp system soon extended to Lower Silesia and the Sudetenland. In that system, the SS commanded the Jewish workers unopposed. Tens of thousands of Jews soon toiled in the Silesian camps for highway or industrial operations and in eastern Upper Silesia's workshops. However, even in that case organization by the SS did not mean that economic interests no longer played any role, for the SS profited financially itself, while serving the Wehrmacht and private enterprises.

The SS did not regain control of forced labor in the General Government until Jews were being systematically murdered in summer of 1942. Usually labor offices still continued to play a role in recruiting and assigning the Jewish forced laborers, even at SS enterprises, but also in making selections for murder transports. Ultimately, the labor administration guaranteed that the extermination program did not collide with labor market interests and armaments requirements in all the occupied Polish territories. As in Germany, forced laborers were consequently the last large group temporarily spared from the extermination transports. At the end of 1942, 300,000 Polish Jews, most of them forced laborers, still lived in the General Government. Because of their importance for the war, labor camps and some ghettos with workshops were excluded from the murder program for a long time. Paradoxically, forced-labor programs actually expanded in many places for economic reasons; in fact, they only reached their peak in 1942, as in Silesia with over 50,000 men and women who performed compulsory labor under the SS Organisation Schmelt. In 1943, various forced-labor camps of industrial operations in Silesia and the General Government even were specially integrated into the SS concentration camp system so that the inmates would not be lost for war production. The Lodz ghetto was not liquidated until summer 1944. Many of the Jews who had survived to that point even were taken to Germany as laborers until the last months of the war. Despite the years of martyrdom often associated with forced labor, for many Polish Jews it thus represented a real chance to survive mass murder.

Conclusion

COMPULSORY LABOR – AN UNDERESTIMATED ELEMENT OF NAZI ANTI-JEWISH POLICY

Until now scholars of history have not systematically compared the forms of Jewish forced labor in Germany, in the annexed territories, and in the occupied countries. Since the 1990s, with the growing number of detailed studies on persecution of Jews, historiography has gained many new insights; at the same time, specialization, isolation, and the wealth of facts now available make a comparative overview difficult. Thus, despite a great deal of new information, the notion is still widespread that the SS and the Security Police, at least after 1938 in Germany and later in the occupied countries, dominated and determined anti-Jewish policies in all matters.[1] As the studies presented here demonstrate, however, in contrast to previous views, forced labor is a convincing counter-example. The forced-labor program for Jews in Nazi-controlled territory was not predominantly organized by the SS. The majority of the forced-labor deployments occurred outside and independent of the concentration camps or other SS camp systems, and the labor administrations planned, established, and controlled Jews' obligation to perform forced labor. That is the case almost universally in Germany, in Austria, in the Protectorate, in the Warthegau, and, during the period from 1940 to 1942, in the General Government.

The National Socialists introduced forced labor as a basic element of anti-Jewish policy in the territories listed, and also throughout Europe. The reasons for that are complex. On the one hand, measures against the particular Jewish population in question, including professional prohibitions, Aryanization, and expropriation of property, produced poverty and unemployment among the victims of the Nazi policies and thus dependency on state welfare. On the other hand, extreme labor shortages developed, first in Germany and Austria, but then also in the occupied countries.

---

[1] For example, recently Musial expressed the view that in Poland, "In the first phase the civilian administration was responsible for anti-Jewish policies, in contrast to the Reich, where the SS and police apparatus controlled this sphere"; Bogdan Musial, *Deutsche Zivilverwaltung und Judenverfolgung im Generalgouvernement, Eine Fallstudie zum Distrikt Lublin 1939–1944* (Wiesbaden, 1999), 341.

GERMANY

Jewish forced labor in Germany still is associated primarily with use of Jews in concentration camps. It was a little known fact that forced labor served as an integral part of Jewish persecution outside that context. After the November 1938 pogrom, the Nazi leadership sought to reorient anti-Jewish policy by forcing emigration with any means available, and by placing Jews unable to emigrate in a forced community to separate them completely from the rest of society. All avenues for Jews to earn a living independently were blocked. Within a central program of persecution organized with distributed responsibilities, the labor administration then was to organize segregated labor deployment for Jews without income or employment. Forced labor was thus not an interim solution but rather the key element in a newly channeled persecutory process after 1939.

The regional and local labor offices implemented segregated labor deployment in Germany. From the outset, Jews were in fact subject to unwritten special law: in being forced to work based on racial criteria, in being utilized in separate columns, and in being allocated to difficult unskilled labor regardless of qualifications and profession. A characteristic feature of segregated labor deployment in Germany was that Jews were still employed under individual work contracts. But such contracts were by no means an indicator of voluntariness, as in the case of Jews, "assignment by the labor office" replaced "the employee's declaration of intention."[2] They were later utilized de facto under special legislation created progressively by decrees of the Reich Trustee of Labor and various decisions of the labor courts, then finally codified by an October 1941 order. Two phases of segregated labor deployment are evident: (1) The December 20, 1938, decree of the Reich Institute for Labor Placement and Unemployment Insurance obligated all Jews supported by government unemployment insurance to work in separate columns on regional and local infrastructure projects, at waste disposal sites, and for municipal administrations cleaning streets. After the rapid takeover of Poland, Hitler dropped the idea of introducing forced labor for all able-bodied German Jews in case of war in favor of the new plan to deport all German Jews to the occupied territories; the labor administration consequently was ordered to continue following the December 1938 decree for the time being. (2) Beginning in 1940, the labor office responded to new labor shortages by recruiting all able-bodied Jews, predominantly for industry or other activities requiring skill. This transformation in labor policy indicates how specific market interests of the labor administration were able to reshape persecutory measures.

Even before the attack on Poland, in summer 1939, German labor offices had pressed more than 20,000 Jews, mostly men, into compulsory labor service. In summer 1941, the number of forced laborers in Germany reached

---

[2] *Jüdisches Nachrichtenblatt*, Viennese edition of January 23, 1942: 1.

its peak with over 50,000, more than half of them women. For countless German Jews, forced labor determined the course of their daily lives for up to four years and at the same time was a structural element furthering isolation and state control. Between 1939 and 1941, dozens of small and large labor camps independent of the SS concentration camp system were established in Germany for this forced-labor program. Countless private enterprises, municipal administrations, and public builders employed Jews who had been robbed of their rights; the work, usually physically difficult or damaging to their health, was performed in isolated columns or separate company departments. In Berlin alone, Jewish forced laborers worked for over 230 companies, among them a number of large-scale operations such as Siemens, and in Frankfurt am Main, for over 220 companies, 80 of them operations "important for the war."

The labor administration had increasingly organized forced labor in Germany to benefit the war economy, especially armaments, without the SS and Gestapo being involved in any way, but this situation changed after fall 1941 with mass deportations of German Jews. As tens of thousands of Jewish forced laborers seemed of marginal consequence – from the standpoint of the national economy – compared to millions of foreign workers, the compulsory employees no longer had any real protection against deportation. Although transport timing compatible with production was to be coordinated with the labor administration and the Wehrmacht offices responsible for armaments, local power relationships were ultimately the decisive factor. Of course the labor administration, enterprises, and the Wehrmacht armaments inspection office responsible for war-time production cooperated in selecting the forced laborers to be deported. In a few cases, transport dates were cancelled; in others, entire companies, mostly in armaments production, were spared removal of their forced laborers for extended periods. After more than a year of deportations, armaments workers in many cases represented the bulk of Jews still remaining in Germany. They were finally pulled from the companies at the end of February 1943 in the big Fabrik-Aktion and deported.

In 1943, the labor administration organized further compulsory labor, modeled on segregated labor deployment, for Jews in mixed marriages. Jews in mixed marriages were assigned to manual labor or, less frequently, to industry. Based on a decision by Hitler in 1942, Jewish Mischlinge were taken to perform forced labor, initially in France in 1943, later in Germany. After Himmler had pushed in fall 1944 for accelerated forced deployment to dozens of newly established forced-labor camps, mostly for Organisation Todt projects in Reich territory, the labor administration employed thousands of Mischlinge.

AUSTRIA

The idea for segregated labor deployment came from Vienna, Austria. Radical persecution of Jews after the Anschluss resulted in mass dependence on public welfare and unemployment assistance. In September 1938, the Austrian labor administration reacted with the novel measure of forcing unemployed Jews to perform excavation work in separate columns. After the November pogrom, the Austrian model became the prototype for segregated labor deployment of Jews in the Reich. From the end of 1938 on, the Austrian labor administration forced thousands of Jews to perform difficult unskilled jobs. As in the Reich, Jews who were registered at the labor offices and received unemployment assistance were taken first, then all able-bodied men and women; this occurred earlier than in Germany, however. The labor offices assigned hundreds of Jews in columns to waste management jobs in Vienna, to brickworks, to gravel pits for the Reich Autobahn, and to Reich road and power plant projects. In cooperation with the regional labor offices in the Old Reich, thousands of Jews were sent from Vienna to the Old Reich to work on road, dam, and dike projects, and even on the harvest. In contrast to Germany, where the labor administration obligated Jews to industry in 1940 because many construction projects had been stopped due to the war, the Viennese labor administration sent an increasing number of Jewish laborers to construct dams and roads inside Austria, where infrastructure modernization was part of war preparations. As the Austrian Jews had been concentrated in Vienna at an early date, outside deployment in camps constituted a much greater proportion of compulsory employment than in Germany, where Jews still lived in many cities. When mass deportations out of Vienna began, postponing transports was relatively rare because in contrast to Germany, industrial work played almost no role at all. By fall 1942 almost all Austrian Jews had been deported and the labor camps closed.

The Ostmark must be considered a regional trailblazer with regard to the ideas, methods, and discriminatory conditions of segregated labor deployment. This was not the case for the phenomenon as a whole, however; as a result of several early deportations, the Viennese labor administration never was able to expand forced labor of full Jews as extensively at the German labor offices. The peak was reached at the beginning of 1941 with 8,000 forced laborers. Only when the Jews in mixed marriages and the Mischlinge became part of the forced-labor program in the last two years of the war did the Austrian labor administration achieve almost total exploitation of the labor pool. Just as were German Jews, Austrian Jews were in fact subject to special law that was initially unwritten and then later gradually codified. Austrian companies, like their counterparts in Germany, formally signed individual contracts with Jewish compulsory employees provided by the labor office during the entire war period. There were a few exceptions to the Austrian rule of segregated labor deployment, for example, in the SD Central Office-controlled retraining camps. In 1942, the Vienna Gestapo bypassed the labor office in arranging special assignments for thousands of people on orders from the city or the NSDAP Gau leadership.

SEGREGATED LABOR DEPLOYMENT AS THE MODEL
FOR DANZIG AND THE PROTECTORATE

In Danzig, development followed a pattern similar to that in the Old Reich. After annexation of Danzig, barely 2,000 Jews still lived there. At the beginning of 1939, the city government introduced laws on the model of the Nuremberg racial laws. The Jews found themselves excluded from the business world. Earning a living independently was no longer possible. Soon half the members of the synagogue community had to rely on support. The Danzig government employed some of the unemployed Jews in a kind of segregated labor deployment. Thus, forty men of the Danzig dike association performed excavation work in a camp in Güttland an der Vistula in August 1939.[3]

After establishment of the Protectorate of Bohemia and Moravia in March 1939 on the territory of the Czech state, systematic anti-Jewish policies were instituted there; the policies were driven equally by the Germans and the Czech government. The gradual exclusion of Jews from employment in administration and the economy resulted in rapid impoverishment of the Jewish population and dependence on social assistance. Up until 1940, Czech Jews could not be deported to occupied Poland as planned in 1939, so the first local measures were introduced. Several central orders in succession created a forced-labor system for unemployed Jews after the beginning of 1941, again based on the segregated labor deployment model. In summer 1941, 11,000 of the over 17,000 registered men eighteen to fifty years old were working, just under 7,000 of them already performing forced labor. In the Protectorate, utilization by the labor offices was extended in September 1941 to all sixteen-to-sixty-year-olds. After a few weeks, forced labor included 12,000 persons. In some labor office districts, that was almost 100 percent of all Jews capable of working; in others, it was more than 50 percent.

On average, more than half of the available Jewish workers were engaged in forced labor, which the labor administration in the Protectorate organized only in columns segregated from other workers. Until fall 1941, women were scarcely recruited, in striking contrast to Germany and Austria at this time. Despite the new mass deportations that had been underway since October 1941, the labor offices were able gradually to expand forced labor. The labor offices assigned Jews not to the countryside and to construction as they had previously, but instead, because of the season, to industry. In spring 1942 that changed once again. The peak was reached here a year later than in Germany and Austria. In May, more than 15,000 men and 1,000 women were forced to toil for private companies and agencies. In July 1942, the

---

[3] Yad Vashem Archive (YV), Jerusalem, 08, No. 21, no folio numbers, Report of the Danzig synagogue community for the August 22, 1939, conference, 2–3; Leo Baeck Institute Archive (LBIA) New York, Wiener Library, Microfilms, Reel 73, Newspaper "*Danziger Vorposten,*" August 4, 1939.

forced laborers were placed on the same footing as those in most of the territories under German rule. Additionally, Jews were excluded from social insurance. The labor administration directed forced labor for Jews in the Protectorate, but diverging from the Reich, the Central Office of the Security Police in Prague took a modicum of control in May 1941. The Protectorate thus held a kind of transitional position with relation to the forced labor introduced in the General Government for the Jewish population.

MODEL FOR THE OCCUPIED EASTERN TERRITORIES

In the eastern territories occupied by Germany, whether in Poland, or in the Soviet Union, forced labor was one of the first measures imposed on Jews of the conquered territories. A frequently encountered misunderstanding is that the SS and Security Police alone determined anti-Jewish policies in the occupied territories from the outset. Persecutory measures usually were organized, as in Reich territory, with a division of labor. Just what concrete forms the first persecutory policies took depended on whether or not deportation was planned for the particular Jewish population group. The same especially applies for planning and organization of forced labor. In regions annexed to Germany where rapid deportation of Jews was planned in order to Germanize the area, compulsory employment initially was not organized centrally or methodically; instead, local measures predominated. However, when transport plans failed, the authorities began in 1940 to recruit Jews systematically for forced labor. In the General Government, which was earmarked as an area to receive Jews deported from other regions, one of the first measures of the new occupying power introduced general forced labor for Jews in an October 1939 order.

Jews' impoverishment and unemployment, coupled with the labor shortages, was a central motive for systematic establishment of forced-labor programs in the occupied Polish territories as well. Social and economic interests again changed political responsibilities. While the Warthegau labor administration controlled and directed Jewish forced labor from the outset, the situation in the General Government was different. In the October 1939 order, the government of the General Government for the first time had transferred official responsibility for Jewish forced labor on German-controlled territory to the Higher SS and Police Leader. However, as the HSSPF did not act in the interests of the labor market, war production, or social services to the employed Jewish population, he surprisingly lost this function to the labor administration in early summer 1940. From then on, the main labor department of the General Government controlled and directed Jewish forced labor. This point, at the latest, was the beginning of systematic organization of forced labor as an element of persecutory policy in the General Government.

From that point on, the labor offices assumed primary responsibility for forced labor in the General Government. The labor officials typically were viewed in Poland as the "front-line soldiers of labor utilization."[4] Other branches of the civilian administration in the occupied Polish territories also participated in organizing forced labor: centrally, the main departments for construction, forestry, and agriculture, and locally, the city administrations and the Kreishauptmänner. The German administration needed workers to modernize the occupied territories' infrastructure with hydraulic, road, and railway construction, especially after starting to ship non-Jewish Poles as forced laborers to Germany. The entire General Government thus had an interest in the exploitation of Polish Jews. At the end of 1940, more than 700,000 Jews are believed to have been engaged in forced-labor program in occupied Poland.

Local and regional ambitions of the SS, the police, the Wehrmacht, and the civilian authorities interfered with labor administration operations. Additionally, the municipal administrations responsible for organization of the newly formed ghettos became increasingly involved. They initiated labor measures, on the one hand to pursue their own economic interests, and on the other to sustain the unemployed ghetto inhabitants. As the inhabitants' welfare was made the sole responsibility of the newly formed Jewish councils, municipal workshops and departments of private enterprises were set up in the ghettos. At the same time, an increasing number of ghetto inhabitants were sent in the early stages to newly established Jewish camps. Thus, the inhabitants of the Litzmannstadt ghetto in the Warthegau worked in Reich Autobahn construction, and the inhabitants of the Lublin ghetto in the General Government worked in hydraulic construction. After the mass murders began, the assumption that forced labor might protect against deportation to extermination camps gave the Jewish council an important motivation for cooperation in forced-labor initiatives.

In the General Government, the SS attempted to put its ideas and interests into effect on a parallel course and to establish its own camps. In some of the occupied territories, at least two forced-labor systems thus actually operated side by side: that of the civilian labor administration and that of the SS. Examples of the latter were the SSPF camps in Lublin district after 1940 and the SSPF camps along Durchgangsstraße 4 in Galicia after fall 1941. However, those camps, like the forced-labor system of the Schmelt SS Office in Upper Silesia, must be viewed as special regional phenomena. The SS often disregarded labor needs as well as the social effects on the Jewish population when forced laborers did not receive at least minimum wages. However, even

---

[4] General Government, Office of the Chief of Krakow District (ed.), *Abteilung Arbeit. Die Aufbauarbeit im Distrikt Krakau* (Krakow, 1940), 21, in United States Holcaust Memorial Museum Archives (USHMMA) Washington, DC, RG-15.041M (Records of the Krakow District Office), Reel 2, no folio numbers.

when such regional SS networks developed, labor offices remained decisively involved in recruiting, selecting, and placing forced laborers. Unlike the SS, the labor administration was able to coordinate economic and armaments needs with persecutory goals, including isolation and control. Overall, the relationship between the two institutions was characterized retrospectively less by conflict than by agreement and cooperation. The further east they were, the more the labor administration acted like the SS. The labor administration made use of the police for recruiting forced laborers, and labor office officials in the General Government also took part in other persecutory measures. In Krakow, the governor charged the labor department in March 1941 with establishing the ghetto.[5] Moreover, regardless of who was responsible for a concrete forced-labor measure, whether a labor office or the SS, the work was usually performed, even in Poland, by public or private enterprises. Large and small construction, equipment, and armaments companies profited from the forced labor of the Jews. Private and public companies maintained many of the labor camps and thus decisively defined the victims' labor and living conditions. Many operations did not pay wages at all or diverted them to civilian or municipal administrations that only supplied starvation rations to the forced laborers or the ghetto.

For organization of forced labor in occupied Poland, the beginning of mass murders of Jews was a watershed. From this point on, the SS dominated forced labor in the General Government, and economic interests had far more difficulty in prevailing. In summer 1942, control over forced labor was officially returned to the SS in the General Government. Under those circumstances, the SS eliminated the last vestiges of wages and in fall instituted a forced-laborer rental system. Nevertheless, the SS still cooperated closely with the Wehrmacht and with armaments companies, taking their interests into consideration when carrying out deportations. At the end of 1942, 300,000 Jews, mostly forced laborers, still lived in the General Government as a result. More than a third of this number surprisingly lived in Galicia district – that is, in the part of the General Government where mass murders had begun the earliest. The labor administration remained involved despite SS control, and not only in recruiting and assigning workers. By classifying Jews into those capable of working and those incapable of doing so, the labor offices defined the groups for deportation and mass killings. Labor officials participated in preliminary meetings before the "evacuation" of ghettos and made themselves available as accomplices for "clearing measures." The main labor department in the General Governor's office regularly received reports about mass murders.[6]

---

[5] *Eksterminacja Żydów na ziemiach polskich w okresie okupacji hitlerowskiej. Zbiór dokumentów*, edited by Tatiana Berenstein, et al. (Warsaw, 1957), Doc. No. 47, 111–113.

[6] Dieter Pohl, *Nationalsozialistische Judenverfolgung in Ostgalizien, Organisation und Durchführung eines staatlichen Massenverbrechens* (Munich, 1996), 287–288.

In contrast, the labor administration at the Posen Reichsstatthalter's office in the Warthegau continued to have the upper hand in organizing forced labor. It placed tens of thousands of Jews with the Wehrmacht and private enterprises. Despite orders in force in the Third Reich providing that forced laborers be paid minimum wages, the labor administration in Warthegau abolished its own regulations on paying minimum wages, which had been in effect since 1940. A June 1942 order put the labor offices in charge of a forced-labor rental system that strongly resembled the parallel SS rental methods developed in the General Government and in Upper Silesia.

SILESIA, A SPECIAL CASE

Upper Silesia and eastern Upper Silesia were consolidated into one territory in fall 1940. Politically and administratively, an occupied Polish area was merged with Old Reich territory. As in the Warthegau, the actual intention was to deport the Polish Jews living there with all haste into the General Government, but those plans had also failed by summer 1940. To avoid wasting the potential of the tens of thousands of workers concentrated in eastern Upper Silesia, Himmler appointed a Special Commissioner for Utilization of Foreign Nationals.

Influenced by events in the General Government, the SS Organisation Schmelt instituted a brutal forced-labor system for the eastern Upper Silesian Jews. From March 1941 on, the special commissioner exercised control over distribution of Jewish forced laborers, at least in Upper Silesia, a departure from the practices in all other territories under German rule. The Reich Autobahn authorities, the companies performing construction under their management, and then later armaments enterprises benefited most from this service. In fall 1941, the system of the special commissioner employed over 17,000 Polish Jews from the eastern Upper Silesian ghettos in the entire Silesian region. Forced-labor camps were established throughout Silesia and the Sudetenland, first at road construction project sites, then in 1942 for armaments construction projects or armaments production.

Officially, the forced laborers earned 70 percent of the wages of non-Jewish workers, but in reality they received only a ludicrous pittance for pocket money; the rest went to the Schmelt organization, in part to finance the ghettos in East Upper Silesia. In the large cities of eastern Upper Silesia, such as Sosnowitz and Bendzin, parallel manufacturing sites had been established for the Wehrmacht and private companies. In these workshops, Jews only received half the wages of comparable Aryan workers, and 30 percent of that went to the SS Schmelt office.

In 1942, the Schmelt agency made the transition from requiring minimum wages to an SS-developed rental system. The enterprises continuing to employ Jews as forced laborers now paid daily rates to the SS. Concentration of forced laborers in the countless camps of the Schmelt system ran counter to the deportation and extermination process. In spring 1942, the camp system encompassed 40,000 people. In summer, Schmelt was even able to select for his camp 8,000 Jews from the western European transports bound for Auschwitz. At the end of 1942, over 50,000 Jews worked under Schmelt control. After a first wave in 1942, the ghettos in eastern Upper Silesia were cleared in 1943 and the Jews still living there were deported. However, many camps were not closed and some were integrated into the concentration camp system until 1944.

Until now the question regarding the relationship of the SS to the labor administration paled beside the horrors of the Schmelt regime. What must be remembered is that the SS regime in Silesia only applied to Polish Jews from eastern Upper Silesia; German Jews from Silesian towns were still employed in the labor offices' segregated labor deployment. At the end of 1942, over 2,000 German Jews still were working in Breslau; furthermore, several camps existed in Silesia for that group. As many of the camps attributed to Schmelt were maintained by the Reich Autobahn authorities, it is unlikely that the SS was in charge of all the Silesian forced-labor camps in every time period. The Organisation Schmelt clearly managed the distribution of Polish Jews from eastern Upper Silesia from 1941 on, but the labor administration remained involved at least in regional transfers. Generally, the SS forced-labor system under Schmelt was an unusual regional case. It was the only one of its kind in the German Reich and its annexed territories; at the same time, it was one of the largest regional SS forced-labor systems for Jews in all of occupied Europe. Nevertheless, as the analysis of the General Government has shown, eastern Upper Silesia was clearly not the area of the former Polish state where forced labor first was used systematically as an instrument of anti-Jewish policy, as Sybille Steinbacher claims.[7] Almost a year before, in spring 1940, both the civil administration and the regional SS in the General Government already had created extended camp systems for Jewish forced laborers based on even earlier German experiences.

CAMP SYSTEMS FOR JEWISH FORCED LABOR

Labor camps for segregated labor deployment had already been established in 1939; they housed unemployed Jews recruited by the labor offices and often living far from home to perform road and hydraulic construction work. German and Austrian Jews were sent to these Old Reich camps maintained by public builders, municipalities, or private companies. The conditions in the camps mostly depended on the attitude of the officials in charge. In summer 1939, hard labor and abuse led to suicides, just as in Kelkheim im Taunus. A total of forty labor camps could be confirmed in Germany for

---

[7] Sybille Steinbacher, *"Musterstadt" Auschwitz. Germanisierungspolitik und Judenmord in Ostoberschlesien* (Munich, 2000), 142.

the period up to 1943. Another camp system was set up in Germany in summer 1941 in connection with the preparations for deportations. Local authorities, in cooperation with the Gestapo, for the first time quartered not only Jewish forced laborers but also entire families in these labor and residential camps. Several thousand Jews from big cities and from entire rural Kreise were concentrated in forty camps, both to bring them together for the upcoming transports and to be able to exploit them as forced labor. These labor and residential camps had Jewish subadministrations. Isolation, malnutrition, and limitations on freedom were part of the everyday routine. After 1943, Jewish Mischlinge were recruited for forced labor; initially, many were taken to labor camps in France. After fall 1944, dozens of camps were established in all parts of Germany, especially near Organisation Todt projects but also close to municipal administrations for which Mischlinge performed forced labor until the end of the war.

Aside from segregated labor deployment, there were three special types of Jewish labor utilization in the Old Reich. In 1939–40, a system was developed to use German Jews in agriculture and forestry. This encompassed about fifty camps maintained by the Reichsvereinigung der Juden in Deutschland; half of them were former training establishments of Jewish organizations and the other half were newly established camps. Bypassing the labor offices, forced labor was initially arranged under Gestapo control with direct collective labor contracts between the Reichsvereinigung and interested municipalities or forestry offices. In spring 1941, the segregated labor deployment program organized by the labor offices absorbed these camps; the usual terms for forced labor determined future recruiting, placement, and wages. Those camps, with the other labor camps for German Jews, gradually were closed by 1943, as deportations progressed.

In the Old Reich, the labor administration also arranged camp work for foreign, mostly Polish Jews from the Warthegau. Over forty camps were set up for that purpose after 1940, most of them in the Brandenburg region, first for Reich Autobahn construction, and later for industrial operations. Many of these camp inmates came from the Lodz ghetto; they were completely excluded from German labor law, even from the special conditions for German Jews. Because of the drastic conditions in the camps, many people had to be returned to the ghetto either prematurely or completely exhausted.

The special regional system of the SS Special Commissioner Schmelt developed parallel to those camps in Old Reich territory beginning at the end of 1940; it ultimately encompassed at least 177 camps for Jews from eastern Upper Silesia. While many of the Schmelt camps initially supported Reich highway construction, they increasingly provided labor for armaments projects and industrial production after 1942. Hard labor and malnutrition resulted in extremely high mortality rates among camp inmates. Starting in 1942, selections took place in the camps; people incapable of working were taken to Auschwitz and murdered there. In 1943–44 many of the camps were closed, but some of them were integrated into the concentration camp system. These camps then functioned as subcamps of Auschwitz or Groß-Rosen, and the inmates were regarded as concentration camp prisoners. Thus, a total of six different camp systems for Jewish forced laborers have been identified today within Germany in the period from 1939 to 1945. They all operated independently of the concentration camp system, and only one was under SS control.

Sixty-five camps established or used for forced labor of Austrian Jews – likewise independent of the concentration camp system – could be confirmed in Austria. In the Ostmark, twenty-nine camps maintained by private companies and public builders, mostly for dam and road construction, existed between 1939 and 1942. Many Austrian Jews were taken to German labor camps in two waves, in 1939 and 1941. There, sixteen camps were established exclusively – and two partially – for Austrian Jewish men and women. Like the Reichsvereinigung camps in Germany, sixteen retraining camps were exceptions to labor-office-controlled segregated labor deployment in Austria: Run by the SD Central Office for Jewish Emigration and subordinate to the Viennese religious community, they supplied labor for agriculture and forestry. The SS also built two camps of its own for forced labor. However, based on the information available today, labor camps for Mischlinge played scarcely any role in Austria. After the Jewish camps were closed, in some Austrian camp towns, for example, St. Valentin, Münichholz, and Eisenerz, subcamps of Mauthausen Concentration Camp were established and the new prisoners had to assist the same companies that had employed the Austrian Jews previously.

For the Jews, the labor camps always meant a harsher form of forced labor. While German Jews still received minimum wages in the camps, Jews in most of the Austrian camps were paid a third of that. In the camps subordinate to the Jewish organizations, the workers only received pocket money. The Polish Jews taken to Germany did not even receive that much. In most of the camps, going out and having contact with town residents were prohibited. The forced laborers in many of the camps were thus performing the most difficult work while in dire need, without adequate food or work clothes. Tallying the labor and retraining camps for German Jews, the dozens of labor camps for Mischlinge at the war's end, the labor and retraining camps for Austrian Jews, and the camps for non-German Jews, yields the depressing result that more than 400, possibly as many as 450, labor camps for Jews independent of the concentration camp system existed between 1938 and 1943 in the Old Reich, in Austria, and in the Sudeten region alone. Many of these camps are forgotten today because they only existed for a short time. They were by no means as well hidden from the population as the concentration camps; town residents often guarded, inspected, or supplied the camps.

Various camps systems for forced labor of Jews also existed in the occupied Polish territories. In the Warthegau, dozens of labor camps clearly not subordinate to the SS at least until 1942 were constructed for agricultural work, improvements, and road construction. In the General Government there were several extensive, partially independent camp systems, with three main networks: the Wehrmacht camps; the forced-labor camps established by civilian authorities for hydraulic and road construction, and so forth; and SS camps such as those in Lublin and Galicia. The inmates lived under far more difficult conditions in the forced-labor camps of occupied Poland than in the Reich's, even if they were not SS camps. The forced laborers received no wages. Hunger was an everyday condition. Many died of exhaustion. After 1941, people unable to work were either deported or shot. Those conditions also led to acts of resistance, as inmates escaped from the camps. According to one estimate, the occupied Polish territories claimed at least 910 camps,[8] but there were probably many more.

If the camps in Germany and Austria are added to that, Jewish workers in the Greater German Reich and in the occupied Polish territories were interned in more than 1,300 separate forced-labor camps mostly independent of the concentration camp system and usually maintained by private and public companies, municipal administrations, the Wehrmacht, or regional SS offices. All the different camp systems intensified the social isolation and physical exploitation of the persecuted, but paradoxically some of the camps provided better chances of survival for the individual Jew as a result of economic interests.

Until the international debate about compensation for forced laborers, most of the survivors had never been indemnified. Because segregated labor deployment, even if performed in labor camps, occurred outside the concentration camp system, it was not recognized either in Germany or Austria as deprivation of freedom. That was the case, despite the fact that many of the laborers had to live in such camps for years and were forbidden to leave for purposes other than work, and despite the fact, that many people, whether in Germany or in the occupied territories, found themselves guarded by police, SS, soldiers, or auxiliary troops in camps fenced with barb wire.

THE MODEL FOR "UTILIZATION OF FOREIGN WORKERS" IN THE REICH

Segregated labor deployment of German and Austrian Jews constituted the model for the Jewish forced-labor program organized by the labor administration in the occupied territories, and for utilization of millions of Poles and "eastern workers" in Germany. The October 3, 1941, order legalizing Jewish forced labor in Germany defined Jewish forced labor as a *"Beschäftigungsverhältnis eigener Art,"* that is, a "special employment

---

[8] Gudrun Schwarz, *Die nationalsozialistischen Lager* (Frankfurt am Main and New York, 1990), 75.

classification." That became the technical term in 1941–42 for utilization of Poles and Soviet citizens carried off to the Reich. Methods developed by the labor administration after the end of 1938 became blueprints for those two groups. After non-Jewish Polish workers had been assigned work in the Reich, the Nazi state endeavored to put them on the same footing as Jews.[9] Polish forced laborers were treated similarly to Jews in 1940, and their downgraded standing was justified with the same racist arguments. After June 1940, German Jews and Poles were both denied contractual and professional allowances in Germany; later, both groups were subject to a special tax, the *Sozialausgleichsabgabe*. After the October 1941 forced-labor order affecting Jews, the same wage tax tables were used for Jews and Poles in the Old Reich. Wages were paid only for work performed.[10] Both groups worked in separate columns or work departments and were marked at work with discriminatory symbols. Even their living conditions were the same. Curfews and prohibitions on use of public transportation and visits to restaurants and churches restricted Jews, Poles, and eastern workers alike. For racial defilement (*Rassenschande*) with Aryans, all three groups were in jeopardy of the most severe penalties; after the end of 1941, they were subject to a special criminal law.[11]

WORK AND ANNIHILATION?

The results of the present studies clearly demonstrate that forced labor in the Third Reich cannot in any case be considered part of the Nazi murder program. The Nazi state had introduced forced labor as an element of their persecutory policy years before the decision to commit mass murder. Contrary to previous assumptions,[12] Jewish forced labor represented from the outset a conspicuous economic factor both in Germany and in the occupied Polish territories, not least of all for war production. At New Year's 1941, the German labor administration employed over 41,000 strategically situated

---

9   For historiography and the state of research on Polish workers in the Third Reich, see Czeslaw Luczak, "Polnische Arbeiter im nationalsozialistischen Deutschland während des Zweiten Weltkrieges," in *Europa und der "Reichseinsatz". Ausländische Zivilarbeiter, Kriegsgefangene und KZ-Häftlinge in Deutschland 1938–1945*, edited by Ulrich Herbert (Essen, 1991), 90–105.

10 For a comparison of the two groups, see Wolf Gruner, "Die Organisation von Zwangsarbeit für Juden in Deutschland und im Generalgouvernement 1939–1943: Eine vergleichende Bestandsaufnahme," in *Die Festung Glatz und die Verfolgung in der NS-Zeit*, published by the Foundation for the Topography of Terror, 78 (1997): 43–58.

11 For details regarding the circumstances of Poles and eastern workers in general, see Ulrich Herbert, *Fremdarbeiter. Politik und Praxis des Ausländereinsatzes in der Kriegswirtschaft des Dritten Reichs* (Berlin and Bonn, 1985).

12 Herbert speaks of an economic significance for Jewish forced labor only after the turning point in the war at the end of 1941; Ulrich Herbert, "Arbeit und Vernichtung," in *Europa und der "Reichseinsatz,"* 417.

Jews, mostly in industry. The labor offices in Austria and the Protectorate of Bohemia and Moravia had placed considerably more than 10,000 forced laborers in agriculture, construction, and industry. Seven hundred thousand Jews in the General Government alone were engaged in forced labor. Jewish forced labor had been expanded even further by the end of summer 1941 in Germany, the Protectorate, Upper Silesia, and Poland. If the Soviet and West European territories with comparable programs but no precise figures are included, the economy had at its disposal more than a million cheap Jewish workers without rights and readily available for socially unrestricted use.

Against this background one must ask what prompted the apparently irrational order to deport and murder the Jewish population, and with it the forced laborers. The decision is clearly attributable to the perspective of the Nazi leadership – a perspective shaped by the special situation in Germany. In summer 1941, Germany had over 50,000 German Jews in forced labor, but already more than a million forced laborers from eastern and western Europe. With that ratio, removal of the Jewish population, including compulsory employees, without detriment to the German national economy, seemed feasible. At the same time, progressive occupation of the Soviet Union with a population numbering in the millions raised the prospect of an immense future army of slaves in the minds of the central officials in charge.

Of course, this policy of the Nazi leadership, with its focus solely on persecutory goals and the national economy, had its shortcomings. It rapidly became apparent that Jewish forced laborers in Germany in the meantime not only had gone to work in production areas vital to the war effort but also in some regions (for example, Berlin), they made up a large proportion of the forced laborers. The problems were even more pronounced locally. Industrial operations proved to be dependent on Jews if they represented more than half the personnel or if they ran entire shifts on their own. After the first intense conflicts between the political and the economic objectives, between the labor administration and the Wehrmacht offices on the one side and the SS and Gestapo organizing deportations on the other, the adversaries began to cooperate. Deportation plans were coordinated, indeed synchronized, locally by pragmatic agreements with the production interests. Labor administrations and Wehrmacht armaments inspection offices, but also private companies and city administrations that employed the forced laborers, worked hand in hand with the Gestapo in many locations. The labor administrations supplied the Security Police with lists specifying the Jews' suitability or importance for labor. Armaments workers received limited-term releases from transports; some companies, such as Siemens, even negotiated limited-term collective guarantees preventing removal of their Jewish forced laborers. In fall 1942 the RHSA itself finally even developed plans for a direct exchange of German Jews for Poles, taking into consideration the learning curves necessary for production. Berlin, a center of industrial concentration, clearly illustrates that economic interests led to decided modifications in the course of deportations. At the end of 1942, 15,000 of 20,000 Jewish forced laborers in the Reich lived there; they were not deported until the infamous 1943 Fabrik-Aktion. That was the case even though Berlin, as the capital of the Third Reich, was the city from which the Jewish population, according to Hitler's and Goebbels' wishes, was to have been deported first and completely.

In the former Polish areas, too, the economic importance of forced labor cannot be overestimated. In 1940 and 1941, the labor administration assigned large numbers of Jewish forced laborers to infrastructure measures important for the war, such as hydraulic, rail, and road construction projects. Because of labor shortages, thousands of Polish Jews were even sent to work in Germany against Hitler's order. After the SS had reassumed control of forced labor in the General Government, Hitler himself promised the army and the economy in September 1942 to guarantee protection of the Polish Jewish skilled workers in the General Government, this time against the wishes of Himmler, who was pushing for total eradication. The SS consequently coordinated its actions with the Wehrmacht (which depended on tens of thousands of Jews, among them many skilled laborers) but also with private enterprises and public builders such as the Organisation Todt. Jews worked on the supply roads leading to the Soviet Union, and they were especially instrumental in providing the Wehrmacht with clothing and other equipment. Labor shortages resulting from transfer of many non-Jewish Poles to forced-labor programs in the Reich, and the large number of Jewish skilled workers employed in the war industry altered the murder process in the General Government. Forced laborers at important production sites were excepted from mass murder; and at the end of 1942, the largest number of Jewish workers in all the districts of the General Government were concentrated in Galicia district, where the SS had the greatest influence on the organization of forced labor. Workers for the camps in Silesia were mustered from the trains coming from western Europe and destined for Auschwitz.

Despite ongoing murder operations, at New Year's 1943 about 400,000 male and female Jewish forced laborers were still living in Germany and in the occupied Polish territories (probably more than 200,000 in the General Government, 70,000 in the Greater German Reich, and 115,000 in the annexed Polish territories). Thus, upon closer examination, the thesis of the total irrationality of the deportation decisions conflicting with the exigencies of war cannot be upheld for Germany, the annexed territories, or Poland.

The same is essentially true for the thesis of "destruction through work." This assumes that the prime objective of forced-labor measures is the death of the persons obligated to perform labor, not exploitation of potential labor. This is definitely not the case for the early systematic utilization of Jews in Germany, Austria, and the Protectorate from 1939 to 1941, but is also doubtful for forced labor in the Polish territories. While many historians still view forced labor in Poland only as an integral component of extermination, and usually justify that on the basis of the SS camps,[13] others in the meantime concede that Jewish forced laborers in camps at least temporarily had better chances of survival than the rest of the population. From that perspective, the situation after 1942 could be described as a compromise between work and destruction.[14] I agree with Christopher Browning's view that destruction through work is not at all accurate, because most of the forced laborers did not die from work but were shot to death or killed in the extermination camps.[15]

Finally, the SS always sought to achieve concrete work objectives such as construction of a street or fortification of a border, even under the cruelest conditions. Jews who died in camps in Poland usually succumbed to malnutrition or miserable hygienic conditions, not senseless heavy labor as used by SS guards against inmates in some concentration camps. For example, in Mauthausen Concentration Camp, the SS forced prisoners to climb up and down a stone stairway carrying heavy loads until the victims were totally exhausted; this often fatal labor had no economic rationale. In Poland, not forced laborers but persons unfit for work were selected at an early point and either shot on the spot or deported and later murdered in gas chambers at extermination sites. If murder had been the only objective, the SS would have been able to arrange that more simply without the detour through forced labor. In the end, housing Jews as forced laborers in camps for an extended period was more expensive than murdering them, because equipment, maintenance, and supplies required investment. It is more likely that mismanagement in combination with the SS belief in its racial superiority resulted in high mortality rates in many forced-labor camps, as did the colonial-master behavior in civilian agencies and companies.

---

[13] Thomas Sandkühler, "Das Zwangsarbeitslager Lemberg-Janowska 1941–1944," in *Die nationalsozialistischen Konzentrationslager. Entwicklung und Struktur*, edited by Ulrich Herbert, Karin Orth, and Christoph Dieckmann, Vol. 2 (Göttingen, 1998), 606; Hermann Kaienburg, "Zwangsarbeit von Juden in Arbeits- und Konzentrationslagern," in *"Arisierung." Volksgemeinschaft, Raub und Gedächtnis*, edited by Irmrud Wojak and Peter Hayes and commissioned by the Fritz Bauer Institute (Frankfurt am Main and New York [Campus], 2000), 226. Likewise, recently Hans Mommsen, *Auschwitz, 17. Juli 1942. Der Weg zur "Endlösung der europäischen Judenfrage"* (Munich, 2002), 135.

[14] Dieter Pohl, *Nationalsozialistische Judenverfolgung in Ostgalizien, Organisation und Durchführung eines staatlichen Massenverbrechens* (Munich, 1996), 335; – , "Die Großen Zwangsarbeitslager der SS- und Polizeiführer für Juden im Generalgouvernement 1942–1945," in *Die nationalsozialistischen Konzentrationslager. Entwicklung und Struktur*, edited by Ulrich Herbert, Karin Orth, and Christoph Dieckmann, Vol. 1 (Göttingen, 1998), 431–432.

[15] Christopher Browning, "Jewish Workers in Poland: Self-Maintenance, Exploitation, Destruction," in *Nazi Policy, Jewish Workers, German Killers* (Cambridge, New York, and Melbourne, 2000), 87–88.

In striking contrast to the thesis of destruction through work, upon closer examination the forced-labor camps were the last places where Jews were exempted, at least temporarily, from the extermination program. In camps and ghettos in Silesia, in the Warthegau, and in the General Government, forced laborers often escaped genocide until late 1943 and even 1944. That was true even in the regional SS strongholds such as Galicia and Silesia, making it clear that the SS itself subordinated the murder programs there to economic objectives. While local persecutory interests of the SS often interfered with the central labor market interests of the labor administration in the General Government during the period before 1942, local and regional economic interests later frequently modified central plans for murder. It is of interest that the latter is true also for the occupied Soviet territories, as Jürgen Matthäus recently revealed.[16] Jewish forced laborers even were transferred by the thousands to the Reich at the end of the war, in direct contradiction to all Nazi plans for persecution. Because of economic interests, many victims lived to see the end of the war and liberation from Nazi terror.

COMPULSORY LABOR AS A BASIC ELEMENT IN PERSECUTION OF JEWS

The forced-labor organization that later spread its tentacles to all of Europe and even to North Africa thus originated in Germany. There the labor administration received instructions after the November 1938 pogrom to organize forced labor for the Jewish population affected by unemployment and the trade prohibition. Forced labor soon dominated everyday life for the majority of the Jewish population in Germany, Austria, the Protectorate, and the occupied Polish territories. The model of forced labor developed in Germany was applied in all annexed and occupied territories, often with much more radical enhancements. In all those territories, the labor administration rather than the SS planned and implemented forced labor, always taking into consideration economic interests. While the SS in the General Government obtained partial control over Jewish labor in 1942 in the shadow of mass murder, and complete control via expansion of the concentration camp system after 1943–44, it never succeeded to that extent in Germany, the annexed territories, or other occupied countries, even toward the end of the war.

Forced labor of hundreds of thousands of Jews, of men, women, children, and the elderly, was an important economic factor for the labor market in Germany and in the occupied Polish territories, not least of all for war production. Thus, the interests of the entire state in their exploitation prevailed;

---

[16] See the chapter by Jürgen Matthäus in Christopher R. Browning, *Die Entfesselung der "Endlösung". Nationalsozialistische Judenpolitik 1939–1942*, with an essay by Jürgen Matthäus (Berlin, 2003), 411 and 431 (English version published by the University of Nebraska Press, 2004).

in the end, those interests altered the course of deportations and at least partially even influenced the program of mass murder. The actual beneficiaries of exploiting cheap labor unprotected by rights were, in all countries and territories, local and regional authorities, especially municipalities and other public builders; state institutions such as the Wehrmacht, the Reich Railway, and the Organisation Todt; and private enterprises, especially for road construction, underground construction, and hydraulic construction, and for industrial operations.

Overall, the leaders of the Third Reich approached anti-Jewish policies very pragmatically. Many contradictions are explained by the extensive participation of various German agencies and institutions. Particular interests, but also cooperation and a division of labor among various authorities, decisively influenced the actual form of Jewish policy and thus the victims' everyday living conditions in the Third Reich. The same is true of forced labor, which was a basic element of this policy from 1938 on. Compulsory employment of hundreds of thousands of Jews in Germany and the territory that it occupied was systematically planned centrally and elaborated locally. It was not simply a preliminary stage or an interim solution before a long-planned murder program. Economic interests influenced not only the kind and form of forced labor, its organization, and the associated responsibilities, but also the development of persecutory policy – and gradually even the murder program. Tens of thousands of Jews survived the Holocaust because they were exempted from genocide due to economic interests and labor shortages.

Forced labor in separate columns and in camps especially established for that purpose allowed exploitation of labor potential, subsistence of Jews who had become unemployed because of persecutory measures, and separation and control of individuals in the Jewish population most capable of offering resistance. With segregated labor deployment, the Nazi state mobilized human labor potential in two ways. For German Jews it meant "selection" and "compulsory employment," but for Aryan Germans it meant the prestige of higher positions in company hierarchies, better compensation, and easier work.[17] At the same time, potential solidarity was forestalled, because Jews performing forced labor never remained completely isolated despite the segregation ordered.[18] The majority of Germans at all social levels either actively supported, approved, or at least accepted the forced-labor program, and only a few women and men refused to do so. Hugo Schriesheimer – who is quoted in the introduction – wrote that the tormentor of the Jewish forced laborers was not pharaoh, but Hitler. Hitler personally defined certain aspects of the forced-labor program. Not just Hitler, however, but tens of thousands of people – officials and employees

[17] See Detlev Peukert, *Volksgenossen und Gemeinschaftsfremde* (Cologne, 1982), 214.
[18] Ulrich Herbert makes similar statements regarding forced labor conditions of Soviet laborers and foreigners in general; Herbert, *Fremdarbeiter*, 156 und 357.

from the labor administration and ministries, local and regional agencies (such as the hydraulic construction, road construction, and forestry offices), city administrations, and the police: members of the Wehrmacht, the SS, the Organisation Todt, and countless employees and workers at small and large private companies and public enterprises (such as the Reich Railway and the Reich Autobahn) – took part in the development of the forced-labor programs. Thus, they shared responsibility for the years of social discrimination and brutal exploitation of hundreds of thousands of Jews in all parts of Europe.

Index of Subjects

Table of Decrees and Orders on Forced Labor

Date	Source	Region	Subject	Pages
May, 1938	Hitler	Reich	on forced labor for "criminal" Jews	108
Dec 20, 1938	Reich Institute	Reich	on segregated labor deployment	See Index of Subjects, Decrees on forced labor
May 19, 1939	Labor Ministry	Reich	on segregated labor deployment	8
Oct 26, 1939	GG	GG	on forced labor for Jews	231, 242
Dec 2, 1939	HSSPF	GG	creating Jewish work columns	231
Dec 11, 1939	GG	GG	implementing forced labor	233
Jun 3, 1940	Labor Ministry	Reich	reducing social benefits	12
Jul 5, 1940	GG	GG	on transition of forced labor	247
Jul 27, 1940	Greiser	Warthegau	on wage scales for Jews	182
Jan 23, 1941	Czech Gov	Protectorate	requiring forced labor for Jews	153
May 9, 1941	Czech Ministry	Protectorate	on forced labor procedures	154
Aug 29, 1941	Czech Ministry	Protectorate	expanding compulsory labor	158
Sep 9, 1941	Czech Ministry	Protectorate	on segregated labor deployment	163
Aug 14, 1941	Rosenberg	Occupied SU	on labor obligation of Jews	255
Sep 20, 1941	GG	Galicia/GG	on labor obligation of Jews	255
Oct 3, 1941	Körner BVP	Reich	codifying special labor law for Jews	See Index of Subjects, Decrees on forced labor
Oct 31, 1941	Labor Ministry	Reich	implementing October 3 decree	22
Jun 25, 1942	Reichsstatt-halter, Labor dep	Warthegau	on employment of Jewish forced labor	186, 191
Jun 25, 1942	GG/Labor Dep	GG	transition of forced labor to SS	
Jul 17, 1942	Czech Gov	Protectorate	reducing social benefits	171
Feb 24, 1943	Gestapo	Reich	ordering Fabrik-Aktion	79
Oct 6, 1944	RSHA	Reich	second Fabrik-Aktion	95

Index of Persons

Index of Places and Camps